# *Cont*

# List of Illustrations

# Acknowledgements

The greatest pleasure in writing this book has been the people I have met along the way. At the National Records Office (*Dár al-Wathá'iq al-Qawmía*) in Khartoum, Dr 'Ali Saleh al-Karrar and his colleagues gave me immeasurable assistance in tracking down the relevant sources from the archives. The late Professor Muhammad Ibrahím Abú-Salím spared me time, despite ill health, to discuss the larger themes of the book; his published works have been central to my research. The hospitality and efficiency of George and Eleanora Pagoulatos at the Acropole Hotel provided, as they have done so many times over the past fifteen years, a peaceful and comfortable home from home. At the Sudan Library of the University of Khartoum, 'Abbás al-Zein was patient and helpful, advising me on the most important books in his extraordinary collection and locating the most obscure documents among his hoard of treasures. Sara al-Mahdi arranged a rewarding visit to Jazíra Aba, where my host was Sheikh al-Núr 'Abd-al-Mahmúd, the imám of the island's main mosque; he looked after me with great kindness and showed me many interesting sights. Other insights into the early life of the Mahdi came from Muhammad Hassan Ihímir, 'Abd-al-Rahmán Birrah, 'Abd-al-Rahmán Muhammad Harún and Suleimán Yusúf Dalil, all at Jazíra Aba. Muhammad Hámid Muhammad al-Fádl kindly translated some important anecdotes. At Jazírat Labab, 'Abd-al-Gádir Muhammad and 'Abdallah Saleh not only provided lunch (on the 'Eid al-Adha to boot) but also rowed me over the river to see the Mahdi's birthplace.

Anyone working on the Mahdía will know how Jane Hogan and her colleagues at the Sudan Archive, University of Durham, are the lynchpin of any serious research effort; her kindness and help were invaluable to me. I would also like to thank the staff of Rhodes House at Oxford University for their friendly service; this was a tranquil haven for writing as well as research. The Library staff at the School of Oriental and African Studies (part of London University) was equally efficient, especially in the Special Collections department. Zoe Lubowiecka at Hove Library gave me the key to the Wolseley Collection, the source of much rich material. At Sudeley Castle in Gloucestershire, Jean Bray, the Archivist of the Emma Dent collection, allowed me to use an important letter of the Mahdi that had somehow escaped even Professor Abú-Salím's net. Heather Sharkey shared published and unpublished work on the historiography of the Mahdía, while Haim Shaked allowed me to use substantial quotations from his condensed translation of Ismail 'Abd-al-Gádir's 'court biography' of the Mahdi. Robert Kramer and Gabriel Warburg offered personal encouragement as well as many fascinating insights from their own works. I would also like to thank Professor Peter Holt, the distinguished doyen of British Mahdía studies, for reading an early draft of the book's early chapters and making many useful suggestions. John Whitehead, Paul Whitehead and Steve Hubbell went beyond the call of familial duty to read various drafts and make immensely useful comments. The spirit of Graham Thomas was an inspiration hovering over my little office. I am grateful to my agent, Mandy Little, and my editors, Jaqueline Mitchell and Hilary Walford, for their belief in what might have appeared a prohibitively 'minority-interest' project. I have been particularly privileged to have the collaboration of Osmán Nusairi, a London-based Sudanese journalist, playwright, editor and friend. I am truly grateful for his accurate and sympathetic work in translating not only the writings of the Mahdi but also a variety of primary source material.

My mother, brothers and sisters have been constantly supportive throughout the writing process. At home, Kate, Flora and James have forgiven me the absences, the enthusiasm for obscure details of Sufi sects and the closed office door, offering instead love and encouragement to see the project through to completion. Finally, in acknowledgement of an older debt of gratitude, I would like to thank three teachers who in different ways helped equip me to cope with life: Fr Adrian Convery, Philip Smiley and Bernard Vazquez.

# Notes on Transliteration and Calendars

Words, titles and expressions that are transliterated, not translated, are rendered in italics at first reference only. The conventional academic approach to transliteration from Arabic is to pick out names in scholarly detail, which can often be dense and unreadable. The Arabic of Sudan is also idiosyncratic. The glottal 'q' (ق – qáf) is pronounced as a hard 'g', 'g' (ج – gím) is pronounced 'j' and 'th' (ث – tha) is often pronounced 's', to cite just three examples. Thus, instead of the academically precise ع‎Uthmān Diqna, I render the celebrated Mahdist general's name as 'Osmán Digna; instead of naming the Kordofani capital al-Ubayyidh, I use al-Obeid. Both examples convey a Sudanese 'feel' while indicating clearly any necessary vocal stresses. The Arabic letters that are most difficult to pronounce, the *ain* (ع) and the *hamza* (ء), are rendered ' and ' respectively. Where locations are prefaced by the definite article *al-*, it is used only at first reference and subsequently omitted; hence, for example, al-Massallamía is referred to as Massallamía at all subsequent references and al-Fasher as Fasher. When names or terms are commonplace to readers in English, I have left well alone; thus, for example, Khartoum, Sufi, Ramadan and jihad retain the conventional Anglicised spellings.

Many Sudanese, Egyptian and Ottoman sources in the archives use the Islamic calendar, which began with the migration of the Prophet Muhammad from Mecca to Medina in 622 AD. The twelve months of the Islamic year (denoted as AH, *Anno Hegirae*) are: Muharram, Safar, Rabí' I, Rabí' II, Jumáda I, Jumáda II, Rajab, Sha'bán, Ramadan, Shawwál, Dhú al-Qaida and Dhú al-Hijja. It is important to stress that the months in the lunar Muslim calendar 'slip' in relation to the longer solar Western calendar. So 11 Ramadan in AH 1298, when Muhammad Ahmad had his first encounter with government representatives, corresponds to 7 August 1881; by his death on 8 Ramadan 1302, the Western calendar would have been open at 22 June 1885.

# Principal Characters

* indicates killed in conflict or in imprisonment

## 1. SUDANESE: THE MAHDI AND HIS FOLLOWERS

| | |
|---|---|
| 'Abdallah 'Abdallah | The Mahdi's younger brother* |
| 'Abd-al-Rahmán al-Nujúmi | Senior Mahdist amír* |
| 'Abdulláhi Muhammad al-Ta'íshi | The Mahdi's first Khalífa* |
| 'Abdulláhi wad al-Núr | Mahdist agent in Kordofan and amír at siege of Khartoum* |
| 'Abd-al-Halím Musá'id | Mahdist amír in Kordofan |
| Ahmad al-Azhari ibn Ismail | Senior judge of Khartoum 'ulamá' |
| Ahmad wad Jubára | The Mahdi's first Qádi al-Islam, 1881–2* |
| Ahmad Suleimán al-Mahasi | Head of Beit al-Mál, or treasury* |
| 'Ali wad Helu | The Mahdi's second Khalífa* |
| 'Asákir wad Abú-Kalám | Názir of Jimi' clan of Baggára |
| Hamdán Abú-Anja | Mahdist amír; head of Jihádía rifle corps |
| Hámid 'Abdallah | The Mahdi's elder brother* |
| Ilyás Ahmad Umm Bireir | Al-Obeid merchant and Mahdist sympathiser |
| Karamallah al-Sheikh Muhammad | Mahdist amír of Bahr al-Ghazál |
| Madibbu 'Ali | Rizeigat Baggára chief and Mahdist envoy |
| Muhammad 'Abdallah | The Mahdi's eldest brother* |

| | |
|---|---|
| Muhammad Ahmad 'Abdallah | The Mahdi |
| Muhammad Badr al-'Ubeid | Mahdist amír from Blue Nile region |
| Muhammad Khálid 'Zugal' | Deputy Governor of Darfur; became Mahdist amír* |
| Muhammad al-Kheir 'Abdallah al-Khojali | Tutor to the Mahdi; appointed amír of Berber |
| Muhammad 'Osmán Abú-Girja | Mahdist amír |
| Muhammad Sharfi | Great-uncle of the Mahdi |
| Muhammad al-Sharíf | The Mahdi's third Khalífa* |
| Muhammad al-Tayib al-Basír | Mahdist amír in Jazíra region |
| Músa wad Helu | Leader of Digheim Baggára |
| al-Núr Muhammad 'Angara | Government commander of Bara; became Mahdist amír |
| 'Omar al-Makáshfi | Mahdist supporter in Jazíra* |
| 'Osmán Digna | Mahdist amír in Eastern Sudan and Karari |
| 'Osmán 'Sheikh al-Dín' | Son of Khalífa 'Abdulláhi |
| al-Quráshi wad al-Zein | Sammanía sect leader based at al-Massalamía |
| Yaqúb Muhammad al-Ta'íshi | Younger brother of Khalífa 'Abdulláhi; senior amír* |
| Zaki Tamal | Amír under Khalífa 'Abdulláhi* |

## 2. EGYPTIAN/OTTOMAN GOVERNMENT, SUDANESE ALLIES AND EUROPEAN EMPLOYEES

| | |
|---|---|
| 'Abbás (Bey) | Secretary to Governor-General 'Alá-al-Dín Siddíq (qv)* |

# PRINCIPAL CHARACTERS

| | |
|---|---|
| 'Abd-al-Qádir Hilmi | Governor-General of Sudan, May 1882 to February 1883 |
| Ahmad 'Arábi | Egyptian officer and revolutionary leader |
| Ahmad Dafa'allah | Pro-government merchant in al-Obeid* |
| 'Alá-al-Dín Siddíq | Governor-General of Sudan, February 1883 to November 1883* |
| 'Ali Bey Sharíf | Mudír of Kordofan |
| al-Amín Muhammad al-Darír | Head of Khartoum 'ulamá' |
| 'Awad-al-Karím Ahmad Abú-Sin | Hereditary chief of Shukría |
| de Coëtlogon, Henry | British colonel, served with Hicks before returning to siege of Khartoum |
| Colborne, the Hon. John | British colonel attached to Hicks' force |
| Farajallah Raghib | Sudanese general in Egyptian army; commander of Omdurman Fort during siege |
| Faraj al-Zeini | Egyptian officer in command of Khartoum's forts during siege |
| Farquhar, The Hon. John | British colonel on General Hicks' staff* |
| Giegler, Carl | German telegraph engineer; Deputy Governor-General of Sudan |
| Gordon, Charles | British colonel; Governor-General of Sudan, February 1877 to December 1879 and February 1884 to January 1885* |
| Hassan Ibrahím Shalláli | Egyptian army general* |

| | |
|---|---|
| Hicks, William | Retired Indian Army colonel hired to lead assault on Kordofan* |
| Hussein Khalífa | Governor of Berber |
| Lupton, Frank | British Governor of Bahr al-Ghazál* |
| Muhammad 'Osmán al-Mírghani | Head of Khatmía sect |
| Muhammad 'Abd-al-Ra'úf | Governor-General of Sudan, 1880–2 |
| Muhammad Sa'íd Pasha | Governor of Kordofan* |
| Muhammad Tawfíq | Khedive of Egypt |
| Nubar Boghos | Prime Minister of Egypt |
| Ráshid Aymán | Governor of Fashoda* |
| Ra'úf Pasha | see Muhammad 'Abd-al-Ra'úf |
| Salih al-Mak | Shaigi officer |
| Slatin, Rudolph | Governor of Darfur |
| Suleimán Niyázi | Circassian major-general; Governor of Red Sea Province |
| Yúsuf Hassan al-Shalláli | Egyptian general* |

BRITISH

| | |
|---|---|
| Baker, Valentine | British Commandant of Police in Egypt |
| Baring, Sir Evelyn | British Consul-General in Egypt (later Earl of Cromer) |
| Dufferin, Lord | British Ambassador to Constantinople; seconded to Cairo |
| Malet, Sir Edward | British Consul-General in Egypt |

## PRINCIPAL CHARACTERS

Power, Frank — Reporter for *The Times*; acting British Consul in Khartoum*

Stewart, John Donald Hamill — British lieutenant-colonel; intelligence officer*

Wood, Sir Evelyn — British general in Egypt

Wolseley, Lord — British general; leader of failed attempt to rescue Gordon, 1884–5

# Introduction

On 26 January 1884, exactly a year before the day he died in Khartoum, General Charles Gordon attended several meetings with British and Egyptian officials in Cairo to discuss his imminent mission to Sudan, a territory in the throes of violent revolution. For Britain, which had recently occupied Egypt and adopted it as a colony, the policy was clear. Sudan, an Egyptian possession since 1821, must be abandoned and Gordon was the man given the job of extricating Egypt's surviving garrisons. For the Khedive and civil government of Egypt, however, abandonment amounted to a dreadful disgrace, compounding the shame of defeat by Britain, and an impermissible dereliction of their responsibilities to the wider Ottoman Empire. Gordon himself, formally employed by the state of Egypt, was pulled between conflicting loyalties and inconsistent in his own opinions. While he had accepted the evacuation mission on the terms dictated to him by officials of the Gladstone government, he had more than a veiled sympathy for the Sudanese revolutionaries who had risen up to replace Egyptian occupation with a doctrinally 'pure' Islamic state. 'Listen,' Gordon now said to the mandarins of Cairo, 'the Soudan is a beautiful woman who gave herself to Egypt. She now asks for a divorce. How will you refuse it?'[1] And so he set off for the south, changing his mind uncountable times along the way, failed either to evacuate the garrisons or to establish a compromise interim administration – and lost his head to the sharp sword of a Mahdist standard-bearer.

In fact, Sudan had never 'given herself' to Egypt; she had been systematically raped for six decades before Muhammad Ahmad, the son of 'Abdallah the boat-builder from a small island in the northern Nile, launched the rebellion that ejected the occupiers and shook governments in London, Paris and Constantinople. From such humble beginnings, Muhammad Ahmad became the single most influential figure in the history of modern Sudan, revered by his followers as *al-Mahdi al-Muntazar*, the long-awaited spiritual leader, selected and guided by Allah to lead them through a time of social, political and spiritual crisis. His aspirations were extraordinary; nothing less than the overthrow of the Ottoman Empire and its replacement with a pure Islamic state along the lines of the Prophet Muhammad's first Muslim community in Arabia in the early seventh century. The seizure of Khartoum must be followed, as domino topples domino, by the fall of Cairo, Mecca, Jerusalem and Constantinople itself.

Muhammad Ahmad's declaration on 29 June 1881 that he was the long-awaited Mahdi set him irrevocably on a course of confrontation with the powers of the Turkía. It also spoke directly to a widespread sense of messianic anticipation in the region. Islamic tradition pointed to the appearance of the *fin de siècle* Mahdi when the world had reached its nadir, when faith and justice cried out to be restored. The thirteenth century since the *hijra*, the Prophet Muhammad's flight to Medina in 622 AD, was drawing to a close and many believed that the hour had indeed come. The tribes of Sudan were scattered over a vast expanse of savannah, desert and riverain territory. The most important groups settled along the northern Nile were the Danágla, the Mahas, the Shaigía and the Ja'aliyín. The immense deserts, too, had their own tribes, especially the 'Abábda in the north-east and the Kabábish in the north-west. At the territory's heart, the rich arable land of the Jazíra, the Haláwiyín farmed and traded alongside many other smaller tribes. The Beja people, with numerous sub-clans, inhabited the eastern Red Sea Hills, while the various clans of the Baggára roamed the plains of Kordofan and Darfur. Pushing south during the early 1800s, these Arab tribes had driven indigenous black Africans –Dinka, Shilluk and Nuer – before them, south into the territories of Equatoria and Bahr al-Ghazál. Now, as they flocked to Muhammad Ahmad's banner, he began the process by which they began to think of themselves as not just Haláwiyín and Baggára, Danágla and Hadendawa but as right-thinking Muslims and as Sudanese.

Through the 1870s and early 1880s, the young holy man had travelled widely, from Dongola near the Egyptian border to Sennar on the Blue Nile and the central heartland of Kordofan. Everywhere he saw proof of what was, by his own puritanical standards, a profound spiritual malaise. He also saw plenty of evidence of social discontent and anger at the corruption, extortion and sheer venality of the occupiers who ruled from Khartoum. The man whose career had begun in the sheltered Islamic schools of an esoteric Sufi sect was transformed into the leader of a pitiless military uprising. The revolution progressed swiftly, assisted by the blunders and inefficiency of Khartoum's commanders, who were 'pacified by the illusion that it was a passing bubble of fanaticism and religious commotion, which is often seen in the East, and, as such, easy to master and extinguish'.[2] While his generals engineered a succession of increasingly remarkable victories over Egyptian commanders and their European employees, the Mahdi sent out letters and proclamations staking his claim to a divine mandate.

> You should know that Allah has guided both me and you to follow his Book and the path of his Prophet. Indeed, the Prophet Muhammad has told me in person that I am the Expected Mahdi. He has given me the sword of victory; with that sword, I am invincible. As another sign, a banner of light flies over me in the hour of war, carried by the angel 'Azrá'íl. It puts fire into my companions and brings terror into the hearts of my enemies. Again and again, the Prophet has said that those who doubt my Mahdía doubt God himself and his Messenger. He who becomes my enemy is an infidel; he who fights me faces defeat in this world and the next.[3]

Such examples make it clear that to describe the Mahdi's campaign as simply one against taxes, deprivation and political oppression would be to misunderstand his personal sense of mission. Not only did he believe in those visitations and instructions from the Prophet Muhammad; he also protested that the country's leaders were no longer real Muslims and therefore no longer had any right to rule. European employees serving Khartoum were denounced as mercenary supporters of the apostate Ottoman leadership as it undermined the true Islamic path. The Mahdi was not a conservative as he saw little worth conserving. He was less a reformer than a revivalist, championing an uncompromising proto-Islamic state, purified of what he saw as the revolting excrescences of modernity. While he established the foundations of a new nation, his was not a nationalist or geographical concept as such; the theological interests of the wider community of Muslims, the *umma*, took precedence over secular boundaries.[4] There was no separation between 'church' and 'state'. The call of the Mahdi's 'sudden, violent and total' revolution demanded complete personal commitment that transcended any previous obligations; those not inside the Mahdi's community (even Muslims) were infidels beyond the spiritual pale and would be fought implacably as enemies.[5] His message was didactic and absolutist, all his puritanical prescriptions modelled on the fundamentals of the Qorán and the customs and traditions of the Prophet Muhammad.[6] In addition, of course, he had his own precise instructions, transmitted personally by the Prophet in visions.

Life is the abode of those who have no abode; it is the prison of the believer. The hereafter is better and longer lasting, the abode of the God-fearing. As the Lord says: 'To Him will be your return – of all of you. The promise of God is true and sure. But those who reject Him will drink draughts of boiling fluids, a grievous penalty, because they did reject Him.'[7]

You must build a mosque in every village and perform your prayers as a community. . . . Stop making, selling and drinking alcohol in the markets. Spill it away and break the jars! Roll up your sleeves and work to entrench the sayings of the Prophet; avoid religious innovations and stray not from the true path. Order your women, sons, daughters and slaves to perform the five mandatory prayers every day and beat them if they fail.[8]

Muhammad Ahmad al-Mahdi *ibn* 'Abdallah, the man who declared himself the 'Successor of God's Messenger' and who modelled his entire adult life on the life of the Prophet, achieved an extraordinary amount in an extraordinarily short time.[9] His military strategies were elementary, his planning rudimentary at best; but they worked well in the terrain and circumstances of the time. Fortified towns and garrisons were patiently besieged until starvation or thirst compelled the defenders to surrender. In the field, harassing guerrilla tactics were employed until the weakened and demoralised enemy was overwhelmed in a sweeping mass attack at dawn. But if the campaign was relatively brief – less than four years from start to finish – joy in victory was even more short-lived. Muhammad Ahmad al-Mahdi survived Charles Gordon by just five months, dying at the beginning of the holy month of Ramadan in Omdurman on the west bank of the Nile, reportedly stricken by typhus. He was forty-one years old and the father of a new nation.

While Gordon has merited the attentions of at least forty biographers (and the exploits of the British army in Sudan at least as many more volumes by members of the military or intelligence services), Sudan's own leaders have remained bit-part players on the stage of their own written history. The cataclysmic events of the 1880s have been viewed through the wrong end of a telescope, the people of Sudan assuming 'the impersonal role of Fate in a real-life drama wherein the manliness and religious convictions of a handful of Europeans were put to the test'.[10] Inasmuch as there has been a literary tussle over the true identity and importance of the Mahdi himself, it has been a clash of extreme views. To his followers, he was a saintly figure, a paragon of justice, of spiritual integrity, with huge charisma and a social conscience. To his detractors, Muhammad Ahmad was a barbarian, an obese psychotic, 'the mad Mahdi', 'the mad mullah', given over to the dissolute pleasures of harem life. These sharp contrasts have rightly been described as a holy war of words, a 'jihad of the pen'.[11] On the one hand, the Mahdist movement has produced its own accounts, less biography than hagiography or propaganda; foremost among them Ismail bin 'Abd-al-Gádir's *Life of the Mahdi.*

> The Mahdi (peace be upon him) has a broad forehead and an aquiline nose. His face shines like the morning star and his complexion is brownish like that of the Arabs. While sitting and walking he is taller than anyone beside him. All Muslims are in duty bound to practise the teachings of the Mahdi, for his deed was like the deed of the Prophet. He had a victorious army, he settled all legal cases with justice and he called the people to God by his guidance and by the sword which destroys oppression. Death and defeat are the lot of anyone who fights him or quarrels with him.[12]

Both Ismail bin 'Abd-al-Gádir's work and the rambling *Fragrances of Roses and the Tree of the Mahdía*, another hagiography, deliberately set out to establish Muhammad Ahmad's credentials on all the key attributes that, according to tradition, defined the 'expected Mahdi'.[13] Constant comparisons were made with the life of the Prophet. Evidence was cited to affirm that Muhammad Ahmed was of the prophet's family and bore not just his name, as his father had the same name as the Prophet's own father, but also the birthmark on the right cheek and V-shaped gap between the top front teeth that marked him out as one favoured by God. Crucially, both books claimed that miraculous signs and celestial visitations accompanied not just the manifestation of the Mahdi and subsequent battles with Ottoman armies, but his earliest years as well. The second part of *Fragrances of Roses* presented sixty-six of Muhammad Ahmad's proclamations and letters.[14] These writings, read alongside the Mahdi's own compilation of prayers and Qoránic quotations, were compulsory reading for his followers and may be interpreted as the canonical texts of the Mahdía, the defining spiritual principles of the Mahdist movement. More recent accounts, such as the writings of Muhammad Ahmad's great-grandson al-Sádiq al-Mahdi, provide a much more measured and factually accurate appraisal but are still to some extent compromised by the author's own political (and familial) agenda.[15]

Conversely, the prejudices of a century ago, the casually demeaning terminology of 'natives' and 'savages', still resonate today as even enlightened authors fall prey to the old sniggering clichés about 'heroic depravity' and write of Sufi adherents 'dancing towards God in a giddiness of eroticism'.[16] Almost every book of the early twentieth century, when memories of Sudan campaigns were still fresh, echoed the negative propaganda of the Mahdi's enemies and revealed an appalled fascination with 'this terrible prophet, plunderer and murderer of so many thousand people'.[17] The same spirit coloured British films about the period. The 1939 production of *The Four Feathers* began with swirling orchestration and a stark caption: 'In 1885, the rebellious army of cruel Dervishes enslaved and killed many thousands of defenceless natives in Sudan.'[18] These commonplaces had their origins in a series of remarkably successful books published in the 1890s, while the death of Gordon was still fresh in European memories. Indeed, it was a military officer who played a large part in stirring up British public opinion to the extent that a fully-fledged campaign to 'avenge Gordon' was mounted in 1895. The publication in English of memoirs by two former prisoners of the Mahdi, *Fire and Sword in the Sudan* by Rudolf Slatin and *Ten Years' Captivity in the Mahdi's Camp* by Fr Joseph Ohrwalder, caused a sensation.[19] They were highly coloured, packed with bitterness and often outright contempt for the Mahdi and all he stood for, and utterly partisan; both were effectively written by Major F.R. Wingate of British military intelligence in Cairo, himself the author of a history of the period.[20] These books certainly provided some plausible eyewitness accounts of key moments in the revolution but their value as independent accounts of the period was compromised by Wingate's involvement.[21] The mirror-image of the versions by their counterparts championing the Mahdi's cause, *Ten Years' Captivity* and *Fire and Sword* amounted to little more than propaganda, the purpose of which was to denigrate the Mahdi, his successor the Khalífa 'Abdulláhi, and an ethos described by Wingate himself as 'the cruel caprice of an Oriental ruler of the most debased and tyrannical nature'.[22] The only existing English-language biography of the Mahdi, now more than seventy years old, is emotionally charged and driven by a genuine fascination for the personality of the Mahdi but fraught with the contemporary obsession with the 'noble savage'.

> They are not your Arabs of the Mediterranean lands who have become half European. They are the same Arab men whom Mohammed led against the whole universe: primitive barbarians, strong and cruel, heroic in battle, ardent in the harem, intent on war and booty, fanatical in their faith and in superstition. . . . Meanwhile in the south, the Negro lives on, remains a creature of the primeval forest, a cannibal sometimes, always an elephant hunter. The Negro hunts the elephant, the Arab hunts the Negro, and all are hunted and harassed by the Turk.[23]

Recent scholarship has gone a considerable way in helping formulate an objective assessment of the Mahdi, his revolution and its fourteen-year aftermath. Since the archives in Khartoum were first organised and a treasure-trove of documents brought to light, scholars have laboured to produce accounts illuminated by the best possible sources, the words of the protagonists on each side. Peter Holt's *The Mahdist State in the Sudan, 1881–1898* still stands out as the definitive work on the period.[24] As Sudanese scholars have intensified their own analyses of the Mahdía's political, legal, religious and social aspects, the amount of objective material available to the wider public has increased. One 1985 biography, *A Portrait of a Sudanese Revolutionary*, set out in methodical detail the backdrop of the Turkía and the world of Sufi Islam before analysing the development of the Mahdist movement from its modest beginnings to a battle-by-battle description of the military struggle.[25] But the most invaluable single contribution has been the compilation of the Mahdi's complete writings in seven volumes.[26] No analysis of Muhammad Ahmad's life and career can now be considered without reference to this comprehensive work.

What follows in this book is an objective examination of the life, character and motives of a remarkable individual – a man who can be described without exaggeration as the father of modern

Sudan. Nor is this dim and ancient history. The al-Mahdi clan still commands considerable support, its political and commercial power-base painstakingly rebuilt by al-Sayyid 'Abd-al-Rahmán al-Mahdi, the Mahdi's posthumous son, during five decades of British colonial rule. Indeed, at the last free election in 1986 the modern-day Ansár gathered comfortably the largest vote, and, were Sudan a democracy today, the Mahdi's great-grandson, al-Sádiq al-Mahdi, would very likely be Prime Minister again.[27] He may be the lesser son of a great dynasty, yet he is still the *éminence grise* of the nation, whose spiritual authority none in Sudan surpasses. The rivalries of the 1880s still resonate, too, in modern Sudanese politics. The Ansár's traditional opponents (in the arena of democratic politics at least) have always been the unionists, ideological descendants of the pro-Egyptian al-Mirghani clan who in the 1880s rejected the Mahdi's call and maintained loyal support to the government of occupation in Khartoum. When a coalition of soldiers and ideologues of the National Islamic Front usurped power in 1989, they claimed to be acting on behalf of the people in overturning a cosy 'family system' that had strangled national development. In reality, it was a *coup d'état* that created an oligarchy, underpinned by the army and conservative Muslim elements, which has since paid the people no regard at all. The Mahdi would look at both with contempt. If he had a grave, he would be spinning in it.

# 'Leaves after a Storm'
## Karari, 1898

The Mahdist forces screamed as they charged and they prayed as they died. Like the waves of a foaming white sea, they came on in their thousands under the dull sky, boiling over the sloping shoulder of Jebel Surkab, their pale and patched smocks spattered with mud kicked up from the damp earth. On that grey, overcast morning of 2 September 1898, they ran into a firestorm of bullets and artillery shells. '*Allahu akbar!*', they screamed, 'God is great!' and '*Jihád fí sabíl Allah!*', a final commitment to holy war in the Lord's cause.[1] The Mahdi himself was fourteen years dead, but his spectre, as well as his army banners, flew over the dense ranks of his followers. They still fought in his name, for his vision of an Islamic world, for his chosen successor. It had worked before, this screaming, defiant charge, against armies of demoralised Egyptians and scared garrisons in isolated outposts. But not on this day, not against Kitchener's battalions, prepared, positioned and fearsomely armed. The newly issued American Maxim guns chattered relentlessly; just one troop of four horse-drawn guns fired 14,000 rounds that day. Pull the trigger, the machinery loads, fires, ejects and fires again, 650 times in a minute – the heavy bullets punching into and through dirty cotton shifts and scrawny dark bodies. Four, five bullets explode into African flesh before the soldier realises he has even been hit. Then he spins away, his spear flying from his outstretched fingers, or is shoved rudely onto his back, to bleed and

1

die. One last finger pointed to heaven, one last strangled coughing of the sacred formula: *Lá illah ill'Allah wa Muhammad rasúl Allah* – 'There is no God but Allah and Muhammad is the Messenger of Allah'. Out of the hot, cloudy September sky came artillery shells, high-explosive 12- and 15-pound shells sending steel fragments, splinters, razors into the massed ranks of the Sudanese foot-soldiers. The Lee-Metford rifles of the infantrymen added to the carnage. The forces of Mahdism withered and died in sheaves, in drifts, in great heaps, the shattered manhood of three generations of Sudanese villagers, traders, merchants, fishermen and farmers; grandfathers, fathers and sons, soldiers for a cause that an army of occupation had vowed to exterminate. The flags of the Mahdi, who had himself promised that they would never be overthrown, were laid low, trailing blood-soaked in the dust of the Karari hills. For the Sudanese, the Battle of Karari was a day of utter, abject defeat. For the army of Major-General Herbert Kitchener, for the British people, the Battle of Omdurman was a day of reckoning, a day of revenge against the savages who had killed Gordon.

☙ ☙ ☙

The road to Karari – littered with rubble, rubbish and stunted bushes festooned with discarded plastic bags – is now a rutted dusty lane leading north out of Omdurman into the desolate plains of the northern deserts. Between the track and the bank of the Nile, which traces a parallel course in a broad green-brown slick, there are one or two newly built mansions, surrounded by high walls and beaten steel gates. New Omdurman stretches this far, nearly ten miles, into yet another new suburb, Madínat al-Níl. Approaching the battlefield, as the bare stunted hills and rocky outcrops of Karari lurk into view in the heat-haze, a huge military compound sprawls along the left side of the road, sheathed in barbed wire. Stripped helicopters and broken-down tanks guard the gates of the barracks. Humourless soldiers of the parachute brigade eye the passing cars; unlike most Sudanese conscripts, these troops are smartly turned out, their boots laced, trousers putteed, rifles oiled. No photographs here, despite the freshly painted tourist sign that proclaims: 'KARARI BATTLE: IN THIS PLACE THE MAHADIST ANSAR FACED THE ENGLISH ARMY IN 1898'.[2] Sketched on the sign in orange is the emblem of the Mahdist cause, a spear crossed with a crescent moon, and a cartoon-like *jibba*, the patched smock decreed as the Ansár uniform by the Mahdi himself. But the sign points straight into the main barracks gate. Historians are not welcome inside and the humiliations of the past are buried beneath today's assertion of military power. On Jebel Surkab itself, where the forces of the Black Flag gathered on that day of death, a Russian-built radar installation now crouches above the west side of the complex. So much for a memorial.

A mile or so away is the only formal monument to the dead of Karari, a modest stone obelisk mounted on a sturdy plinth: 'In memory of the officers, non-commissioned officers and men of the 21st Lancers who fell here Sept. 2 1898'.[3] Strangely, the monument is almost impossible to read, surrounded as it is by not one but two green steel fences. The outer ring is high and spiked, set firmly into four stone pillars at the corners of a square. The inner fence is taller still and meshed. Then it becomes clear: the fences are there to protect the memorial from the public. But the ground within is littered with stones flung by Sudanese resentful that, while their war dead are forgotten, this obelisk remains as an ever-present reminder of Britain's victory that day more than a century ago. Even the small space around the monument *inside* the inner ring is choked with skilfully aimed rocks.

ψ ψ ψ

It was the Mahdi's heir and former lieutenant, the Khalífa 'Abdulláhi, who led the Ansár to disaster that day. He was a proud and stubborn man who had ruled the Sudan with ruthless authority since his master's death in June 1885. Unlike the Mahdi, however, he was never good at taking strategic advice and his failure to heed the unanimous recommendations of his most

3

experienced commanders, voiced at a council of war on the eve of battle, was his undoing. Under Kitchener, the British had pursued a dogged campaign, fighting their way down from the Egyptian border over the previous two and a half years.[4] Their army, consisting of two British brigades, four Egyptian brigades and both British and Egyptian cavalry, was now encamped in a tight semi-circle at al-'Ijeija, the soldiers' backs to the west bank of the Nile a little way north of Karari village. The Khalífa's final council took place shortly before midnight in his personal tent as drumming rain pounded down on the white canvas. His generals were desperate to avoid another daylight encounter with the British and pressed him to endorse a night attack. The most articulate advocate of this strategy was Ibráhím al-Khalíl, a young amír from the nomadic Rizeigát clan of the western territories. He was supported by the most celebrated Ansár general, 'Osmán Digna, the hero of the Red Sea uprising years before. 'By God, these English,' he said; 'I have known them for fifteen years and I think we should attack them by night. You cannot beat the English without deceit.'[5] 'Osmán Digna argued that the Ansár had always won in battle with a combination of surprise and shock, creeping forward, using darkness and natural cover where possible, before launching the final charge from close quarters, usually as dawn was breaking. To attack in open terrain in broad daylight would be brave but suicidal. The counter-argument was led by the Khalífa's son, 'Osmán 'Sheikh al-Dín', commander of his father's personal bodyguard, the *Mulazimín*, under the Green Banner. The dispute became heated, before the Khalífa – supported, as always, by his brother, Yaqúb, commander of the Black Flag division – issued the final order: 'We fight in the morning after dawn prayers.'[6] His enemy was armed with artillery, machine-guns and repeating rifles. This disastrous decision was all the British could have desired.

The Khalifa could not have played our game better if the Sirdar had told him what he wanted done by him. . . . He never harried us on the march . . . then he came and attacked us when were entrenched in an admirable position to give the best field of fire to all our guns and rifles. If he had taken a position and made us attack him or worse if he had stayed with all his men in Omdurman our losses would have been very heavy.[7]

Much has been written about the battle, detailing the manoeuvres and counter-thrusts from the first Ansár attack, led by Ibrahím al-Khalíl and 'Osmán Azraq at 5.20 in the morning, to the rout that came before noon.[8] The Mahdists scored one small victory – negligible in the scale of the full battle – when 'Osmán Digna's Hadendawa tribesmen successfully ambushed a British cavalry unit, the 21st Lancers, which had mounted a wholly redundant charge on the fringes of the battlefield, in the *Khor Abú-Sunut*, a deep watercourse running into the Nile. It was otherwise a one-sided affair. The British troops who shot so efficiently were only too aware that they were shooting for their lives. They would be given no quarter and were not expected to give any in their turn. But they were endowed with the very best in late-nineteenth-century weaponry; their opponents were using the techniques of twelfth-century warfare and had pitifully inadequate firearms. Many of the Ansár were still using ancient flintlock rifles and even those who had Remingtons, captured from Egyptian garrisons more than a decade earlier, were carrying weapons that were no longer accurate. Sights had been knocked off, rifling was worn away to nothing and proper ammunition was in short supply. Some used .303 ammunition in the .450 chamber, padding out the cartridge with dried mud, while others shot balls of lead, brass or even wood.[9] One Royal Artillery officer, in charge of the horse-drawn 'galloping Maxims', confessed later that he quailed at the prospect of describing the destruction of the Mahdist army, whom he thought 'utterly grand and magnificent'.

On our left the ground was clear and the guns simply mowed them down, and they never got within 800 yards. . . . The gallantry of them was perfectly magnificent. You would see 10 or 12 men with big flags in a bunch right ahead of the whole rush on and on and on, and they would come without a check or waver till every man of them was shot down. Perfectly fearless and even breaking into a walk and walking on to certain death all together. . . .

Then came a charge of Begara horsemen. You never saw anything so stirring and so recklessly brave. These picturesque wild Arabs, absolutely racing to meet death, on and on they came through the hail of bullets as if they had charmed lives. Then suddenly the deadly hail seemed to catch them, like a sudden gale striking a ship, about 200 yards from us. You saw the mass stagger and horse after horse and man after man come down. . . . They came on and on till they seemed to melt and finally break to pieces and disappear, leaving nothing but dead strewn like leaves after a storm.[10]

It was a scene that was repeated many times during the day as the British responded to wave after wave of Mahdist attack with rifles, cannons, Maxims and the guns on board the *Melik* and the *Fateh* standing off al-'Ijeija. Each phase of attack, by the Green Flag and the Black, met the same relentless firepower. The amír Yaqúb was machine-gunned from his horse. Ibrahím al-Khalíl met the same fate. Around them, their men died in thousands. In the storm of bullets there was no time to pick up the dead. When the Black Flag itself finally fell, the British found more than 100 dead and more than twice as many wounded around it. Of the Khalífa's 52,000-strong fighting force, an estimated 10,800 were killed and as many as 16,000 wounded.[11] Casualties in the British brigades amounted to 28 killed (21 of them in the 21st Lancers' pointless charge across the khor) and 147 wounded. Among the British officers and 'native troops' of the Egyptian and Sudanese regiments, the losses were barely higher: 20 killed and 281 wounded.[12] Small wonder, then, that their commanding officer was moved to issue a ringing declaration of victory.

The Sirdar wishes to congratulate the Troops, British and Egyptian, on their excellent behaviour during the general action of to-day, which resulted in the total defeat of the Khalifa's forces, and has worthily avenged Gordon's death.[13]

The question of behaviour, however, dogged Kitchener for years after the battle. There were ugly scenes in the aftermath of the slaughter as the victors moved among the dead and wounded. 'Several dervishes whom we passed as dead, or beyond harm, slashed at our legs with their swords, or rose and charged,' wrote one British officer. 'One hurled himself at an Egyptian company, speared two men, and created some confusion.'[14] Such unwelcome surprises occurred many times as fighter after fighter, feigning injury or surrender, took his personal jihad to its inevitable conclusion. British forces in the east of the Sudan had had this experience in earlier campaigns; to go near a wounded man to help him or offer him water was to invite a sudden and lethal attack. So, after the battle of Tamai in the spring of 1884, British soldiers had gone round the battlefield, and 'shot every wounded or shamming man they found'.[15] This was regarded as a 'fairly safe amusement when indulged in in couples', but not so safe when followed by one man alone. So one soldier with a bayonet poked all prone Ansár fighters; if they moved, the second trooper shot them. Now, after Karari, the same policy was followed, if only informally. Winston Churchill noted that it was 'a pity' that Kitchener had not repeated his formal warning to the troops on the eve of battle on the River Atbara (in April 1897, during the advance south) that the wounded were to be spared. Strident British press coverage of the Mahdist rebellion, coupled with a popular desire to avenge General Gordon, Churchill believed, led many in the army to regard the Ansár as 'vermin – unfit to live'.

I must personally record that there was a very general impression that the fewer the prisoners, the greater would be the satisfaction of the commander. . . . The result was that there were many wounded killed. . . . A certain number – how many I cannot tell, but certainly not less than a hundred wounded Arabs – were despatched, although they threw down their arms and appealed for quarter. . . . Nearly all who perished were killed by the Soudanese and Egyptian troops. . . . Such are what I believe to be the actual facts, and I also record in contradistinction, that thousands of wounded Dervishes survived the day, that many were succoured by the soldiers, and that upwards of 5,000 prisoners were taken.[16]

Kitchener himself robustly denied what he called 'the cruel and, to my mind, disgraceful charges against the troops under my command'. In a formal report to his superiors, he categorically denied that he had 'ordered, or [given] it to be understood, that the Dervish wounded were to be massacred' or that the soldiers under his command, 'whether British, Egyptian, or Soudanese, wantonly killed wounded or unarmed Dervishes *when no longer in a position to do us injury*'.[17] In that same statement, Kitchener also denied that Omdurman had been looted in the aftermath of the battle or that civilians had been shelled in the town's streets by his gunboats. Sudanese eye-witnesses, however, made detailed assertions to the contrary.

We suffered a number of vexations during the three days during which the town was turned over to the soldiers. They entered our houses and took and ate everything within reach of their eyes and hands. No one cared to offer any opposition, for exaggerated accounts of murders and beatings up, savage enough to break a bone or two, were circulating. People preferred to bear patiently whatever might befall. However, we had one thing to be thankful for; the invaders left our womenfolk untouched, and satisfied their greed by carrying off mere possessions, such as furniture, fittings and jewels. We had to leave doors, cupboards and boxes unlocked and the street doors open.[18]

The vicissitudes of war meant that many of the Khalífa's own elite corps of bodyguards, the *mulazimín*, were taken on by the British as an urban police force. These fighters, mostly southerners, were tasked with conducting house-to-house searches and locating any fellow-southerners who might be assumed to be slaves. These, under the new British authorities, would immediately be liberated. This brought a dual misfortune to the notables of Omdurman, even those who had opposed the Mahdi and had become reluctant subjects of his successor.

> To the Sirdar of the Army,
> We beg most respectfully to state that the best help the Government could give to the natives to ameliorate their present state and save them from danger of want and hunger, is to keep to them their black servants, male and female. But what is going on at present by the entrance of soldiers to the house with the Dervish blacks, has caused the greatest confusion in the town. Many Arabs, because of their black complexion, have also been taken with blacks as blacks – and the Dervish blacks who were the Khalifa's mulazimin and who now accompany soldiers to search the houses for blacks are, for personal enmities, leading the soldiers to commit many irregularities.[19]

Sweeping into Omdurman as the surviving Ansár melted away into the desert to the south and west, the victorious army found a scene of devastation, death and squalor. Bodies lay scattered in the narrow dusty lanes. There was barely a household without its dead and dying, either soldiers from the battlefield or their relatives, struck down by shells pounding the town from the Nile.[20] The British pushed on towards the brown clay-brick dome of the Mahdi's tomb, towering over the drab landscape of Omdurman's single-storey houses, shacks and huts. The tall gubba was the symbol of the Mahdi and all he had stood for, the holiest shrine in the country for hundreds of thousands of his followers. It had not escaped the attention of the gunners on Kitchener's flotilla. Pierced by several well-aimed shells, the dome was smashed; sunlight flooded through the jagged holes to illuminate the damage within. It was, wrote one British officer, 'a splendid target and was hit plumb in the center [sic] of the dome at the 3rd round'.

It is beautifully built of red brick and lime and took some demolition. You are at liberty to assign any cause you please to its removal. We may say that so long as it stood it was a menace to our rule and an inducement to a removal of fanaticism. We may say that in its semi-demolished state it was a danger to life and living, anyhow so long as it stood it was a conspicuous memorial to celebrate the victory of the Savage over us, and now that it ceases to exist our disgrace may be forgotten and atoned for.[21]

One more thing was required to eradicate Britain's shame at that earlier 'victory of the Savage'. The dome of Omdurman had been raised above the body of Muhammad Ahmad al-Mahdi, the man who had achieved that victory fourteen years earlier and left such lasting scars on the British psyche. Not content with destroying the tomb, Kitchener now resolved to dispose of the body. To the horror of his defeated enemies, the General ordered that the Mahdi's bones be exhumed, freed from the tattered remains of their funeral shroud and thrown into the Nile. Some officers on Kitchener's own staff saw this as 'rather bad form'.[22] Churchill, who admired the Mahdi, noted with genuine outrage: 'Such is the chivalry of the conquerors!'[23] The Mahdi's skull, however, was detached from his skeleton and retained by the General, perhaps to mirror the fate of Gordon, whose head had been cut off after the Ansár capture of Khartoum. Among other officers, however, there was little sympathy for the bewilderment, shock and anger felt by most Sudanese and most Muslims.

The poor devil's bones are gone too and quite right. Many folk wonder where they are, so just let them wonder. I wonder what happens when you can't find your complete set at the Last Parade?[24]

The outcry in Britain at Kitchener's decision reached Queen Victoria herself. Whether the Sirdar had planned to set the skull in silver as an adornment for his mess table or to despatch it to the Royal College of Surgeons in London, there to be held in posterity, royal intervention ensured that some small measure of dignity was returned to the last remnant of Sudan's Muslim revolutionary leader. Kitchener was compelled to write to the Queen, justifying his destruction of both body and tomb. The Mahdi's skull was quietly buried in a Muslim cemetery at Wadi Halfa on the Egyptian border, base-camp for the British assault on Sudan. Halfa, its cemetery and the head of the Mahdi are now drowned deep under the waters of Lake Nasser.[25] The body of the man born by the Nile was returned to the Nile.

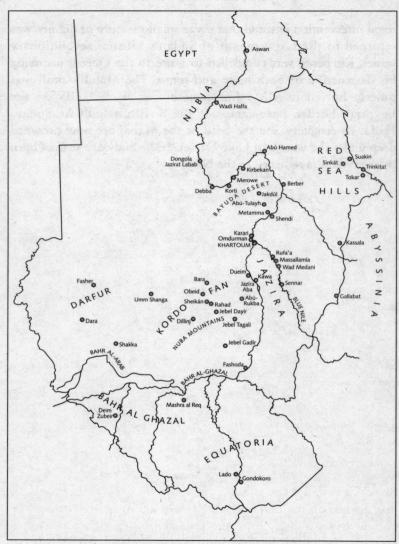

Sudan (with modern frontiers).

# ONE

## *The Boat-Builder's Son Labab Island, 1844–1849*

Heavy with silt, the Nile flows through Nubia in a turgid mud-brown stream. Thousands of miles to the south, the Blue Nile has risen in the mountains of Ethiopia, bringing the rains from the highlands to the dusty Nubian plains. From the high, forested lake lands of central Africa, the White Nile has forced its way through swamps and savannah to converge with the Blue at Sudan's heart, cutting the deep riverbanks that separate Khartoum, Omdurman and Khartoum North. The conjoined torrent, the artery of life in much of Sudan, swirls north past Dongola in a rich chocolate stream, forming a majestic snake across the miles of arid terrain. In a particularly intense rainy season, the Nile flood can become awe-inspiring and dangerous, capable of carrying away crops, orchards and homes.

At *Jazírat* Labab, a small island in mid-river ten miles south of Dongola itself, little now remains of human habitation. Severe floods devastated the island community in 1975. Farmers built new homes on the east and west banks and now row across the current to tend their crops of wheat and beans. When the water recedes after each annual inundation, ebbing back to leave sculptured terracing layered with alluvial silt, the farmers of Labab plant their crops as they always have, on the island, feeding their families and animals and perhaps profiting a little from trade with the villagers on the other river-islands at Badín and Argo and at Dongola itself. In the season of low water, the banks of the Nile become an irregular chessboard of small square fields, each contained by its own mud embankment. Minor masterpieces of amateur engineering haul the muddy water up from the river, letting it fall with gravity along a network of elegantly graded channels into the fields. With the passing years, only the mechanism of lifting the water has changed, from oxen pacing with limitless patience around the creaking *ságiya* waterwheel, or the elegant sweep of the *shádúf*'s bucket on its swinging pole, to today's dull chugging of two-stroke motors.

In a cool grove of date-palms in the centre of the island, a modest memorial marks the exact place where Muhammad Ahmad, the third of four sons of 'Abdallah Fahl the local boat-builder, was born on 12 August 1844.[1] In a low-walled yard, shaded by the thick green fronds waving above, sits a small stylised dome, just three feet high. This little structure contains nothing but a short steel spear, pointing upright, with a crescent moon across the shaft forming an elegant hilt. This, the emblem of the al-Mahdi clan, is judged to suffice; there is no name, no date, no rehearsal of the title – al-Mahdi al-Muntazar – under which Muhammad Ahmad would preach salvation, Islamic revival and holy war. But, for the contemplation of the visitor, there is a simple slogan scratched rustily into the blue paint on the crescent, *Allahu akbar wa-illahu al-hamd*: 'God is great; thanks be to him'.

Little enough has changed in the life of a rural Sudanese artisan in the long years since the birth of Muhammad Ahmad.[2] His father, 'Abdallah Fahl 'Abd-al-Walí, owned a successful business making Nile boats in a variety of sizes, as well as water wheels.[3] He fulfilled orders from local fishermen, traders and farmers (that is, all the viable commercial enterprises in the immediate vicinity) as well as working to commission from merchants further afield. At his yard on the northern point of Labab Island, the rhythms of the working day began with a shared meal, scooped steaming from the communal clay bowl on chunks of rough unleavened bread. 'Abdallah's older sons, Muhammad and Hámid, both some years older than Muhammad Ahmad, sweated alongside their father and his employees. They used basic tools, a curved adze, hand-drills and rough iron spikes, to construct the crude but rugged vessels of Nubia out of thick planks of acacia wood. At 'Abdallah's boatyard, the massive *nugúr* and the twin-masted *gyássa* took shape, as well as smaller passenger boats, all broad in the beam and sturdy, hardwearing and reliable, capable of carrying thousands of sacks of cross-river merchandise.

Muhammad Ahmad learned to walk and talk in this rustic, hard-working environment, tottering around the stacked planks and mounds of sawdust, his hand held by his sister Zeinab.[4] He was by accident of birth a member of a proud community of riverside artisans and farmers. He was a *Dongoláwi* – a term of pride among the Nubian community but, as he would discover in later life, a term of abuse elsewhere.[5] More specifically, in the complex tribal structure of the northern region, Muhammad Ahmad was of the Kunúz family of the Nubian Arab Berábera.[6] But there was more to this family than was at first apparent. Muhammad Ahmad's father used the honorific *al-Sayyid* (something like 'the honourable') on the strength of a genealogy reaching back to 'Ali bin Abí Tálib, the son-in-law of the Prophet Muhammad himself.[7] This extraordinary claim of a family of boat-builders in a humble Nile-side community to be *Ashráf*, blessed descendants of the House of the Prophet, may have stretched credulity.[8] On the west bank of the Nile opposite Jazírat Labab, however, the arid rocky landscape is scattered with the domed tombs of Muhammad Ahmad's ancestors, all still known individually and celebrated not just as ashráf but as holy sheikhs, fluent in the Qorán and pillars of the community. As an adult, Muhammad Ahmad would sign himself 'al-Sayyid' in letters written as early as August 1877, nearly four years before his declaration as the Mahdi.[9] He would also expand his personal claim, asserting that he was directly descended from the family of the Prophet not only on his father's side but also his mother's.[10] The authorised biographies of the Mahdi have all the details to hand. As a small boy, they claim, he had his glorious heritage drummed into him, generation by generation: he was Muhammad Ahmad, son of 'Abdallah, son of Fahl, 'Abd-al-Walí, 'Abdallah, Muhammad, Haj Sharíf, 'Ali, Ahmed, 'Ali, Hasb al-Nabí, Sabr, Nasr, son of 'Abd-al-Karím, Hussain, Awn-Allah, Nejm al-Dín, Osmán, Músa, Abú al-Abbás, Yúnis, Osmán, Yaqúb, 'Abd-al-Gádir, Hassan al-'Askarí, Ulwan, 'Abd-al-Baqí, Sakhra, Yaqúb, son of Hasan al-Sibt, son of *al-Imám* 'Ali, himself the son of the Prophet's paternal uncle.[11]

Those same biographers, whose endorsement by the Mahdi's descendants and followers compels us to suspect their work of being propaganda, struggle to convey much information about Muhammad Ahmad's earliest years. Physically, he grew to be tall for his age; powerfully built, strong in the shoulders, a tendency to portliness averted by an abstemious lifestyle. All who met him confirm that he had a distinctive birthmark, possibly a mole, on his right cheek, which was regarded as a holy sign. Muhammad Ahmad carried to his dying day the facial striations peculiar to his clan, three vertical scars down each cheek. The hagiography by Ismail 'Abd-al-Gádir, a highly educated and distinguished Islamic scholar from Sudan's central Kordofan province, sketches a brief and saccharine portrait of a studious, self-contained little boy.

Nothing was so dear to the Mahdi, from the beginning of his life, as isolation and keeping a distance between himself and the people – especially when they were without principles as were the people of that time. In isolation, the heart becomes pure. So, from his childhood, he was fond of seclusion and private worship. He was, from his childhood, the greatest in loyalty and the most perfect in religion.[12]

Such sanctimonious sentiments were quite possibly ascribed retrospectively, the characteristics of the adult extrapolated back to the child. But even compliments of that nature were dwarfed by the extravagances of 'Abd-al-Rahmán al-Jabri's biography, in which the boy's early childhood was blessed with a succession of miracles; all proof, al-Jabri insists, that Muhammad

Ahmad was destined for great things. Thus, in one such wonder, a young virgin woman was carrying the baby boy home when he turned in her arms to suckle her breast. God caused it to yield milk. As the miracles unfolded, the prodigious lad was able to speak to his mother when he was just fourteen days old and once, when a toddler, he trod on a thorn while playing beside the river. A bird flew down and plucked it out.[13] Another twenty-nine miracles are listed by al-Jabri as having occurred in the Mahdi's adult life. Other works list still more, while his followers still celebrate occurrences such as the time when Muhammad Ahmad was walking with a teacher on a particularly hot summer day; a single cloud appeared, they say, to shelter this remarkable boy.[14]

It is all too easy to decry these stories as laughable invention and plenty have done so. A typical commentary by a British colonial administrator in the 1920s poured scorn on al-Jabri's 'unscrupulous license'. 'No honest zealot could have resorted to the deliberate forgeries with which he supports his argument of such accounts,' the commentator observes before noting that while such 'impudent forgeries . . . would fail to deceive those natives of Sudan who lay any claim to learning, it is equally certain that they would be blindly accepted by the ignorant'.[15] Which is exactly the point. Westernised readers might be alienated by accounts of miracles but to dismiss them unsympathetically would be to underestimate both the power of popular superstition and the importance of miracles, *karámát*, in the religious life of nineteenth-century Sudan. The vast bulk of the Mahdi's followers were villagers and rural nomads who shared the belief of the Sufis in saints living and dead – saints who studied the Holy Book, led often excessively ascetic lifestyles and occasionally saw visions. Miracles were seen as proof positive of a saint's holiness, or *baraka*. Some sophisticated townspeople in Khartoum may have scoffed, but few were immune to the temptation to invoke the names of saints to avert trouble or illness and make pilgrimage to the tombs and shrines that dotted the countryside. Anyone whose baraka had produced such wonders at such an early age, the logic ran, must be pure indeed. His protection must be worth seeking, his teachings worth following.[16]

ψ ψ ψ

At the time of Muhammad Ahmad's birth in 1844, the town now known as Dongola had another name.[17] It was a military camp, established by well-armed refugees from Egypt who had fled up the Nile into Nubia. They called their fortress, a few hours downstream from the ancient Christian city of Dongola, *Úrdí al-Manfúkh*, 'Fatty's Camp', after their leader Muhammad 'Fatty' al-Manfúkh. The settlement that inevitably grew around the fortress became known first as al-Úrdí, then Dongola al-Úrdí, then simply New Dongola.[18] It was a settlement of modest, mostly single-storey houses, built of mud-brick, leather or goat-hair matting, their roofs flat palm-leaves or straw cones. Each house was separated from its neighbour by at least one large courtyard, used for keeping animals; the result was a maze of irregular lanes and alleys, blind corners and abrupt cul-de-sacs.[19] European travellers passing through were not impressed. 'New Dongola is a miserable place,' wrote a French draughtsman, Louis-Maurice Adolphe Linant de Bellefonds, travelling up the Nile with an Egyptological expedition. 'These are really bad houses, built of mud. The village sits in flat, open country which is unhealthy because of the plants and trees that cover it.'[20] When the American Quaker adventurer Bayard Taylor arrived at Dongola on camelback in 1851, he was scarcely more impressed.

About two o'clock, we descried the minaret of El Ordee, its sugar-loaf top glittering white in the sun. . . . As we approached, it presented the usual appearance of the Nubian towns – a long line of blank mud walls, above which rise, perhaps, the second stories of a few more ambitious mud houses; here a sycamore, there a palm or two, denoting a garden within; a wide waste of sand round about, some filthy people basking in the sun, and a multitude of the vilest kind of dogs. . . . The town may be seen in an hour. It contains no sights, except the bazaar, which has about twenty tolerable shops, principally stocked with cottons and calicoes. Outside are a few shops, containing spices, tobacco, beads, trinkets and the like small articles. Beyond this was the *soog*, where the people came with their coarse tobacco, baskets of raw cotton, onions, palm-mats, gourds, dates, faggots of fire-wood, sheep and fowls.[21]

There was a simple explanation for the dismal scene that awaited Taylor in the 'melancholy, deserted region' around Dongola, where 'untenanted villages line the road . . . palms growing wildly and rankly, water-courses broken down, sakias dismantled, and everywhere dwellings in ruins'.[22] The little settlement, surrounded by farmers and merchants of the Danágla, Kabábish and Bisharín tribes, should have been poised for growth. The Nile itself was the main north–south artery for trade and communication. Striking west into the Nubian Desert, a traveller would bisect the *Darb al-Arba'ín*, the legendary forty-day caravan route linking the western lands of Sudan with the Egyptian Nile at Assyút. Dongola should have naturally evolved into a provincial crossroads, a destination for settlers and regional hub of trade and administration. But twenty-three years before the Mahdi's birth, war had come to the northern Sudan.

Far from this negligible dot on the map of geopolitical change, the tectonic plates of Europe were shifting. The nineteenth century was the age of European domination, driven by industrialisation, economic boom, exploding population growth and aggressive imperialist expansion. In the 1840s, Italy was rebelling against Austro-Hungarian imperial rule; Britain had seized Natal in southern Africa; Prussia was resisting attempts to form a united Germany; France, under the elected monarch Louis Philippe, had built its first railway; and Karl Marx was hard at work on his *Communist Manifesto*. The Ottoman Empire was no longer the military or cultural force it had once been; yet its arm was still long. From the 'Sublime Porte' at Constantinople, named after the lofty *Báb al-'Ali* gate of the Grand Vizier's residence and administrative headquarters near Topkapi Palace, administrators and soldiers dispersed to do the bidding of the Sultan across the reaches of an empire that, even in decline, still stretched from northern Romania to Aden, from Tunis to Kuwait.[23] Even a small Nile-side town, apparently so far from the machinations of Europe's political elite, would not be immune when invading Ottoman troops left their mark.

In 1820–1, the territory now known as Sudan was invaded by an army from Egypt, itself a satellite of the Ottoman Empire. The mastermind behind the invasion was Muhammad 'Ali Pasha, technically Governor of Egypt and subordinate to the Sultan but in reality the ambitious viceroy of a nation that was independent in all but name.[24] His own relationship with the sultanate in Constantinople – the Porte – was ambivalent. On the one hand, successive Sultans could depend on Muhammad 'Ali to crush dissent in Egypt. Most notoriously, in 1811, he ordered the massacre in Cairo's citadel of several hundred Mamluk chiefs, influential warlords whose families had controlled Egypt for centuries and whose remaining members were forced to flee south into Nubia.[25] Muhammad 'Ali could also be relied on to pay to the Porte an annual tribute gathered in the territory under his control, as well as contributing troops to Ottoman campaigns. But behind the mask of obedience lay Muhammad 'Ali's desire to carve out an empire for himself, over which he and his descendants would rule; what seemed like loyal service was designed to help him realise this ambition. The eradication of the Mamluks effectively sealed his own authority in Cairo and he was able to get rid of troublesome and disobedient Albanian troops within his army by sending them to their deaths in the Sultan's campaign to suppress a rebellion by Wahhabi adherents in Arabia. But if he were to entertain any plausible aspirations to empire-building, Muhammad 'Ali knew that he had to have a disciplined army, a new force that would be forcibly conscripted and trained along French and Ottoman lines.[26] Reluctant to conscript Egypt's own rural labourers, the *fellahín*, he looked instead further south, where slaves might be found in their thousands.

It was Muhammad 'Ali's third son, Ismail Kámil Pasha, who led the first of two expeditionary forces that swept down through the northern and central territories of Sudan, toppling the existing order.[27] Egyptian historians have insisted that this was a legitimate annexation, carried out on the explicit orders of the Sultan, the Commander of the Faithful.[28] But the campaign was more pragmatic than idealistic, such disingenuous claims screening the reality of an all-out hunt for slaves and loot. For Muhammad 'Ali, there were additional fringe benefits. Elements in the Egyptian army hostile to his planned changes might fall as casualties during the campaign; it was also a good opportunity to smash for good the Mamluk chieftains still surviving in Nubia.

♱ ♱ ♱

The shadow of the occupation fell lightly over Muhammad Ahmad's earliest years. The provincial Governor at Dongola al-Úrdí, Hassan Rifa'at al-Stanali, maintained a garrison, oversaw the collection of taxes and watched for any signs of local disaffection.[29] But it was not until Muhammad Ahmad's father, 'Abdallah Fahl, took his three sons, his daughter and his pregnant wife south in 1849 that the family moved into the Sudanese heartland, where powerful political forces were at work and resentments against the Ottoman–Egyptian occupiers were more sharply focused.[30] There were two compelling reasons for the move to a new home, less than a day's journey from the capital at Khartoum. 'Abdallah had won a contract to build boats for the government. The Ottoman occupying force controlled the northern and central districts but was set on further expansion, south and west. Pushing upriver into the territories around the Gazelle River (*Bahr al-Ghazál*) and into Equatoria, the occupying force needed boats of all shapes and sizes to ship soldiers, civilian administrators, weapons, ammunition and food.[31] Once the campaigns were over, remote outposts would need supplying. And in the wake of conquest, the merchant tribes of the north – the Danágla and the Ja'aliyín – were quick to migrate, following fresh opportunities to expand their trade. It all depended on river transport. Powered steamers would not be brought to Sudan until the 1860s and, until then, boats were big business. The second reason for the move was that timber in the quantity needed for boat-building was in increasingly short supply in the Dongola region. Date palms there were aplenty, as well as 'dense forests of mimosas', but *sunut* wood, heavy, hard and essential for a tough boat, was scarce.[32] Future business prospects in Dongola appeared limited at best, while proximity to Khartoum promised lucrative trade after the completion of the government contract. 'Abdallah's planned destination was Karari, on the west bank of the Nile a short way north of Omdurman and an easy journey upstream to Khartoum, where forests of acacias remained unexploited.

The family's journey up-river by boat was made in four stages, although the precise timescale is not clear. For Muhammad Ahmad's heavily pregnant mother, the rigours of travelling by open boat, often cooking and sleeping on board, were even more arduous than usual. Their first stop was at the house of 'Ali wad Tanír, near Shendi. Then came the village of Sayyál, where the family disembarked at the house of Munír Muhammad. It was on the third stage of the journey, when they were resting at Umm Karábíj, that a shattering blow befell the family: 'Abdallah the boat-builder fell ill and died.[33] From this time on, the small boy Muhammad Ahmad was taken care of by his elder brothers. The eldest, Muhammad, took over as head of the family and clearly became a father figure to his younger brothers. Within a few weeks of their arrival at Karari, a younger brother was born, named 'Abdallah after the father he would never know. Muhammad and Hámid set about establishing the family business in this new location, compelled by the pressures of the government contract to settle in rapidly, recruit competent local carpenters and get down to work. The tragedy of a father's loss must have affected the five-year-old boy greatly. It certainly increased his tendency to seclusion, prayer and intense meditation. At this extraordinarily young age, Muhammad Ahmad embarked on a long road of spiritual development and scholarship, subsidised by loyal and loving brothers. If, as al-Jabri put it, the Mahdía was a tree, then the sapling was taking root close to the heart of enemy territory.

# TWO

# *The Shadow of the Saráya*
# *Khartoum, 1849–1861*

If a suggestion from Satan should assail your mind, seek refuge
with God; for he hears and knows all things. Those God-fearing
people who remember him when an evil thought from Satan
assaults them, lo! they see aright![1]

A soft, musical murmur pervades the *khalwa* attached to the al-
Mahdi family mosque in Omdurman's Wad Nubáwi district.[2] The
boys in this Qoránic school, clustered on mats of straw and
sackcloth in whatever shade they can find in the mosque's dusty
courtyard, try to memorise the Sura of the Heights.

When the Qorán is read, listen to it with attention, and hold your
peace that you may receive mercy. And remember your Lord in
your very soul, with humility and in reverence, without loudness in
words, in the mornings and evenings; do not be among the
heedless. Those who are near the Lord do not disdain to worship
him; they celebrate his praises and bow down before him.[3]

Heads bent over their writing-boards, chanting and rocking
rhythmically, the boys embed in their memories the concluding
verses of the sura. The most confident sings out the melodious
verses in a strong voice, not even glancing at the text scribbled in
jet-black ink across his wooden writing-board. When the verses

are thoroughly mastered, they will be washed off and a fresh
section of the holy text dictated. Sheikh Bábikr al-Yás, the
strikingly handsome imám presiding over the khalwa, watches the
boys with care. He and Sheikh Abú-Bakr Yáhya have more than
250 students in their care; some are teenagers but many are as
young as six.[4] It is easy to imagine the young Muhammad Ahmad
in just such a place, industriously cramming, dreaming of the day
when he will be tested and found not wanting, his knowledge of
the Qorán complete. And perhaps this very sura, the Sura of the
Heights, had special significance for him. It has a simple enough
message: Learn from the past. Illustrating man's spiritual history
from the time of Adam, the sura expounds the doctrine of holy
revelation through various apostles to the time of the Prophet
Muhammad – at whose hands, Muslims believe, God's revelation
was completed. For Muhammad Ahmad, this would be a message
to take to heart in later life. The predecessors of the Mahdi had
consistently been resisted and rejected but truth triumphed in the
end and evil was humbled. For a believer, the *Súrat al-'Aráf* leaves
no room for doubt: God's plan never fails.

With the family now settled at Karari, Muhammad Ahmad's
education became a priority. His brothers Muhammad and Hámid,
hard at work in the new boatyard on the west bank of the Nile,
consulted friends, relatives and other members of the Danágla
diaspora in the Khartoum–Omdurman region in their search for
ideal teachers. There were many scholars and holy men to choose
from and the serious little boy was apt for religious study and
abstinence. But not all schools were good. The territories of Sudan
lay on the fringe of the Muslim world; books were scarce and
teachers with a substantial grip on more than basic Qoránic
studies (leavened with indigenous, African-influenced traditions)
were scarcer still. Young boys often had to travel away from home
for extended periods to study particular subjects under particular
masters, boarding at distant schools. In Khartoum itself,

Muhammad Ahmad studied under Sharaf al-Dín Abú-al-Sádiq, a traditional holy man known as a *faqí*.[5] Other tutors during Muhammad Ahmad's earliest school years included faqí Mahbúb al-Habáshi and Sheikh Mahmúd al-Mubárak at Burri, a village to the east of Khartoum on the bank of the Blue Nile.[6] He appears to have been an exemplary student during these years. His followers say he became a *hafiz*, a student who has memorised the entire text of the Qorán by heart, a formidable task demanding exceptional application, by the age of eleven.[7]

The life of a boarding-school student of the Qorán was hard. The day began as early as 4 a.m., with practice and recitation of the previous day's lessons. Once correctly recited, the verses were washed off and replaced by new verses to be committed to memory. Then followed lessons on critical explanation of the Qorán, on Islamic law, on the life of the Prophet, the early years of Islam and even military theory.[8] At intervals through the long day, studies were interrupted for communal prayers.[9] There was little time for sleep; the *masháyikh* and *fuqara'* were demanding masters, dictating lessons from their own prodigious memories from the vantage point of a wooden rope-strung bedstead, on which they sat cross-legged.[10] Errors were punished with beatings. Some students were sent out to beg for food in the local market. Pupils would also be expected to hunt for firewood, cutting it from nearby forests or fishing driftwood from the Nile.[11]

☙ ☙ ☙

During Muhammad Ahmad's childhood at Karari, Omdurman was a small community in the growing shadow of the new administrative capital at Khartoum, on the other side of the river.[12] Yet, of the two, Omdurman was the more ancient, lying at the junction of three important trade routes: west to the savannah of Kordofan and its main town, al-Obeid; north downriver to Shendi and Dongola; and east to the Red Sea Hills and Abyssinia. Migrants had settled here at the confluence of the Niles for at least 200 years, though by the time Muhammad

Ahmad's family arrived, in the footsteps of many Danágla and Mahas tribal émigrés from the north, it was still just a small settlement of twisting alleys and simple houses, surrounded by peaceful fields and citrus orchards.[13] As an obvious strategic rendezvous point, its merits were recognised not just by Ismail Pasha's invading Ottoman army, which camped at Omdurman on 18 May 1821 on its way to toppling the Funj capital at Sennar, but by the Kurdish cavalry commander, Maho Bey, who made Omdurman his temporary capital five years later, as the development of Khartoum began.[14]

The name 'Khartoum' itself means simply 'Elephant's Trunk'; with a stretch of the imagination, the junction of the two Niles could be seen to resemble the delicate cleft in the tip of such a trunk.[15] Its location was perfect for the establishment of a new capital, the river on the western and northern sides offering not just access but additional protection. As Ottoman colonial grip tightened on Sudanese territories, so Khartoum grew to fit its role as the hub of an authoritarian and centralised administration, whose twin *raisons d'être* were slavery and taxation. The invading army had found little but 'three huts and a large cemetery' when they first reached the confluence of the rivers in 1821; marauding Shilluk tribesmen from up the White Nile had destroyed an earlier settlement.[16] But, as with Dongola to the north, what began as a military camp started to attract civilians to service its needs. As the historian C.E.J. Walkley has written, the community grew into a small settlement of modest houses, made of mud-brick, hair matting and cowhide, clustered around a central mosque.[17]

Khartoum had no attractions in itself, no industries, and no inherent source of wealth; the tribes around breathed malevolence towards the hated 'Turks', their new masters. Moreover, with deserts for hundreds of miles to the north, the Viceroy of Egypt sent to this 'Soudan graveyard' his unruly Arnauts, disaffected officers, civilians and convicts.[18]

In spite of all the settlement fortuitously led to commerce, which gradually expanded. Merchants, adventurers and others were attracted later . . . Egyptians, Greeks, Italians, Maltese, French and others sped up-stream, so that by 1840 there was a population of 30,000, afterwards doubled, though fluctuating according to the exigencies of war and trade.

Dongola boatmen flocked thither, first for honest toil, but later with others, as lawless buccaneers, bound for their El Dorado, the White Nile slave-raids. To these were added Blue Nile and Berber traders, river men and freebooters who formed a large class. The fleets of sailing-boats brought in their train boat-builders and sail-makers, while the military forces needed forage, artificers, gunsmiths, saddlers and tailors. The mercantile community had its scribes, tinsmiths, filigree goldsmiths, bakers, pipe-makers and water-carriers. . . . But this semblance of civilisation was only a film concealing corruption and savagery.[19]

By the time Muhammad Ahmad began his studies at the school of Sharaf al-Dín Abú-al-Sádiq in 1850, most of the Khartoum township was still a ramshackle maze of zigzagging lanes. There was a huge gulf between the lifestyles and housing of the rich and the poor. Most citizens had to be content with a single low-roofed room and a small yard, or *hosh*, for the donkey, sheep or goats. Accommodation for the slaves who worked for the urban elite sprang up like mushrooms on the outskirts of the city, the nineteenth-century equivalent of the slums and shanty-towns of today's displaced or migrant-worker communities. The wealthy of Khartoum, by contrast, lived in considerable style. The town's political and commercial dignitaries had sprawling and luxurious accommodation, well staffed with employees and slaves who cleaned, looked after the horses and prepared lavish meals. The few really lavish private houses built in Khartoum before 1860 were modelled, like the splendid mansions at Suakin on the Red Sea coast, on Arabian styles imported from Jedda; after that date, European influences began to filter down from Egypt.[20] Courtyards, stores and stables surrounded the inner sanctum of *diwán*, family rooms and sleeping chambers. Quarters for servants and slaves, kitchens and other unsightly parts of the house were safely partitioned off. With such comfortable dwellings went an equally lavish lifestyle. Senior government officials maintained substantial harems of wives and concubines, slaves and free women from as far apart as Georgia and Abyssinia, often installing them up-river at leafy Wad Medani, where the Pasha's women could enjoy a cooler climate beside the fast-flowing Blue Nile. These richly dressed ladies were often draped in 'diamonds, notes of gold tissue and large cashmere shawls'.[21] Money changed hands in a bewildering variety of currencies. Ottoman, Egyptian, Spanish and Austrian coins in gold, silver and copper, in pounds, dollars, guilders, piastres and riyals, passed between the wealthiest merchants.[22] Despite the fact that Khartoum was a small settlement with few roads (none of them paved), status had to be flaunted and so horse-drawn carriages were commissioned from Paris for senior officials, shipped in pieces and reassembled in Khartoum. These were elegant, luxurious vehicles, with well-sprung chassis, embossed leaves and scrolls on the coachwork and a scalloped seat for the distinguished passenger's personal bodyguard.[23] The most stylish residence in town, of course, was the *Saráya*, the spacious palace housing the Governor-General himself on the bank of the Blue Nile. By the time of Bayard Taylor's visit in 1852, it was the centrepiece of a town that presented 'a picturesque and a really stately appearance' to the visitor.

The line of buildings extended for more than a mile along the river, and many of its houses were embowered in gardens of palm, acacia, orange and tamarind trees. The Palace of the Pasha had a certain appearance of dignity, though its walls were only unburnt brick, and his *hareem*, a white, two-story [*sic*] building, looked cool and elegant amid the palms that shaded it. Egyptian soldiers, in their awkward, half-Frank costume, were lounging on the bank before the Palace, and slaves of inky blackness, resplendent in white and red livery, were departing on donkeys on their various errands. . . . For Soudan, it is a building of some pretension, and the Pasha took great pride in exhibiting it.[24]

28

Small as Khartoum was, it was the capital of an enormous territory; not as big as Sudan today but still hundreds of thousands of square miles, larger than France, one of Europe's leading imperial powers. In this huge land, the Pasha in the Saráya was the supreme authority. When Muhammad Ahmad came with his family to Karari in 1849, Khálid Khusraw, a native of Constantinople, was *Hikimdár* (Governor-General) of Sudan Districts.[25] In November that year, at the conclusion of his four-year term, the Governor-General handed over to 'Abd-al-Latíf 'Abdallah, a Circassian naval officer of a violent temper who had commanded the Ottoman imperial fleet.[26] These were the latest in a succession of military men from all over the empire – Turks, Kurds, Syrians, Albanians and Greeks – summoned by the imperial viceroy in Cairo to administer his Sudanese territories. The occupation may have been launched from Egypt but it was largely staffed by the empire's Turkish-speaking elite. Egyptians in the army could not expect to rise above the rank of major; their civilian counterparts were similarly restricted to subordinate duties. Indigenous Sudanese almost never managed to rise above the lower layers of administrative bureaucracy. As for the top job, in the early years of the occupation at least, the authorities rarely promoted anyone to be Governor-General without a good track record in military campaigning, provincial administration elsewhere in the empire or experience in the territory of Sudan itself. Such rigorous criteria did not last. Cairo used Sudan increasingly as a dumping-ground for incompetent lesser officials, disaffected army officers, deportees and even criminals. On one occasion, the ruler of Egypt himself was forced to write to Khartoum after three undesirable individuals had been sent packing from Sudan: 'You say that you wish the three persons to be returned to Egypt on the ground that they are deportees. This is a misapprehension; we sent them to Sudan not as deportees but as governors.'[27] By 1852, an American visitor noted that Egyptian officials in Khartoum 'generally consider themselves as exiles, and a station in Soudân carries with it a certain impression of disgrace'.[28] Small wonder, then, that, so far from Cairo and in the absence of any lines of communication more efficient than the Egyptian postal service, the rulers of this lucrative new acquisition were occasionally tempted to line their own pockets. Even for highly competent officials and military officers, this uncomfortable exile might be made more bearable by the opportunities for financial gain. So, even as popular discontent with the occupying powers swelled, the administration in what would be the waning years of Ottoman rule was delegated to substandard Egyptian officers and bureaucrats or to foreign employees and attachés. Many foreigners made their way to Egypt and its dependencies to seek their fortunes, driven south by conflict, instability or social constraints at home: Italians and Frenchmen after 1815 and Americans after the Civil War. Individuals who did not quite fit into the establishment back home, were too restless to accept a conventional career or were simply too eccentric similarly turned up in Cairo and Khartoum. The names of Baker, Messedaglia, Lupton, Hicks, Gessi, Slatin, Giegler and, of course, Gordon echo through the chronologies of late-nineteenth-century Sudan.

Thus it was that throughout Muhammad Ahmad's childhood, the administration in Khartoum tirelessly pursued the original and brutally commercial mandate of the occupation, which the ruler of Egypt had described as 'this capital matter', the procurement of 'negroes'.[29] Their predecessors had been as industrious, mounting seasonal raids against the tribes of central and eastern districts for thousands of men, women and children.[30] The explicit policy was twofold: the forcible recruitment of slave-soldiers for the Egyptian army and the maintenance of a steady supply for both domestic and export markets.[31] Slave conscripts made surprisingly effective soldiers. Indeed, the most courageous, loyal and efficient soldiers in the government army during Muhammad Ahmad's later uprising were the slaves captured in the south, entrusted with the best firearms and trained together to form battalions of *Jihadía*, 'holy warriors'. The Ottomans had systematically enslaved conquered peoples in the Caucasus, the Balkans and North Africa for centuries to supplement, replace and, when necessary, subdue Turkish soldiers with slave battalions.[32] In Sudan, their obedience and loyalty appears to have been greater than even their Egyptian officers. As successive Governors-General expanded their conquests southwards, opening up Equatoria and Bahr al-Ghazál in the late 1860s, the trade took off like wildfire. One calculation of 'this new and infamous traffic' by a European administrator in the service of the Khedive estimated that, from 1860, 'in the brief space of fourteen years more than four hundred thousand women and children were taken from their native country, and sold in Egypt and Turkey, while thousands and thousands were massacred in the defence of their families'.[33]

Sudanese society in the northern provinces was anything but averse to this immensely lucrative trade. Long before the Egyptian invasion, the indigenous authorities in Sudan had made a tidy profit from the export of slaves over the Red Sea to Jedda.[34] The societies of many tribes who lived on the river, including the Danágla and the Ja'aliyín, were built around slavery and the Baggára nomads of Kordofan and Darfur 'devoted themselves essentially to hunting – hunting slaves and hunting ostriches or elephants'.[35] Capturing slaves was an accepted side effect of inter-tribal fighting and completely acceptable in religious terms.

For Muhammad Ahmad himself, slavery was part of normal life. Indeed, the earliest surviving example of his personal seal is on a document in which he witnesses the legal transfer of a slave woman between two of his brothers and his aunt.[36] That acceptance reflects exactly the attitude of the Qorán, which guided Muhammad Ahmad's every decision. The Holy Book may have sought to mitigate the effects of slavery but the several matter-of-fact references amounted to an endorsement that was quite satisfactory for him.[37]

# THREE

# *The Handclasp*
## *Al-Kawa and Berber, 1861–1868*

The year 1861 was a pivotal time in Muhammad Ahmad's life. By the age of seventeen, he had explored thoroughly all the traditional Islamic sciences.[1] As well as the Qorán itself, assumed to be the foundation of all his learning, he studied *fiqh*, the philosophy of Islamic Sharí'a law. He took additional courses in theology and the doctrine of Allah's unity (*tawhíd*), in critical explanation of the Qorán (*tafsír*), in the sayings and traditions of the Prophet (*Hadíth*), in Arabic language and grammar, mathematics and astronomy. Far from being the illiterate barbarian subsequently depicted by his enemies, he was, for a Sudanese of his time, broadly educated, well read and possessed of the faculties that would be necessary when it came to arguing his case coherently with state-sanctioned Muslim scholars and judges. As his education had progressed through his teens, he had become familiar with the works of theologians and scholars, militants and mystics from across the spectrum of Islamic philosophy.

The young student devoured manuscripts, hand-copied and passed down from teacher to student, by a variety of authors who helped shape his religious and political thinking.[2] Perhaps the most militant influence was Ibn Taimía, a thirteenth-century legal scholar who lived in Baghdad (like Khartoum, a city under occupation) and who had himself been greatly influenced by the ninth-century legal scholar, Ibn Hanbal.[3] His core ideas – a belief in the ideal Muslim community in the image of the original community surrounding the Prophet Muhammad in Medina, and contempt for contemporary Muslim leaders who had failed to ensure proper standards of faith and practise among the people – remained undiluted by the passage of a millennium. In a precedent echoed by his many followers through the centuries, Ibn Taimía issued a *fatwa*, a legal ruling, against the occupying forces in Baghdad, denouncing them as apostates and infidels and calling on all true Muslims to revolt in order to establish a truly Islamic state. The Mahdi's own teachings would follow these lines closely.

But Muhammad Ahmad's influences were not all militant revivalists. Other thinkers, such as Mohi-al-Dín ibn 'Arabi, Ahmad ibn Idrís and Muhammad 'Ali al-Sanúsi, focused more on the spiritual development of the individual and his personal relationship with God. Ibn 'Arabi was a poet and philosopher, celebrated by his admirers as one of the world's great spiritual teachers, and the author of more than 350 volumes of fine poetry, compilations of prayers, and philosophical treatises.[4] The influence of Ahmad ibn Idrís and Muhammad 'Ali al-Sanúsi stemmed from their founding of influential and pervasive sects, whose followers spread from Arabia across north Africa and down into Sudan. These were the Sufi brotherhoods, to which Muhammad Ahmad would devote the next phase of his life.[5] Ahmad ibn Idrís never travelled from Morocco to Sudan but his students, migrating into the Nile Valley, established indigenous Sudanese branches of the sect – and his Sufi litanies were taught to Muhammad Ahmad by one of his followers, 'Abdulláhi al-Dufáni.[6] The followers of Muhammad 'Ali al-Sanúsi, whose proto-nationalist activism was also influenced by the teachings of Ibn Taimía, settled mainly in what is now Libya. Sheikh al-Sanúsi's writings were widely available in Sudan.[7]

Such reading material may have influenced Muhammad Ahmad to become a disciple of a Sufi brotherhood, or *taríqa*.[8] His tutor, in the Sammánía order, was Sheikh Muhammad al-Sharíf Núr al-Dá'im, a religious figure of considerable stature and distinguished ancestry, who taught in a small community near al-Kawa on the west bank of the White Nile, 100 miles south of Khartoum.[9] The sheikh's new *muríd*, or disciple, would serve him with devotion and submission, for the sheikh of a taríqa had absolute authority and was believed to be infallible, guided personally by Allah. For an aspirant Sufi, the journey towards perfect knowledge of God could only be undertaken under the watchful guidance of an appropriately qualified sheikh. Or, as one early Sufi teacher, Abú Yazíd al-Bistámi, has been quoted as saying: 'He who has no Shaykh, his Shaykh is Satan.'[10] Each sheikh received his licence to preach from his own master and a chain of spiritual authority passed inherited and infallibly validated rites from generation to generation.[11] Muhammad Ahmad's initiation would have featured an essential rite, the oath of allegiance accompanied by a handclasp, placing the novice's hand between those of his new master. This oath, the *bay'a*, is widely used in Islamic countries as a sign of formal recognition and loyalty; it was modelled on the oath sworn by the followers of the Prophet himself and referred to explicitly in the Qorán.

> Verily those who swear their loyalty to you do no less than swear their loyalty to God. The hand of God is over their hands. Then anyone who violates his oath does so to the detriment of his own soul; anyone who fulfils what he has sworn to God will win from the Lord a great reward.[12]

Muhammad Ahmad's novitiate in the taríqa lasted seven years, a period that took the young student into his early twenties and during which he began to acquire a reputation for extreme asceticism. One particular habit became ingrained and appears to have been the first conscious imitation of the Prophet Muhammad, who is celebrated by Muslims for having prayed more frequently and intensely than even the mandatory five daily prostrations. Beginning after the *'asha* prayers at around nine in the evening, Muhammad Ahmad would stand in a secluded spot and recite the Qorán to himself through the night, from memory, until the pre-dawn prayers at around four in the morning. This was another conscious imitation of the Prophet, who had resorted to a cave at Hirá, a few miles north-east of Mecca, to pray in solitude, waiting

for the revelation that would come to him 'like the break of day'.[13]
After praying with his fellow-students, Muhammad Ahmad would
resume his intense solitary meditations, reciting traditional Sufi
invocations and elements of the sect's special rites handed down
from his masters.[14] Given such ardent meditations, as well as a
near-starvation diet and a roster of menial duties performed as a
demonstration of his humility, it is hardly surprising that
Muhammad Ahmad was the apple of his master's eye. Sheikh Núr
al-Dá'im would later compose an elegant tribute to his pupil.

> He came to me near Jebel Sultan on the riverbank,
> Desiring to follow the right path, guided by me.
> So I accepted his oath, to obey my orders and my prohibitions.
> He pursued the path of praiseworthy deeds in all sincerity,
> Regularly invoking God in his prayers, in silence and aloud.
> He exerted his efforts on the path of praiseworthiness
> And I, not knowing what the consequences would be, promoted
>   him.
> He stayed with us, performing services too humble even for the
>   lowliest,
> Like grinding grain and gathering firewood.
> He gave to the needy, as if he never feared poverty.
> How he fasted! How he prayed! How he recited the word of
>   God, tears running down his face.
> How he prayed long into the night, through to mid-morning.
> Thus he quenched his thirst from the spring of the people
> And his goodness won him the admiration of the people.[15]

Like every other taríqa, Sheikh Núr al-Dá'im's sect had its own
colourfully hand-stitched banner, bearing the Muslim's declaration
of belief, 'There is no God but Allah and Muhammad is the
Messenger of Allah', and the names of the brotherhood and its
founder.[16] Idiosyncratic dress, too, characterised the adherent to
most Sufi brotherhoods. Befitting their aspirations to humility,
poverty and asceticism, novices wore simple shifts of rough,
homespun cotton, similar to the knee-length *arrági* still worn by

rural Sudanese today.[17] This tunic, known variously as a *muraqqaʿa* or a *jibba*, had been the uniform of Sufi orders for centuries and represented contempt for the material things of this world; as the cotton frayed and tore, the garment was not replaced but repaired with patches of coarse wool or felt.[18] The abstemious novice was known as a *darwísh*, a word whose simple meaning of a 'poor fellow' acquired, among Sudanese, very positive spiritual implications. Among foreigners, the word 'dervish' quickly acquired a strongly pejorative sense, denigrating and dismissive.

Central to Muhammad Ahmad's prayers, both solitary and communal, was the *dhikr*, literally, 'remembrance' or 'recollection' of Allah. Like his fellow novices, he was required to know and use all the correct litanies and formulae of Sheikh Núr al-Dáʿim's branch of the taríqa, repeatedly chanting fixed phrases in a fixed order, especially the 99 names of Allah and verses from the Qorán.[19] For an individual, the dhikr is the hallmark of an intense, internal version of Islam, achieving knowledge of God by prayer, meditation, physical movement and spiritual ecstasy – a practice endorsed repeatedly in the Qorán itself.[20] Sufis have traditionally stressed 'inwardness over outwardness, contemplation over action, spiritual development over legalism and cultivation of the soul over social interaction'.[21] The taríqa's prayers, then, were 'planned with careful gradation and exercises, with the help of group suggestion, of rhythmical speech and breathing and of rhythmical movement, so as by a kind of self-hypnotism to banish any external sight or sound or thought'.[22] Many fraternities collated these repetitive litanies into small volumes or prayer books. Such a collection was known as a *rátib*, a word giving the sense that the prayers were 'ordered' and 'arranged'. These meditations could become extremely intense. Indeed, traditions dating back to the time of the Prophet refer to the trance-like state into which the Sufi worshipper may work himself through relentless chanting and swaying. Muhammad is said to have urged his followers to 'be abundant in the mention of God the Most High to such a degree that men call you demented'.[23]

Orthodox Muslims were not the only ones who heartily disapproved of such excesses. Clarence Brownell, a Connecticut-born explorer who passed through Khartoum in 1862, noted in his diary: 'The mosk is lighted up tonight, and a great drumming, chanting & howling of Dervishe at their Ziks is going on; making night hideous.'[24]

�™ ☙ ☙

Sheikh Núr al-Dá'im did not personally teach all his young charges at Kawa. For the first two years of his novitiate, Muhammad Ahmad studied under Sheikh al-Amín al-Suwayli in the central Sudanese Jazíra region.[25] Then, in 1863, he was despatched north to the khalwa of Muhammad al-Dikkeir 'Abdallah Khojali, a sheikh based at al-Ghobosh near Berber, north of Khartoum.[26] It appears that Muhammad Ahmad was ambivalent towards this move. On the one hand, he was happy to stay away from Khartoum, where he had been shocked by official corruption and what were, to him, lax standards of religious devotion.[27] Sheikh Muhammad al-Dikkeir, who had himself been taught by a highly distinguished graduate of Cairo's al-Azhar University, Sheikh al-Hussein Ibrahím wad al-Zahrá, impressed his own pupil.[28] Indeed, Muhammad Ahmad's veneration of his tutor was such that in subsequent years he accorded the sheikh the honorific *al-Kheir*, 'the Good', and appointed him his representative in the Berber region. But there was a problem with the khalwa itself, inasmuch as it was subsidised by the government in Khartoum. A commonly told story relates how the zealous young student refused to eat the food provided at Ghobosh 'since it was derived from oppression'.[29]

Sponsorship of Islamic schools through government subventions was not yet an institutionalised policy, though it did become so in 1866 when Ja'far Mazhar became Governor-General. The Egyptian general was a highly educated and cultured man who developed a literary circle of poets and scholars in the capital and 'instituted a system of subventions to mosques and religious schools in the bigger towns, to be qualified for by examination'.[30]

Ja'far Mazhar's motives were genuinely altruistic and his education policy (along with the telegraph system, the fleet of Nile steamers and similar progressive ideas in trade) helped bring Sudan closer to the rest of the educated, sophisticated Muslim world – a beneficial side effect of colonialism.[31] But for most of his predecessors, controlling the centres of religion and education was just another way of controlling an occupied territory. The true heart of the state-approved religious fraternity was the corps of 'ulamá', scholars who had been educated at al-Azhar, the highest authority in Sunni Islam.[32] These men were steeped in knowledge of the Qorán, the traditions of the Prophet and Islamic Sharí'a law.[33] Preachers, judges, scholars and administrators, they were appointed to posts across the Ottoman Empire and paid by the central government, enjoying a status parallel to that of politicians, bureaucrats and diplomats.[34] It was also their job to persuade the occupied that the occupiers were there in the interests of a genuine 'Commander of the Faithful', that is, the Sultan in Constantinople.[35]

The 'ulamá' took their duty as guardians of community morality seriously, doing their best to encourage orthodox Islamic practices among the conquered natives and to undermine the leadership of the traditional fuqara'. But the indigenous holy men, despite being scattered and unorganised, remained hard to co-opt into collaboration and were not wholly eclipsed by the 'ulamá' imported from Egypt and further afield. They certainly lost their exclusive status as interpreters of Islam but the fuqara' and Sufi masháyikh retained popularity and prestige. The people were quite content to continue visiting the tombs and shrines of their saints while according respect to the legal expertise of the 'ulamá'. So, since total domination by the 'ulamá' over the traditional interpreters of Islam was not possible, mutual cooperation became a question of pragmatism on both sides.

As well as government grants, the brotherhoods could win status and privileges from the government. Alongside them, leading merchants and tribal chieftains were merged into the new establishment; they recognised the new order, collaborated with it and developed vested interests that were to be threatened by the

Mahdi's uprising. Some taríqa leaders, like Hassan Muhammad al-Mírghani of the Khatmía sect, gained economic opportunities and rank as intermediaries between the new regime and the occupied.[36] His father had founded a political and religious dynasty that remains central to Sudanese politics today, rivalling the influence of the al-Mahdi clan. The Khatmía brotherhood was based at al-Sanía, a village in the eastern Kassala region, and had been granted privileged status in the early days of Ottoman administration.[37] Other influential figures that collaborated enthusiastically and became local proxies for the new regime, filtering orders from the centre, included Zubeir ʿAbd-al-Gádir wad al-Zain, a Yaqúbábi from Sennar district. He inherited the title of *sheikh al-masháyikh* ('sheikh of all sheikhs') from his father, who had been so appointed back in 1826.[38] Another senior personality was ʿAbd-al-Gádir Muhammad ʿAbd-al-Rahmán, a Sufi adherent who took an active part in government in the Blue Nile region during the Turkía. After the overthrow of his patrons, ʿAbd-al-Gádir paid his respects to the Mahdi in Omdurman and was rewarded with senior rank. Such conversions, however, went against the general trend of unswerving loyalty on the part of those tribes who took the government's side when it came to the conflict with the Mahdi. Tribes like the Shaigía, the Shukría and the Kabábish all rejected the Mahdi's call and all proved their fidelity to their patrons in Khartoum.

ψ ψ ψ

With his life so narrowly dedicated to scholarship and religion, it is hardly surprising that Muhammad Ahmad grew up to be a priggish and sanctimonious young man. As he cast his puritanical eye over the society around him, he reacted with disdain and censure. His clan followers today still pass around anecdotes of his student days, chuckling to themselves as they reflect on the difficulties faced by the scholar as he tried to earn a living in the world outside the khalwa walls, struggling to develop money-making ventures that did not collide with his Islamic principles. One story describes how Muhammad Ahmad went into business with a man from al-Gateina, a small town outside Khartoum where ferries carrying slaves from the south would dock. The venture involved trading *durra* (wheat), the staple food of the Sudanese. But it swiftly collapsed when the partner (who evidently had a firmer grasp of the laws of supply and demand) proposed concealing their stock until prices were driven up. Muhammad Ahmad was apparently shocked by such a nefarious proposition and abandoned the partnership. Another version of the same story describes how the partner simply argued that the further downstream they travelled the better profit they would make; Muhammad Ahmad retorted waspishly that 'such effort and zeal should never be exerted for such a worldly mission'. His prospects as a fisherman, too, foundered on his refusal to bait the hook, as that would be 'cheating' the fish. And a stint as a charcoal vendor came to an abrupt end after an intense haggling session with a female customer, which was progressing well until she revealed that she was planning to use the charcoal to prepare *marísa*, a heady sorghum beer.[39]

His religious strictures made it impossible for him to be part of normal society. As he saw it, the moral compromises necessary for survival would put him at odds with his own vows to obey God in all things. He was not, however, a monk. For Muslims, a life of asceticism does not necessarily involve celibacy. In 1866, at the age of twenty-two, he accepted his social obligations and was married for the first time.[40] His first wife, Fátima bint al-Háj Sharíf, was a young Dongoláwía from the community of his 'Ashráf' expatriate cousins at Karari.[41] She would bear him four daughters (all of whom would be married off to important personalities in the Mahdist movement) but no sons.[42] Muhammad Ahmad travelled to Karari from Muhammad al-Dikkeir's khalwa at Ghobosh for the ceremonies and returned to his simple khalwa lodging with his young bride.

The formal end of his novitiate in 1868 and his formal appointment as a sheikh of the Sammánía order by his Sufi mentor, Sheikh Muhammad al-Sharíf Núr al-Dá'im, gave Muhammad Ahmad considerable new freedoms: freedom to travel, freedom to preach his own message and, above all, freedom to set up his own establishment and recruit his own followers. In a subsequent letter, he described how Sheikh Núr al-Dá'im had granted him his own preacher's certificate, just the latest in a succession of mentors and students dating back to the Prophet himself. The letter quotes the exact wording used by Sheikh Núr al-Dá'im.

> I have witnessed that this muríd, who loves God and His messenger, is worthy of this great rank and blessing, the licence of the Sammáni order. He is qualified to teach tawhíd. I have placed on him as a precondition sole devotion to God, to be broken and humbled before him and to serve other fuqara' . . . If time permits, he will be enough for all of us, as an Islamic jurist of authority. I hereby grant him the licence and make him a *khalífa*, a successor in our order. This licence is absolute regarding the teaching of novices, guiding eager disciples . . . and wearing the jibba, the patched rag for which he is qualified.[43]

Now, at the age of just twenty-four, Muhammad Ahmad judged that it was time to set up on his own, to build his own mosque and khalwa, preferably in a remote location. When necessary, he could always travel further afield, to preach and to learn more about the sordid vagaries of the secular world. This marked the final occasion on which he turned his back on an alternative, orthodox course. Some Sudanese of similar education were accepted at Cairo's al-Azhar institute to pursue their theological training; there, Muhammad Ahmad would have lived among men of a similar background in nationality-based accommodation blocks and found more qualified teachers.[44] Why Muhammad Ahmad rejected this option and maintained his concentration on the more esoteric spiritual aspects of Islam is unclear. His dislike of the Ottoman state and its colonial institutions, both religious and temporal, was perhaps already ingrained. Perhaps he was already convinced of the hypocrisy and spiritual shallowness of the 'ulamá' and their mentors in Cairo. Perhaps, despite his impressive Qoránic knowledge (and purported distinguished ancestry), he was refused entry. Two reasons are given by Mahdist followers today:

Sheikh Muhammad al-Dikkeir begged him to stay, insisting that he could match anything on offer at al-Azhar; in addition, Muhammad Ahmad's brothers refused to accompany him to Cairo and he was too accustomed to the emotional support network afforded by having his extended family around him. Besides, given the influence of thinkers as diverse as ibn Taimía and the Sufi founding fathers, a combination of disgust for the contemporary orthodoxies on the one hand and the appeal of the poetic mystics on the other, the lure of autonomy is quite understandable. Education at al-Azhar might well have resulted in the young ideologue being co-opted into a state role, any revolutionary tendencies extinguished.[45] So, by choice or circumstance, Muhammad Ahmad remained outside 'the system', a figure on the margins.

Travelling to Cairo, though, would have opened the young Muhammad Ahmad's eyes to the rest of the world, enabling him to place Sudan in both contemporary and historical contexts, giving him the scope to understand the wider Islamic world, its culture and literature. The Egyptian Sudan was still isolated and its colonisation, ironically, had given its inhabitants an improved opportunity to learn more about the outside world. Staying in Sudan meant retaining an essentially blinkered worldview. He knew about Mecca, Constantinople and Jerusalem, of course, but only inasmuch as they merited attention in the Qorán and the Hadíth. Nothing in his letters or proclamations suggests the least interest in contemporary Islamic leaders or influential thinkers. Even as Muhammad Ahmad was honing his own social and religious ideas, activists such as Jamál al-Dín al-Afghání and Muhammad Abdúh were seeking the renaissance of a purer form of Islam and the liberation of the larger Muslim community in the face of European domination.[46] Many of their theories were similar to those subsequently proposed by Muhammad Ahmad al-Mahdi – the revival of Islam in its original state and the rejection of contemporary decadence and division – but he was simply not looking abroad. As his studies progressed and he rejected all local alternatives, an obdurate revivalism became the focus of Muhammad Ahmad's message. As always, Sudanese have a proverb for the occasion: *Fás al-má waráha nás*, 'Fez, beyond which there are no people'. For Muhammad Ahmad, it was not necessary to visit the uncharted territory beyond the Red Sea Hills, the Nubian Desert, Darfur and the swamps of Bahr-al-Ghazál; for now, the map was labelled simply 'Here be dragons'.

# FOUR

# The Voice of the People
## Jazíra Aba, 1868–1878

In the bleak landscape of the central White Nile region, Aba Island comes as a welcome relief to the traveller. The countryside on both sides of the river is blank, utterly featureless, the dun dust stretching flat to the horizon under a relentless sun. There are far fewer trees on Jazíra Aba now than there were when Muhammad Ahmad and his family arrived but there are palm groves and citrus orchards, bean fields and simple housing. Linked to the main Khartoum–Kosti road by a causeway on the eastern side, the island, three miles wide and thirty-five miles long, is still the spiritual home of the Mahdi's descendants and followers. The heart of the community itself is clustered on the western shore. Single-storey mud-brick homes lie on rutted alleys; local landmarks include the dilapidated al-Imam al-Mahdi College and the main mosque in the village's market square. The Imám at the mosque, Sheikh al-Núr 'Abd-al-Mahmúd, is proud to show off to visitors the landmarks of the Mahdi's life here, including the blue-painted and pillared prayer-hall inside a second, smaller mosque to the west. Inside, a stylised concrete depression is all that remains of the spot where Muhammad Ahmad prayed and chanted in solitude for hours, even days at a time.

There were, the sheikh said, three such locations, all known in Arabic as a *ghár*, a cave or, more likely in this flat, sandy country, a pit.[1] The ghár here by the river was preferred in summer, close as it was to the breezier riverbank; it was also near Muhammad Ahmad's house and the khalwa where he preached. In autumn, he would also pray at another location, now inside the al-Mahdi College complex.[2] And in winter, he would cross by boat to Tawíla on the west bank. This third ghár really was a cave in the rocky riverbank; these days it lies deep under the Nile, drowned in the 1930s as the Nile backed up behind the new Jebel Aulia dam.

The network of Sammanía masháyikh and disciples was scattered across the central Sudan, especially the Jazíra and White Nile regions but also west into Kordofan's main towns. This community of colleagues, friends and fellow believers would later be crucial to Sheikh Muhammad Ahmad's call, his *da'wa*; for now, it was those contacts in the taríqa who pointed him towards Jazíra Aba. The densely wooded island was inhabited by a clan of the southern Dinka tribe, headed by their traditional chieftain, *Mek* 'Ali, but was also used for summer pasture by many local tribes, including the Hassanía and Ahámida.[3] The plentiful timber helped Muhammad Ahmad's boat-building brothers overcome any opposition to the move and, once installed, the family immediately began to establish links with the local dignitaries in the most effective and binding way. Muhammad Ahmad took for his second wife Fátima, the daughter of his great-uncle Ahmad Sharfi who had lived on Jazíra Aba for some time, part of the Danágla diaspora in the south and centre of the country. According to the precepts of the Qorán, polygamy is permissible providing that each wife – to a maximum of four – is treated with equal fairness. The Prophet himself had been happily married to one woman, Khadíja bint Khuwaylid, for twenty-five years; after her death, he treated marriage as one part of his religious, social and political mission, marrying a variety of women for a variety of practical reasons.[5] Muhammad Ahmad now began to do the same and Fátima soon achieved what her namesake, his first wife, had failed to do; within three years she had borne him two sons, Muhammad and al-Bushra. She then became known as *Umm al-Mu'minín*, 'Mother of the Faithful', a title originally given to the first wife of the Prophet.[6] Further cementing cross-community ties, his eldest brother, Muhammad, also married the daughter of the Dinka chieftain 'Ali, effectively their host on the island.[7]

Muhammad Ahmad spent several years settling into Jazíra Aba, building a new community of followers around him. His earliest surviving letters give us a clear hint as to the extent of his influence and reach. These letters, long before the days when his proclamations would be copied by secretaries and mass-produced by the hundred, were written in his own dense, unpunctuated *riq'ah* script.[8] In one letter, Muhammad Ahmad wrote to the chief Judge at Fashoda, *Qádi* al-Daw ibn Suleimán, in an attempt to secure release from military service for one of his new followers.[9] 'I beg you, my beloved brother, to help our son in the order, 'Abd-al-Nabi,' he wrote. 'He is a sergeant in the army but his love of God and preoccupation with him has distracted his heart from the government's business. . . . You must secure his release on grounds of his age or any other defect . . . so that he can engage fully in serving God.'[10]

Muhammad Ahmad also wrote out many special blessings and quotations from the Qorán as amulets for his followers to carry, usually in tiny leather lockets, to ward off 'diseases and all wants of human life'.[11] None of these scraps has survived, although one much more forceful document which has indicates clearly the kind of influence wielded by the young sheikh. In this *laissez-passer*, Muhammad Ahmad invoked the status of his own family as descendants of the House of the Prophet by signing himself 'son of al-Sayyid 'Abdallah' and begged 'the sanctuary of God and his protection for the Batta family, their brothers, offspring and property'.

The aforementioned are associated with friends of Allah and are admitted under their protection. He who honours them honours the people of God; God shall in turn honour and support him. We appeal to God to bring distress and humiliation to anyone

who assaults the Batta family, in this life or the next. Beware!
Beware of abusing them. Anyone who does so harms himself in
this world and in the world that is to come.[12]

Muhammad Ahmad's rapidly ascending status within the
Sammánía was reflected in the tone of his earliest proclamations.
These manshúrát were closer to official notices than letters,
designed to be read openly and passed around. It was a means of
communication on which he would depend more and more as he
broadcast his call to a larger and larger audience. In his capacity as
an imam licensed by his own mentor, Sheikh Núr al-Dá'im,
Muhammad Ahmad was qualified to endorse one of his followers,
Siráj al-Dín Ahmad al-Jinaid, the son of a traditional faqí, as a
fully-fledged Sammáni sheikh.[13] But even as his personal authority
and reputation gradually grew, the relationship with his mentor
was deteriorating. The precise reason for the final schism is
unclear. Some have suggested that Sheikh Núr al-Dá'im's move to
establish a subsidiary branch of his Kawa khalwa at al-'Aradaib,
close to Aba Island, in 1872 was unwelcome. There was also
growing political factionalism within the taríqa.[14] It is clear,
however, that the pupil had simply outgrown the master, who in
turn became embittered and envious of his former protégé's
growing reputation.[15] Mahdist followers at Jazíra Aba today like
to relate a story to illustrate the hostility they say was felt by
Sheikh Núr al-Dá'im towards Muhammad Ahmad, even in the
days when he was still a muríd. Like many such anecdotes, the tale
is told with relish for detail (amid exclamations of approval from
those gathered around) and the kernel of truth in the story, the
personal animosity between the two men, is embellished with
fanciful flavours of a miraculous nature.

Sheikh Muhammad Núr al-Dá'im once had a vision in which
the Prophet said: 'The Mahdi is with you; he has two names in
one name.'[16] Enraged with jealousy, Sheikh Núr al-Dá'im sent
his obedient pupil to a small village on the Nile where the
people had complained of a huge crocodile that had been

carrying off their livestock. Sheikh Núr al-Dá'im commanded Muhammad Ahmad to wash his master's clothes in the river: 'Not by the bank but out in deeper water,' the sheikh said, 'where the current is cleaner.' Before long, Muhammad Ahmad's fellow disciples rushed back to the khalwa to tell their tutor that Muhammad Ahmad had been snatched by the crocodile. But imagine Sheikh Núr al-Dá'im's amazement when he learned that his pupil, instead of being drowned and devoured, had been carried gently in the jaws of the beast to a small island further south, where he was able to finish his laundry chores in peace![17]

If Muhammad Ahmad was taken aback at his superior's increasingly evident jealousy, he was shocked by what he saw as shortcomings in Sheikh Muhammad Sharíf's own lifestyle. The crucial incident that precipitated the split came in the spring of 1878: a lavish circumcision ceremony for Sheikh Núr al-Dá'im's son, complete with parades, music and dancing, all *harám*, taboo, to the stern standards of the pious young Sufi.[18] In typically forthright manner, he did not hesitate to speak his mind. The senior sheikh was bitterly angry at such outspoken criticism from a subordinate who should have treated him with the respect due to the infallible. He insulted Muhammad Ahmad in deeply personal terms and cast him from the brotherhood.

Begone, for you show the truth of the saying 'The Dunqulāwī is the devil in the skin of a man'![19]

Muhammad Ahmad in turn attempted to appease his irate mentor with sometimes extravagant demonstrations of humility. He prostrated himself, lashed into a *sheiba*, a forked yoke used to punish a runaway slave, at his master's doorway. In an effort to offset the shame caused by his earlier criticism, he also composed a poem lauding the sheikh's supreme qualities.

Muhammad Sharíf, relief of our time; I am satisfied with him as my sheikh and my support in God's presence.

By God, I remain solemnly bound to my oath until the day of
resurrection.
I am fully aware of his love, which is good for me before God.
Satan had wrestled with me, to my horror, but that white hand
came to my rescue; thanks to it I have been guided along the
right path.
Muhammad Ahmad is your slave, your dependant;
Relieve him from all life's difficulties.[20]

It was all to no avail. But if Sheikh Muhammad Sharíf Núr al-
Dá'im hoped that excommunication would result in Muhammad
Ahmad's downfall, he was mistaken. There were, after all, two
other branches of the Sammánía brotherhood and Muhammad
Ahmad had only to look a little to the east, to al-Massallamía on
the Blue Nile, to find the khalwa of Sheikh al-Quráshi wad al-
Zein.[21] Sheikh al-Quráshi's credentials, as favoured pupil of the
brotherhood's founding father, were at least as distinguished as
those of Muhammad Sharíf. Nor, perhaps surprisingly, was
Muhammad Ahmad deterred by the fact that Sheikh al-Quráshi's
khalwa (whose students were largely Ja'aliyín) was subsidised by
the ruling family of the Shukría tribe. The Shukría, under the
leadership of the Abú-Sinn clan, were the government's staunchest
supporters in the Blue Nile region.[22] But Sheikh al-Quráshi was, at
eighty-six, very elderly; Muhammad Ahmad's reputation made it
highly likely that, despite his own youth, he would inherit the
leadership of the taríqa when the old holy man died. In the
meantime, Muhammad Ahmad's prospects were markedly
improved by taking the sheikh's daughter, al-Ni'ma, as his third
wife.[23] It was a further example of shrewd network building, the
development of a wide community of unquestioningly loyal
partisans whose make-up transcended traditional clan divisions.[24]

☙ ☙ ☙

Muhammad Ahmad had always planned to travel, not just to
teach but also to listen to the voice of the people. From his secure

base at Jazíra Aba, he now began to tramp the countryside, covering great distances overland and taking the family's boats up and down the Nile: from Sennar to the south up into the northern territories, the country of his birth; from the Blue Nile west into the heartland of Kordofan. It appears, however, that his eyes did not look much to the eastern hills or Red Sea districts; he travelled no further east than al-Rufa'a and Massallamía. Astonishingly, too, Muhammad Ahmad appears to have made no attempt to make the holy Haj pilgrimage to Mecca. But on the journeys he did undertake he took with him a coterie of followers and novices, a delegation that found a ready welcome in the homes and mosques of Sammánía members across the country.[25] These were, above all, religious missions. As he walked from mosque to mosque, he exhorted the people to pray and to exercise their personal and social obligations as laid down in the Qorán and the traditions of the Prophet. But these tours also reinforced his outrage against government abuses, cementing a belief that social and political issues had a part to play in his ideological battle. Everywhere he went he encountered people who lived in misery, ignored by the hated 'Turks' in central government except as a source of crippling taxes.

Taxation was as larcenous as it was systematic and compounded by corruption and extortion. Ostensibly levied on the basis of acreage or production, the actual cost to the tribute-payer rose exponentially as each bureaucrat in the hierarchy skimmed off his own profit. Dishonest clerks wrote bogus bills for illiterate farmers, dishonest merchants used illicitly weighted scales and dishonest provincial governors issued credit slips for advance tax payments, only to refuse subsequently to recognise that an instalment had been paid. Nor were the authorities concerned about how the tribute was paid, in cash or kind. Nomadic tribes were a valuable source of camels for troop transports and forced levies were made of wheat, butter, cotton, wool, leather, and gum arabic as well as livestock and slaves.[26] Merchants were content to act as middlemen for the government, bartering corn for these various products. The government could then use the corn in lieu of cash payment to provincial soldiers and officials.[27] Ruinous taxes imposed on everything from date palms to ságiya water wheels had broken many a farmer and contributed to the migration of many Danágla and Ja'aliyín from the north. Cornelia Speedy, hunting with her husband in the eastern hills, saw the tax collectors in action for herself.

> I cannot but believe that the stories we hear on all sides of the tyranny exercised by these tax collectors must be true. The people assure us that over and beyond the lawful rates they are obliged to pay, almost every farthing they can make is demanded of them, and seized by force. They have no incentive consequently to cultivate their land, and thence arises their wretched state of poverty, and the degraded condition of deceit engendered by oppression, in which they habitually live.[28]

The taxes were thus mercilessly collected by irregular cavalry troops from the northern Shaigía tribe, known variously as 'Bashi-bazouks' and 'Sanjaks'.[29] The Shaigía had opposed Ismail Pasha's invading army in two pitched battles in 1820, but discovered that their spears and swords were ill matched against firearms and artillery. Thereafter they signed on as a local militia, losing their political independence but benefiting from proximity to power and from the occupation of large tracts of land between Khartoum and Shendi.[30] Each province maintained its own force of these irregulars, who were widely loathed and described in one official report as 'swaggering bullies, robbing, plundering, and ill-treating the people with impunity . . . a constant menace to public tranquillity'.[31] Non-payment was rewarded with a few lashes of the *courbash*, a hippopotamus hide whip, or imprisonment. Huts were pulled down and fields dug up in case a few meagre coins were hidden. At Obeid, the largest town in Kordofan, the rigours of tax collection in the late 1870s were witnessed by Yúsuf Mikhail, a student who helped illiterate villagers write petitions against corrupt officials.

Complaints and petitions to the Government about the increasing injustice of tax collection increased . . . especially against the Shāigī a soldiers. Some people even said: 'Better for us to be buried ten in a grave than pay the tax.'[32]

For Muhammad Ahmad, the tributes and taxes levied by the 'Turks' were wholly unacceptable and not only because they wreaked such misery. The only tax a Muslim should be obliged to pay was the *zakát*, a donation that was carefully calculated to be 2.5 per cent of excess income, in other words after a full year's subsistence had been taken into account.[33] Unlike the taxes plundered by the dreaded sanjaks, which lined the pockets of an occupying force, the zakát was authorised under Sharí'a law as a contribution to the whole community.

Another reason why anti-government feeling was on the rise, even among the wealthy, was a slowly intensifying campaign to expunge the slave trade. Khartoum, like its rulers' mother-city Cairo, owed much of its prosperity to the slave trade. Almost everyone at every level of society in the city had at least one slave, stolen in armed raids from the forest and swamps of the south or the Nuba Mountains and sold in the markets of the capital. The luxurious households enjoyed by the government's senior officers and officials were wholly run by slaves; Egyptian soldiers brought slaves as well as wives with them even to the most far-flung garrisons. The campaign to end the trade was forced upon a reluctant government in Cairo by Europeans who were appalled to read of the 'horrors' of the trade – let alone to see it for themselves.

Every year more than one hundred vessels leave Khartoum for the purpose of hunting down the negroes; and slaves, who formerly were brought in by stealth, are now dragged publicly along the highways of the country, and even through the streets of Khartoum, with the yoke upon their necks. Assured of impunity and of the inefficiency of the law, the slave-dealers have thrown off the mask. It is an everlasting scandal to civilised

Europe thus to authorise, by her silence, the infamous piracy which has stained the White Nile with blood.[34]

Sudanese slavers recognised no law. Even when successive viceroys in Egypt responded to heavy financial pressure from Britain and other European nations and ordered an end to the raids in the deep south, efforts in the field were half-hearted at best. The earliest serious efforts to stamp out the trade were made by Sir Samuel Baker, a British explorer who was appointed Governor of Sudan's southern Equatoria province in 1869 by the new ruler in Cairo, Ismail Ibráhím.[35] Baker's heavy-handed techniques and huge expenditure endeared him to no one and little was achieved; indeed, his generous funding, the provision of a small fleet of paddle-steamers and more than a thousand Egyptian

Ismail Ibrahím, Khedive of Egypt 1863–79.
(Illustrated London News, 28 February 1885)

and Sudanese troops leads to a suspicion that opening new territories and taming them for Cairo's long-distance administration was a greater priority than quelling the slave trade.[36] When Baker left the provincial capital, Gondokoro, in May 1873, progress had been minimal; even his colleagues recognised that 'the supposed conquests and suppression of slavery were proved a chimera; the trade flourished more than ever'.[37]

His successor as Governor-General of Equatoria was another Briton, beginning an acquaintance with Sudan that would absorb six years of his life and ultimately claim it. Lieutenant-Colonel Charles Gordon, a short, stocky, bewhiskered officer of the Royal Engineers who had won renown in the Chinese war of the early 1860s, arrived in Khartoum in February 1874 bearing an explicit decree from Khedive Ismail.

> The province which you are to administer is a territory scarcely known. Until very recently, it has been exploited by adventurers who traffic ivory and slaves in equal measure. Your primary concern, *Monsieur le Colonel*, is to apply the following stricture absolutely: Once the dominance of the brigands is over, free commerce can proceed in safety. Everyone down there must be made to understand that a man is not a commodity just because he is of a different colour. Life and liberty are sacred.[38]

Gordon spent nearly three years in the depths of equatorial Africa, with minimal success. He achieved much in developing the province as an effective network of military posts but did little to 'suppress the slave trade over 200,000 square miles of thorn-scrub and swamp'.[39] Unlike Baker, he never bothered to learn Arabic or any southern language. At his disposal he had insufficient men, whose low morale was exacerbated by not having been paid for four years, and the administrative support of a few Europeans and Egyptian officials of shady character.[40] His best soldiers were southern troops who had themselves been in the service of the slave-dealers. These men, known as 'bazingers', were armed with double-barrelled guns and, unlike their Egyptian colleagues, trained to shoot straight. 'They are very reliable troops, have no fear, and fight like lions,' noted a British abolitionist touring the south; 'and, what is most noteworthy, they can live on two or three handfuls of grain a day, and never grumble for their pay, however long in arrear [sic] it may be'.⁴¹ Gordon may have succeeded in closing off the Nile to some of the traffickers but he was powerless to weaken the stranglehold on the south maintained by one of the government's own senior officials. Al-Zubeir Rahmatallah Mansúr was a powerful slave-trader who ran his own private army, mounted slave-raids (known as 'razzias') through unarmed villages and administered his own fiefdom in the Bahr al-Ghazál region.⁴² His ruthlessness in destroying a government force sent to rein him in was rewarded by that government in its weakness with a formal civilian posting as provincial governor's agent. Further self-enriching advances into Darfur, in which he killed Sultán Ibráhím Muhammad al-Hussein, netted further promotion. It was only when the adventurer travelled to Cairo in 1875 to plead against his rival, the Governor-General Ismail Ayúb himself, that he fell victim to the old rule of suppressing the potential usurper and was forcibly detained in exile.⁴³

Despite his frustrations and poor health, the mercurial Gordon, always fired with a Christian missionary zeal, allowed himself to be persuaded by the Khedive Ismail to accept a rapid promotion and stay on in Sudan. He served as Governor-General of Sudan for nearly three more years, struggling to tackle the slavers in Bahr al-Ghazál and Darfur, struggling to cope with inefficiency, corruption, debt and substandard colleagues. There were no conclusive inroads into the wider trade, despite the execution of Zubeir Rahma's son, Suleimán, who had taken over his father's mini-empire, and a mass liberation of slaves in Kordofan.⁴⁴

Large chains of slaves, male and female, with their children, in innumerable numbers came out, playing the flute and making the *zaghárít* [ululation], and showing immense joy . . . Only a few slaves remained by their own choice with their masters . . . who had treated them well. The Danáqla retained very few. . . .

On arrival in El Fasher [the capital of Darfur] he found that there were many *jallāba* who had innumerable slaves, and slave-dealers who wanted to buy them.[45] He immediately issued an order to all parts and to all governors in the west to give freedom to the slaves.[46]

Such flamboyant gestures did nothing to undercut the root of the problem, the fact that Sudan was the source of supply for the lucrative Egyptian trade. A journalist for *The Times* newspaper commented, on reviewing 'Colonel Gordon's most recent reports, that his work of extermination of the slave-traders in their strongholds in the Gazelle River' was close to completion.

No doubt a terrible blow has been struck at the great source of supply to the Egyptian slave trade. But people must not be too sanguine of immediate results. The treaty which the Khedive made with England in August 1877 fixed seven years as the limit during which slavery may still exist in Egypt, 12 years as the period for the Soudan. It remains to be seen whether at the expiration of these periods public opinion in Egypt will have changed sufficiently to permit this reform.[47]

Gordon's own musings on the subject reflected the mixture of the pragmatist and the zealot in the man: 'Consider the effect of harsh measures among an essentially Mussulman population carried out brusquely by a Nazarene – measures which touch the pocket of everyone,' he wrote. 'Who that had not the Almighty with him would dare do that? I will do it.'[48] But with the officials of the state, the urban elite, the jallába and the rural nomads all against him, it was an impossible task and his efforts only added to the popular sense of grievance against a hypocritical government and its Christian hirelings.

The appointment of a *nasráni* – a 'Nazarene', as Gordon put it – to the Saráya for the best part of three years marked a radical change in the politics of the territory, ruled for so long by the cream of the Ottoman military, and could not have escaped the notice of Muhammad Ahmad, another man who was supremely confident of having God on his side.[49] It seems certain that he would have known of Gordon, though Gordon may not have learned much about the holy man of Jazíra Aba. During the late 1870s, Muhammad Ahmad was living a quiet life of prayer and preaching on the island; Gordon was rarely even in Khartoum and had more pressing problems. He travelled obsessively during the first eighteen months of his rule, to Darfur, to Berber and even to Abyssinia; anything was better than the tedium of administrative chores in the capital. By the end of 1879, he was a beaten man, defeated by ill health and immense frustration. On his return to Alexandria, a medical examiner found him 'suffering from symptoms of nervous exhaustion . . . the effect of continued bodily fatigue, anxiety and indigestible food'.[50] Muhammad Ahmad, by contrast, was approaching the peak of his powers. His sermons took on a new urgency, a new stridency. The breadth of his education and his years of listening to the grievances of the people enabled him to tailor his style according to his audience. He could address uneducated farmers in simple, colloquial terms and Islamic scholars of the state with a grasp of theological and legal detail that they respected. In his writings, similarly, he substituted rustic colloquialisms for sophisticated internal rhyming schemes to convey his message most effectively to a given audience. In the words of one influential sheikh in today's Mahdist community: 'He was a psychologist!'[51]

# FIVE

# 'A New Dhikr'
## Jazíra Aba and Kordofan, 1878–1880

In July 1878, just months after Muhammad Ahmad joined his branch of the Sammánía, Sheikh al-Quráshi wad al-Zein passed away at Massallamía.¹ Already a man of regional influence and respect, the 24-year-old sheikh of Jazíra Aba was now accepted as the leader of a taríqa in his own right, commanding a much larger following and quite the equal of his former mentor, Sheikh Muhammad Sharíf Núr al-Dá'im. A tall, powerfully built man, he had developed a constant smile that displayed a conspicuous gap between his top front teeth. He dressed like his followers in a simple cotton shift, its tears repaired with dyed woollen patches, baggy knee-length trousers, a straw skull-cap and a broad white turban. His life now alternated between that of a hermit, praying alone at immense length, and an itinerant preacher, sermonising to the community. The deference of the student coupled with the humility of the perpetual house guest combined to shape a personality of remarkable politeness and calm. The fact that he had three wives at such a young age in no way detracted from his followers' acclaiming him as 'the Renouncer', who had turned his back on the world and its material rewards.² His followers frequently observed him weeping. The tears – prompted by fear of God or grief at the state of the world around him – were interpreted as a demonstration of the utmost piety. From Jazíra Aba on the White Nile and Massallamía on the Blue, his reputation for asceticism, spirituality and even sanctity spread like ripples over smooth water. Before long, rumour began to spread among the naturally superstitious people of the countryside that the Sheikh of Jazíra Aba had remarkable, indeed miraculous powers.

Government steamers, passing the island on their way between Khartoum and Fashoda, would often stop to take on wood for fuel. For the curious, especially among Sudanese and Egyptian passengers and crew, the young holy man was a local celebrity worth visiting. Captain after captain paused to seek 'his blessings for safe voyage . . . for which blessings nice presents were handed to him'.[3] In 1880, Major Gaetano Casati, an Italian explorer and mapmaker making his way upriver with a government delegation to the south, described the miraculous feats popularly ascribed to the young sheikh on the island.

We arrived before the island Abba, which nearly faces the territory of Koweh; the steamer here slackened speed, and the whistle of the engine blew four times with a very prolonged sound; the captain, the crew of the vessel, and the passengers offered prayers to God, turning towards the island. 'What are they doing?' I asked of a Greek merchant, who was sailing with us to the province of Bahr-el-Ghazal . . . 'They are rendering homage to a holy man who dwells here; he is immortal, report says. Once already, without passing through death, he has ascended to God, from whom he returned seven hundred years ago.' . . .

Michael Saad (a Copt), Chief Accountant of the Equatorial Province, told me that when he was sailing up the stream in company with the Egyptian expedition under Sir Samuel Baker, he with others landed at the island Abba to pay their respects. . . .[4] Mohammed Ahmed received them very courteously, and, as is usual, complimented them by offering then *eau sucré* and sweet milk, the recipients amounted to over forty; every one drank to satiety, notwithstanding which the contents of the cups were not in the least diminished – a wonderfully miraculous performance, and a still more wonderful credulity, in those who believed it.[5]

Muhammad Ahmad's spiritual mission was not yet overtly political but his drive had begun to establish an Islamic renaissance, to get religion literally 'straightened out'.[6] In social terms, this meant the establishment of a community on the pure, definitive, primitive Islamic model, underpinned by the teachings of the Qorán and the application of the Sharí'a. Muhammad Ahmad felt nothing but contempt for the compromises adopted over the centuries as the world of Islam, especially the Ottoman caliphate, came to terms with the Western world, compromises he denounced as innovations, bid'a. 'Permission has been given to us to revive religion among Muslims', he wrote in early October 1880. 'Innovations have spread through the land and are being followed by both 'ulamá' and people. . . . Nothing is left of Islam but its name; nothing of the Qorán but its Arabic script.'[7] He began to solicit supporters in earnest and letters streamed out from Jazíra Aba to a remarkable network of religious notables and tribal elders. Carefully testing the waters before jumping in with a call to outright revolution, he called on the families of influential holy men, teachers and tribal chiefs to join him. 'Those whom we call to join us and who refuse regret it greatly,' Muhammad Ahmad wrote on 20 June 1880; 'with their refusal they incur the displeasure of God, his Prophet and us.'[8]

> With God's grace, those who join us will not fear the trials and miseries of life. The Prophet himself conveyed to me the good news that angels will be our guardians and that he himself will be with us. . . . Beware! The good of both this world and the hereafter lies in what I have instructed you to do. It pleases God, his Messenger and the holy men. Heed not what people say; they know nothing. . . . There is no prospect of success in religion except by joining the people in charge of it, for the behaviour of one influences that of another and man adopts the religion and customs of those around him. It is indeed as God said:
>
> 'Ye who believe! Fear God and be with those who are true.'[9]
>
> We have had good omens and clear instructions from the Prophet himself. You must, my beloved ones, respond to my

order and come to us promptly in Ramadan, for the Prophet has given instructions that we congregate in the month of Shawwál.[10] Attend to this matter for it is a direct order from God and his Messenger. So beware, beware and may peace be upon you.[11]

Another letter written two days later suggests that Muhammad Ahmad had selected Abú-Dom, a small village on a hill in eastern Kordofan, as his meeting-place.[12] It was the choice of a cautious man: in the foothills of the Nuba Mountains, it was far from the prying eyes of government agents or soldiers. 'Our set date must not be forgotten,' he urged, calling on the recipients to spread the word among the network of fuqara'; 'it has been repeated and confirmed'.

Convey my greetings to the sheikhs who are responsive to God and his Prophet . . . Let there be no indifference! Sheikh Muhammad al-Tayib al-Basír, successor of our grandfather Sheikh al-Basíri, has already arrived with a number of Halawiyín elders and dignitaries and sworn the oath of allegiance.[13]

The declared support of Sheikh Muhammad al-Tayib al-Basír was a significant coup. The grandson of the Sammánía founder and the leader of the third surviving branch of the taríqa, he was an exceptionally influential religious figure. His support was crucial in the early stages of the Mahdía.[14] As before, Muhammad Ahmad confirmed their close relationship by marrying his daughter, al-Surra.[15] Before long, a series of delegations was making its way to Jazíra Aba. The Dighaim, part of the larger Baggára clan of the White Nile, were the first, followed by a group of Kinána elders, hastening north-west from Sinja on the Blue Nile to join the movement. Many of these first recruits would become trusted companions and generals in the imminent uprising; many of them would die in battle.[16] After the Kinána came the Husunát, the Amárna, the Duwayh and the 'Falláta', West African Muslims who had settled in Sudan on their way to or from performing the Haj at the holy sites of Arabia.[17] For all these arrivals, the oath of allegiance to Muhammad Ahmad was solemn and uncompromising, pledging a commitment to spiritual fidelity, social responsibility, non-materialism and dedication to the cause.

> We pledge our allegiance to God, His Apostle and to you that we will uphold the Oneness of God and will not set up associates to Him. We will not steal, commit adultery, make slanderous allegations or disobey the command to do what is good and honourable. We pledge our allegiance to you to renounce and forsake material things, to be content with what lies with God and the next world – and not to shirk from jihad.[18]

Many still had reservations; after all, to ally oneself in public with an alternative claim to power invited real trouble from the authorities in Khartoum. The hardest to convince were those masháyikh with established ties to the government. It is not known whether Sheikh Muhammad al-Izayriq of Wad Medani received either a personal visit or a written summons from Muhammad Ahmad but he certainly received a government subsidy for his khalwa and developed an immediate antipathy to a man he denounced as a fraud. Sheikh al-Izayriq subsequently wrote and circulated a terse poem denouncing the *Mutamahdi*, the 'False Mahdi', of Jazíra Aba.

> Praise to Allah! the ruinously mighty,
> Creator of all, destroyer of thrones,
> Who folds night into day with no help or supporter.
> I beseech you to bring down the utmost suffering
> On this group of ruffian Arab nomads.
> For they have been led astray by the man of Aba
> Who says he is the Mahdi!
> God forbid, God forbid![19]

It is not known why the gathering did not take place in Ramadan or Shawwál but a month after the appointed rendezvous the 36-year-old sheikh on Jazíra Aba was still banging the drum.[20]

'It will not have escaped your attention, my beloved,' he wrote, somewhat sarcastically, 'that we are calling the people to God'.

This time, matters have reached the point of suffocation. The drum is beating, calling on you to entrench happiness and leave behind misery and wretchedness. We consider you in the forefront of those who care for religion and its supporters. So read this letter and come to us speedily with your people, family, brothers and all those who bear any love for their faith. Don't be delayed, my beloved! For as Allah says:

'Be ye helpers of God! As said Jesus the son of Mary to the disciples: "Who will be my helpers to do God's work?" And the disciples said, "We are God's helpers".'[21]

This is the hour of need for which you have been created. Do not ignore it because of worldly considerations or terrible atrocities will befall you. I am your council and loving carer. Let the remainder of your life be dedicated to supporting the religion of God and the establishment of the Sunna.[22]

That same month, Muhammad Ahmad wrote again to Sheikh Muhammad al-Tayib al-Basír. Referring to an 'intercession' by his own late mentor, Sheikh al-Quráshi wad al-Zein and to a 'signal' from the Sammánía founder, Sheikh al-Basír, Muhammad Ahmad indicates that he is poised to share a great secret. He begins by apologising for not visiting him in person, explaining mysteriously that he is 'preoccupied by a hidden mission'.

Lights, good omens, prophetic secrets and instructions, divine revelations, all have appeared to me repeatedly. I wrote to you earlier, before receiving the supreme command, which has now happened. Happy are those who took an early initiative in joining our movement with their families, sons and property. Those who do not heed this command are outcasts, whom God and his Prophet will judge to determine their punishment.

This affair is secret, a secret which is not meant to be revealed. It must be kept secret, for your eyes only, until God himself reveals it. . . . I have the sworn allegiance of about 20,000 people to carry out this matter, which has been brought upon me all of a sudden by God and his Prophet.[23]

That truly impressive figure of 20,000 followers is not an impossible estimate if those tribal leaders who had made their way to Jazíra Aba to swear the bay'a in person brought with them, in spirit at least, their entire clans. In reality, though, the actual community surrounding Muhammad Ahmad was still small and, in both political and military terms, powerless. Even the most devout adherent might have asked where it was all leading and by what authority their master spoke of Islamic revival in such absolutist and unsettling terms. Before declaring what was on his mind, however, he would need to canvass opinion much further afield.

ۺ ۺ ۺ

Muhammad Ahmad certainly made a big impression on the communities he visited as he travelled around the Jazíra and into Kordofan, lobbying influential merchants and tribal leaders. At Rufá'a, on the Blue Nile, he would stop to visit relatives, always accompanied by an escort of disciples. His leadership of the evening communal prayers was witnessed by Babikr Bedri.

Often when we were students we would attend the sunset prayer with him and listen to him reciting the Koran in his reverent, humble voice. Once when he was reciting the Chapter of the Calamity during the first part of the service, and when he came to the verse 'A day will come when mankind will be as a cloud of scattered moths', he fell down unconscious in a trance, and one of his disciples came forward in his place to finish the prayer.[24] I was among the worshippers, and when we left he was still unconscious.[25]

Muhammad Ahmad had made his first prolonged tour of Kordofan province during the dry season in March 1880.

Kordofan was crucial to any successful movement because the region was home to two important but mutually hostile groups, the Ja'aliyín and the Baggára. The Ja'aliyín jallába were a powerful presence in Kordofan's main town, Obeid. Obeid was a prosperous trading hub, rich in gum arabic, ostrich feathers, tamarind and mercury, gateway to the western reaches of Darfur and home to as many as 50,000 people, most living in straw huts. The chief merchant, wad al-Irayiq Muhammadein, was an essential local proxy for the Egyptian provincial governor, Brigadier Muhammad Sa'íd Wahbi.[26] He collected the taxes levied on the merchants and had, under the law, the power to impose fines or even, in collaboration with the governor, to order prison sentences.[27] But the jallába, constantly vying among themselves for influence, were bitterly divided between two faction leaders. Ahmad Dafa'allah and Ilyás Ahmad Umm Bireir were both rich and powerful merchants.[28] Ilyás had been removed from the provincial governorship the previous year by Governor-General Charles Gordon and replaced by Muhammad Sa'íd because the protracted vendetta with Ahmad Dafa'allah, fuelled by 'their mutual hatred and intense aversion to each other', had spilled over into open conflict.[29] But Ilyás was a wily old fox, content to bide his time. One scurrilous story widespread in Kordofan for decades related how he bribed the incoming Governor with a sack of gold coins to ensure that he, Ilyás, did not lose too much status in the town.[30] The arrival of Muhammad Ahmad on the scene served his purposes perfectly. His guest, too, ignoring traditional animosity between the Ja'aliyín and his own Danágla, had made it a priority to woo Ilyás Umm Bireir (though there is no record of his having a daughter available to marry).

This was a visit for laying foundations, especially among supporters of the various Sufi sects, the Sammánía, the Ismailía and the Tijánía. Building lasting support could wait for a second tour. But this first tour of Kordofan stirred up great popular interest. For many in Obeid, the first they knew of the preacher from Jazíra Aba was the mysterious sound of late-night Sufi ritual. Gossip quickly spread. A darwísh had arrived from the river, surrounded by novices and pupils. He had been seen visiting all the famous local mashàyikh and fuqara', including al-Makki Ismail al-Wali, whose father had founded the Ismailía brotherhood in Sudan and who became Muhammad Ahmad's 'most trusted confidant' in Obeid.[31] Yúsuf Mikhail remembered his arrival clearly.

> Then one day we heard, after midnight, recitation of a new dhikr which came from the outskirts of the town. . . . In the middle of the night he would start with his disciples and circle round the town until dawn, when it would be time for morning prayer, and then he would stop the recitation of dhikr. . . . Sheikh Muhammad Ahmad was a good-looking man, a pleasant speaker and eloquent, with a magnetic power of attracting people . . . He was, so to speak, watering parched soil, until he planted love for himself in their hearts. . . . He did not leave any prominent person without paying him a visit and delivering sermons; he endeared himself to the high and the low, both young and old.[32]

For a Dongolàwi like Muhammad Ahmad, to woo the Ja'aliyín was straightforward compared to forging ties with the Baggára. Settled tribes, both along the two branches of the Nile and in the towns of the hinterland, were highly suspicious of the Baggára, cattle-herding nomads spread over a huge area of Kordofan and Darfur. The cultivators of the Nile valley regarded the Baggára clans as barbarians, uncouth and unwelcome.[33] Another Sudanese proverb asserts: *Jamal fí al-hosh wa lá sheikh al-'arab*, 'Better to have a camel in the yard than even a sheikh of the nomads'.[34] The Baggára were hardened fighters, experienced slavers and resilient people of the countryside but they had also suffered from Gordon's attempts to expunge the slave trade, from abusive tax collectors and from the oppression of routine government corruption.[35] Certainly, no revolution could succeed without their support and, returning through eastern Kordofan, Muhammad Ahmad solicited the friendship of influential figures on the west bank of the White Nile such as Sheikh al-Manna Ismail of the Jawama'a and Sheikh 'Asákir wad Abú-Kalám of the Jimi', both clans subsumed into the larger Baggára tribe.

Such deep-seated rivalries and animosities between the tribes had helped the Ottoman occupiers hold on to power. To bring them together under one banner took immense effort and great charisma. It was an essential step towards a viable movement and Ismail 'Abd-al-Gádir, the court biographer of the Mahdía, justly celebrated Muhammad Ahmad's success in unifying the disparate groups.

> Despite the tribes' violence, scorn, mutual enmity, raids, lack of common language and disregard for punishment, God united their hearts through His Mahdi and they became brethren and ardent supports of the Mahdi's cause. They . . . sacrificed their lives and properties in support of the Mahdi, without him offering them any material inducement.[36]

It was not, however, so straightforward in all cases. The Shaigía and the Shukría had served the government loyally for decades; they would not be won over by Muhammad Ahmad's arguments. Nor would Mek Adam of Tagali in the Nuba Mountains, a traditional tribal chieftain who coexisted peacefully with the government in Khartoum despite refusing to pay tribute.[37] Muhammad Ahmad travelled to meet the Mek on Kordofan's southern fringes and was welcomed courteously as an honoured guest at Adam's personal compound. But the Mek remained ambivalent about throwing in his lot with what appeared even then to be a nascent rebel movement.[38]

# SIX

# 'From the Mouths of Babes'
# Jazíra Aba and Kordofan, 1880–1881

A momentous meeting in late 1880 focused Muhammad Ahmad's ambitions and provided him with an irreplaceable right-hand man gifted in administration, a close personal companion – and an heir apparent. Muhammad Ahmad was at Massallamía on the Blue Nile, working beside his Sammánía disciples to finish the tomb of his late mentor, Sheikh al-Quráshi wad al-Zein. Perched on rough wooden scaffolding, the sheikh and his followers were tidying the final details on the gubba, the characteristic dome that marks the resting place of many a Sudanese holy man, when 'Abdulláhi Muhammad Túrshein al-Ta'íshi arrived.[2] The stranger was 'tall and thin, somewhat pale in countenance, with thin pointed face and big beard. He was quiet, and at that time seldom spoke unless another addressed him.'[3] This man, a Baggára from the western reaches of Kordofan, had made a long and arduous journey specifically in search of Muhammad Ahmad. But westerners were not welcome among the people of the Nile and, as he related in later years, 'Abdulláhi al-Ta'íshi had been abused many times by the local people as a thief and a ruffian.

At length I reached Messallamia, and here I found the Mahdi busily engaged in building the tomb of the late Sheikh el Koreishi. On seeing him I entirely forgot all the troubles I had suffered on my journey, and was content to simply look at him and listen to his teaching. For several hours I was too timid to dare to speak to him; but at length I plucked up courage, and in a few words told him my story and I begged him, for the sake of God and his Prophet, to allow me to become one of his disciples. He did so, and gave me his hand, which I kissed most fervently, and I swore entire submission to him as long as I lived.[4]

A relationship of spontaneous affection and mutual admiration arose between Muhammad Ahmad and 'Abdulláhi al-Ta'íshi immediately. They were, after all, alike in many ways. They were of similar age, 'Abdulláhi being the elder by three years, and from similar backgrounds.[5] Muhammad Ahmad had already proven himself immune to the normal prejudice of the Nile-side tribes against western nomads and he recognised spiritual pedigree. 'Abdulláhi's father, Sheikh Muhammad Adam ibn 'Ali al-Karrár (nicknamed *Túrshein*, 'Ugly Bull'), had been the head of a Darfur branch of the Sammánía taríqa.[6] 'Abdulláhi's childhood education had included the basic formal schooling in the Qorán and traditional religious sciences in the brotherhood khalwa, alongside his three brothers.[7] The family had been driven out of Darfur, their original home, in 1874, when the Ta'íshi and Rizeigát clans tried to prevent the slaver and titular Governor of Bahr al-Ghazál, Zubeir Rahma Mansúr, from annexing Darfur. 'Abdulláhi himself only narrowly avoided execution by Zubeir.[8] Now, from his deathbed in exile, at Abú-Rukba among the Jimi' Baggára of eastern Kordofan, 'Abdulláhi's father urged his son to search for the Mahdi, for the man who would bring back the days of Islam's glorious past. Perhaps, he told 'Abdulláhi, it might indeed be this Muhammad Ahmad, this holy man of Jazíra Aba, whose asceticism and piety had won such widespread fame.[9]

'Abdulláhi al-Ta'íshi was not the only man in Sudan looking for the Mahdi. For Muslims, the year 1297 was drawing to a close and, with a new century approaching, talk of a Mahdi arising was swirling excitedly. Waves of 'Faláta', Sudanese of West African origin who were among Muhammad Ahmad's earliest admirers, had come to Sudan precisely because they had been warned to expect a Mahdi to arise in the east.[10] Nor were the people of Obeid immune to a prevailing obsessive speculation about an imminent Mahdi. Rival gangs of children from different neighbourhoods of the town fought each other under home-made banners, representing 'Turks' and followers of the Mahdi. When their elders discovered this rather bloody game (which the 'Mahdists' always won), they took the boys to task but muttered among themselves the proverb *akhdhú fálkum min awládkum* – 'Draw your omens from what your children say and do', in other words, 'From the mouths of babes . . .'.

> One would hear nothing but curses on the rulers and on everyone who controlled one of the Government departments. Indeed, by the will of God most high, most people, both men and women, began to ask: 'Isn't there a Mahdi for us? Isn't it said that this is the right time for the appearance of the Mahdi?'[11]

ψ ψ ψ

The concept of the Mahdi, a divinely guided deliverer who would restore the world to the true path of Islam, complete with justice and faith for all, cannot be traced to the Qorán itself, which never mentions the word. It seems to derive from an honorific without any messianic significance given to the Prophet Muhammad himself, as well as to his four deputies, the *Khulafá al-rashídún*, by Muhammad's earliest followers. There are different traditions within the Sunni and Shí'a branches of Islam and, over the centuries, there has been considerable debate over which part of the Prophet's family, the 'People of the House', a bona fide Mahdi might descend from.[12] Since its first documented use in the year 685 AD, the term 'Mahdi' has been variously used for propaganda purposes and to give credibility to political underdogs.[13] Citing a range of endorsements sourced to the ever-growing body of Traditions ascribed to the Prophet, members of the Fátimid, Abbásid and Ummayad dynasties produced their own 'Mahdis' at different times. Not all collections of Hadíth contained references to the Mahdi but some unequivocal messages could be found.

> The Prophet said: 'The Mahdi will be of my stock, and will have a broad forehead and a prominent nose. He will fill the earth with equity and justice as it was filled before with oppression and tyranny, and he will rule for seven years.'[14]

Common themes run through the different traditions: As well as being descended from the Prophet's family, the Mahdi would bear his name and his father would bear the Prophet's father's name, Muhammad ibn 'Abdallah. Appearing at the end of a century when the Faith had reached its nadir, he would restore justice and peace, divide fairly the wealth of the Muslims and defeat the enemies of Islam. In 1377 AD, 'Abd-al-Rahmán Wali al-Dín ibn Khaldún produced a highly complex and detailed analysis of Mahdist beliefs and traditions, especially among Shí'a and Sufi communities.[15] Scrutinising the arguments and counter-arguments to be construed from the Hadíth, ibn Khaldún was explicit in his declaration of a general belief in the Mahdi.

> Know that it has been commonly accepted among the masses of the people of Islam throughout the ages that there must be at the end of time the appearance of a man from the People of the House (ahl al-beit) who will help the Faith (al-dín) and make justice triumphant and whom the Muslims will follow and who will gain control over the Islamic lands, and who will be called the Mahdi.[16]

Across a vast territory, from the west of the Sahara through Sudan and into Arabia, Mahdist expectation and belief reached a peak in the thirteenth Muslim century, which was even now drawing to its close.[17] Traders, settlers, pilgrims travelling to and from the holy sites of Islam in Mecca and Medina, all carried messages of Islamic revival across vast distances. Three movements in particular, the Sanúsis in central North Africa, the Wahhabis in

Arabia and the Fuláni of West Africa's Hausaland, contributed to the growth of Sudan's own movement towards an Islamic renaissance. The Wahhabis in the Arabian Hejaz disapproved of deviation from the 'true path' of Islam as laid down in the Qorán and the Sunna of the Prophet and had rebelled against the Ottoman Empire in 1813.[18] True fundamentalists, they insisted that traditional Islamic law was not being adhered to with sufficient rigour; religious devotions and mandatory prayers were being neglected. To the north, where Libya lies today, the Sanúsía brotherhood had followers scattered along the Mediterranean coast and down into the central Sahara. Its founder, Muhammad ibn 'Ali al-Sanúsi, had visited the Wahhabis in Arabia; he, too, placed great emphasis on the life and example of the Prophet and ran a highly conservative, ascetic taríqa. Because its khalwas and lodgings were spread along trading routes, the brotherhood helped foster trans-Saharan commerce – and itself expanded as many merchants joined the order.[19]

The most compelling precedents for Muhammad Ahmad, however, came from a territory far to the west of Sudan, where Usman dan Fodio had led a revivalist jihad against the corrupt and decadent rulers in what is now northern Nigeria.[20] It was a strikingly successful revolution, resulting in the establishment of the Islamic Sultanate of Sokoto. Usman dan Fodio was a Sufi of the Qádiría brotherhood, a poet and often-reclusive mystic whose disgust for violations of Islamic precepts by the orthodox 'ulamá', as well as lax practices by society in general, prompted rebellion and military conflict.[21] The sheikh's core demands were straightforward enough. He called on the Hausa rulers to allow him to call people to God throughout the country; not to obstruct anybody responding to this call; to free all political prisoners; and to cease burdening the people with taxes.[22] Usman dan Fodio never claimed to be the Mahdi but he did claim that his call to jihad was expressly mandated by the Prophet in visions.[23]

Returning with his new mentor to Jazíra Aba after a month on the Massallamía building-site, the forty-year-old 'Abdulláhi al-Ta'íshi was afforded the honour of carrying one of the taríqa's banners, stitched with verses from the Qorán. Because of his recent arrival, this privilege was unexpected and caused resentment among Muhammad Ahmad's followers. As they walked, however, the two men talked at great length and at Aba Island itself, 'Abdulláhi was allotted a small straw hut close to that of the sheikh. The new man was able to watch his master closely as he reverted to his habits of intense prayer, meditation and solitude in the riverside cave. Many believe that it was the arrival of 'Abdulláhi al-Ta'íshi at his side that prompted the specific idea of being the long-awaited Mahdi in Muhammad Ahmad's head, helping him to reach a remarkable conclusion to his own internal existential debate. According to Mahdist followers on Jazíra Aba today, however, the young sheikh had for some time been giving serious thought to the question of the Mahdi. The list of possible candidates to emerge as the *fin de siècle* Mahdi must have been short. Muhammad Ahmad's geographical isolation had kept him ignorant of current leaders in Islamic thought, orthodox or otherwise, outside Sudan, although he briefly considered Muhammad al-Mahdi al-Sanússi, the head of the order at Jaghbúb in the northern Sahara region, as a possible saviour of Islam.[24] The idea that he himself might be the Mahdi came to him late, after he had visited all his previous mentors in turn, asking each whether he was the one.

He said to each sheikh, even to Muhammad Sharíf Núr al-Dá'im: 'If you are truly the Mahdi, I shall support you and assist you.' He went to the 'ulamá' in Khartoum too. There was mutual respect between them in those days. But none of them was really competent to be the Mahdi. They knew the theory but they had never really sought to live their entire life according to the ways of the Lord.

Then Muhammad Ahmad retreated to his ghár by the river with no food or water. He stayed there, concealed from view, from

Saturday to Thursday. When he emerged, dazed and weak, he said simply: 'I am empty. I am powerless. But I have received an order from Allah through his Prophet. I am al-Mahdi al-Muntazar.'[25]

These prophetic voices, possibly brought on by prolonged self-denial and deep meditative trances, came to Muhammad Ahmad frequently in the long hours of meditation and prayer.[26] Going far beyond his earlier hints about 'good omens' and unspecified revelations, he now described to his followers detailed and extraordinary personal audiences with the Prophet Muhammad, often featuring appearances by lesser prophets, angels and saints. In July 1881, he wrote again to Sheikh Muhammad al-Tayib al-Basír, describing a typically dramatic vision.[27]

One of the good omens that has occurred since we last met was that I saw the Prophet in a vision, attended by our brother the faqí 'Isa. He sat by me and he said to our brother 'Isa: 'Your sheikh is the Mahdi.' He replied: 'I believe in him.' The Prophet again said to him: 'He who does not believe in him, believes neither in God nor his Prophet.' This he repeated three times.[28] Then my brother 'Isa said: 'O Messenger of God, the 'ulamá' mock us, and we fear the Turks.' Then the Prophet said: 'By God, if your belief is strong, you can achieve any objective, with the help of even a piece of straw.' . . .

Then Sheikh al-Tayib appeared and addressed 'Abdulláhi: 'No sooner was your sheikh born than the people of the interior recognised him as the Mahdi.[29] When he was just 40 days old, the plants and even inanimate objects knew him as the Mahdi. Your taríqa is based on six virtues: Humility, meekness, little food, little water, endurance and visiting the tombs of holy men. There are also six further virtues: War, resolution, prudence, trust in God, surrender to God and unity of opinion. These 12 virtues are to be found in no other man but you.' Then the sheikh added: 'Advise your followers to avoid three vices: Envy, deceit and neglect of their prayers.' . . .

Then the Prophet commanded 'Azrá'íl, the Angel of Death, to accompany me and my people.[30]

Such an audience with the Prophet, known as a *hadhra*, was an immensely powerful weapon in the hands of a plausible and charismatic figure. It set out in irresistible terms a divine mandate and an unimpeachable authority. According to the Hadíth, the Prophet himself said: 'Whoever sees me in a dream, surely he has seen me, for Satan cannot impersonate me.'[31] In staking this claim, Muhammad Ahmad seized the holy high ground. To declare himself the Mahdi meant that he was, at a stroke, placed not only above the 'ulamá' and the entire hierarchy of the Ottoman Khalifate but also above the petty wrangling and animosities dividing Sudan's own tribes, clans and turuq.

And so the great secret was revealed, initially only to Muhammad Ahmad's closest companions, during March 1881.[32] 'Abdulláhi al-Ta'íshi, already becoming established as Muhammad Ahmad's right-hand man, claimed to have been the very first to hear the sensational revelation.

> He now used often to come and talk privately with me, and one day he entrusted me with the secret of his divine mission. He was appointed as Mahdi by God, he said, and had been taken by the Prophet into the presence of the apostles and saints. But long before he entrusted me with his secret – indeed from the first moment I beheld his face – I knew that he was the messenger of God – el Mahdi el Muntazer. Yes, these were indeed happy days, and we had then no cares or troubles.[33]

It is, of course, impossible to speak with objective certainty about the validity of Muhammad Ahmad's claim, especially since those waking dreams in which he received the 'instructions' of the Prophet lay at the heart of his claim to the allegiance of all Sudanese, indeed all Muslims. The immense power of these visions was such that an explicit endorsement by higher powers effectively nullified the requirement for the traditional requirements and attributes of the Mahdi to be fulfilled.[34] Since the Qorán itself establishes the precedent that rules set in one part of the Holy Book can be abrogated by subsequent verses, Muhammad Ahmad would have argued, what could be more persuasive evidence of my being the Mahdi than the word of the Prophet himself?[35] Why, he may have added, should Allah be constrained by rules laid down by men? Muhammad Ahmad ibn 'Abdallah may have been able to recite a plausible family history and he may in subsequent months and years fulfil many of the other Mahdist expectations but any man who dared claim that he spoke personally with the Prophet was unassailable.

Two counter-arguments might, however, be made; one, that he wasn't the Mahdi but *believed* he was, in which case he may have been mentally unsound; or that he wasn't but he thought that such authority would be *politically* useful in the context of the rebellion. Muhammad Ahmad himself addressed both arguments. In a letter written nearly two years later, he insisted that he had been of totally sound mind when he saw those prophetic visions.

> All that I have told you regarding my being the Successor and the Mahdi and other matters were communicated to me personally by the Prophet while I was awake and in good health. I was not asleep or in a trance, nor under the influence of intoxication or madness. No, I was in possession of all my faculties of reason – prepared to command what he commands and prohibit what he prohibits.[36]

And, rejecting charges of political opportunism, Muhammad Ahmad told even his most loyal followers in later years that he had begged to be excused the Prophet's mission so that he might dedicate himself more devotedly to personal worship.[37] This insistence that he had tried to turn down the position of Mahdi was something he repeated to the public in Kordofan.

> He then said to the people: 'I was terrified and tried to refuse it, but the Apostle of God said: "There is no-one for it except you, Muhammad Ahmad." So I have been commanded in this cause by the Messenger of God.'[38]

Kordofan was selected, once again, as the ideal spot to test opinion before declaring openly that he was the Mahdi. With anti-government feeling still high in Obeid, Muhammad Ahmad was accorded hospitality, as before, by a succession of influential religious and business personalities. On this second tour, he also tried to win over members of the state-sponsored 'ulamá', including Ahmad bin Ismail al-Azhari, the Cairo-educated chief judge of western Sudan.[39]

This time he came with the aim of the secret propagation of the mission of Mahdism. He circled round the town, just like the previous time, and said in the same manner: 'The Everlasting is the Everlasting God! He is the Everlasting!' . . . As before, he would preach and admonish and teach religious subjects to the learned people, and little by little he would propagate his mission. . . .

As regards the ordinary people who heard about the arrival of the darwīsh Muhammad Ahmad, they came to him in large numbers to ask for his blessing. . . . During the sermon he would weep with one eye only, from which tears would flow onto his cheek. The masses loved him enormously and when he was assured of their love he revealed the cause of Mahdism to them. . . . Then he gave them the bay'a, which was written on paper, in secret, and they were told to keep it until his cause was revealed.[40]

۝ ۝ ۝

The final revelation, or *zuhur*, came on 29 June 1881 with the public manifestation of the Mahdi at Jazíra Aba.[41] Four days earlier, Muhammad Ahmad had marked his thirty-eighth birthday. This was the defining moment in his life, the open declaration of a hitherto underground ideological revolution against the government. By setting out an alternative to the existing political and social system, an alternative that centred on an ideal proto-Islamic society governed by Sharí'a law, he declared himself a revolutionary.[42] The administration in Khartoum might have the authority of the Khedive; he, by contrast, had the authority of higher powers. From now on, his letters and proclamations would be signed, simply, 'Muhammad al-Mahdi'.

Following another precedent from the life of the Prophet, Muhammad Ahmad set about appointing four deputies.[43] Each named for their 'predecessors' at the right hand of the Prophet, these men became the first layer of both the military high command and civilian administration; each brought with him a substantial tribal following. 'Abdulláhi al-Ta'íshi, a disciple of fewer than seven months' standing, was the most senior; he could bring the Ta'íshi and Rizeigát clans and other western Baggára tribesmen under the Mahdi's banner.[44] The second was 'Ali wad Helu, a small, wiry and very hairy individual who, as well as being an influential chief among the Dighaim and Kinána clans of the Baggára, had been educated at al-Azhar in Cairo and had 'considerable knowledge' of Islamic theology.[45] The fourth was Muhammad al-Sharíf, the Mahdi's ten-year-old son-in-law; also of Dongoláwi descent, his family could command the loyalty of clansmen from Berber, the Jazíra and Dongola itself.[46] Because he was so young, he was entrusted to the care of one of Muhammad Ahmad's earliest followers, 'Abd-al-Rahmán wad al-Nujúmi, a Ja'ali merchant who had travelled from Massallamía to join the sheikh of Jazíra Aba.[47]

In an attempt to spread his revolution further afield, the Mahdi wrote and offered the position of third Khalífa to the 35-year-old leader of the Sanúsía in the northern Sahara region, Muhammad al-Mahdi al-Sanúsi (who, despite his name, had never claimed to be *the* Mahdi).[48] No reply came from across the Nubian Desert, forcing the Mahdi to write again the following year. In that second letter, he rehearsed his own claim to be the Mahdi and repeated in detail the visions underpinning that claim. He summoned Muhammad al-Sanúsi to support the uprising, either by joining the hijra to Kordofan or by launching his own jihad from the north.

I wrote to you earlier when I heard about your proper ways, your preaching of the true path towards God and your readiness to revive the religion . . . You did not reply, so I assume that you did not receive that letter. . . . I have experienced a hadhra, during which the Prophet seated my four Khalífas on the thrones of their predecessors. . . . Your spirit was attending that audience. . . .

The Prophet has instructed me to migrate with my people to a mountain west of here called Gadír, next to Mount Mássa. This hijra is imposed on us by the Book and by the Sunna, as God says:

'To those who leave their homes in the cause of God, after suffering oppression, we will surely give a good home in this world. But truly the reward of the hereafter will be greater!'[49]

The Turks have mobilised their armies and now attack us repeatedly, so God has killed them and burned their bodies. This . . . is a sign of the wretchedness of those who disbelieve in my Mahdía.[50]

No reply to this second appeal, if indeed there was one, has survived. But confirmation that Muhammad al-Mahdi al-Sanúsi had rejected his namesake's call was not long in coming. When Khedive Ismail in Egypt wrote to al-Sanúsi, demanding whether reports alleging that a 500-strong cavalry contingent had been sent to the Mahdi under the leadership of al-Sanúsi's own son, Mahmúd, were true, al-Sanúsi replied angrily that the self-professed Mahdi was an 'apostate of religion and renegade' whose prophetic revelations were nothing more than 'idle yarns, fables and falsifications'.[51] That conclusion was reached after his envoy, sent nineteen months after the first invitation from Jazíra Aba, reported back from a territory at war, 'a burning country, dying and reeking of death'.[52] Witnessing the scene after the capture of Obeid, amid scenes of devastation and despair, the envoy concluded that no one responsible for such slaughter could truly be the Mahdi. Al-Sanúsi's letter to the Khedive was followed by a more widely distributed statement, picked up by the British press, declaring that 'the Sheikh Senoussi has . . . sent a circular to the religious heads of his tribe directing them to inform the Mussulmans that the Mahdi is a false prophet and an adventurer, and that they should on no account follow him'.[53]

Within Sudan, however, news of a new Mahdi spread like wildfire and people began to talk of unnatural wonders and miracles. As the Mahdi, his status eclipsed that of even the most revered saints and his baraka was correspondingly on the rise. Stories circulated about limitless food and drink being dispensed at his hand.[54] Excitable followers, including Babikr Bedri, began finding the name 'Muhammad' or 'Muhammad Ahmad' on eggs, stones and leaves.

> One day we bought a watermelon, and found that on every seed in it there were lines of writing. On the one side of the seed was written 'There is no god but God', but the writing on the other side was indecipherable except for the one word 'Muhammad'. I took some of these melon-seeds and showed them to our teacher, who read the writing on the one side and then turned the seed over and said, 'And what have we here?'
> 'That is "Muhammad",' I said.
> 'And what about the rest of the line?'
> 'Naturally,' I replied, 'it will be "the Mahdi"'.
> 'And why won't it be "the Prophet of God"?'
> 'The Prophet of God,' said I, 'has no need of miracles in this Muslim land'.[55]

Muhammad Ahmad had gathered a considerable following, of which the central government was just becoming aware. His companions believed in him as their spiritual mentor and believed in his revolutionary mandate. But more than charisma and visions were required. For Muhammad Ahmad to be truly accepted as the Mahdi, success in the material world, political and military, was needed to buttress his religious authority. He had been planning for at least a year to lead his community to a more isolated and secure base, emulating the Prophet Muhammad's own strategic withdrawal. There had already been many delays and it would take military action by the government to force the issue.

# SEVEN

# The Sword of the Prophet
## Jazira Aba, August 1881

By the summer of 1881, responsibility for the government in Khartoum had passed into the hands of an Egyptian army general, Muhammad 'Abd-al-Ra'úf, who had left Cairo to take up the post of Governor-General the previous spring.[1] Ra'úf Pasha had a long record of Sudan service, mainly in the southern equatorial province and mainly undistinguished. Charles Gordon, as Governor-General, had himself sacked Ra'úf twice, from provincial governorships in Equatoria and Harar, and back in the 1860s, Sir Samuel Baker had shared that low opinion of Ra'úf, then a scheming subordinate. Few in Sudan administration, however, lost their jobs for inefficiency or even failure and Ra'úf was still well placed when two key events occurred – the resignation of an utterly exhausted Gordon and the summary dismissal of the Khedive in Cairo.

The welfare of the Khartoum administration depended wholly on the will of Egypt to maintain its colonial holding. But Egypt was a nation crippled by debt, much of which had been incurred in Khedive Ismail's attempts to develop the country as a modern, Westward-looking state. Ismail had built schools and hospitals, a railway running the length of the nation and, in opening the Suez Canal in 1869, he had made Egypt a crucial junction on the map of modern global trade.[2] But the money going out far exceeded the cash coming in and Sudan, where expenditure consistently exceeded revenue, had helped drive Egypt into a state of financial crisis. Egypt's creditors were the merchant banking houses of London and Paris; the Rothschilds, Frühling and Göschen and others. They obliged with loan piled on loan but on ruinous terms.[3] When it came to pressing for their money back, the banks had the full support of their governments, culminating in a situation where European 'financial advisors' were commanding the Khedive to pay nearly 50 per cent of his treasury revenues immediately over to Egypt's foreign creditors. Cairo's insolvency enabled Britain and France to exercise a direct influence over not just Egyptian finances but also key policy issues. Egypt's humiliation was compounded when the British and French governments leaned on the Sultan in Constantinople to dismiss Ismail, pointing out that the Ottoman ruler's own debt repayments to the Bank of England might be jeopardised if the Egyptian tribute to the Sultan, more than seven million pounds a year, were to dry up. Sultan Abdülhamit II, who already suspected that Ismail had bribed 'traitors' in Constantinople to shut their eyes to underpayment of the tribute, was easily persuaded.[4] On 26 June 1879, Khedive Ismail was sacked by telegram. Having had the foresight to arrange the immediate succession of his son Muhammad Tawfíq (by dint of further judicious 'gifts' to senior Ottoman officials), Ismail went into exile.[5] Britain had begun to interfere in the running of Egypt and anything that affected Egypt affected Sudan.

Distracted by these traumatic events, the Egyptian government struggled to find an adequate replacement for Charles Gordon when, exhausted by months of non-stop campaigning against the slave-traders of Bahr-al-Ghazál and Darfur, by thousands of miles on camel-back and by financial and administrative problems in Khartoum, he resigned in late 1879. 'I have pleasure in once more acknowledging the loyalty with which you have always served the Government,' the new young Khedive wrote to Gordon. 'I should have liked to retain your service, but, in view of your persistent tender of resignation, am obliged to accept it. I regret, my dear Pasha, losing your co-operation.'[6] In Cairo during January 1880, Gordon had himself lobbied hard for the return of Ismail Ayúb, his predecessor at the Saráya, a versatile and highly experienced Circassian officer.[7] The reappointment of Ismail Ayúb was formally gazetted on 15 January but then, in a disastrous volte-face, the decision was formally rescinded eleven days later and the promotion of Muhammad Ra'úf was gazetted instead.[8]

So it was that the earliest phase of the Mahdi's revolution was handled, or mishandled, by Muhammad Ra'úf, a man more *au fait* with baccarat than battalions, instead of Ismail Ayúb, the man who had crushed mutinous troops in the east, cut through the weed-infested swamps of the south, redesigned the streets of Khartoum and, as Governor-General, added Darfur to Egypt's southern dominions. It was Ra'úf who now had to address the shocking news from the Jazíra region. For years, Khartoum had known of the sheikh on Jazíra Aba but neither government nor 'ulamá' had any reason to fear that this faqí would pose any greater threat than his many predecessors – until his declaration that he was the Mahdi. That public manifestation, known to and supported by so many tribal elders and religious leaders in the Jazíra and Kordofan, changed everything and the authorities had to act. In fact, Muhammad Ahmad had already been betrayed by his former mentor, Muhammad al-Sharíf Núr al-Dá'im, a bitter man who told Ra'úf that his former pupil had become conceited, persuaded by 'the Satan of arrogance' that he was the Mahdi.[9] Given the background of unconcealed animosity between the estranged sheikhs, Hikimdár Muhammad Ra'úf may have been tempted to dismiss such whispering as pure vindictiveness. But then an extraordinary document was brought to his attention, a manshúr from the Mahdi, his first propaganda leaflet for public consumption. The proclamation repeated verbatim many of the details from earlier private letters of Muhammad Ahmad's audience with the Prophet Muhammad, an audience which culminated in the Prophet 'outlining the series of events up to our entering Mecca and receiving the oath of allegiance from the Sharíf of Mecca himself'.[10]

Gingerly engaging this mysterious sheikh, Muhammad Ra'úf wrote a cautious letter to Jazíra Aba, expressing the goodwill of the government and its desire to welcome Muhammad Ahmad

among the ranks of Sudanese loyalists. He received a swift reply at
the beginning of the holy month of Ramadan. A personal telegram
arrived, dictated to a clerk at the government's own telegraph
station at Kawa and laboriously transmitted by Morse code.[11] The
Mahdi's challenge to the authorities could not have been more
explicit. In the telegram, he stressed his divine mandate and
threatened that 'whoever does not believe in my Mahdía will be
purified by the sword'.

To the Hikimdária,
In reply to your letter, I should reveal to you that my call to re-
establish the Sunna and reclaim our religion from its present evil
ways is mandated directly by the Prophet Muhammad. I declare
that I am the Expected Mahdi and my arrival was heralded by
heavenly signs. He who follows me will be victorious. He who
refuses will be punished by God in this world and the next . . .
The sermons preached to the faithful have been crystal clear. He
who does not believe will be purified by the sword.

You should know that in my two audiences with the Prophet
a sword was brought to me; as long as I have it, I was told, no
one can defeat me. The Prophet also told me that whoever
comes against me will be humiliated by thunderstorms or by
drowning. It is well known that God says:

'If you assist Allah's cause, he will assist you and make your
foothold sure.'[12]

From the servant of the Lord, Muhammad al-Mahdi son of
al-Sayyid 'Abdallah.[13]

Ra'úf Pasha determined to summon Muhammad Ahmad to
Khartoum to face a delegation of senior 'ulamá', whose job it was
to scrutinise and refute the pretender's Islamic credentials. At
worst, reasoned Ra'úf, his curiosity about the celebrated mystic
would be satisfied and if the man were indeed to reveal himself as
a threat to the established order, his detention might nip revolt in
the bud. The man entrusted with the mission and despatched by
steamer up-river to Jazíra Aba was Muhammad Bey Abú-al-Su'úd,

a friend of the Governor-General's since their schooldays in Egypt and, during the 1870s, one of the busiest slave-merchants in Equatoria.[14] To a European government colleague, Abú-al-Su'úd was an 'intriguer, with his one, somewhat squinting, eye, whom no-one trusted and whom everyone feared because of his friendship with Ra'úf'.[15]

This first encounter between the Mahdi and the representatives of the order he was pledged to overthrow took place at Jazíra Aba on Sunday 7 August 1881.[16] Sitting barefoot on a rush mat on the floor of Muhammad Ahmad's khalwa, the two men had an intense argument. The envoy first told his host of the Governor-General's joy in hearing the news that the long-awaited Mahdi has arisen at last; only come to Khartoum, he says, and lend your prestigious support to His Excellency Ra'úf Pasha as is your duty. 'You misunderstand', Muhammad Ahmad replied: 'Who can be set above the Mahdi, personally selected by the Prophet? It is Ra'úf who is duty bound to obey me, along with the rest of the community of the faithful.' And the sheikh of Jazíra Aba began to explain his revolutionary mandate in language that even a simple-minded Turk could understand. At this point, the visitor lost patience. 'How can you hope to fight the government with this meagre following?' Abú-al-Su'úd demanded.

Pointing to the senior Khalifa 'Abdalláhi and the other Khalifas and veteran companions who were present in council . . . the Mahdi answered, smiling, that if need be he would fight the government only with those present. The Mahdi then asked them whether they were content to die for the cause of God (*fī-sabīl Allāh*). The Khalifa promptly declared that they were ready to die for God, His Messenger and His Mahdi, and all the others answered likewise.[17]

Abú-al-Su'úd made his way back to Khartoum to explain the failure of his mission and to prepare a more forceful reaction. The government's almost comically incompetent handling of what was not, then, even a crisis was observed from a distance by the Deputy

Governor-General, Carl Giegler, a German telegraph engineer working at Obeid. He was among a number of officials in the provinces to receive coded telegrams alerting them to the Jazíra Aba dissidents.

In my diary I wrote briefly, 'Received news per telegraph of a row at al-Kawwa where some impostor pretends to be the Redeemer (Mahdi).' Since at that time I was ignorant of many of the details of what happened at al-Kawwa, I was not greatly impressed by the news. Much more serious happenings had taken place from time to time which had seemed far more serious such as military revolutions and revolts of whole tribes. Indeed, in relation to the means of power at the command of Sudan Government, this episode was an unpleasant, but not an important, far-reaching matter. Yet it became both important and far-reaching due to the stupidity with which the authorities in Khartoum handled the matter.[18]

The very day that Giegler received the telegram, Abú-al-Suʿúd (who had taken the Mahdi's threat equally lightly) was overtaken by disaster. Having made his report to his friend at the Saráya, he was sent south again, this time at the head of a company of 200 men.[19] With him travelled Ahmad Ismail al-Azhari, the scholar and jurist whom Muhammad Ahmad had met at Obeid the previous year. Al-Azhari's presence, at the specific request of the Governor-General, was designed to bolster the Islamic credibility of the raiding force, assuming that he could not help negotiate a last-minute surrender by the sheikh of Jazíra Aba. The expeditionary force left Khartoum on 11 August on the steamer *Ismailia*.[20] Reaching Jazíra Aba in 15 hours, they tied the boat to a large tree a quarter of a mile north of the settlement, disembarked and advanced in heavy rain towards the residence of the Mahdi.[21] They then blundered into a trap.

Since the departure of the frustrated emissary, the Mahdi had not been idle. He knew that the authorities would have to respond in force to such an explicit challenge. Urgent messages went out, carried by trusted followers, calling for reinforcements from the

Dighaim, Husunát and Falláta communities along the east and west banks of the White Nile. They came swiftly to his call. Sword in hand, the Mahdi, assisted by his two senior deputies, 'Abdulláhi and 'Ali wad Helu, took personal command of the disposition of his forces. Deployed in units of ten, his untrained army of a little over 300 men concealed itself among the reeds and bushes to wait in the drumming rain for the arrival of the 'Turks'.[22] Despite the slightly superior numbers at the Mahdi's disposal, it should still have been an easy victory for a trained government force, equipped with firearms. For their weaponry, the Mahdists had spears, swords, stout sticks and farmers' tools. For motivation, they had the prophetic reassurance of their master that the enemy would be 'as weak as a reed pen' and a slogan that they were instructed to chant three times as the fighting began: 'O God, Thou art our Lord and their Lord; we entrust ourselves and them to Thy hand and it is Thou who will slay them.'[23]

Night had fallen by the time the government force landed on the island, forming the regulation military square. The soldiers, like the Mahdi's companions, broke their Ramadan fast after sunset prayers, eating their first meal for around twelve hours. Dividing into two groups, under the leadership of two Egyptian adjutant-majors, they advanced confidently towards the Mahdi's village.[24] Suddenly they found themselves surrounded by what seemed like several hundred of his followers. In panic, disorientated in the darkness and terrified by the screams of their hidden enemy, the Egyptian troops fired wildly, one volley and to negligible effect. Before they had time to reload their cumbersome rifles, they were set upon and almost immediately overpowered. Driven back in disorder towards the water, harried all the way by the rebels and hampered by trees, bushes and muddy terrain, the Khartoum detachment fell back on the steamer, where they were able to put up some semblance of resistance. But, even as Abú-al-Su'úd's men fired from armoured positions on board the vessel, the positions had changed. The Mahdists were now on the offensive – and they now had rifles with which to return the fire of the 'Turks'.

As dawn broke, the Mahdi led his followers in the prayers that marked the beginning of Ramadan's mandatory daily abstinence from eating, drinking and sex. Like many of his followers, the prayer-leader himself was bandaged. Despite the advice of the Khalífa 'Abdulláhi that he should remain well behind the front line of his own army, Muhammad Ahmad had been wounded in his right shoulder, grazed by a bullet from the government's first volley of shots. On this embattled morning, the prayers were performed in a special way, in another conscious imitation of the life of the Prophet Muhammad. On the eve of an important battle at Najd, four years after the flight to Medina, Muhammad's companions had been camped in the hills, preparing to fight. Fearing that the enemy would attack them during prayer, the Prophet had arranged his men in ranks and divided them into two groups. The Prophet performed one prayer-cycle with one group while the other group stood guard, weapons in hand; the groups then changed places for the second cycle. This was called the Prayer of Fear and the Mahdi, for the first and only time in his campaign, now used the same cautionary tactic.[25] The official biographer, Ismail 'Abd-al-Gádir, later reported on the details of the skirmish.

> After the prayer, the Mahdi and his Companions joined those who were fighting the Turks in the steamer. When the firing intensified, the Khalifa pleaded with the Mahdi to take shelter . . . The battle continued until sunrise; then the Turks were defeated and – after a group of them had been killed by the Companions' bullets – they started to flee aboard the steamer.[26]

The Battle of Jazíra Aba was, for the Mahdi's followers, a victory that was nothing short of miraculous. Despite their overwhelming advantage in weaponry, the government troops left behind 120 of their party dead. Abú-al-Su'úd and Ahmad Ismail al-Azhari survived to relate a second failure to Governor-General Ra'úf. Losses among the Mahdi's improvised army were minimal, a dozen men acclaimed as martyrs of the cause. These twelve followers were buried within the day, as prescribed by Islam, in the

Mahdi's own ghár, the pit where he retreated to pray in privacy. But the event was a glorious victory, to be celebrated in verse.

> Jazíra Day! A day so pure, worthy of our sacrifice.
> May you be greeted with a rattling, cheering heavy rain!
> Twin of Badr of old, brother of that famous victory,
> You have a blessed spot, which remains throughout the ages.
> Through you, God replaced a wanton simpleton with the Mahdi
> And protected the Sharí'a with sharp swords.[27]

Word of the incident trickled only slowly out into the world. Ten days later in London, those interested in Foreign and Colonial News had to burrow at the bottom of page three of *The Times*.

> Intelligence from the Soudan reports an affray between the population and the military, caused by the preaching of a 'false prophet'. One hundred and twenty Egyptian soldiers were killed. The rise of the Nile is satisfactory.[28]

# EIGHT

# Hijra to Jebel Massa
## Nuba Mountains, 1881–1882

Mohammed Abú-al-Suʿúd's attempt to bring him to heel and to Khartoum gave the Mahdi proof that his fledgling uprising was too exposed at Jazíra Aba. It was time to take to the hills. The flight to Kordofan began within hours of the *Ismailia*'s ignominious retreat to Khartoum. The community was well prepared for the trek into the hills of southern Kordofan. Theirs was not a luxurious lifestyle, they had few enough possessions to take with them and, thanks to the advance work done by Muhammad Ahmad in wooing the peoples of the region, they could count on a friendly reception and ample food en route. And with the rainy season at its peak, the Mahdi's followers had a valuable advantage over the government force that they knew the Governor-General must send after them. The army would be encumbered with the full impedimenta of a campaign: backpacks, heavy serge uniforms and firearms. Baggage-camels and mules would have to drag artillery-pieces through the muddy and inhospitable terrain. Unaccustomed to the climate, many Egyptian soldiers would succumb to malaria and intestinal disorders. The Mahdi's companions, meanwhile, in their patched smocks, sandals and light cloaks, were ready for rapid movement, in territory where they or their allies were completely at home. The fact that the trek began while Ramadan was still underway posed few additional constraints or personal difficulties as the rigours of fasting are mitigated during journeys.

Central Sudan, showing route of the hijra.

For Muhammad Ahmad, this migration or *hijra* marked another milestone in his emulation of the life of the Prophet Muhammad. He had built the foundations of a viable movement and had spread his message far and wide. Assuming the hijra were to proceed successfully, he would expect it to be followed by jihad and – God willing – the establishment of a new caliphate. The Prophet's own hijra, prompted by the persecution of himself and his followers at the hands of rival, non-Muslim clans in Mecca as they struggled to win converts to their new religion, took him to Medina. More than 200 miles north across the burning wasteland of the Rahat lava fields, the secretive and arduous journey took ten weeks. There in the southern Hejaz, he and his fellow refugees made formal alliance with those Medina residents who made them welcome, a group Muhammad dubbed the Ansár, or 'supporters'.[1]

To begin his own hijra, the Mahdi was faced first not with a traverse of burning desert but a river crossing. From Jazíra Aba he, his brothers and the Khalífa ʿAbdulláhi organised the shipment of men, women, children and supplies across the broad stretch of the White Nile on to the western bank. For a family of boat-builders, this was easy to accomplish. The boat-yard run by his brothers Muhammad, Hámid and twenty-year-old ʿAbdallah had been working overtime in the construction of a small fleet of passenger and cargo carriers, which were gathered at Tawíla, the long inlet on the west bank of the White Nile where Muhammad Ahmad had prayed and where women fetched water. This was the nucleus of the Mahdi's Nile fleet, which would subsequently grow to number more than 70 large and 1,300 smaller wooden vessels.[2] For the purposes of the hijra, though, a handful of sturdy boats were enough to ferry the small Jazíra Aba community into exile. Muhammad Ahmad had a narrow escape almost immediately. In Jimiʿ country, still on the first stage of the journey, they camped near a group of sixty government bashi-bazouks, out on a tax-collecting mission under the leadership of Adjutant-Major Muhammad Juma. To the great good fortune of the migrants, the officer decided to send for instructions from his commanding officer at Obeid, instead of attacking an unknown group of travellers. Many years later, Muhammad Juma would find himself a prisoner of the Mahdi in Omdurman, rueing the day he had let such a 'golden opportunity' slip through his fingers.[3]

From his earlier travels, the Mahdi knew where he could count on support, where tribes disaffected with the government or won over by his own claims to be their deliverer might provide sanctuary for him and his fellow refugees. From Dár Jimiʿ, the planned route cut through eastern Kordofan and down into the Nuba Mountains, via Abú-Dom, Gardúd and Jebel Tagali.[4] The latter lay within the domain of Mek Adam, the local chieftain whom Muhammad Ahmad had wooed assiduously. Since his last visit in March, Adam had resolved not to get involved, beyond offering Tagali as a staging post where the Mahdi's footsore companions could recuperate on their marathon journey south. The chief, in fact, had been urged by his tribal counsellors to kill the upstart from the river before his movement could develop. He did not take their advice but he did adopt a 'passively hostile' position.[5] One local Tagali faqí, Dafa'allah Bigwi, was particularly vehement in his opposition to Muhammad Ahmad and no amount of personal correspondence from the Mahdi could persuade him to join the cause.[6] Instead of welcoming the travellers, Adam would send out his son 'Umar to meet them with a gift of sheep and corn, bearing also a message from his father that retreat further south into the hills might be a wise precaution.[7]

Nor were other local chieftains always eager to embrace the travellers. At Jebel al-Jaráda, a full two-and-a-half months after setting out from Jazíra Aba, Muhammad Ahmad's followers were forced to fight their way through the territory of a chief of the Kinána clan, Mukhtár wad Zubeir, who refused to accept the Mahdi's mission. After a tense standoff, Chief Mukhtár ordered his men to open fire on Muhammad Ahmad's companions. It was a mistake; after a short skirmish, the chief and thirteen of his clansmen were dead and their village looted.[8] But by then they were nearing their destination and a week later the weary migrants heard their master announce that they had at last arrived. They were at Jebel Gadír, where they were welcomed by the local chief, Mek Násir, who had been briefed by messenger of the Mahdi's imminent arrival. Work began immediately on building a mosque and new homes for the community. The hijra had taken seventy-nine days. Those who had made the trek were dubbed *muhajirún* while, as in the days of the Prophet, those who welcomed them were dubbed the new Ansár. But it was to Ansár, followers or followers-to-be, that Muhammad Ahmad addressed many of his proclamations and that was the name that stuck for the whole community.

The name of the hijra's destination had special importance in Mahdist tradition. Since the early tenth century, when Muhammad 'Ubaid'allah, founder of the Fatimid dynasty, had declared himself the Mahdi in north-west Africa at a place called Jebel Massa, tradition had pointed to that being the name of the spot where any bona fide Mahdi might manifest himself. Muhammad Ahmad's hijra in Sudan ended at Jebel Gadír but he promptly renamed the hill 'Massa' to conform to both tradition and popular expectation. And, in keeping with the Prophet's precedent on completion of the original hijra, Muhammad Ahmad now decreed that his own followers and those who came to join him at Jebel Gadír should also be styled Ansár. It was an astute way of blurring tribal boundaries, unifying Sufis and non-Sufis, followers of a variety of brotherhoods and potentially rival sheikhs, under his own banner. A subsequent, draconian proclamation explicitly stated that the traditional label of 'dervish' should be replaced.

> All my beloved and all the faithful have already been notified not to call 'dervishes' the Ansár whose hearts are sharply aware of God and who know that this world is doomed to extinction . . . Such a man is not to be called 'dervish'. Rather he should be described as a man of reason and insight, clear-headed and a true supporter of religion . . . Indeed, anyone who does call such a man 'dervish' is to be punished by whipping. I have specifically banned you from calling Muhammad al-Badawi Abú-Safiya a 'dervish'.[9] He is to be called Sadíq, 'the Righteous', and anyone calling him 'dervish' – even by a slip of the tongue – is to be given a punishment of 100 lashes and three days' fasting.[10]

At Jebel Gadír, the Mahdi now had a short breathing space to rest his weary soldiers and a new base from which to send out his letters and proclamations, the propaganda that would convert many to his cause. The successful conclusion of the hijra marked the formal beginning of what he confidently expected would be his long reign as the *Khalífat rasúl Allah*, the Successor of God's Messenger.

The defeat at Jazíra Aba enraged and alarmed Governor-General Ra'úf in Khartoum. In his reports to his superiors in Cairo, however, he played the incident down, describing it as an 'affray', still underestimating the seriousness of the uprising.[11] Ra'úf pinned the blame for the disaster squarely on the expedition's officers, who, he insisted, had been ordered to escort the Qádi of Kawa to Jazíra Aba for further peaceful negotiations.[12] But, set on revenge, the Governor-General began his deployments. With uncharacteristic foresight, Ra'úf began work on increasing his Nile fleet. Several brand-new paddle steamers had been commissioned in 1877 by Colonel Gordon during his tenure at the Saráya. The vessels had been shipped in pieces from London and carried by camel over the desert from Suakin on the Red Sea to the capital. Now Ra'úf set the engineers at the Khartoum boatyards to work, reassembling the *Abbas* and the *Mohammed Ali*. These would serve alongside the dozen other vessels, including the *Ismailia*, the *Bordein* and the *Safia*, already plying the Nile between Dongola in the north and Gondokoro in Equatoria.[13] Many of these had been built for Sir Samuel Baker's early campaign against the slave trade in the 1860s and 1870s but would now become invaluable troop and food transports as the conflict intensified. More immediately, Ra'úf ordered the Governor of Kordofan, Brigadier Muhammad Sa'íd, to gather forces sufficient to crush the dissident group. For Carl Giegler, still at Obeid, the telegram he had received on 12 August alerting him to the 'row at al-Kawwa' had also presented immediate deployment orders.

The telegram . . . ordered me at the same time to mobilize all the troops I had at al-Ubayyid and send them under the command of Muhammad Sa'id Pasha to the White Nile in order possibly to capture the Mahdi . . . before he fled. . . . I armed the troops – four infantry companies [i.e. 800 men] – for him. Everything necessary was collected in three days so that the expedition, well-equipped as far as transport and provisions were concerned, could depart on 15 August.[14]

The Mahdi and his followers were still mid-hijra, on the river Zamzía in Chief Adam's territory, when word reached them that Muhammad Sa'íd had reached Jazíra Aba. Frustrated at his enemy's escape, he torched the buildings of the Mahdi's settlement and destroyed the island's farms and orchards. Then he set out in pursuit, recrossing the river and following the rebels' trail into the Kordofan hills. Spies among the local tribes kept the Mahdi up to date with Muhammad Sa'íd's every move. But the time spent gathering the force and the delay at Jazíra Aba itself frustrated any hope of catching up with the Mahdi's community; before the end of September the force had returned tamely to Obeid without even encountering the rebels. Mahdist historians insist that the governor fled in the face of a determined rebel attack near Abú-Shudeira in the Tagali region. But the account of a senior bashi-bazouk officer, Major 'Abdallah Muhammad, makes it clear that the unwieldy force, more than a thousand men, supported by pack-camels to carry the ammunition and by additional cavalry from the loyal Jimi' clan of the Baggára, was driven back to barracks by the heavy rain after twenty-two miserable days. 'The rains were frequent, all the khors [seasonal water-courses] were full and the roads were difficult as there was so much grass,' he wrote later.[15] Governor Muhammad Sa'íd certainly had professional anxieties about his substandard scratch force; he told Cairo that the subjugation of the Tagali region required six full battalions of infantry and another six companies of Shaigía bashi-bazouks. Back at Obeid, he instead despatched the son of the influential merchant Ilyás Ahmad Umm Bireir to try to persuade Mek Adam to seize the Mahdi. This tactic, however, was never likely to bear fruit as both the envoy and his father had already gone over to the Mahdi's side.[16] It had been a wasted opportunity. If the Jazíra Aba community had been resolutely attacked, the mystique of the self-proclaimed Mahdi could have been challenged and would-be followers dissuaded from joining a short-lived rebellion.

As the weeks passed, Ra'úf, focusing on the uprising as just the latest expression of popular frustration and political discontent and overlooking or misunderstanding the Mahdi's message of Islamic revivalism, dared to hope that the threat might pass. Surely, he thought, traditional tribal divisions and jealousies would appear to undermine the unity of the faqí's following. Instead, the Mahdi not only held his tribal coalition together, he attracted more to his banner. In September, Carl Giegler returned to Khartoum to find the Governor-General 'in a very despondent mood, making plans continuously but never coming to a decision'.[17] In the military arena, much worse was to come. This time, the man to blame was the Governor of Fashoda, Ráshid Aymán.[18] As the year was drawing to a close, Ráshid decided, without checking with Khartoum, to exploit the end of the rainy season to take the rebels at Jebel Gadír by surprise. But it was, as Giegler said 'a mad escapade'. A network of Ansár spies and loyalists among the region's tribes meant that surprise was impossible. Ráshid's force, too, was simply inadequate. Two companies of 200 regular troops apiece, even with the support of Shilluk tribesmen from the Fashoda area under Chief Kaikun, could not hope to defeat the Mahdi's fighters, fired with ideological zeal and hardened by their long journey. Ismail 'Abd-al-Gádir may not have been far off when he noted with derision that 'Ráshid's boldness, insolence, love of authority and avidity for promotion' led him to conduct a campaign that was 'contrary to Turkish military rules'.[19] Ráshid marched north-west from his base on the White Nile with reckless haste. His passage through Kinána territory was observed by many and it was a woman named Rábiha *bint* 'Ali who brought the news to the Mahdi's settlement.[20]

As in Jazíra Aba, the Mahdi and his companions deployed their men with patience and strategic skill, setting their trap well away from their own village. On the morning of 8 December 1881, immediately after the dawn prayer, the Ansár were arrayed in a crescent, centred on the Mahdi's brother, Muhammad.[21] Dighaim tribesmen stood to the north, their Kinána allies to the south. There they waited.

At sunrise on Friday, the enemy's army rose. The Companions waited patiently until the enemy was closer than bullet-range. On Ráshid's order, his army fired at the Companions, who charged and annihilated them. Only those who fled – and they were few – survived. Rāshid was killed and 111 men were taken prisoner. About 30 of the Companions died as martyrs . . . An eyewitness told the author that the Mahdi's sword and garments were bloodstained but he had not seen the Mahdi actually fighting. . . . The Mahdi then ordered the martyrs to be buried with all their clothes, save the weapons. As for the prisoners, some of them reverted to the Turks and some accepted the Mahdi.[22]

ψ ψ ψ

This easy victory netted the Ansár a considerable windfall of firearms, pack animals and other booty and enabled them to enjoy a period of consolidation. The Mahdi chose not to press home his advantage against the now almost defenceless riverside town of Fashoda or against any of the other government garrisons on the White Nile, undermanned and falling into demoralised disrepair. Instead, he began to put his social agenda into practice in the context of a real and growing community. More and more local chieftains, including those who had wavered when success looked doubtful, now agreed to commit themselves to the revolution, though in many cases material grievances against the occupiers were a far greater prompt than the less than perfect adherence of the 'Turks' to the right ways of Islam. The nomadic Baggára, the most suspicious of other tribes but the most liable to be impressed by military prowess, began to arrive in considerable numbers.[23] Their presence began a gradual process of change within the movement, as the predominance of Nilotic tribes was matched, then eclipsed, by the fighting clans from the west. Many important tribes and rival Sufi sects, however, still refused to join the Mahdi. Alongside the Shaigía and the Shukría, the Kabábish and the Jimiᶜ clans on the Kordofan side of the White Nile were still providing support to the government. As Muhammad Ahmad intensified his propaganda offensive from Jebel Gadír, firing off letters and proclamations to spread his message as widely as possible, he attempted to browbeat personalities such as Sheikh 'Asákir wad Abú-Kalám, tribal chieftain of the Jimi', into making the hijra to Jebel Gadír.[24] Sheikh 'Asákir had personally led the contingent of cavalry that had accompanied Governor Muhammad Sa'íd on the first abortive pursuit of the Mahdi's followers from Jazíra Aba. Now, accusing the sheikh of hypocrisy for first embracing the Mahdist cause then changing his mind, of being 'blinded by overweening ambition and misled by the Devil', the Mahdi warned him not to incline towards the Turks, 'whose crescent is on the wane'.[25]

As new recruits flooded to the Nuba Mountains, some responding to miraculous stories of Egyptian bullets turning into water at a word from the Mahdi, they were bound into a cohesive community by their new clothes. The jibba was mandatory attire, which blurred the traditional visual markers differentiating the fractious tribes. Coupled with the abstemious lifestyle enjoined upon the members of the Jebel Gadír community, this tatterdemalion patchwork smock helped Muhammad Ahmad 'enforce unity and cohesion amongst his followers and at the same time they had the effect of hardening them to undergo the perils of war without complaint'.[26] To those who objected to this rude garment, the Mahdi insisted that the jibba had been authorised by a vision in which the Prophet had drawn a deft analogy. 'The body of every man is made up of patches,' he said. 'His head [face] is a black patch, the skin of his lips is a red patch, his teeth are a white patch and his fingernails are yellow patches.'[27]

Communal prayers were another binding agent. In addition to the five daily prayers, every important Sufi fraternity had its own collection of supplications. As sheikh of a large Sammánía taríqa, Muhammad Ahmad had already begun to distil key elements of the sect's dhikr, as well as quotations from the Qorán, into a small, concise volume of mandatory prayers known as a *rátib*. With the Mahdi settled at Jebel Gadír, his Rátib took its final shape and hand-copied editions began to circulate almost immediately, carried by the Ansár in tiny leather satchels slung close to the body on braided leather straps.[28] The chanted meditations of the Rátib, repeated in stipulated multiples of 3, 7, 10, 21, 100 or 101, became mesmeric with repetition.

> I seek refuge in God. I commit myself to God. How good God is. There is no power but with God (three times). There is neither might nor power but with God, the sublime and greatest (21 or 101 times). Praise be to God the great (100 times). God is our sufficiency and excellent substitute (7 or 70 times). I ask pardon of God the most knowing (100 times). He gives life and deals death and is almighty (100 times).[29]

The text of the Rátib makes clear that the invocations are there, at least in part, to 'purify our thoughts in order to perceive the sweetness of the Qorán'; 'I am poor,' the preacher says, 'and hope that you will favourably grant me the mysteries of your dear Book'. Included are the final verses of the Qorán, which the worshipper is instructed to repeat seven times.

> Say: I seek refuge with the Lord of the dawn, from the evil of what he has created, from the mischief of the utterly dark night when it comes on, from the evil of those who blow upon knots and from the evil of the envious one when he envies.
> Say: I seek refuge with the Lord and cherished of mankind, the ruler of mankind, the judge of mankind, from the evil of the Whisperer who slinks off, who whispers into the hearts of mankind from both jinns and men.[30]

꙳ ꙳ ꙳

At the core of Muhammad Ahmad's social plan were belief, prayer, poverty and morality, all embraced by the principles of jihad. The concept of jihad was at least as important as an internal struggle against disobedience and desire as a battle of the sword against the 'Turks'. 'Those who love me love to follow the two virtues of poverty and holy war,' he would later write, quoting the Prophet.

Those who follow these virtues are happy in themselves, and the light of God is poured down upon them. . . . But those who do not follow these virtues are ever in trouble, in whatever station they may be they are never satisfied. It is said, 'If a man possesses two valleys of gold he will wish for a third. Nothing satisfies him but dust.'[31]

From the arrival at Jebel Gadír, the Mahdi's public proclamations, marked by an absolute intolerance of disobedience, set out a range of social and behavioural taboos. 'Anyone who deviates from good manners should be chastised', he wrote. Drinking alcohol, smoking, taking snuff, swearing, using abusive names, shirking the mandatory prayers, all were *harám*, forbidden, and good citizens shouldn't hesitate to inform on a neighbour who didn't toe the line. The behaviour of women, a term that applied to any female over the age of five, was remorselessly circumscribed.

Women who are too old for marriage should make every effort for the jihad. As far as the young ones go, they should control their natural desires, confine themselves to the home and not go out unless strictly necessary. They should whisper, they shouldn't let men hear their voice except from behind a veil. They should pray and obey their husbands. A woman with uncovered hair, even for the blink of an eye, deserves 27 lashes. A young lady heard speaking with a loud voice or immodestly should also receive 27 lashes. For obscenity, man or woman, the penalty is 80 lashes.

He who calls a fellow Muslim a dog, a pig, a Jew, a pimp, a dissolute, a thief, an adulterer, a fraudster, cursed, an infidel, a Christian or a sodomite should be punished with 80 lashes and seven days' imprisonment.

The penalty for a man caught talking to a woman who is not his relative is 27 lashes. Smoking, chewing or sniffing tobacco – all deserve 80 lashes.[32] As for alcohol, the penalty is 80 lashes and seven days' imprisonment. Refusal to pray can be punished by death or confiscation of your assets or a combination of 80 lashes and seven days' imprisonment.[33]

The Mahdi appointed Ahmad Jubára, a Syrian whose family had lived in Sudan for sixty years and who was one of Muhammad Ahmad's earliest followers, as Qádi al-Islam, responsible for overseeing the application of Sharí'a law.[34] Ahmad Jubára was made an honorary Dongoláwi when he was presented with a banner by the clans grouped under the flag of the Khalífa Muhammad Sharíf, the Mahdi's son-in-law.[35] The appointment marked the start of the Mahdi's own legal system; all cases prior to this date were declared null and void, unless they involved fraud, debt, the property of orphans or the freedom of slaves. To offset the temptation of illicit sex in what was at that stage a large informal encampment of many mutual strangers, Muhammad Ahmad ordained that marriage dowries should be set at an affordable level: ten rials for a virgin and five for a non-virgin.

While the original religious impulse of the movement had clearly not diminished in the mind of its leader, he was aware that he had also created a resistance movement. Until now, his forces had been dedicated but not disciplined, enthusiastic but not organised. Much is made, in Mahdist literature, of the allure of paradise, the certain fate of a Muslim believer who dies in battle during a jihad. When Muhammad Sa'íd had failed to engage the fleeing community in battle in the early stages of the hijra, the Mahdi's companions were said to have wept in 'grief at missing the jihad, which is a means for the attainment of martyrdom – the ultimate aim of the Companions'.[36] But the more astute among the rebels, including Khalífa 'Abdulláhi, realised that structure would be needed as well as strategy. Bigger and better armies would be sent against them by the authorities in Khartoum. After the battle of Jebel Gadír, the role of *Amír juyúsh al-Mahdía*, 'Commander of the Armies of the Mahdía', was given to the Mahdi's older brother, Muhammad, whose standard was a white banner, stitched with the shahada and the declaration that the Mahdi was the Successor of the Prophet.[37] The Mahdi's fighting force, by now numbering several thousand, was divided into three great divisions, each under the banner of a Khalífa. Men loyal to the Khalífa 'Abdulláhi, Baggára from the west of Kordofan and Darfur, marched under the Black Flag.[38] The Kinána and Dighaim followed 'Ali wad Helu under the Green Flag. The Red Flag flew above the division commanded by Muhammad al-Sharíf, representing the peoples of the Jazíra and further north, as well as the Mahdi's own clansmen, the Ashráf. Borrowing the symbol of authority from local chieftains in the region, each Khalífa had a war-drum of beaten brass and leather skin.[39] Below them in the new military order were a variety of tribal chiefs and commanders known as *umará'*; as the uprising spread into the north, west and east of the territory, celebrated umará' such as 'Osmán Digna and 'Abd-al-Rahmán al-Nujúmi acquired great stature and de facto regional autonomy.

Each flag commander equipped his men with the best weapons they could obtain, with one important exception. The Mahdi stubbornly refused to let the Ansár use the firearms captured from the government forces they had defeated. For him, the purity of the mission required that the weapons of the 'infidel Turk' must not be used. This policy was explicitly articulated in a proclamation the following spring, addressed to the three flag commanders and their subordinate officers.

The Prophet has repeatedly informed us that our victory is through the spear and the sword and that we have no need for the rifle . . . Had it been of any merit, it would have given aid and succour to those who carried it before . . . [but] God defeated and subdued them. He stripped them of their robe of majesty and prestige . . . though we were extremely weak and had no power but our reliance on God.

Now I see that you are inclined towards carrying firearms, having abandoned your big spears and swords . . . The Prophet himself has urged strongly that bamboo sticks be used for spear-shafts . . . As the Lord has said:

'Against them make ready your strength to the utmost of your power, including war-horses, to strike terror into your enemies.' . . .[40]

I instruct all my generals . . . to gather all their lieutenants and inform them of our instructions so that each may carry it out with his subordinates and collect all the firearms in their possession.[41]

No one has permission to leave uncollected any firearm, small or large. Every amír is to make a precise inventory, itemising each weapon. All this should be done under the supervision of the Khalífa 'Abdulláhi or anyone whom he deputises for that purpose. After the collection, we shall see what God wills.[42]

Notwithstanding the prudent precaution of hoarding the firearms (and keeping them out of the hands of tribesmen whose loyalty had not yet been proven), this was a tactical mistake that would not be rectified until the siege of Obeid later that year, when even Muhammad Ahmad was persuaded that men armed with spears and sticks could hardly be expected to prevail against rifles, rapid-fire Nordenfeldts and artillery.[43] For now, though, his fighters used swords, spears and even throwing-knives. These wicked looking triple-bladed weapons, cut from a piece of steel, came originally from the Zande people in the forests of central Africa to the south. The rank-and-file Ansár were not above assimilating any practical weaponry into their arsenal. Cavalry horses were given rudimentary protection with quilted armour. Select leaders had the real thing, armourers beating out ringlets for chain mail tunics. From Darfur in the west came the inspiration for plate metal helmets, complete with chain mail fringe and cotton padding. From the blacksmiths' forges, too, came new swords, especially the *kaskara*, a straight metre-long blade, its steel often acid-etched with propitious designs, thrust into a leather scabbard of flared design.[44] Several tribal chieftains even wore genuine medieval armour that had somehow made its way down to Sudan in the centuries since the Christian Crusades in the Levant. Europeans who encountered such anachronistic visions always reacted with astonishment.[45]

# NINE

# Jihad
# Jazíra and Nuba Mountains, 1882

The defeat and death of Ráshid Aymán, Governor of Fashoda, in the battle at Jebel Gadír threw Khartoum into still greater confusion. The Governor-General, Muhammad Ra'úf, still complaining that Ráshid had specifically disobeyed his order to stay in Fashoda, was left with no alternative but to appeal to Cairo for reinforcements and endorsement of his handling of the rebellion thus far.[1] He received neither; nor would Cairo permit the redeployment of three battalions serving on the frontier with Abyssinia. A report in *The Times* shortly after the death of the Governor of Fashoda predicted, instead, the end of Ra'úf's reign in Khartoum.

> Serious troubles have again broken out in the Soudan. The false prophet, to whom attention was called some time ago, at the head of 1,500 men, has totally annihilated a force of 350 Egyptian troops, whom the Governor of Fashoda was leading against him. The Governor himself was among the killed. The Governor-General of Soudan, who alleges that the expedition was undertaken against his orders, has sent an urgent application for reinforcements. . . . It is thought that he will be dismissed from his post.[2]

Muhammad Ra'úf was indeed promptly sacked by Khedive Tawfíq and summoned back to Cairo. His replacement, gazetted on 16 February 1882, was Major-General 'Abd-al-Qádir Hilmi, originally from Homs in the Ottoman province of Syria. 'Abd-al-Qádir Pasha, then forty-five years old, had already seen administrative service in Sudan, as well as combat experience in Egypt's war with Abyssinia in 1875–6.[3] But he needed time to return to Cairo from his posting as Governor of Port Said and the Canal Zone before travelling south. To fill the gap of several weeks, Carl Giegler was designated Acting Governor-General. A tall German with a red beard, Giegler had already been deputised at the Saráya once before, during Charles Gordon's temporary absence in Darfur at the end of 1879.[4] Now, for a few weeks, he had the authority to reverse the passive and complacent policy of Ra'úf, which he had so trenchantly criticised in the aftermath of the first encounter at Jazíra Aba. Watching his disgraced commander depart by steamer on 4 March, Giegler reflected that he now had 'the whole thing in my own hands'.[5] Unlike Ra'úf, Giegler was confident that he could suppress the rebellion with the manpower already under his command in Sudan, without the aid of reinforcements from Egypt. So, having prudently secured the backing of his superiors in Cairo, he moved swiftly, gathering troops on the White Nile from wherever he could find them. His strategy was to launch a large force under an experienced general directly at the Ansár stronghold in the Nuba Mountains; smaller contingents, meanwhile, would crush Mahdist supporters in the Jazíra. If necessary, a further offensive in Kordofan might be necessary. By the time 'Abd-al-Qádir Pasha himself arrived in Khartoum in May, his stand-in had already set in motion a substantial campaign. It was a policy that went against 'Abd-al-Qádir's more cautious, defensive instincts and brought mixed results. Spring and summer brought the government a few minor victories and one devastating defeat.

The first campaign against the rebels came in the Jazíra region, where minor uprisings had burst into flame like scattered bushfires, carefully kindled by Muhammad Ahmad's agents, including Sheikh Muhammad al-Tayib al-Basír. The town of Sennar, capital of the pre-occupation Funj rulers, had been under siege by the Mahdi's followers since early spring of 1882.[6] Their leader was Sheikh Ahmad al-Makáshfi, another early supporter of Muhammad Ahmad.[7] The governor, Hussein Bey, sent Khartoum an urgent telegraph message, confirming that the thousand or so rebels surrounding the small town had called on him to surrender promptly, in the name of the Mahdi. A sortie was driven back by the Mahdist attackers and the small garrison, equipped with just one artillery piece, was forced to take refuge in its own barracks. But help was at hand. Giegler diverted a company of 200 men from its planned rendezvous with the main force gathering on the White Nile for the assault on Jebel Gadír. It was a small force but, in its company commander, Salih al-Mak, it had valiant leadership.[8] Relieving the Sennar garrison on 13 April, Salih al-Mak demonstrated calm authority and practical application of his superiority in weaponry. The Acting Governor-General was justifiably proud.

What a marvellous exploit! . . . It was a very dangerous operation since the whole Jazira . . . was more or less in revolt. But at that time all had to be dared, though it may seem foolhardy to have sent such a small detachment against some 10,000 enemy . . . The march over the Jazira lasted 10 days till they reached the town of Sinnar. With great cunning he then played the role of the disenchanted commander whom his superiors had wanted to send to Jabal Qadir to fight against the Mahdi. He told all the people whom Ahmed al-Makashif [*sic*] had sent to meet him that he only wanted to wait till he came to Sinnar before showing his true allegiance, and joining al-Makashif so that together they could drive the 'Turk' out of the country. And so he was able to get into the town with the help of the rebels. . . .

When he . . . was about 200 metres from the rebel army, he halted his men, said a few encouraging words and ordered them to fire. All had Remingtons. . . . The panic among the rebels must have been great at first when they saw their people falling in heaps. More orderly counter-attacks which followed were easily beaten off. After two hours it was clear who had won. Salih had not lost a single man. Thousands of the rebels lay dead or wounded on the ground. The remainder now fled horrified. Salih and his people then entered Sinnar where he was honoured like a god.[9]

Giegler, meanwhile, was personally leading an expedition against another Mahdist supporter in the Jazíra, Sheikh al-Sharíf Ahmad Taha. Giegler collected his force – regulars from Khartoum, bashi-bazouks from Gedaref to the east and stragglers from the Kordofan force – and embarked on the steamer *Abbas*. Morale was badly affected when rumours began to swirl through the ranks that a command from the enemy sheikh would turn the government's bullets to water, that cannons had been miraculously transported through the air from the Mahdi himself. Giegler himself was outraged when he was ordered to stand down by 'Abd-al-Qádir Hilmi, by now making his way up the Nile. The Hikimdár signalled his stand-in from Berber that an Egyptian infantry major should lead the attack on Sheikh Taha's positions at Massallamía, not a German civilian. The attack, before dawn on 3 May, failed badly. The government infantry square was penetrated, the cavalry joined the headlong retreat and the Mahdists gained yet another artillery piece. Giegler then recruited a militia of Shukría tribesmen under Sheikh 'Awad-al-Karím Ahmad Abú-Sinn, hereditary chief of a clan that had, like the Shaigía, remained loyal to the central government since the occupation in 1821.[10] On 5 May, an army of 2,500 Shukría, their chiefs 'all dressed in mediaeval breast-plates with steel helmets and arm and leg protections', moved decisively against Ahmad Taha near Abú-Haráz. This time, wrote Geigler, everything went well. The rebels were driven back with heavy losses. Sheikh Taha, the only man on horseback, initially seemed immune to the government bullets.

All around him fell but he remained unharmed. But his horse seemed to stumble; he bent forward and a bullet struck him in the head . . . When the Sharif and all his men had been killed, I had his head sent to Khartoum and placed on a spike in the market place. This was quite a barbarous thing to do but quite in place at that time. People now came from all sides to congratulate me for having destroyed the destroyer of peace.[11]

The Mahdi at Jebel Gadír was furious to hear of the Shukría involvement in the defeat of Sheikh al-Sharíf Ahmad Taha's army. He wrote immediately to 'Awad-al-Karím Abú-Sinn and another government ally, Sheikh Hamad al-Níl. 'You have killed the son of Taha,' he berated them, 'a setback to the faith and a triumph for the unbelievers. Know well that you shall hear of this later.'[12]

Giegler's main army was put under the command of Brigadier Yúsuf Hassan al-Shalláli, a rarity in the government's regular army in that he was himself Sudanese. He had served with distinction in several campaigns against slave-traders in Equatoria, Bahr-al-Ghazál and southern Darfur in 1878–9 when Colonel Gordon had been Governor-General in Khartoum.[13] His second-in-command was Colonel Muhammad Suleimán, another Sudanese from the Shaigía tribe who had served in the regular army with distinction since 1846. The core force set out from Khartoum on 15 March but was then compelled to wait idly at Kawa on the White Nile for the reinforcements that Giegler had ordered from Obeid. Morale declined and there were frequent desertions. By 7 April, when Carl Berghoff, a German photographer employed as government Inspector at Fashoda, wrote to friends in Alexandria, Shalláli's force was still waiting.

We have here about 2,000 soldiers, regulars and irregulars, and we are still awaiting reinforcements from Sennar and Kordofan before marching against the Mahdi, Muhammad Ahmad, at Gebel Gedir. The effective force will consist of 3,000 men, including 500 cavalry, 600 camels for the baggage and water, four guns, two rocket-tubes, &c. In a month the expedition will be ready. Yussuf Pasha, who was with Gessi Pasha in the Bahr Ghazal, will have the command-in-chief.[14]

The Governor of Kordofan had been ordered to send one battalion of regulars and two squadrons of Shaigía cavalry. But the expedition got off to an inauspicious start. The traditional *noggára*, a large wooden war-drum, fell from the camel ridden by 'Abdallah Dafa'allah, the brother of the influential merchant Ahmad. The accident was interpreted by the men, women and children watching the departure as a dreadful omen. After slaughtering a bull to divert the evil eye, the army set out to join their colleagues at Kawa, the riders showing off their horsemanship in a last act of bravado, 'as if they were departing finally with no hope in life any more'.[15] From there, after further delays, they proceeded upstream to Fashoda, whose garrison had been obliterated six months before.

The march into the hinterland was an exhausting one, covering 100 miles of difficult terrain in sixteen days before they approached the main Ansár force at Jebel Gadír. Setting out on 4 May into the wooded hills, Shalláli Pasha had to coordinate the most numerous force assembled since the days of the Ottoman invasion, a complement of between 4,100 and 6,000 men.[16] As they passed through the region of Jebel Fungur, now well into the Nuba Mountains, four of the Mahdi's spies were handed over to them. The spies were captured by tribesmen loyal to the government, who had earlier helped Ráshid Aymán on his disastrous expedition by providing him with men, pack animals and provisions. On that occasion, the Mahdi had led a punitive raid on Jebel Fungur but had relented and granted them his forgiveness. Now, with a substantial government army again on their territory, the tribesmen proved willing to renege on their pledge of allegiance to the Mahdi and betray his agents. The spies' punishment was swift and brutal; in front of the assembled army, Shalláli had their arms and legs cut off one by one. This move misfired badly; the government soldiers were greatly impressed by the stoicism with which the Ansár met their gruesome death and correspondingly apprehensive about the resolute nature of the thousands of men that awaited them.[17]

During a rest stop of eighteen days at Jebel Fungur, Shalláli Pasha wrote a long letter to the Mahdi. The brigadier accused the Mahdi of wrongfully killing faithful Muslims at Jebel Jaráda and

treacherously ambushing the original government detachment back
at Jazíra Aba, which had, he wrote, only been seeking to persuade
Muhammad Ahmad to come to Khartoum for a substantial debate
with the 'ulamá' over his claim to be the Mahdi. Shalláli also
challenged his adversary about his use of scouts; surely, he taunted,
if you are the Mahdi, you must know everything anyway. Deriding
Muhammad Ahmad's followers as little more than cattle-stealing
Arabs and idol-worshippers, Shalláli concluded by offering the
Mahdi an all-expenses-paid trip to Mecca. These and several other
points, which revealed a dishonest appraisal of the military
situation, a less than competent grasp of Muslim theology and
fundamental contempt for the Ansár, were tackled head-on by the
Mahdi in a sharp riposte. His rebuttal, written on 22 May and
peppered with Qoránic quotations, is worth quoting at length.

Your letter has reached us and we would like to point out, with
definite proofs, your mistakes in all the points you raised and
show you where you have gone wrong in your presumptions.

To begin with, your statement that we killed those soldiers in
the two battles treacherously, before they had started to fight, is
clear lies, because in both encounters they fired first so we
fought and killed them. Your statement that they had been sent
by the government to peruse the evidence [of our claim] is also
false. If the government had wanted an exchange of views and
to peruse the proofs we possess, it would have sent pious men
and 'ulamá' – men who are capable of coherent deliberation on
these matters – instead of stupid soldiers.

Your statement that we killed Muslims in this region
unjustly is also false. We only fought and killed those people
at Jebel Jaráda after they denied our Mahdism and fought us.
The Prophet has told us . . . that those who doubt our
Mahdía, deny it and disagree with us are infidels. It is
legitimate to shed their blood and their property becomes our
bounty. As to your statement that the ones we killed were
Muslims and followers of the teachings of the Prophet and
that God will hold us to account, this too is null and void. It

has been written . . . that the princes of Egypt, all their soldiers and followers, are to be fought because they have stolen the wealth of the Muslims. Killing them is permissible because the Book says:

'The punishment of those who wage war against God and his Apostle, and strive with all their might for mischief across the land is execution, crucifixion or cutting off the right hand and left foot.'[18]

Moreover, the Prophet commanded us explicitly to fight the Turks, telling us that they are infidels as they disobeyed his own order to follow us and wished to extinguish the light of God through which he wanted to reveal his justice. And a number of our brothers clearly saw fires burning the bodies of the infidel soldiers who were killed – hastening their punishment and demonstrating their true worth.

Turning now to your capture and injury of the four scouts, you should know that earlier friends of the Prophet suffered imprisonment, beatings and death. But they will be recompensed, while you will surely see God's retribution for what you did to them. As to your statement that the use of scouts is incompatible because a true Mahdi should know the unknowable, you are clearly ignorant of the life of the Prophet himself. Since he used scouts, how could it be incompatible with our Mahdism?

Next let me deal with your statement that my only followers are ignorant Baggára Arabs who used to worship stones and trees, while the rich, the powerful and the pampered stayed away until their homes were destroyed and their best leaders killed. You are just like the chiefs of the unbelievers who said to Noah:

'Nor do we see that any follow you but the most abject among us, those of immature judgement.'[19]

We pray to God that you and all who follow you will be booty for those 'ignorant Baggára' whom you deride.

Let us turn next to your invitation to come first to you then proceed to the place of guidance, the blessed Mecca. You should know that our progress towards Mecca is guided by the Prophet at the time ordained by Allah, not at your whim. And as to your suggestion that we send an angel as proof of our Mahdism, this again simply shows your ignorance. God himself told Muhammad that even miracles are no guarantee of real faith:

'Even if we were to send you a message written on parchment, so that the unbelievers could touch it with their own hands, they would be sure to say: "This is clearly nothing but magic".'[20]

Finally, you say that His Highness the Khedive has ordered you not to fight us until we transgress – we hardly believe this! Your fear and despair were the only reasons holding you back. After all, we have transgressed your laws and contravened your wishes since we were at Jazíra Aba; how dare you present an argument that could only come from the weak-minded? So hurry along and fight us so that you may secure the promotion with which the Devil has enticed you. And do not write again. We shall not reply. As long as you disbelieve in our Mahdía we have nothing for you but pointed spears and sharp-edged swords.[21]

After delivering this uncompromising rebuke, Muhammad Ahmad awaited the arrival of the government army. Increasingly exhausted, hungry and thirsty, Shalláli's men pushed forward through the rough, wooded terrain. When night fell on 29 May, they were encamped behind a strong square zaríba of thorn bushes, each corner protected by an artillery detachment. The Mahdi, meanwhile, was gathering his forces under cover of darkness; the infantry under their new divisional flags complemented by 200 men mounted on captured government horses. After staging a night march and resting his men close to the enemy position, Muhammad Ahmad launched his attack immediately after the dawn prayer on 30 May.[22]

The bewildered government troops were woken by the screams of their attackers, pouring forward in their thousands with complete disregard for the thorns of the zaríba or the bullets of the defenders. Artillery was next to useless at such close range. Once the zaríba was penetrated, the government force was at first trapped within its own defences, pressed back against the thorns.

But a large number of Egyptians managed to break out, only to be followed, tracked and slaughtered by the gleeful Ansár. This enthusiasm for the chase nearly cost the life of the Mahdi. With so many of the rebels now pursuing the fleeing Egyptians, Muhammad Ahmad was left with few companions around him; those government troops still inside the zaríba were able to concentrate their fire on the group surrounding the Mahdi until, their ammunition spent, they were hacked down where they stood. The Battle of Massa, as Muhammad Ahmad called it, was the greatest victory yet in the uprising against the Khartoum authorities. It stiffened the resolve of tribesmen whose commitment to the revolt was doubtful and transformed the enthusiasm of the zealots to unswerving dedication. Because it ensured the safe continuity of the nascent Mahdist community, it also marked the formal beginning of Muhammad Ahmad's self-proclaimed Mahdist state.[23]

But casualties were high. Ismail 'Abd-al-Gádir reported that 200 Ansár were killed, among them the Mahdi's older brother, Hámid. On the government side, losses were far higher. Brigadier Yúsuf Hassan Shalláli would not return to Khartoum, nor 'Abdallah Dafa'allah to Obeid. Egyptian officers and men, many of them reluctant conscripts, were massacred in their thousands alongside their Shaigía and Kordofani allies. There were few prisoners. Mahdist propaganda insists that this was one of the first occasions on which the corpses of the defeated enemy were consumed by fire, one of the many karámát attributed to the Mahdi.[24] This belief in spontaneous combustion may not be as absurd as it seems. It was noticed at the Battle of Atbara in April 1898, for example, that British lyddite shells not only set grass huts alight but 'the cotton clothes of some of the killed and wounded Dervishes had caught and they were horribly burnt'.[25] This unpleasant phenomenon seems to have been appropriated and retrospectively applied to the enemy, even in battles where artillery was not deployed.

The spoils of battle or *ghaníma* – weapons, slaves, animals, food and clothing – were divided according to the Mahdi's new rules, designed to emphasise the sense of Ansár community and counteract the predatory tendency of those tribesmen whose motives for joining the jihad was largely self-enrichment. A fifth of the booty (presumably the best fifth) was allocated to the Mahdi himself as imam of the community; the rest was commandeered by a new communal treasury, the *Beit al-Mál*, for eventual distribution among the Ansár fighters and the families of those who had been killed.[26]

۝ ۝ ۝

When 'Abd-al-Qádir Hilmi finally arrived in Khartoum on 11 May, the Shalláli force had already assembled at Fashoda on the White Nile and set off on its doomed expedition into the Nuba Mountains.[27] Although Geigler's gambit had failed, he was not disgraced or removed from government. He was removed from his position as deputy Governor-General on 2 June, the day he returned to Khartoum, but appointed instead Inspector-General for the suppression of slavery.[28] Now, 'Abd-al-Qádir abandoned the strategy of aggressive search-and-destroy missions. He was determined to pursue a new three-pronged strategy, consisting of a defensive military deployment, a propaganda offensive and covert efforts to assassinate the Mahdi.

The defensive posture implied an acceptance at the Saráya that government control of key urban centres must be maintained at the expense, if necessary, of large expanses of rural Kordofan and the Jazíra. In the early summer of 1882, Obeid was still held by a strong government garrison; the towns of Darfur, too, were secure. Unrest had yet to stir in the east on any threatening scale. There were dissident elements in Jazíra, but they could, the Governor-General calculated, be contained. With all this in mind, three battalions of regular troops, supported by Shaigía cavalry and totalling 3,500 men, were transferred from the eastern Red Sea districts. Two more battalions were made up from slaves donated by merchants and tribal chiefs from Khartoum, Berber and Dongola.[29] All the main towns – Khartoum, Obeid, Sennar, al-

Dueim, Fashoda and al-Fasher – were ordered to improve their defences. According to a British intelligence report completed the following year, a 'state of siege' was proclaimed in the capital.

> Five forts had been constructed, each armed with one gun.[30] The town was divided into four military sections, and picquets patrolled the streets both day and night. A rising in the town was expected, simultaneously with an attack from without. As a further protection, it was decided to cut a canal south of the town, joining the two branches of the Nile, but the commencement of this work appears to have been delayed until November.[31]

The government's propaganda counter-offensive was mounted on two fronts. On a political level, the Governor-General appealed to the patriotism of the key tribes that still remained loyal, including the Shukría, most of the Kabábish and the Dabaina. In return for helping the government against the rebels, 'Abd-al-Qádir offered to let them off a full year's tax. And, in addition to letting them keep any spoils of war, he would pay blood money: two pounds for every Mahdist fighter, dead or alive, and 18 pounds for a chief.[32] With so many letters and proclamations from the Mahdi now in circulation, the orthodox 'ulamá' in Khartoum were faced with a serious challenge to their own legitimacy. For Muhammad Ahmad, repeated and venomous denunciations of what he called *al-'ulamá' al-sú'*, 'the evil scholars', spiritually deficient academics subservient to their precious texts, had become a recurrent theme.[33]

> Ye 'ulamá' of evil, who pretend to pray, to be charitable and to study religion, but who do none of these things. You pretend to repent and return to the truth but in reality you follow your own amusements and ambitions. Your words are the words of wisdom, but your heart is the heart of wickedness. I tell you: In making your provisions for this life you have destroyed your hope in the world to come. You are indeed the most wicked of men. You are but slaves of the world. Your sins will take hold of you and they will drag you by your hair and drive

you barefoot and naked into the presence of the great Judge, who will punish you eternally for your evil deeds.[34]

The religious counter-attack was overseen by Sheikh al-Amín Muhammad al-Darír, a religious figure from Tuti Island whose rank as 'Distinguished Chief of Sudanese Ulamá' (*Ra'ís mumayyaz 'ulamá' al-Súdán*) had been endorsed nearly twenty years earlier, specifically and exceptionally, by the Sultan in Constantinople himself.[35] Three manifestos, commissioned to refute the Mahdi's authority on legal grounds, were written by Sheikh al-Amín al-Darír himself, by the Mufti of the Appeal Court in Khartoum, Shákir al-Ghazi, and by Ahmad Ismail al-Azhari, the 'álim who had met Muhammad Ahmad in person at Obeid and Jazíra Aba.[36] None of these manifestos tried to deny the concept of the Mahdi as a heresy; instead they focused on finding proofs that Muhammad Ahmad was an impostor.[37] Sheikh al-Amín published a 'Guide for Him Who Seeks Guidance on the Clarification of the Mahdi and the False Mahdi'.[38] Shákir al-Ghazi's 'Message on the Call of Muhammad Ahmad the Mahdi' stressed the legitimacy of both the Sultan in Constantinople as the defender of the Islamic faith, the leading Imam and Khalífa, as well as his subordinate, the Khedive in Cairo.[39] He denounced the followers of the 'False Prophet' as *khawárij*, 'rebels'. Ahmad al-Azhari's 'General Advice to the People of Sudan on Disagreement with Rulers and Disobedience of the Commander of the Faithful' was more elaborate, taking on the Mahdi's on his own terms.[40] He scrutinised and, in a precise twelve-point argument, rejected Muhammad Ahmad's claims to have met the requirements and attributes set out in the Hadíth in terms of his place of birth or manifestation, his physical attributes, his lineage or even the contemporary circumstances that were supposed to have triggered the appearance of the Mahdi. 'You and I live in comfort, safety and quiet,' the judge told his reader; 'our refuge, the refuge of all, does exist. It is the Khedive and His Excellency the Governor-General of Sudanese provinces, 'Abd-al-Qádir Pasha . . . who grasp the oppressed by the hand and take vengeance upon the oppressor.'[41] In addition, Muhammad Ahmad's claim to have received the personal endorsement of the Prophet Muhammad, which in theory might have overridden such criteria, was emphatically denied on the grounds that any claimed revelations that differed from the law must be cast aside. Finally, the 'ulamá' ruled that the murder of Muslims constituted apostasy, as did the crime of causing a schism in the *umma*, the community of Islam.

> Now this pretender to the office of Mahdi is causing schism in the congregation and has broken the staff of Islam, and has ruined the abodes of the Muslims, plundered their property, dishonoured their women, and made some tyrannise over others, as is in accordance with their apostasy, because they have made lawful the killing of the faithful . . . though these are observing the laws of religion . . . [42]

Other influential personalities deployed in the Governor-General's propaganda campaign included Sheikh Muhammad 'Osmán al-Mírghani of the Khatmía sect and Muhammad Ahmad's old mentor, Sheikh Muhammad Sharíf Núr al-Dá'im. British newspapers illustrated the work done by the Khatmía leader, especially in the eastern districts. One lithograph in *The Graphic* depicted the sheikh in a rattan rocking chair, receiving the oath of allegiance from a group of Beja tribesmen, while European colonial officers in fezzes and topis looked on approvingly. The caption reads: 'The Soudan – Friendly natives doing homage to the Sheik el Morgani'. In another, a scribe sits cross-legged on a small rug in the centre of a *diwán*, or reception chamber. 'Sheik Morgani dictating letters to the rebel leaders, advising them to submit to the Khedive', reads the caption.[43] As for Sheikh Núr al-Dá'im, he was put to work, at the personal behest of 'Abd-al-Qádir Pasha, on a long poem, comparing the saintly early life of Muhammad Ahmad (quoted in chapter 3) with what the poet characterises as the arrogance and evil of the man who had declared himself the Mahdi.

> He lived on our hand-outs as our servant for 20 years
> But in 1295 destiny caught up with him,

As he has previous knowledge of evil.[44]
Accompanied by a devil from the world of the jinns
And one from the world of mankind, both joined him in evil-
doing.[45]
Forget not the call of need; many a man fell into evil because of the
pain of poverty.
So when he said 'I am the Mahdi', I told him to straighten his
ways,
For that status is reserved for those who know.
He insisted: 'Your son is the Mahdi,
So let us rise up to bring about the victory of our faith,
Killing those who disobey.
You take the throne here and I will rule other countries.'
So I said to him: 'Forget what you desire to do;
It is an evil that only leads to loss.'
But Satan said to him: 'Be courageous ! Fear not for you
Will be victorious on both land and sea' . . .
And he said: 'I am like water:
Cool in temperament but, when heated, like fire' . . .
From that time he rejected me and I him
And I declared a fatwa that he had gone astray and become an
infidel.[46]

Evidence of the Governor-General's third tactic, secretly trying
to kill the Mahdi, has been uncovered in the khedivial archives in
Cairo. In July 1882, 'Abd-al-Qádir Pasha sent a telegram to
Tawfíq outlining various possible methods of assassination,
including poisoned dates and sending a murder squad of two
government agents to Jebel Gadír. In addition, he requested a
'dynamite envelope', a prototype letter bomb, which he hoped to
have manufactured in Cairo.[47] It is not certain that any of these
ideas were even tried, although one account describes how the pair
of assassins was discovered on their way to Jebel Gadír. When the
Mahdi was informed, he bided his time until they arrived, then
revealed that he knew exactly who they were. The would-be killers
were so confounded that they converted to the Mahdist cause on

the spot.[48] There is another report of an assassination attempt, when the Mahdi was at Kába in Kordofan the following year. One 'Abdallah wad Ibráhím fired six shots at the sleeping imam. All six bullets misfired. Instead of punishing his assailant, the Mahdi is said to have forgiven him and presented him with a banner of the Ansár.[49] It is not clear that the Kába incident was sponsored by the government or simply a case of an individual with a personal grievance. But 'Abd-al-Qádir's schemes were desperate measures at a desperate time.

# TEN

# 'Star with a Tail'
## Obeid, 1882–1883

The holy month of Ramadan was drawing to a close when, in the late summer of 1882, the main rebel army – as many as 50,000 men – began the descent from its encampments in the hills of southern Kordofan and marched on Obeid.[1] Muhammad Ahmad ibn 'Abdallah al-Mahdi travelled in their midst. He alternated between moving on foot like his followers, as a gesture of humility, and riding an unusually beautiful white camel named 'Debelan' after her slender build.[2] Above the forest of spears, blades glinting dully in the overcast muggy air, and shouldered muskets, multicoloured banners waved, their slogans picked out in clumsy hand-stitched lettering:

O God the merciful and compassionate
O eternal, O everlasting, Lord of majesty and honour
There is no God but Allah! Muhammad is the messenger of God
Muhammad al-Mahdi is the successor of God's messenger[3]

Obeid was a rich prize. Apart from its commercial wealth and the potential loot from the town's Egyptian officials, it would provide a strong operational base from which to launch an assault upon Khartoum itself. But taking this strategic target would not be easy; Obeid was home to a substantial garrison of around 6,000 Egyptian troops, armed with new Remington rifles that had been sent there in June by the Governor-General in anticipation of a siege. The garrison, though, was badly demoralised by the succession of shameful defeats that their colleagues in the government army had suffered at the hands of the Mahdi's ramshackle but now enormously numerous forces.

By the time the Mahdi established his temporary headquarters at Kába, six miles from the walls of Obeid, no one was in any doubt about the deadly intent of this incursion. Local chiefs and sheikhs, for reasons variously ideological, political or simply opportunistic, declared themselves for the rebellion. Many influential figures in and around the city – tribal chiefs, politicians, merchants and religious dignitaries – had already struck up strong personal relationships with Muhammad Ahmad during his two visits to Kordofan the previous year. Those who did not support the Mahdi had two options: To make their way hastily inside the garrison fortifications or head east to the safety of Khartoum. But, as the teeming, ill-disciplined masses of the Mahdi's army stirred up the dust in plain view of Obeid, everyone who could leave town fled. The mob scene at Kába was witnessed by Fr Joseph Ohrwalder, an Austrian missionary who had been captured by Mahdist loyalists further south at Dillinj.[4]

As we approached the camp, at every step the crowd grew denser. El Obeid was now visible a short way off, and the sight

Obeid, main town in Kordofan, effectively a collection of huts with government buildings at the centre.
(Illustrated London News, *8 December 1883*)

of the houses and trees was a pleasant break in the monotony of this desolate wilderness. The continuous rattle of the bullets, interrupted by the thunder of the cannon, was an indication that a brisk engagement was going on. As we entered the camp, the crowd was so enormous that we were almost choked with the dust that was raised, and soon became thoroughly exhausted . . .

The fanatics now completely surrounded us, and kept on threatening us with their lances, clubs and sticks . . . The exertions of the last few days, the heat, the yelling of the crowd, the monotonous chants of the Dervishes, and finally the din of this enormous camp of over 100,000 men, exclusive of women and children, reacted on us to such an extent that we were well-nigh speechless.[5]

This vast gathering of soldiers and camp followers had been roused by the Mahdi's summons to jihad, a summons that was now sent to the defenders of Obeid, one last chance for those who may yet be convinced to change sides. The Mahdi went on the propaganda offensive; on 30 August, he sent two emissaries into the city, bearing a long letter. One copy was addressed to the provincial governor, Muhammad Sa'íd, the other to the people of the town.[6] The letter clearly staked Muhammad Ahmad's claim to superiority over the clerics of Obeid's orthodox hierarchy, the 'ulamá'; it also presented an explicit final choice: Join us or die.

To the community of 'ulamá', to the merchants and city officials, to the humble and the destitute of Obeid,

This letter is a sign that I have faith in your good qualities. When I say that the Prophet has told me in person that I am the Expected Mahdi, I have told you the unvarnished truth. I am no impostor or pretender.

So do not be deceived by those evil 'ulamá' and their sermons of hate and calumny. It is as the Prophet says: 'Love of money and prestige produced hypocrisy in the heart as surely as water makes plants grow.' Those 'ulamá' are highwaymen blocking the true path of my worshippers.

Leave behind your children and families! Come unarmed to meet us outside the city and join the Ansár. If you do, we pledge safe passage and guarantee the security of your families and property. If you do not, we will fight you, scatter your ranks, destroy your homes and make an example of you for surrendering to the unjust.

The Lord says: 'Incline not towards those who do wrong or the fire will seize you.'[7] Let this serve as ample warning. Peace.[8]

This ultimatum was spurned by the embattled garrison, as was the inviolable status of the envoys. Apparently enraged by the arrogance of the Mahdi's representatives and by their lack of fear at being in their enemy's camp, Muhammad Sa'íd had them both hanged.

☙ ☙ ☙

Inside Obeid, the arrival of the army of Ansár worsened a sense of already profound anxiety among the civilian population. The whole of central Kordofan was in ferment, stirred up by a Mahdist agent named 'Abdulláhi wad al-Núr, who had been inciting the tribes to attack government tax collectors, rip up their account registers and steal the money from the collectors' coffers.[9] All through the summer of 1882, garrison after garrison in towns such as Abú-Haráz, al-Birka and al-Tayára, as well as Dillinj in the hills to the south, had come under attack and been defeated by increasingly well-organised members of the Jawáma', the Habbanía, Bidiría and other tribes in staggering numbers. In June, Bara, an important town thirty miles to the north of Obeid on the main trade routes to Khartoum and al-Debba, was besieged by 'Abdulláhi wad al-Núr at the head of at least 50,000 fighters. The government defenders managed to score some early victories.

The Arabs attacked the fortifications of Bara from every direction on the morning of Saturday 7 Sha'bán [23 June] and opened fire . . . The soldiers replied with a defensive volley and discharged their guns, which were eight in number – four mountain guns and four rocket-guns. After a short fight lasting about an hour, the Arabs were compelled to retire and withdrew, leaving on the battlefield about 9,000 killed. The Shaigieh and Turkish went out in their rear to pursue them, killed a large number of them and seized many of their camels and all the provisions and animals they had left in their camp.[10]

For every such account, however, the refugees pouring into Obeid brought a dozen tales of the rebels' suicidal bravery in mounting headlong, screaming charges against better-armed defenders, as well as accounts of atrocities perpetrated by the Mahdists in victory, including the slaughter of women and children. These stories fuelled the fears of the people of Obeid. Particularly terrifying to the townspeople were the nomads of the Baggára tribes. Even in times of peace, they were feared and despised, regarded as dangerous hunters, slave-raiders and contemptible 'Arabs' by those who lived in towns or in settled Nile-side communities. Now, fired by greed for loot (and, occasionally, religious fervour) the tribesmen were the stuff of urban nightmares. So those townspeople who had not already joined the Mahdi or escaped east set to with a will when pressed into service by the garrison to help dig defensive trenches. The longest trench, known as a *geiger*, ran right around the town. As a precautionary measure, an inner trench encircled a cantonment of key garrison facilities, including the arsenal, the barrack-blocks housing men of the 1st and 2nd Battalions, the Governor's and Deputy Governor's houses, the prison, food-stores, three large wells and administrative buildings. Obeid's wells were very deep and the water had to be pulled up with windlasses; supply was poor in spring but the autumn rains would at that time have replenished the ground water.[11] A thick zaríba was hauled into place in front of each trench and an earth parapet built up behind it as additional deterrents. Government firearms were handed out to loyal civilians.

The outer entrenchment by the white house was guarded by the bashibuzuqs and the townsmen. They were armed with long rifles. The second entrenchment was guarded by the soldiers from al-Jíra, Sinheit and Kassala, armed with Remington rifles. The depth of the entrenchment was two feet; there was a zeriba outside the entrenchment and inside the zeriba a parapet, loopholed for rifles.[12]

The beginning of the battle for Obeid, after cautious weeks spent gathering men and *matériel*, nearly brought complete disaster to the Mahdi's forces. He had completely under-estimated the garrison's determination to resist, their preparedness and their firepower. And, for the first time, Muhammad Ahmad had come up against a competent Egyptian army officer, a true leader who could not be relied on to snatch defeat from the jaws of victory. The locals may have derided Muhammad Sa'íd as *Jiráb al-Fúl Pasha*, 'Bag of Beans', but he was a general with campaign experience who had served the occupying government with distinction in Kordofan.[13] In Muhammad Sa'íd, the Mahdi met a worthy adversary – and, very nearly, his match.

On Friday 8 September, after leading the dawn prayer, the Mahdi launched a full frontal assault on the government positions.[14] The huge assault force had strict instructions to penetrate the 'Turkish' defences from the east in successive waves. Many, however, simply disregarded their orders and attacked where they though the best looting might be had. They came under withering fire from rooftop positions, out of reach of their spears. And when one contingent of Mahdists, led by the Mahdi's own brother, Muhammad, succeeded in penetrating both trench and zaríba, Muhammad Sa'íd triggered a lethal trap, signalling by bugle for fresh forces to emerge from hiding to pour down more fire upon the invaders.[15] Inside the fortifications, a young resident named Yúsuf Mikhail watched the stubborn defence. It was a bloodbath.

The spear-heads, which were very close to one another, glittered and clinked like thunderbolts falling from the sky. Then they began to attack us, but we waited and endured patiently until they came near to us and then the four sides of the trench fired all at once.

126

Fire poured on them from cannons, rockets and Remingtons, while we, the whole lot of us, stood up shoulder to shoulder because at that hour master and slave behaved like brothers and the soldiers and the local people behaved like twins . . .

We killed hundreds and thousands of them, though they continued to fall upon us, fearless and dauntless. We answered them with bullets: 'Look, you Arab rogues, here are gallant warriors and men of destiny who offer you certain death' . . . The firearms, owing to constant firing, became so hot that they had to bring water . . . so we could wet our handkerchiefs and put them in our hands . . .

Fighting continued between the two parties and the raven of separation croaked . . . and one could see nothing but dead people heaped everywhere.[16]

This 'Friday Battle' was a devastating military reverse for the rebels after a year in which success had followed success. By the time the army bugles blew the ceasefire at sunset, casualties among the attackers were massive, as many as 10,000 men killed and wounded.[17] It was also a personal tragedy for the Mahdi. His two remaining brothers, Muhammad and 'Abdallah, as well as his nephew Ahmad, were mown down by the gunfire from the Obeid rooftops.[18] This came as particularly hard news as the Mahdi's only other brother, Hámid, had been killed in battle the previous May. The Friday Battle also cost the Mahdi's chief deputy, 'Abdulláhi al-Ta'íshi, a brother and, in a further setback to the organisation of this fledgling movement, the leading jurist and newly appointed Qádi al-Islam, Ahmad Jubára, was also shot dead.[19] There was nothing for it but to fall back on Kába and reassess strategy. The Mahdi issued a stern rebuke to his ill-disciplined force.

He then said that the Prophet had told him: 'If not, and if not, and if not – victory would have been attained.' The Mahdi explained this as meaning: 'If *not* for the disobedience of your companions and their not entering the city in an orderly manner from the eastern direction as you ordered them, *and if not* for their seizing the booty whilst entering the trench and their being preoccupied with it, *and if not* for their being flabbergasted by its abundance – *victory would have been attained* by them.'[20]

After sustaining such terrible losses, the rebellion would have been stopped in its tracks had the government pressed home its advantage. But Muhammad Sa'íd, who had lost just 288 men in the battle, was anxious about exposing his remaining troops, outside the protection of the walls, trenches and zaríba.[21] But news of the Mahdi's first serious reverse spread quickly through the countryside. At Bara, besieged for nearly a month, 'a salute was fired and the Arabs temporarily discontinued their attacks but kept their stations'.[22] In Khartoum, 'Abd-al-Qádir Hilmi was struggling to rebuild some kind of army that could relieve the pressure on Obeid and reverse the Mahdi's advances in the Jazíra and Blue Nile regions. A relieving force of two regular infantry battalions and 750 bashi-bazouk irregulars was despatched from the capital in September, under the leadership of Lieutenant-Colonel 'Ali Bey Lutfi, widely known by the undignified nickname, 'Abú-Koko' or 'Big Balls'.[23] The expedition suffered from acute water shortages because the Mahdi had ordered the desert wells to be filled in. Ambushed just eight hours from Bara, they were cut to pieces by a Mahdist force under the Jawáma' clan leaders al-Manna Ismail and Rahma Muhammad Manúfal. Leaderless, around 1,200 survivors of the original 2,500-strong force struggled on and into Bara, where they joined the besieged garrison. As well as offering the rebel generals the chance to assimilate survivors into their own ranks, such delays and failures on the part of the government gave the Mahdi time to develop at Obeid the tactic that would serve him well for the rest of the uprising: siegecraft.

These were protracted, bitter and often deadly months for the people and garrison of Obeid. Looking out from the town, they saw the feared Baggára and their tribal allies encamped in such numbers that Obeid, in Yúsuf Mikhail's words, 'looked like a white spot in the middle of a black cow'.[24] And, looking *up*, there was worse to see. In the middle of September, a comet suddenly appeared just before dawn and was visible for several nights. This *najma umm dhanab* – 'star with a tail' – was instantly understood by both sides as a harbinger of momentous change. It was a signal to assure believers and convince sceptics that the true Mahdi was among them and that the days of the 'Turks' were numbered.[25] Omens aside, the government garrison managed the early months of siege without too much difficulty and with adequate food. Muhammad Sa'íd organised armed sorties to seize cattle from surrounding villages and nomad camps; he also ordered his troops to empty the homes of those who had gone over to the Mahdi of grain and other provisions. But as winter passed, supplies dwindled and prices rose until few could afford the little remaining meat and grain.

> For the first two months provisions lasted, and then we had to eat camels, horses, dogs, cats, etc. A month before the town fell we were reduced to eating the fibre of palm tree, gum, skins, and even the leather of our 'angaribs' (native couch).
>
> We lost a number of men daily from the enemy's fire, but towards the end of the siege thirty or forty used to die of starvation at their posts. The men fought well, but we were all heartbroken from want of food. Besides, the men of the garrison of Bara, who had already surrendered, had joined the enemy, and used to call out to us from outside the fortifications that we had better surrender.[26]

Those taunts from the hated 'dervishes' and their new recruits outside the walls, enjoying an abundance of food, only rubbed in the grim predicament of the defenders. After the abortive 'Friday Battle', the Mahdi had sent for rifles from Jebel Gadír; now Ansár snipers picked off unwary defenders. Fr Ohrwalder, still a captive in the vicinity, related gruesome tales of the diarrhoea and death brought on the besieged by eating gum and animal dung. Each night, soldiers and civilians roamed their cantonment prison in desperation, ever searching for something, anything to eat.

129

And now the deaths by starvation had reached an appalling figure. The dead and dying filled the streets; the space within the fortifications being so limited, there was not room for all the people, and in consequence many lay about in the streets and open spaces. The air was poisoned by the numbers of dead bodies lying unburied, while the ditch was half full of mortifying corpses. Scurvy and dysentery were rife; the air was black with the scores of carrion-kites, which feasted on the dead bodies; these ugly birds became so distended by constant gorging that they could not even fly away, and were killed in numbers by the soldiers, who devoured them with avidity.[27]

The garrison's spirits were further depressed by the news of the surrender of Bara on 6 January 1883. The hunger among the defending garrison there was as acute as at Obeid because a Mahdist sympathiser had torched the straw huts containing grain and other provisions before fleeing. The Bara garrison resorted to eating horse, mules and even dogs.[28] Surrender negotiations had been conducted by al-Núr Muhammad 'Angara Bey, commanding officer of the town's bashi-bazouk contingent, who had drawn out the diplomatic procedures for as long as possible in the hope of last-minute relief from Khartoum. His counterpart for the Ansár had been 'Abd-al-Rahmán al-Nujúmi, a senior amír sent specially by the Khalífa 'Abdulláhi.[29] From further east, however, there was much better news for the government garrison. After the disastrous Friday Battle, the Mahdi had ordered two sheikhs, Ahmad al-Makáshfi and 'Abd-al-Básit al-Jamri to fan the embers of rebellion on the White Nile, partly to maintain pressure on surviving garrisons at Dueim, Fashoda and Kawa and partly to impede any relief forces that might be sent to Obeid. But two attacks on Dueim failed to penetrate government defences. Sheikh 'Abd-al-Básit's 400-strong force had been easily crushed by Carl Giegler on 11 November and the rebel sheikh was taken in chains to Khartoum and hanged.[30] In the Jazíra, where the jihad had first exploded, Governor-General 'Abd-al-Qádir Hilmi was scoring victory after victory against the Mahdists, culminating in the relief of Sennar and the destruction of a substantial Ansár force.[31] The rebels had indeed been badly 'cut up'.[32]

Back at Obeid, in utter despair, Muhammad Sa'íd now schemed to blow up the garrison arsenal, an explosion that would have destroyed much of the cantonment and killed almost all the remaining soldiers and civilians. Dissuaded by his senior officers, he finally accepted the Mahdi's final, mildly worded demand for surrender.

> You have been under the authority of the Turks, loyally exerting yourselves and your property for someone other than God . . . So what do you think of my calling you to God, improving your lot and bringing eternal profit and luxury to you ? As you are reasonable . . . it is better that you surrender to my command and prohibition – yourselves, your property and your families – without any charge or accusation but rather with love and friendship, as I am the one in charge of God's affairs concerning you and the successor of the Prophet.[33]

On 19 January 1883, sixty-seven days into the new Islamic century, Obeid fell into the hands of the rebels.[34] Of the 6,000 original defenders, Egyptians, Shiagi militiamen and southern slave-soldiers, some 3,500 had survived. Their remaining alive depended on an oath of fidelity to the Mahdi and compulsory enlistment into the swelling rebel army. The Mahdi had learned many valuable lessons from the struggle for the town. With the luxury of time, manpower and local support, he was able to mount a patient siege. Firepower was essential, he had realised, especially when it came to harrying the garrison defenders as they reinforced their trench-system and sniping at unwary sentries inside the town. No longer would guns be treated as despicable and alien tools. Retreat from this widely publicised point of principle was handled with discretion. In a formal memo to the Khalífa 'Abdulláhi, now effectively his field marshal, the Mahdi stressed the pure principles of carrying out the jihad according to 'God's far-reaching wisdom' before going on to note that, 'trickery being allowed in wars, we desire to make artful acts of deception' against the enemy. That meant arming a squad of 100 picked men with the best available rifles and plenty of ammunition and placing them under the command of a Syrian officer known only as 'al-Shámi', presumably a government soldier who had joined the Mahdists.[35] Most of the soldiers in these special battalions of riflemen were captured southern conscripts or slaves who formed the nucleus of a new force, the Mahdi's own black 'holy warriors', the Jihadía. The surrender of the Obeid garrison provided them with no fewer than 6,000 rifles. Under the leadership of Hamdán Abú-Anja, a half-breed Ta'íshi from the west, those weapons would be put to devastating effect.[36] The Mahdi's new Egyptian artillery commander, Yúsuf Mansúr, captured and forcibly converted to the cause, like the other garrison survivors, brought with him not only his professional expertise and another colleague, Sikander Bey, but another five cannon.

Obeid's most senior commanders did not survive the surrender for long. Governor Muhammad Sa'íd Pasha, his deputy 'Ali Sharíf, the prominent merchant Ahmad Dafa'allah and Muhammad Yassín (the last man to have held the Ottoman position of Sheikh al-Masháyikh, 'Sheikh of all Sheikhs') were among the civic and military leaders who secured safe conduct out of the town.[37] At first, the Ansár treated them relatively gently. Along with every other surviving citizen and soldier, they were searched for valuables, 'standing in the sun . . . hungry and thirsty, as if for Judgement Day', as Obeid was stripped bare.[38] The Ansár and their Baggára allies plundered the town and the loot piled up in fantastic quantities, coins of gold and silver, jewellery. An estimated 7,000 pounds sterling in pure gold was found concealed in the house of the Governor alone, despite his declaration that he had no money.[39] Trying to conceal their treasures from the Ansár was enough to ensure that the senior officials, who had surrendered on the understanding that they would be well treated, would be divided up and ruthlessly executed – although an attempt to smuggle a letter through to Khartoum was also discovered. Factional jealousies also raised their heads. Ilyás Umm

Bireir was eager to take revenge against his former rivals for influence in Obeid. Thus Governor Muhammad Sa'íd was handed over to Sheikh Ismail of the Ghudayát at Alloba and beheaded.[40] Sheikh Madibbu 'Ali at Shakka in Darfur took care of Muhammad Yassín and Ahmad Dafa'allah.[41] As for 'Ali Sharíf, he fell into the hands of the Mahdi's supporters at Birka, as an eye-witness later recalled.

> Muhammad wad Bellal was the executioner, and he struck him on the neck with a sword. But his head was not severed, so they threw him into a well, and all the people crowding round the mouth of the well watched his death struggles in the water. The wife and young sons of the prisoner were also present, and these were later brought up by the Mahdi.[42]

And, half a world away in London, even readers of The Times would learn of the Khartoum government's discomfiture.

> The town of El Obeid, with its garrison, was unconditionally surrendered to the Mahdi on the 17th [sic] inst. Dissension is, however, stated to exist among the False Prophet's followers, and many are expected to join the [Khartoum government] troops when they advance.[43]

Such optimism was groundless. The Ansár now had an operational base from which they could strike west into Darfur, south into Bahr al-Ghazál and north-east towards the capital itself. The Mahdi was master of all Kordofan and the mopping up proceeded apace.

# ELEVEN

# 'The Rapacious Grasp of Foreigners'
## Egypt, 1882–1883

Every official and soldier in Sudan administration, from the Governor-General to the lowliest bazinger, must have asked himself during this time when help would come from Cairo. A single-minded and financially solvent government in Cairo should have been able to quell the Mahdist rebellion. Egypt had a massive standing army and the routes south, via the Nile and the Red Sea, were tried and tested. But Egypt in 1881–2 was a nation embroiled in a profound crisis, a crisis that would end in revolution and foreign occupation. Put simply, British involvement in Sudan would not have happened without British involvement in Egypt. Popular discontent in Egypt was widespread, the army was on the verge of wholesale mutiny and the government coffers were bare. Small wonder, then, that increasingly urgent telegrams from the Saráya in Khartoum received ever more distracted and non-committal replies from the Khedive's office. Cairo had far greater and more immediate crises to wrestle with than the suppression of an insurrection by a motley gathering of disaffected tribes in Sudan. The disastrous timing of the Mahdi's uprising was compounded by the fact that Sudan, where expenditure consistently continued to exceed revenue, had helped drive Egypt into its financial crisis. The occupation had been launched on the assumption that Sudan would yield riches but, by 1882, most provinces consistently lost money. That year, revenue amounted to a little over half a million Egyptian pounds, while expenditure ran to well over 600,000 pounds.[1] Such losses only added to the debts run up by the Khedive Ismail as he tried to Europeanise his country. Egypt, wrote one contemporary British analyst, patronisingly yet perhaps accurately, 'suffers from the ignorance, dishonesty, waste, and extravagance of the East, such as have brought her Suzerain (The Turkish Empire) to the verge of ruin, and at the same time from the vast expense caused by the hasty and inconsiderate endeavours to adopt the civilisation of the West'.[2]

For the Egyptians, subject on an individual basis to delayed or non-existent salaries, their country was humiliatingly in hock to foreigners. Secret associations, some with revolutionary leanings, began to meet. Foreign interference, coupled with Egypt's own autocratic khedivial regime, helped bring political parties into being. Among them was *Hizb al-Watani*, the National Party, which declared its opposition to Ismail's government, denouncing it as a puppet controlled by outsiders, and began to campaign on a platform of liberation from foreign oppression.

> Must Egypt be nothing but a geographical expression? Must her five million inhabitants be as cattle over which are imposed drovers at will? What they ask is to be treated as their brothers in Europe would wish to be treated if placed in the same position as Egyptians are placed . . . Egypt wishes to liberate herself from her debts on condition that the powers leave her free to apply urgent reforms. The country must be administered by Egyptian personalities . . . She does not always want ministers representing this or the other European influence.[3]

Khedive Tawfíq, young and experienced, found himself as constrained as his father Ismail had been by the French and British representatives on the Council of Ministers.[4] The priority of the 'great powers' was, as before, the satisfaction of the creditors; the ministers' method was to dictate the debtor's financial and political decisions. It was, after all, business – but because business decisions took no account of political, social or military factors, outside interference prompted internal upheaval. By an extraordinary coincidence of timing, Egypt was forced to neglect revolution abroad because of revolution at home.

Financial straits inevitably resulted in cuts and by 1881 the Egyptian army had been subjected to the most painful measures. Salaries were slashed, thousands were dismissed and native Egyptian officers found their promotion prospects curtailed. Officers from elsewhere in the Ottoman Empire had always found preferment over Egyptians in the khevidial army, although Ismail at least had allowed them to hold ranks up to the level of colonel, a rank previously permitted only to Turks or Circassians. There was even systematic discrimination against officers who spoke Arabic.[5] When the army finally snapped and turned on the Khedive Tawfíq, they found their spokesman in Ahmad 'Arábi, a forty-year-old colonel in the 4th Regiment whose career had been retarded by his own nationality.[6] He had some limited experience of Sudan, having served as a commissariat officer during 1875–7 in what was then the Sudanese provincial capital at the Red Sea port of Massawa. 'Arábi himself belonged to a secret nationalist society, 'Powerful Egypt', established by a fellow officer in Alexandria.[7] In early 1881, he presented a petition to Tawfíq, demanding redress of the army's grievances. The young Khedive, caught between the demands of the foreign powers and his own army, gave way to each, as and when the power-balance shifted; on this occasion, he buckled in the face of army pressure.[8] 'Arábi's status as a popular nationalist hero was growing, for revolutionary thinking extended far beyond the officer corps. Cairo intellectuals, leading merchants, village chiefs, editors of new opposition newspapers such as *Egypt*, *The Commerce* and *The Patriot*, all were delighted to have a focus for their resentment at the ruling elite – as a British official in Cairo observed.

His ['Arábi's] point was to show that up to the present the Egyptians have had no security of life or property. They were imprisoned, exiled, strangled, thrown into the Nile, starved, robbed, according to the will of their masters . . . The most ignorant Turk was preferred and honoured before the best of the

Egyptians . . . Tewfik, while heir-apparent, had been loudest in complaints of his father; but since he had come to power, he had tried to get power into his own hands and to exercise it in the old Turkish way.[9]

'Arábi's nationalist credentials were boosted when, on 8 January 1882, Britain and France presented a 'Joint Note' formally pledging their support to the Khedive as the legitimate ruler of Egypt.[10] That merely confirmed the popular impression of Tawfíq as the creature of the foreign powers; 'Arábi, abandoning any pretence at loyalty, was established as a powerful counter-force. The nationalist slogan 'Egypt for the Egyptians' began to echo across the country and, by February 1882, 'Arábi was Minister for War in a new cabinet.[11] 'The authority of the Khedive is annulled, and the chamber of Notables is under the pressure of the military party,' noted the *Levant Herald*. 'Amid all this excitement, it is satisfactory to learn that order is not disturbed, and that the security of Europeans is nowhere menaced.'[12]

It was as War Minister that 'Arábi first became privy to the extent and details of the military disaster unfolding in Sudan. He received the news of the Shalláli massacre two weeks after the event. In his reply to Khartoum, 'Arábi said that, 'owing to the troubled condition of Egypt', 'Abd-al-Qádir Hilmi would have to settle for a shipment of arms and ammunition, not reinforcements.[13] Locked in a power-struggle with both the Khedive and foreign officials, 'Arábi was able to give Sudan even less attention than his predecessors. Indeed, he made the situation worse by ordering Khartoum not to recognise the authority of the Khedive. In the face of the growing threat of the Mahdi, this demoralised government officials and made them ask in whose name they were risking their lives.[14]

As the spring of 1882 passed, public discontent in Egypt itself worsened; the country moved closer to open civil war. As tension rose, 'Arábi began to receive explicit statements of support from Sultan Abdülhamit II in Constantinople. Correspondence from senior officials in the imperial capital to 'Arábi in early 1882 revealed deep dissatisfaction with Tawfíq's unreliable nature and profound anxiety over 'the seditious projects of foreigners'. But, amid the declarations of trust and admiration for 'Arábi, there was one important caveat. Above all, the officials in Constantinople wrote, do not give those foreigners an excuse to intervene with force.

> It is incumbent on every Egyptian to strive earnestly after the consolidation of [the Sultan's] power to prevent Egypt from passing out of [his] hands into the rapacious grasp of foreigners. . . . That country – Egypt – is of the highest importance to England and France, and most of all to England; and certain seditious intriguers in Constantinople, following in the path of these Governments, have for some time past been busy with their treacherous and accursed projects . . . According to the telegrams and news sent by the Khedive Tewfik, one of this party, we see that he is weak and capricious . . . The man who thinks of the future of Egypt and consolidates the ties which bind him to the Caliphate . . . who is versed in the intrigues and machinations of our European enemies, who will watch against them, and ever preserve his country and his faith intact – a man who does this will be pleasing, agreeable to, and accepted by our great lord, the Sultan.[15]

That spring and summer, therefore, came a succession of firmans from the Sultan's palace ennobling the Sultan's own appointed replacement viceroy. On 14 March, Colonel 'Arábi, lauded in the proclamation as 'one of the princes of our imperial army in Egypt, as a man of reputation and dignity', was promoted to Brigadier-General and awarded the honorific Pasha.[16] And on 24 June, as a reward for 'honesty, zeal, talent and perfect intelligence', the Order of the Medjidieh, 1st Class, followed.[17] Such honours improved 'Arábi's standing still further in relation to the Khedive but it would prove much harder to prevent the 'European enemies' marching in.

In Britain, both politicians and public were taking an active interest in Egypt. The Prime Minister, William Gladstone, was pleased enough to see 'real movement towards institutions & local self-government' but he did not think that 'Arábi had much to do with either. 'I am wholly at a loss to view Arabi's recent conduct as having any relation to them,' he wrote to a friend. 'He seems to me to represent at this time military violence and nothing else. I may of course be in error but it is not for want of taking impartial pains to inform myself by hearing all sides.'[18] As spring passed into the summer that marked the beginning of the end of Ottoman rule in Egypt, editors on newspapers like the *Illustrated London News* became instant experts on the 'Crisis in Egypt'. Between 13 March and 14 October, not an edition was published that was not filled with news, comment and analysis.

> The state of affairs in Egypt . . . has assumed a very alarming aspect. Arabi Pasha, the leader of the military party . . . though compelled on Saturday afternoon to resign the office of Minister of War, did so under protest, declaring that the Khedive was acting under the control of France and England, and without regard to the Sovereignty of the Sultan, which Arabi Pasha now affects to uphold. . . . Five British ships of war, under sealed orders, have left Suda Bay, the headquarters of the Mediterranean fleet, for Alexandria.[19]

As disorder worsened in the provinces, the coastal port city of Alexandria became the focus for uncontrolled nationalist agitation, often blurred with calls for the expulsion of the foreigners in the name of Islam. On 11 June 1882, fifty foreigners were killed in the city in riots. The British Vice-Consul in the city reported to London: 'Governor promises public security, but is, I think, quite powerless to maintain order'.[20] Foreigners began to flood out of Egypt in their thousands; Cairo's central station was a scene of total confusion. 'The trains . . . taxed to their utmost capacity, were running day and night,' wrote an American in the city, 'carrying their human freight packed like sardines in a box'.[21]

Manifestly something had to be done, for the whole framework of society in Egypt was on the point of collapsing. By June 17, 14,000 Christians had left the country, and some 6,000 more were anxiously awaiting the arrival of ships to take them away.[22]

Even with the security of the Suez Canal at stake, Gladstone was reluctant to stage a military intervention without international support. But this was still the era of gunboat diplomacy and the governments in London and Paris – supported by American, Austrian, Russian and Italian warships – promptly moved naval squadrons across the Mediterranean to stand off Alexandria. Despite 'panic . . . among the natives, many of whom are leaving the town for the interior', 'Arábi loyalists held their ground.[23] Their morale boosted by propaganda leaflets describing unspecified triumphs over the foreigners, they refused to remove their new fortifications on the seaward side of the city, particularly the new artillery batteries pointing out to sea. The slogan 'God grant you victory, 'Arábi' was taken up on the streets of Alexandria and Cairo with renewed fervour.[24] A letter signed by all Alexandria's leading citizens neatly sums up the strength of feeling in the city, referring back specifically to January's notorious Anglo-French 'Joint Note'.

We verily believe that the presence of the fleet off our city can be for no other purpose than to carry out the Note . . . In the demands set forth in this Note, an attempt is made to strike at the rights of the people and their country, to annul the firmans of the [Sultan], and openly and plainly to intervene in affairs of purely internal administration . . . We have heard that His Highness the Khedive has accepted the note in question without finding fault with a word of it . . . We of Alexandria reject the Note of the Powers, and he who accepts it must absolutely and for ever sever his cause from ours. We refuse to separate ourselves from the Porte, to attach ourselves to any foreign power, even should we die for it, for better is it to die for the life of the country than to live while the country is dying.[25]

On 12 July, the Royal Navy began an intense naval bombardment, reducing several parts of Alexandria to rubble and ruin. As the nationalists fled, the British landed their first troops on Egyptian soil, men of the Black Watch and Indian cavalry. The destiny of not just Egypt but also Sudan was suddenly to change. Tawfíq, always weak, now bereft of his army and wholly powerless, threw in his lot with the British. Sacking 'Arábi as Minister of War was irrelevant when the bulk of the army was already firmly behind the rebellion. Continuing khedivial authority depended absolutely on the British troops who not only guarded Tawfíq at the Rás al-Tín Palace outside Alexandria but who now sought actively to destroy the 'Arábi uprising. As for the Sultan in Constantinople, his plans were about to come completely unstuck. Abdülhamit II had hoped to use 'Arábi to undermine the authority of the Khedive and restore Egypt to direct Ottoman rule. He anticipated, mistakenly, that the European powers would be so alarmed by the instability caused by the 'Arábi uprising that they would ask Constantinople to restore order. He did not predict that the British would move in – and stay.

On 13 August, General Sir Garnet Wolseley arrived at the head of a substantial expeditionary force.[26] His thirty-day campaign was efficiency itself, staffed by 'Wolseley's Ring', a group of trusted senior officers who had been by his side for several years.[27] Stealing overland by night from Ismailia on the canal, on 13 September his force surprised and destroyed 'Arábi's army in a single encounter on a prominent hill, Tel al-Kabír, near the railway line and sweet water canal linking Cairo and Suez. 'Arábi and his senior officers fled, while his soldiers capitulated almost immediately.[28] It was a sorry showing for an army that claimed to enforce a popular revolution. So, while Queen Victoria congratulated General Wolseley on a 'glorious and well-deserved success', some British officers felt ashamed of the fuss made over the easy victory against 'skulking cowards'.[29] 'It was magnified to make political capital for Mr. Gladstone and cover his former failures – honors [sic] and decorations in bushels conferred to keep men silent,' wrote one British Colonel. 'Wolseley's speech about it being "the first time since the Crimea that the British Forces have met a *disciplined* Army in the field" was enough to make one sick.'[30]

Brigadier 'Arábi salvaged some measure of personal dignity from this ignominious defeat. He was tried under Article 96 of the Imperial Ottoman Military Code, which forbade armed revolt, and Article 59 of the Ottoman Penal Code, which forbade the assumption of 'the command of a division, a fortified place, or city, &c.'. Both offences carried the death penalty. On Sunday 3 December, the state court pronounced a guilty verdict and a sentence of death against Ahmad 'Arábi but it was promptly commuted by executive order of the Khedive, no doubt under pressure from both London and Constantinople. The Sultan had lost forever the chance to replace Tawfíq with a loyal Egyptian; he had no desire to lose the man himself. Nor did the British, now effectively running Egypt, want a martyr around whom nationalist rebellion might rally. 'Arábi was put on board the steamer *Mareotis* and sent, with six of his closest companions, into exile in Ceylon.

🕯 🕯 🕯

Despite the coincidence of timing and despite the frequent use of Islamic slogans to rouse popular sentiment, Ahmad 'Arábi's revolution was not like the Mahdi's. There was popular, military and religious resentment at the overbearing Ottoman presence in all the machinery of state, but 'Arábi never sought to change the relationship between Egypt and the Sultan in Constantinople, let alone overthrow the Sultan. The nationalists determined to defend the rights of Egyptians and to overturn the rule of a corrupt Ottoman viceroy over what was essentially a huge but private estate. But they explicitly and sincerely acknowledged Sultan Abdülhamit II as their spiritual and temporal master and they accepted his right to demand both legal tribute and military assistance in case the Ottoman Empire found itself at war. Unlike Muhammad Ahmad, too, 'Arábi had the 'ulamá' of the Islamic establishment on his side. Their reasons were less theological than pragmatic, grounded to a great extent in the same resentments at Ottoman favouritism, even in the schools of Islamic law, that had prompted army officers and urban intellectuals to revolt.[31] Al-Azhar, too, had suffered swingeing cuts; enrolment of new students fell by the thousand every year between 1876 and 1880.[32] In harmony with Colonel 'Arábi's army mutiny, the 'ulamá' staged rallies and demonstrations against Khedive Tawfíq and, in the summer of 1882, reached a formal legal opinion that, for pandering to Christians at the expense of his fellow-Muslims, the Khedive was an apostate. It was, the 'ulamá' said, time to declare jihad against the foreigners. The formal question that led to the fatwa was put to the 'ulamá' in the name of 'the Egyptian Nation'.[33]

> What say you of a Sovereign who, being named by the Prince of the Faithful to govern his subjects with justice, and to act according to the rules of God, has violated the compact and sown dissension among the Moslems, and has broken their staff of unity? This so-called sovereign has even gone so far as to prefer the government of the Infidels to that of the Faithful . . . He has been the cause of making his subjects bend before the force of the stranger, and has even gone so far as to use every effort to defend that force.[34]

The fatwa came back swiftly, signed by the eight most senior scholars at al-Azhar. Short and sharp, the ruling was buttressed by no fewer than ten relevant quotations from the Qorán.

> In this case he shall be cast out, and in his place shall be named one who will watch over the law and defend it, and respect the rights of the Prince of the Faithful, our Lord the Caliph . . . The Most High has said:
> 'O ye who believe! Take not the Jews and the Christians for your friends and protectors; they are but friends and protectors to each other. He among you that turns to them is one of them.'. . .[35]
> And: 'Tell the deceitful that they shall have a terrible punishment, those who take for friends unbelievers rather than the faithful. Do they seek honour among them? All honour belongs to God alone.'[36]

While the Egyptian and Sudanese revolutions appeared to be connected by a common hostility to foreign domination, the position of the 'ulamá' was not the only difference between 'Arábi and the Mahdi. From a Mahdist perspective, the fact that 'Arábi's mutiny tied up so much of Egypt's military resources was undoubtedly useful but the Ansár would have suspected 'Arábi's secular motives. To the Mahdi, who sought to establish a new religious supremacy far beyond Sudan, 'Arábi would eventually have got in the way. For his part, Ahmad 'Arábi sent out conflicting messages. On the one hand, he did own at least one Mahdist legal book.[37] The book, found in his campaign tent after his defeat at Tel al-Kabír, expounds 'the Mahdist view on how the Muslim community should behave towards non-Muslims, especially those invading their territory, and the justification for that outlook according to the Sharí'a'.[38] On the other hand, he told his defence lawyer that he rejected the call of the Mahdi, a man who would, he said, 'sweep Tewfik and Arabi alike into the sea' – a conclusion with which his lawyer concurred.

> Any attempt to attribute a community of ideas to Arabi and the Mehdi must arise either from a wilful intention to mislead or a profound ignorance of the subject. I remember talking over the matter with Arabi at the time. He said that the disbandment of the army laid all Egypt at the mercy of the Mehdi, except so far as she could rely for protection on the British troops. 'The Mehdi of the Soudan,' said Arabi, 'is the enemy of the Arabs because we know him to be an impostor. . . . The Egyptians must all resist the Mehdi as a dangerous foe, but the disorder which reigns throughout the country will give even this African dervish a chance of success.'[39]

☙ ☙ ☙

Some elements in Gladstone's government assumed that Britain could enter Egypt in force, replace the Khedive on his shaky throne and leave again. There appears to have been no secret plan to stay.

But the Khedive now had no popular support, a bankrupt treasury and no army. After Tel al-Kabír, the mutineers were paraded for the last time and disbanded in disgrace. To Alexander Broadley, the British lawyer who conducted Brigadier 'Arábi's defence, the treatment meted out to the beaten nationalist troops smacked of an 'inordinate thirst for vengeance' and a 'suicidal policy of retaliation'. 'It was not deemed sufficient to exile and degrade Arabi,' he wrote. 'The shame and disgrace of the chief, it was said, must be shared by every subordinate officer, and even by every common soldier who followed the standard he had raised.'[40] Little did those responsible for this policy suspect how soon they would need to re-recruit the men they had just humiliated and sent packing. More than three months after Tel al-Kabír, the British Foreign Secretary, Lord Granville, was no closer to identifying a departure date.

> Although for the present a British force remains in Egypt for the preservation of public tranquillity, Her Majesty's Government are desirous of withdrawing it as soon as the state of the country and the organisation of proper means for the maintenance of the Khedive's authority will admit of it.[41]

So, *faute de mieux* and pending a long-term political decision, British soldiers and administrators moved in to new premises in Cairo. Major-General Sir Evelyn Wood was brought in to reconstruct an Egyptian army as its Commander-in-Chief, or Sirdar.[42] His civilian counterpart as Consul-General was Evelyn Baring (later Earl of Cromer). In addition came Lord Dufferin, the British Ambassador to Constantinople who had been redeployed by the Foreign Office to recommend ways of reorganising the Egyptian civil service.[43] Baring had already been working in Egypt since 1877, first as British commissioner of the *Caisse de la dette*, the Egyptian public debt office investigating the bankrupt administration of Ismail Pasha, then as Controller-General under Khedive Tawfíq.[44] Both Baring and Wolseley were adamant that the civil and military reforms with which they had been entrusted would be impossible without a strong British presence. In his diaries, Gladstone continued to reflect on 'how to plant solidly western & beneficent institutions in the soil of a Mohamedan community?'[45]

It was at this point that the Sudan crisis became apparent to the British. The problem they now faced – that getting out of Egypt was so much harder than getting in – was compounded by Khedive Tawfíq's refusal to abandon his rebellious satellite state to the south. For Tawfíq, a solution to the Sudan crisis might mean a boost to his domestic credibility. Cairo's new masters, however, firmly refused to be drawn in. Gladstone himself was unequivocal.

It is no part of the duty incumbent upon us to restore order in the Soudan. It is politically connected with Egypt in consequence of its very recent conquest; but it has not been included within the sphere of our operations, and we are by no means disposed to admit without qualification that it is within the sphere of our responsibility.[46]

That refusal meant that British or Indian troops would not be sent to help 'Abd-al-Qádir Hilmi in Khartoum, despite his increasingly desperate appeals. Just five days after Tel al-Kabír, completely unaware of the rout and dissolution of the Egyptian army, the Governor-General was still begging for four battalions of reinforcements, supported by 2,000 Turkish cavalry, 10,000 Remington rifles and artillery.[47] A further telegram arrived on the Khedive's desk on 24 October. Instead of sending help, the British representatives in Cairo began to consider 'Abd-al-Qádir's immediate replacement. Sir Edward Malet, the British Consul-General, met the new Minister of War, 'Umar Lutfi, to discuss candidates and the names of two previous incumbents at the Saráya, Ismail Ayúb and Charles Gordon, came up.[48] Neither, however, could be persuaded to return to Khartoum. Indeed, Sir Evelyn Wood subsequently wrote that Ayúb, 'the Turkish [sic] Pasha who had been serving in Khartoum', flatly refused, making unpleasant observations about 'Englishmen putting Turks in posts of danger'.[49] By early November, it was decided to promote instead the Governor of Sudan's eastern coastal region, ʿAlá-al-Dín Siddíq, a Circassian major-general in the Egyptian army.[50] The firman confirming this appointment followed on 20 January 1883.[51]

In addition, a trusted officer, Lieutenant-Colonel Donald Stewart of the 11th Hussars, was sent on an urgent and secret fact-finding tour of Sudan. Neither the Egyptians nor their representatives in Khartoum were forewarned of the mission. Stewart's brief was simple: Dig up as much background information as you can, as quickly as you can, and come up with specific recommendations for a revised strategy. Accompanied by Giacomo Messedaglia, an Italian soldier, administrator and draughtsman who had served as Governor of Darfur and who contributed finely drawn maps to the report, Colonel Stewart set off immediately, arriving in Khartoum on 16 December.[52] The same day, a telegram from Cairo arrived at the Residence: a message from Tawfíq ordering ʿAbd-al-Qádir to keep the British investigators under discreet surveillance.[53]

# TWELVE

# *A New Order*
# *Obeid, 1883*

Even as the British were consolidating their grip on Egypt, the Mahdi was deliberating his next moves in widening the jihad. The capture of Obeid was but the first step on a long journey and he made it clear to his followers that, once the government in Khartoum had been overthrown, his ambitions would reach far beyond Sudan. The Prophet Muhammad, he told them, had ordered him to kill three cows to celebrate the victory in Kordofan and spelled out in uncompromising terms the road ahead.

> The Prophet then appeared to me in another vision and said: 'As you have prayed in the mosque of Obeid, so you will also pray at Khartoum, then you will pray in the mosque at Berber, then in Mecca, then in the mosque at Medina, then in the mosque at Cairo, then in the mosque at Jerusalem, then in the mosque of Iraq and finally at the mosque of al-Kúfa [near Baghdad].' May God grant that we do indeed pray in all these mosques and finally die as martyrs at the hands of the infidels. Amen.[1]

This was a staggering list. For Muhammad Ahmad to pray in all these mosques – as imam of each community, he would have assumed – would mean the overthrow of the entire Ottoman Empire and the establishment of a new order across the entire Islamic world as he knew it. The inclusion of the mosques at both

Baghdad and Kúfa suggested that he also planned to reunite the Sunni and Shí'a traditions under his banner.[2] It was incredibly ambitious. The Mahdi's fame had certainly spread beyond the borders of Sudan and even Egypt; he had sent his own emissaries to the north and east. Yet his knowledge of events or political currents in the territories beyond Sudan was negligible; the aspiration to spread his message was a leap of faith. Indeed, that faith was apparently rewarded when delegations began to arrive at Obeid, not just from the great Muslim cities of North Africa such as Tunis and Fez but from as far afield as the Hejaz in the Arabian Peninsula and even India.[3] These pilgrims made the arduous trek to hear the teachings of the man who had scored such extraordinary, even miraculous, successes against the forces of foreign rule. Many in the wider Islamic world shared the sentiments of the Egyptians, that European Christians were exercising an unwelcome degree of influence and control in Arabia, the Levant and Raj India.

> In Syria, Egypt, the Hedjaz, at Konieh, at Constantinople, and even in India itself, ardent prayers are addressed to heaven for the success of the African Mahdi.[4] If the heads of Government, if the princes and learned doctors of Islam, who are the slaves of authority, are hostile to the Mahdi, if the Sultan of Morocco excommunicates him, if the Sheik of the Senoussi, who himself claims the title of Mahdi, denounces his rival as a false prophet and impostor, if the Sultan Abdul Hamid in his quality of Caliph, hurls anathemas against him from his throne, yet the solid masses of the Mussulman people bless the Mahdi and give him all their sympathy.[5]

Such earnest good wishes and prayers were all very well but they did not translate into material support within Sudan itself. Not a single Indian, Syrian or Konya Sufi came to Obeid to fight for the Mahdi's cause. There were, however, promising early signs that the 'solid masses' in other countries might successfully import the Mahdist agenda, religious or political, to their own homes. The strongest indications of dissent emerged in Syria and the Hejaz, both Ottoman provinces, and in French-controlled Algeria. The population on the west of the Arabian peninsula was 'highly inflammable' and there was reported to be 'anxiety in high official quarters' in Constantinople that 'the Mahdi may find means to bring about a disturbance on the eastern shore of the Red Sea, and reports have reached the Porte that his emissaries have already appeared in the Hedjaz'.[6] By way of reinforcement for the Turkish garrisons, four cavalry squadrons were rushed south on the troop-transport *Babel*. As for Syria, a Damascene merchant trading in Darfur, 'Abdallah al-Kahhál, was given propaganda letters by the Mahdi, summoning the Syrians to rise against their rulers. Carrying the letters as his guarantee of safe conduct, the Syrian made his way home from Obeid by a long and circuitous route. First he travelled west, through Ansár-controlled territory, through Darfur and into Wadai, a small independent Islamic sultanate in what is now eastern Chad. He then turned north to the Mediterranean at Benghazi.[7] The result, when he reached Syria itself, was 'a dangerous agitation'. 'At Damascus,' reported an American officer in Egypt at the time, 'notices have been placarded all over the city calling the population to revolt against the Turks'.[8] In North Africa, meanwhile, the French Ministry of War was reconsidering its planned redeployment of troops in Algeria to other colonial duties in the Far East because 'Mahomedan fanaticism is reviving in consequence of the Mahdi's success'. According to French press reports, 'marabouts and emissaries from the Mahdi were already reported to have reached Tunis and to be on their way to South Oran'.[9] The Great Powers were beginning to hear – and fear – the name of the Sudanese Madhi.

The Mahdi still hoped to use Sheikh Muhammad al-Sanúsi as his proxy in the pursuit of the jihad against Egypt. He had still received no reply to his repeated offer that the leader of the Sufi sect in Libya be his third Khalífa. So he wrote again, urging Sheikh al-Sanúsi to support the uprising, either by joining the hijra to Kordofan or by launching his own jihad from the north.

Let me remind you that God, through our hands, has conquered many territories and many people who had previously been under the government of the Turks. If this letter reaches you, join in the jihad against Egypt and in the surrounding area, if they do not convert to true Islam or come to join us. But your migration to join us would be better still.[10]

Like the Syrian trader, the messenger carrying the letter to the Sanúsi leader at Jaghbúb took a long and circuitous western route, avoiding either Egypt itself or the heavily patrolled Red Sea. So Muhammad Ahmad took the opportunity to direct letters to the leaders along that western route, in the hopes of spreading the call into the further reaches of Africa's Muslim community. In his second letter to Muhammad Yúsuf of Wadai – the territory immediately to the west of Darfur – the Mahdi explicitly avoided the title Sultan (a title that, by his reckoning, none but God may claim), but compensated by addressing him as 'the venerable and exalted'.[11] The Sultan had replied to an earlier letter from Muhammad Ahmad, enclosing 500 rials as a contribution to the cause. So, as an addendum, the Mahdi also wrote that such gifts were all very well but were no substitute for making the hijra to Obeid.[12] Further west still, Muhammad Ahmad had already targeted the disaffected great grandson of the great eighteenth-century revivalist Usman Dan Fodio, Hayatu ibn Sa'íd, who had fallen out with the reigning Sultan of Sokoto – a substantial territory in what is now northern Nigeria.[13] Theirs was an intense correspondence, bearing all the hallmarks of an exchange between a loving master and a dedicated follower. Hayatu Sa'íd promised unequivocal support.

We warmly welcomed your kind letter. . . . We have been given water after suffering from thirst and given life after wretchedness and death. We have a guide after being led astray. You, my lord, have come with the truth of God's word: 'The froth disappears like the scum on boiling ore; that which benefits man remains on the earth.'[14]

I, my father and all our relations swore the ba'ya to you even before you appeared as the Mahdi. . . . Usman dan Fodio urged us to migrate to join you, to support you and accompany you, as soon as you should appear. We are with you from the core of our beings, to help you achieve victory for God's true religion and the Sunna of Muhammad. . . . I am following directly behind this message.[15]

ψ ψ ψ

Securely established at his temporary capital, the Mahdi also turned his attention to the consolidation of his new administration. The state he had begun to create was fundamentalist and anachronistic, in which the revival of a pure historical Muslim community was to be brought about by rigid, indeed puritanical, conventions. It has been argued that the Mahdi's political, social and economic programmes were 'the weakest of his intellectual links'.[16] But a series of decrees beginning at this time indicate that the Mahdi intended to implement a clearly defined and radical overhaul of the key structures of state.

In the new order, the Mahdi was supreme, the apex of the hierarchy, the interpreter of God's holy word and the Prophet's instructions. Befitting his status, the ranks of his wives and concubines had swollen during the months of campaigning and victory. Among the harem were Umm al-Hassan, the daughter of the late Ahmad Dafa'allah, Aisha bint Muhammad Umm Bireir, from the other most influential Ja'ali family in Obeid, as well as the women captured from the camps of the Mahdi's defeated enemies Yúsuf al-Shalláli and Muhammad Bey al-Shaigi.[17] As each wife and concubine had her own premises, usually a straw hut with its own fenced hosh, Muhammad Ahmad presided over a substantial family community. His eldest children were now teenagers and some of his daughters were already married. His status was reinforced by praise singers, poets who helped the propaganda effort by eulogising Muhammad Ahmad and his cause in elegant verse. The poets used both religious and revolutionary imagery and, as the Mahdi had banned the use of the traditional tambourines and cymbals, had to resort to the power and melody of their own voices.[18]

> Al-Mahdi, the one whose speech is pleasing
> No sooner had he come to us that our difficulties vanished. . . .
> The Rátib of late afternoon is a must;
> By it, you gain palaces and mansions. . . .
> Al-Mahdi, possessor of glory,
> The one on whom our hopes are founded,
> Go, my friend, to him as soon as you may
> And be saved from these conditions. . . .
> You are the eye of life itself
> For people everywhere.
> Seeing you, O decent one,
> Is enough to wipe the burden of our sins away.[19]

Below the Mahdi in the new hierarchy came the three khulafá', then the increasing number of umará' with battlefield experience. Always at Muhammad Ahmad's right hand was his trusted lieutenant, 'Abdulláhi al-Ta'íshi. Just ten days after the surrender of the Obeid garrison, the Ansár were put on notice that 'Abdulláhi's authority was absolute, by direct mandate from the Prophet via his Mahdi.

> Know, my beloved, that the Khalífa 'Abdulláhi is . . . endowed with the adornments of truthfulness and trustworthiness. He is the amír of the Mahdi's armies, referred to in prophetic visions. As such, he is part of me and I am part of him . . . So serve him the way you serve me, surrender yourselves to him as you do to me; believe what he says and do not suspect his actions. Everything he does he does at the order of the Prophet or with my permission – neither by his own choice nor haphazardly . . . As God says:
>
> 'It is not fitting for a believer, man or woman, when a matter has been decided by Allah and his messenger, to have any

opinion about their decision. If anyone disobeys Allah and his messenger, he is indeed on a manifestly wrong path.'[20]

If anyone harbours doubt in his heart . . . it is because of a lack of faith; he has departed from the true faith because of his inattention . . . All the Khalífa 'Abdulláhi's decisions are correct because he has been given the wisdom and authority to finalise matters – even if his decision is a matter of your life and death or the seizure of your property.[21]

In addition to this stark clarification of 'Abdulláhi al-Ta'íshi's authority, Muhammad Ahmad appointed as the new Qádi al-Islam (replacing Ahmad wad Jubára, who had died breaching the zaríba at Obeid) Ahmad 'Ali, a distinguished Islamic jurist who had served as a government district judge at Shakka in Darfur until he deserted to the Mahdist cause.[22] Muhammad Ahmad resolved that it was time to cast aside the orthodox legal system founded on the four accepted schools of Sunni Islam, symptomatic of the division of the unified faith, and replace it with a purer version of the Sharí'a. His decision to ignore the legal literature of the four madháhib, evolved by the finest minds over twelve centuries, as well as the opinions of the 'ulamá' who interpreted it, resulted in an unsophisticated but flexible mixture of the Sharí'a and traditional tribal law – with the Mahdi himself as the sole arbitrator.[23] The abrogation of the orthodox schools of law meant that any books that taught them had to be burned, along with any other religious or academic tracts (except the Qorán and the Hadíth).[24] The various Sufi sects, too, were deemed to be potentially divisive and were abolished. They had outlived their usefulness and the influx from the Western province had made them less important. When baffled members of the Tijánía brotherhood wrote to the Mahdi to ask if their taríqa had really been banned, they received a terse reply from the Khalífa 'Abdulláhi. 'What you have been told is correct,' he wrote on behalf of his master; 'it is the true position and must be followed. So adopt it and end your adherence to that sect. . . . It has been promised that the Mahdi would remove all schools of law and purify the earth from disagreement, so that only pure religion remains.'[25]

Muhammad Ahmad also realised that the disciplinary problems that had nearly brought disaster in the attack on Obeid now needed to be addressed with severity. The problem lay with unruly elements among the Baggára nomad tribes, who had seen in the Mahdist campaign welcome opportunities for self-enrichment. In addition to shirking their responsibilities in the actual fighting because of their keenness to get their hands on the loot, they were now seizing other men's wives and making off with them as well as the material spoils of war. The Mahdi charged 'Abdulláhi to put a stop to the wife snatching, which he blamed generally on 'the disobedience of the Ansár' and specifically on 'the nerve of the nomad tribes in neglecting my orders'. He set the tariff of punishment for wilful neglect of his orders at one month's imprisonment and forty lashes every day, 'as a penalty to the sinner and as a warning to others'.[26] As for those Baggára and other tribesmen who were now returning to their homes without a second thought for the next stage in the jihad, the Mahdi issued a stern injunction against looting. A strongly worded manshúr from early February 1883 made it clear that all captured goods, weaponry, livestock and cash must immediately become communal property, held at the Beit al-Mál.

I notice that your ardour for fighting the battles of the Lord is abating. You have escaped with a burden of booty, which is the fire lit by the Lord – the fire of poverty as well as scorpions and snakes. By doing so, you have exchanged blessings for calamities and if you are not careful, God will overwhelm you with hardships and sufferings – directly or through me. You will be swallowed up by his terrible thunders. . . . He, moreover, granted you the possession of things that were far beyond your reach. You have preferred this life to the eternal one and you, with all your power, endeavour to get the booty and thus satisfy your ambition and love of worldly things, which are not worth an insect's wing in the eyes of God.

Those of you who believe that I am al-Mahdi al-Muntazar should remit all that they have or can procure of this dangerous booty – money, slaves, horses, weapons, etc. – and if you repent and deliver up all the booty you have I will pardon you. But if you refuse to do so, the anger of God and his Prophet will fall on you. I should also add, my friends, that this is your last chance. You cannot resist the troops of God who *do* obey my orders.[27]

Oversight of the Beit al-Mál was entrusted to one of the Mahdi's loyal companions, Ahmad Suleimán al-Mahasi, another member of the diaspora of northern tribes who was described in the announcement of his appointment as 'most able, honest and upright'.[28] Opposition to the new commissioner's decisions, cautioned the Mahdi, would be severely punished.[29] Cementing the political alliance, the Mahdi took Ahmad Suleimán's daughter Safía to be his wife.[30] The extraordinary wealth discovered in Obeid after the surrender, gold, silver and jewellery, all fell into Ahmad Suleimán's care. At one point, an eye-witness marvelled, the treasury commissioner had in his charge 'several sacksful of chains of gold which filled the room'.[31] Apart from the spoils of conflict, a new system of taxation would be needed for the Beit al-Mál to run smoothly. Citizens in the territories now controlled by the Ansár were now expected to contribute zakát, technically a voluntary charitable donation but effectively a compulsory tax of 10 per cent. While Ahmad Suleimán oversaw the administration of the Beit al-Mál and the dispensation of grants to those in the community who had no source of income or subsistence – those, for example, who had travelled far from their own homes and farms – the actual collection of the zakát fell to the Khalífa 'Abdulláhi and his tribal followers, who could be depended upon to bring their considerable zeal and expertise to the business.[32] Zakát became one of the points on which the Mahdi felt he had to educate followers who were less than thoroughly grounded in the core principles of Islam. In a brief letter to Sheikh 'Asákir wad Abú-Kalám of the Jimi' Baggára near the White Nile, he informed the recipient that he was sending one Sheikh Ahmad al-Hajj al-

Badri to supervise the construction of a new mosque and to educate the Jimi' in 'all matters of Sharí'a', including the duties of zakát and of saying proper prayers.[33]

Turning next to the merchants of Obeid *súq*, the Mahdi decided that the market men needed instruction on the basics of honest trade in the proper Muslim manner. His message echoed his earlier indication that financial fraud, one of the crimes for which there had been no 'statute of limitations' set at Jebel Gadír to impede the prosecution of the corrupt, was among the most grievous of sins.

> Know, my beloved ones, that the world with all its flourish and luxury does not weigh, in God's scales, the wing of a mosquito . . . God has shown you the course of what is right so that you may abide by it and weigh everything justly in your business. . . . God warned you against lying, cunning, cheating, breach of trust and breaking pledges, especially lying under oath, for he says: 'Woe to the falsehood mongers.'[34] This means: May liars be cursed. What a serious warning for everyone with a sound heart! . . . Accordingly, this is a call to all those who receive this proclamation and who understand it not to lie on oath, nor cheat anyone, nor be cunning or fraudulent, not to break a pledge in order to gain the debris of this enchanting world. He should not fix his scales or deliberately measure incorrectly so as to give less . . . Do not breach this order of ours lest the fury of Allah and that of his Prophet befall you![35]

The tariff of punishments prescribed at Jebel Gadír was carried out strictly – as were new regulations governing social behaviour. Thieves had their right hands cut off for a first offence, their left foot for a second. To be caught drinking *marísa*, the local home-brewed alcohol, was to invite a merciless whipping. Married, widowed, or divorced women caught having sex were executed 'by burying them to their necks in the earth, when they were either stoned or horsemen galloped over them until they were dead'.[36] One Obeid proclamation set out at considerable length the civic and social responsibilities, behavioural norms and religious practices enjoined by the Mahdi, in an unusually concise series of commandments. The new proclamation amounted to a Mahdist manifesto for the state that was to replace the occupation of the hated 'Turks'. 'I have led you to nothing but that which serves your salvation,' Muhammad Ahmad writes; 'but you must obey my orders and write proclamations like this one to all the villages near you, spreading my commands and prohibitions'.

You must build a mosque in every village and perform your prayers as a community. You must recite from my prayer book, the Rátib . . .

Stop making, selling and drinking alcohol in the markets; spill it away and break the jars! Purify your homes and your mosque. Roll up your sleeves and work to entrench the traditions of the Prophet; avoid religious innovations and stray not from the true path . . .

Do not show tolerance when God's due prayers are ignored. Restrain your followers from temptation and intrigue, from theft and fraud. Order your women, sons, daughters and slaves to perform the five mandatory prayers every day and beat them if they fail. Do not be moved by compassion . . .

You must refrain from fornication, taking snuff or smoking tobacco. Punish the guilty! Keep up congregational prayers; they are the very pillar of religion.

Pay zakát on everything as decreed by God, in full honesty in his sight. Beware of faithlessness and treachery in failing to pay zakát or in concealing booty.

Follow the Lord's verse: 'Prophet! Tell thy wives and daughters and all women who believe that they should cast their outer garments over their persons when abroad.'[37]

Refrain from wailing for the dead and refuse to allow funeral processions to the graveyard . . .

Make dowries easy – 10 rials for a virgin and five for a divorcee or widow. Ban your wives and daughters from going out into the grazing pastures where they may meet men.

Do not have children out of wedlock! . . .

Be like a building, well made of brick, in which each wall holds the others together – or like two hands, each washing the other clean.[38]

Many of these new regulations were probably highly unpopular. But the Mahdi was in no mood to compromise. This was the blueprint of a new society – and he had the unquestioning loyalty of his khulafáʾ and their men to enforce the new law.

# THIRTEEN

## *Hicks Pasha*
## *Cairo, Khartoum and the*
## *White Nile, 1883*

All Kordofan was now in the Mahdi's hands. In the Jazíra and White Nile regions, the rebellion had been controlled but not quenched. Now, in response to the desperate calls from the Khartoum Saráya, the Egyptian government set about reconstructing a relief force for Sudan – despite the refusal of the British, who otherwise dictated policy in Cairo, to offer more than minimal assistance. British officials made it quite clear to Tawfíq that London was still not interested in contributing to any adventure beyond the frontiers of Egypt itself. Sir Evelyn Wood's priority, with a budget of £200,000, was building a new, modern army for Egypt itself from scratch, as Muhammad 'Ali Pasha had done sixty years before, from similarly dismal resources.[1] Most of the British in Cairo, too, were convinced that defending more than the central territories of Sudan was a lost cause. In early 1883, a senior official wrote that it would be 'wise of the Egyptian Government to abandon Darfour and perhaps part of Kordofan, and be content with maintaining her jurisdiction in the Provinces of Khartoum and Senaar'.[2] The Khedive, then, had little choice but to interrupt the process of disbanding Ahmad 'Arábi's disgraced soldiers and, instead, collect them as hastily as was convenient. He was further impeded by the British determination to sell off Egypt's surplus weapons and military stores.[3] More than 2,000 men were press-ganged into the army barracks north of Cairo near the 'barrage' on the Nile.[4] Desertions were frequent. For the men who had fought under Ahmad 'Arábi, defeat and humiliation was to be compounded by a long, uncomfortable journey into exile: from Cairo by train to Suez, then down the Red Sea to Suakin, followed by the arduous desert trek to Berber and finally up-river to the capital. For most of the conscripts, the only reward for this unpleasant experience would be long marches, food shortages, acute thirst and violent death. Even their departure from the capital, at Cairo's Buláq dockside, was a memorably dismal experience.

The Egyptian soldiers were placed in vans and cattle-trucks like animals. They quitted the capital without arms, as prisoners, and with all the circumstances of dishonour. Their native officers were selected from those who were most obnoxious to the new regime, and their very appointment was an avowed and undisguised measure of punishment and repression. . . . When subsequently it became necessary to send further reinforcements to the Soudan, they were provided after the same fashion. Soldiers were again despatched to the front unarmed, beaten, and in chains. Even [the] black regiment, once considered the flower of the Egyptian army, were sent to fight against the Mehdi with every aggravation of ignominy, and thereby predisposed to desertion and mutiny. It is not surprising that Colonel Hicks was unable to hold his own with the aid of such unpromising material.[5]

Colonel William Hicks was the officer selected by the Egyptian government to lead this motley array and to say that he was 'unable to hold his own' was an understatement. At fifty-three, Hicks was a tall, handsome man with stern features and a jutting grey beard. He had retired from the Indian Army after seeing active service during the 1857–9 Mutiny and the 1867–8 Abyssinia campaign, during both of which he was decorated and mentioned in despatches.[6] Like so many foreigners with few alternative

prospects but prepared for a challenge, he had found his way to
Egypt. Of his actual selection for khedivial duty in Sudan, one
British officer recalled that Hicks' name was literally pulled out of
a hat at Shepheard's Hotel in Cairo by General Valentine Baker,
Commandant of Police.[7] Baker himself was probably the most
competent and experienced British officer in Cairo but, because he
had been cashiered for indecently assaulting a young woman in an
English train in 1875, other British officers were barred from
serving under his command.[8] The government in London was swift
to make it clear that the fact that Hicks was British in no way
implied British endorsement of the campaign that he was to lead.
The Foreign Secretary, Lord Granville, wrote that 'HM
Government [was] in no way responsible for the operations in the
Soudan, which have been undertaken under the authority of the
Egyptian government, or for the appointment or actions of
General Hicks'.[9] Despite such protestations, Hicks' appointment
was vetted by Lord Dufferin in Cairo, who found the General 'a
grave, sober-minded man . . . the choice was excellent'.[10]

For Hicks himself, the attractions of the appointment –
elevation by the Khedive to the rank of Major-General and the
possibility of campaign glory – were offset by the risks.[11] With no
experience of Sudan, he was expected to lead an army of defeated,
demoralised and mutinous troops in extremely inhospitable terrain
against fiercely committed and well-armed rebels on their own
territory. He spent his time in Cairo consulting anyone familiar
with the dramatic developments in Sudan. Like most outside
Khartoum itself, Cairo-based British journalists had ignored or
underestimated the impact of the Mahdi's rebellion over the
preceding eighteen months. Now, with the 'Crisis in Egypt' safely
over, London editors began to fill their readers in on some of the
background to the 'Crisis in the Soudan'. Their accounts were
often highly coloured and riddled with propagandist distortions
and factual errors.

The Mahdi is described as one Mohamed Ahmed, a Dongolian.
He is illiterate, but has studied religion, has been ordained a

sheikh, and has gained a reputation for sanctity by playing the hermit. He has increased his influence by marrying numerous wives among the wealthy families, keeping within the prescribed number of four by a resort, when necessary, to divorce.

Like most prophets, he was denounced by his own townsmen, who proclaimed him mad. In appearance he is tall and slim, and he wears a black beard. He reads and writes with difficulty, is head of a local order of Dervishes, and has shown much tact in uniting the discordant tribes. The number of tribesmen following him Colonel Stewart estimates at about 338,000 souls.[12]

Hicks was a fundamentally decent and honest man but too weak and indecisive to seize control of a problem as manifold and ingrained as the uprising in Sudan. A soldier of the old school who remained alternatively bewildered and outraged by inefficiency and disobedience, he was subject to often wild mood swings. In his letters to his wife, Sophia, he endlessly lamented the incompetence of his officers and shabby quality of his men but never lost altogether his hope that some good might come of it all. At times he fantasised about a knighthood, 'some wonderful decoration' and even '£10,000 backsheish from the Khedive for having settled the Soudan'.[13] Before his departure from Cairo, he felt self-doubt and foreboding. After meetings with a succession of Cairo VIPs, including the Khedive Tawfíq, Sir Evelyn Wood, Sir Edward Malet and Lord Dufferin, Hicks confessed to Sophia that 'at present I can't help feeling anxious as to my ability to conduct all this . . . it is rather formidable'. But the very next day, flush with optimism, 'some men are born great, others achieve greatness, some have it thrust upon them. I am to be of the last!!'[14] Hicks clearly listened to advice from his superiors in Cairo, especially Baker, and assessed the political aspects of his mission with pragmatism.

There is no element of success or even safety unless a *high* Sheik or Priest of the Mahomedan religion, a *holy* man, descendant of the Prophet, is sent up *with me* to preach against the Mahdi, to issue proclamations that the English are the protectors and friends of the Mahomedans, by going *with* me to show the alliance between us and Mahomedanism . . .

If I could only buy the Mahdi's head I would. In the cause of humanity it would be justifiable, for hundreds and *thousands* are losing life through him and the rebellion. I anticipate a world of anxiety there for it is a web of intrigue I am going into.[15]

When the planning of the Hicks mission began, it was determined that it would be an aggressively offensive campaign to secure the central region around both Blue and White Niles, relieve the besieged garrisons of Obeid and Bara in Kordofan and eradicate the rebels as a military threat.[16] These ambitious targets were set in Cairo, without regard to the expressed opinions of 'Abd-al-Qádir Hilmi in Khartoum, who was still convinced of the merits of a cautious, defensive deployment. The Governor-General supported the reassertion of government control over the provinces east of the White Nile, but took a dim view of a Kordofan campaign. Unlike Hicks or the armchair warriors in the Khedive's Abdín Palace, 'Abd-al-Qádir Pasha had already suffered the destruction of one expeditionary force (even though he bore no personal responsibility for the Shalláli disaster). His refusal to support the Hicks campaign no doubt made the Egyptian government all the more determined to see him replaced as Governor-General. His successor, 'Alá-al-Dín Siddíq, was formally notified that on the strength of his experience in running the vital ports of Massawa and Suakin along the Red Sea coast he had been promoted to oversee Sudan's entire civil administration. Military duties would be taken on by another Circassian veteran of Ottoman rule in Egypt's dominions, Major-General Suleimán Niyázi, who also had campaign experience in the eastern Sudan.[17] General Niyázi's priority was to assemble forces on the White Nile to avert a Mahdist push into the Jazíra and Blue Nile territories from Kordofan.

A specific decision was made in Cairo not to notify 'Abd-al-Qádir Hilmi until 'Alá-al-Dín reached Khartoum from Suakin on 21 February, 'his firman in his pocket'.[18] By that time, however,

'Abd-al-Qádir was again out campaigning successfully against the Mahdists in the Sennar region, while Carl Giegler, reappointed Deputy Governor-General, was again occupying the Saráya in an acting capacity. The resulting confusion and political intrigue in Khartoum – two Governors-General, one deputy and two Commanders-in-Chief – hampered decision-making for nearly six weeks. It was not resolved until 'Alá-al-Dín was formally proclaimed Hikimdár in a big ceremony at the Saráya on 26 March. 'There is no doubt,' Hicks noted in a letter the same evening, 'Khartoum is full of disaffected men and the Government hated'.[19] The professional relationship between the elderly Niyázi and Hicks soured immediately. Hicks spoke neither Turkish nor Arabic; neither 'Alá-al-Dín nor Niyázi spoke English. So at the most basic level, contact between General Hicks and his senior colleagues depended on the service of a Welsh civilian interpreter, Edward Evans, who had interpreted for Ahmad 'Arábi at his trial.[20]

Lieutenant-Colonel Stewart, meanwhile, was as convinced as 'Abd-al-Qádir Hilmi that the Kordofan campaign was an extremely poor strategic decision. He and Hicks met face-to-face in Khartoum between the General's arrival on 4 March and the Colonel's departure four days later but Stewart's trenchant advice appears to have gone unheeded.[21] In his final report, the investigating officer recommended in brisk, no-nonsense language not strategic redeployment but total withdrawal from western and southern Sudan.

I am firmly convinced that the Egyptians are quite unfit in every way to undertake such a trust as the government of so vast a country with a view to its welfare, and that both for their own sake and that of the people they try to rule, it would be advisable to abandon large portions of it. The fact of their general incompetence to rule is so generally acknowledged that it is unnecessary to discuss the question. . . . I am not altogether sure if it would not in the end be better for all parties if the Mahdi or some other leader were successful, and the Egyptians compelled to restrict their territory to the east bank of the White Nile. . . . I have been asked to select a strategical frontier to the west, but it is quite impossible to do so, as the country is a barren open plain, almost devoid of features.[22]

Hicks and his senior colleagues remained determined to press on with a Kordofan campaign, despite such explicit advice and despite their lamentable resources. The capacity of the Mahdists thus far to wreak havoc on Egyptian forces that were greatly superior in numbers and weaponry was brutally illustrated in mid-March by new government estimates of battlefield losses since August 1881. The figures were simply staggering. The number of dead, missing or captured, including the garrison at Obeid, was put at 16,296 men. In terms of matériel, the rebels had gained 17,669 rifles, sixteen artillery pieces and nearly five million rounds of ammunition.[23] On the government side, there were no apparent grounds for optimism. An official British report described the state of affairs at the main camp at Omdurman, where as many as five battalions of new conscripts from Egypt (who did not even have military uniforms) were undergoing rudimentary training.

The troops were working at elementary drill and tactics, and making some progress, but the Officers were, as a rule, ignorant, and incapable of grasping the meaning of the simplest movement, unwilling to assume any responsibility, and totally devoid of initiative. Many of the troops had superstitious ideas regarding the power of the Mahdi, and other thought that the Khedive had only sent them to Sudan to get rid of them.

They were dressed in long white cotton shorts and native cotton trowsers [sic]. Most of them wore coarse leather sandals. Each man had a grey overcoat and hood. The Infantry were all armed with Remington rifles. The tactics of the Egyptians in the presence of the enemy were to form battalion or double company squares. The troops were formed in three ranks to give them confidence. Each man was provided with four or five crow's feet (iron spikes with four points), which he was instructed to throw in front of him on the approach of the enemy.[24]

Relationships between all the senior officers degenerated into petty squabbling, relentless backbiting and mutual recriminations. Hicks was outraged that, though his own salary was double that of his most senior British officers, some of them were making as much as £700 extra by writing reports for British newspapers.[25] Carl Giegler drew some sharp pen-portraits in his memoirs: 'Alá-al-Dín Pasha is described as 'a good, pleasant and amiable gentleman but of rather limited intelligence'. Suleimán Niyázi was 'an old wreck . . . an appropriate commander to lead the kind of troops who had been sent from Egypt'. The Deputy Governor-General, however, liked Hicks and saw quickly that he regretted taking on this most difficult task, though he was perplexed that the General wasted so much time and emotional energy on incomprehensible trifles.[26] Again and again, Hicks confided to Sophia his anxieties about his European staff officers ('as helpless as babies') and Egyptian NCOs and men.[27] Attempts to impress the Pashas of Khartoum with displays of fire-power went badly wrong when the Nordenfeldt gun-teams botched the manoeuvre, spilling ammunition on the ground and jamming the machine-guns. In comparison to his beloved Indian army, the troops were dismissed as a useless shower.

> I reduced a Capt. to the rank of Lieut. the other day but it seemed to have no effect for I caught him neglecting his duty next day. The Egyptian is the most hopeless man to make a soldier out of: he has no patriotism, no loyalty, no courage; there is no discipline amongst them, and neither officer or man has any feeling of honor [sic]. It is simply heartbreaking to try to do anything with them – there is nothing to work upon. I cannot tell you how disgusted I am with everything in this place. I am surrounded by intrigue, deception, and liars. The situation is too disgusting. I cannot believe a single thing I hear and I cannot get anything done I order, procrastination is the rule – and there is *no shame* in anyone. One party is intriguing for Abd al-Qadir and the other for Ala al-Din and they tell me tales and lies of one another; they hide information from me to bring the opposite party into disfavour, and they won't work

together. It is too distracting and my English officers are no help to me – they want judgement and many of them increase my difficulties . . .

Here I have 4,000 of Wolseley's *enemies* under my command. He got great kudos for breaking them – my great anxiety is lest they should run away when I take them before the rebels . . . I am instructing them daily and this morning I rode amongst them and made several men aim at my eye and pull the trigger so that I could see if they raised the muzzle of their rifles. Who would have thought a short time ago when they were behind the trenches at Tel el-Kabir that an English officer would be asking them to pull a trigger at his eye at two feet distance – and they wouldn't slip a cartridge in.[28]

Despite these many frustrations, Hicks managed to assemble an expeditionary force for a short preliminary campaign on the east bank of the White Nile. Their target was a substantial force of several thousand Ansár, led by Músa wad Helu, a Baggára of the Digheim tribe and brother of the Mahdi's second Khalífa, and 'Umar al-Makáshfi, an important faqí whose brother Ahmad had been killed by Salih al-Mak, the talented Shaigi officer, at Sennar the previous summer. The rebels, sent by the Mahdi to take Dueim, were massing at Jebelein, more than a hundred of them armed with breech-loading Remingtons, the spoils of victory at Obeid. The Egyptian contingent of 3,200 infantry was supported by 300 Albanian cavalrymen, the only men that Hicks appeared to trust. For additional fire-power they had a battery apiece of Nordenfeldts and small brass 2.5-inch calibre cannon, known to Indian frontier veterans like Hicks as 'mountain guns'; both were mounted on mule-drawn field carriages.[29] Departing from Khartoum on 4 April, Hicks made rendezvous with another 1,600 troops under Brigadier Hussein Mazhar at Kawa, close to Jazíra Aba. In a technique deliberately copied from the Mahdi, the general prefaced his advance by having a proclamation translated into Arabic and carried by spies into the rebel camp.

I, Major General Hicks Pasha, give notice to all persons that I, an English officer, have come by order of the Khedive to the Soudan with a large Army. I have come to put down rebellion, which assuredly I will do; and to punish evil doers; but I have also come on behalf of the Khedive to redress wrongs and oppression, and give justice to all. . . . It is only against rebels in arms that I make war; peaceable people will be protected. . . . It is the custom of the English to be just and generous and all may be sure of forgiveness and of getting justice if they return to obedience and communicate with me.[30]

Despite continuing grumbles about inefficiency, the heat and inadequate funds to settle six months of arrears still owed to the Kawa contingent, General Hicks planned his offensive meticulously from his base on board the small veteran paddle steamer *El Fasher*.[31] He divided his forces effectively into land and river contingents and steered them forward with caution and coordination. He anticipated correctly the line of a probable rebel retreat, which took them directly into the line of artillery fire, and he cut off another possible escape route by burning the rebels' rafts. An ideal position was selected in which to await the inevitable full-frontal Ansár rush and, perhaps even more importantly, the senior officers cooperated closely. On 29 April, this careful planning was rewarded with complete success, a fine birthday present for the commanding officer. Attacked by some 4,000 Ansár at al-Marábi, between Kawa and Jebelein, the Egyptians held their positions and destroyed the oncoming Mahdists with disciplined fire. '"Vive la guerre" they say,' commented the General; 'but it is sickening to kill so many in such a one-sided affair, for we only lost 7, and 5 the day before, when they lost shoals'.[32] Colonel Colborne, a British officer seconded to Hicks' Soudan Field Force, vividly described the massacre that followed.

Breaking from cover, the enemy sweeps with an inward curve right and left, his extreme flanks converging towards the opposing angles of our square. Now file-firing commences from the front directly assailed, the men having been cautioned to aim low. Nearer they swept, horse and foot closing on either flank, but as they came within our zone of fire, they butted forward, hit to death. The Nordenfeldts have now got to work, and within a few minutes the leading mob . . . fell in piles. But fanaticism knows no check. The chosen chiefs of the Mahdi were there, followed by their own chosen henchmen. They staggered to the front, to break into a furious gallop straight for our death-dealing square, while in their rear swiftly sped the faithful spearman.

Onward they came, waving their banners inscribed with the Mahdi's own rendering of the Koran . . . Right up to the cannon's mouth, right up to the rifle muzzle, dauntless they rode, encouraging their followers with the promise of paradise, to break our square. But Nordenfeldts and Remingtons are no respecters of creeds or fanatical idiosyncrasies. Sheikh after sheikh went down with his banner, although the Mahdi had assured each he was invulnerable, and their faithful but misguided followers fell in circles around the chiefs they blindly followed.[33]

Hicks' fragile confidence surged. His command techniques had been vindicated and his men had been shown that fire-power could prevail if discipline were maintained. The surviving rebels, utterly demoralised, had cast aside their banners, jibbas and turbans, a sign, Hicks was convinced, 'that the False Mahdi's declarations were so many lies'.[34] The victory at Jebelein prompted the general staff to begin planning seriously for a Kordofan campaign in the autumn.

# FOURTEEN

# *'The Sunset of Their Lives'*
# *Kordofan, 1883*

As a result of his brisk victory on the White Nile, General Hicks acquired a new nickname among Sudanese on both sides: 'Strong-arm'.[1] But the problem of his rivalry with General Suleimán Niyázi was not resolved until late summer. Again and again, Hicks threatened peevishly to resign if he was not given explicit superiority. In July, to his horror, Hicks discovered that one of the general staff in Cairo had leaked all his confidential telegrams complaining about Niyázi to the *Egyptian Gazette*. But at last, in August, a week after he telegraphed his formal resignation to the Minister of War, Hicks received the news he had awaited for so long. General Niyázi was to be sent off to the Red Sea district and he, Hicks, was in sole military command. 'All today,' he wrote on 4 August, 'I have been feeling like Judas Iscariot . . . Hundreds of people came to say goodbye to him and he embraced me at the river side. I felt like the school boy who had told tales of his school fellows.'[2]

Hicks himself was quite clear about his strategy for the Kordofan campaign. The straightest and most pragmatic route was a direct run from the White Nile to retake Bara, then on to challenge the full force of the Ansár at Obeid. Stewart himself had estimated the distance from Khartoum to the Kordofan capital as a mere '12 caravan marches, 5 post marches', although the Hicks 'caravan' was so vast that more than 12 days would have to be budgeted.[3] Frank Power said the force carried food for three months, as 'we can only march

171

seven miles a day'.[4] Every precaution would be taken at the nightly campsites. As well as the obligatory zaríba of thorns there would be 'wires stretched to trip the natives, and the whole ground strewn with crows' feet (caltrops) – eight iron spikes in a cluster – to tickle the bare feet of the Kordofani.'[5] Along the route, Hicks would leave as much as 30 per cent of his enormous force in detachments of at least one company in small fortified posts between ten and thirty miles apart. In this way he could keep open a secure line of communication, down which messages could pass, as well as ammunition, dried meat, biscuit and of course water, carried in large wheeled metal water-tanks.[6]

This route passed through the territory of three important clans, who now found themselves pinned between two enormous armies, neither of which was willing to grant them neutral status. Government contacts with these tribes had been sporadic and inconclusive but Hicks now hoped to woo Sheikh 'Asákir wad Abú-Kalám of the Jimi' and Sheikh al-Manna Ismail of the Jawama'a with letters promising pardon and full government support against the Mahdi. The British general also needed to confirm the loyalty of Fadlallah wad Sálim, Názir of the Kabábish, who had held a government concession in the territory to the west of Omdurman since the 1870s.[7] In June, Sheikh 'Asákir had welcomed messengers from Khartoum, pledging to submit to the government and receive the formal pardon of the Khedive. And, to the government's delight, it had emerged that there was another significant element further south ready to turn against the Mahdi. Chief Adam of Tagali in the Nuba Mountains, who had been so ambivalent about hosting the Ansár during the hijra, had finally decided to cast his lot with the authorities, as Colonel Hicks described in a letter home.

> King Adam . . . had received letters from the Mahdi telling him that he was sending his baggage, treasure (plundered at Obeid), wives, and children to Gebel Tegella; asking King Adam to take charge of them; and to join with the Mahdi and fall upon Asakir. King Adam went on to write [to] Asakir to come to

Tegella . . . with a view of uniting their forces and falling upon and plundering the Mahdi's family and baggage and making war on the Mahdi himself. . . . This is very good news and I am expecting something sensational when I meet Asakir or his son. There is no doubt about the enmity of the King of Tegella . . . of Asakir and his tribe, and of Manna's tribe, to the Mahdi. . . . If these Chiefs unite I believe they *will* crumple up the Mahdi and his Dervishes in a very short time.[8]

According to a letter from the garrison commander at Dueim, Sá'íd Pasha, on 13 June, King Adam had indeed ambushed the Mahdi's family and baggage, incurring Muhammad Ahmad's lasting hostility.[9] Sa'íd's spies had told him further that Muhammad Ahmad was recalling his emissaries from every direction to Obeid, in order to hold a council on the Tagali question.

His optimism renewed by the apparent cooperation of the Jimi', the Jawama'a and the Tagali chieftain, Hicks began moving his force down from Omdurman to his advance base at Dueim on the White Nile. Had the army been competently led, it should have been formidable: 8,300 regular infantry, 1,100 bashi-bazouks, 100 further cavalry, 800 Shaigía irregulars, 16 artillery pieces and 6 five-barrelled Nordenfeldt machine-guns. To carry the baggage, Hicks had some 5,000 camels at his disposal and a vast number of camp followers. Along to observe was a new arrival, Frank Power, a 25-year-old cub reporter for *The Times* of London, who had travelled to Sudan with the veteran *Daily News* correspondent, Edmund O'Donovan. Joining them in the travelling press corps was Frank Vizetelly, correspondent and artist for the *Illustrated London News*.[10] At the last minute, another civilian from Khartoum was added to the complement of Hick's general staff: Walter Glass Chiene, a young Superintendent Engineer at the Khartoum Arsenal.[11] For the journalists, this should have been an unbeatable front-line assignment with front pages guaranteed; but, despite his unexpectedly comfortable quarters in the Saráya, Power was ambivalent about joining the Hicks expedition into the interior. 'The Mahdi, the "False Prophet", is in possession of the country ten miles from this city,' he had written to his family in Ireland, 'and in about two weeks . . . we march on a campaign that even the most sanguine look forward to with the greatest gloom'.[12]

The preliminary march to Dueim, through a featureless and drab terrain, justified that pessimism. It was a fiasco, reducing the expeditionary force to total exhaustion. Under a searing sun and with temperatures rising to 127°F (50°C), the troops achieved fewer than ten miles a day, pitifully short of Stewart's estimate. It took twelve days to cover the 110 miles south, the soldiers tramping across a seemingly endless dusty plain where the landscape stretched bleakly to the horizon, only alleviated by the occasional tree or patch of prickly bushes. Frank Power was prostrate with dysentery, only able to complete the journey by being lashed on to a gun carriage, 'which eight horses drew over rocks, stones, trunks of trees, &c., so it was no easy mode of travelling'.[13] One piece of impedimenta too many, he was promptly sent back down-river to the capital from Dueim. More serious for Hicks was the loss of camels. By the time he arrived at Dueim on 14 September, 157 beasts had died, most due to plain neglect. The thousands of beasts marshalled in Omdurman had been fed on grain rather than their natural diet of forage. 'Abbás Bey, Secretary to the Governor-General, related in his campaign diary a telling incident that illustrated the rivalry between Egyptian officers and their inability to show the least bit of initiative. After a full twenty-three hours in Dueim, Hicks discovered that the camels had still not been fed and watered since the twelve-day trek from Omdurman. The senior Egyptian officers responsible, Brigadier Hussein Mazhar and Rajab Bey Siddiq, blamed each other and showed little interest in resolving the problem.[14]

At Dueim, Hicks was joined by the Governor-General, 'Alá-al-Dín Siddíq, who had brought with him by steamer several Khartoum dignitaries. These men, certainly supernumeraries on a military campaign, were hostages whose lives would be forfeit if their followers were to foment disturbances in Khartoum during their absence. In addition, the Governor-General brought a group of experienced administrators who would be placed in charge of re-establishing government control of Kordofan once Obeid was retaken. These included Busati Bey Madani, a former Inspector of Finances, Mahmúd Ahmadáni, a former Governor of Khartoum, Hamad al-Tiblib, Chief of the Appeals Court in the capital and Ginnáwi Bey, a leading Khartoum merchant whom 'Alá-al-Dín intended to send on to govern the already unruly southern province of Bahr al-Ghazál.[15]

As the most senior officers in the land gathered in council, 'Plan A' rapidly evolved into 'Plan B' and then, as swiftly, into 'Plan C'. Each change compromised Hicks' original plan more dangerously. First to be abandoned was the simple Dueim–Bara–Obeid route; instead, the army would follow a more elaborate curve to the south. This, the commanders hoped, would bring two advantages. Water would be more plentiful along the khayrán, the seasonal watercourses where the recent rains should have replenished the wells. If the army could make their way to al-Rahad, they could rendezvous with Chief Adam of Tagali, who had promised assistance if the Hicks force were willing to attack Obeid from the south. Hicks also hoped that Sheikh 'Asákir would stop prevaricating between the government and the Mahdi and finally decide to 'come in when we get to his country'.[16] The General's last official despatch itemised the posts along the revised route and the distance separating them.

> I decided that my line of communications should be secured by posts of 200 men each, left in strongly fortified positions in the following places:- Shatt (16m), Zeraiga (16m), Sarakhna (32m), Nurabi (16m), Agaila (24m), Johan (32m), Abli (28m), Beliab (22m), Um Sheikh (12), Rahad (14), Khashil (14m), Melbeis (25m).[17]

The second, fatal strategic compromise was the abandonment of that plan to establish fortified posts in the rear of the advancing army. This reckless and disastrous decision was made two evenings into the march, at a council of war attended by Hicks, 'Alá-al-Dín Siddíq, his new deputy Brigadier Hussein Mazhar, and two senior colonels, Salím Auni of the 1st Battalion and Rajab Siddiq of the 4th Battalion.[18] The two colonels, perhaps knowing their men best, immediately voted against the system of fortified posts. Hussein Pasha Mazhar supported Hicks in the 'yes' camp but only if more men from the 5th and 6th Battalions in Khartoum were sent as reinforcements. But the strongest pressure came from Governor-General 'Alá-al-Dín, who had absolutely no confidence in the troops. It would be impossible, he argued, to expect contingents of Egyptian soldiers, even at company strength, to maintain isolated positions in enemy territory, with large numbers of hostile tribesmen prowling around in the wake of the army's passage – let alone ask them to escort convoys of stores or messages between the staging posts. This was the moment where Hicks displayed a fatal weakness. He accepted, though he had premonitions of disaster. 'It is too disgusting', he wrote. 'So I have now to cut myself adrift from communication with the outer world, and from my supplies. . . . I am commanding an Army officered by men who will not undertake the ordinary risks of warfare.'[19] Large supplies of stores, including 'thousands of tons of biscuits, &c.', had to be left at Dueim.[20] The General was not alone in his anxiety. A slave boy in the service of Muhammad Bey, one of the Egyptian officers, later reflected on that momentous decision.

We plunged into the desert, having turned our backs on the Nile that the greater part of our soldiers were to see no more. They had commenced their last march, the march from which there was to be no returning. No more would they greet the rising sun, with backs turned to the east; every step they traced on the sand led to the sunset – the sunset of their lives.[21]

☙ ☙ ☙

Such a huge force could hardly be amassed in secret. Indeed, the muster of the battalions at Omdurman was known to the Mahdi at Obeid as early as July.[22] After consultations with his khulafá' and umará', Muhammad Ahmad evolved a simple plan and issued swift orders. The 'Turks' would be lured into a trap, drawn forward into increasingly empty terrain – free from resistance but also free from opportunity to resupply – and harried from the rear. At a point of the Mahdi's own choosing, the government army would be confronted by the main Ansár force and crushed between the hammer and the anvil. On 29 September, Muhammad Ahmad ordered his army to set up camp outside the walls of Obeid and a vigorous programme of daily manoeuvres and exercises was begun. The effusion of propaganda from his new capital to the tribes of the region had brought in thousands upon thousands of new supporters. So that they should be spiritually prepared, he ordered them to perform the dhikr and proclaim the greatness of God constantly in the *takbír* prayer.[23]

> To these assembled multitudes he now preached more fervently than ever, urging them to renounce the pleasures of this life, and think only of the life to come. 'Ana akhreb ed dunya wa ammer el akhera' ('I destroy this world, and I construct the world to come'), was his endless theme. To those who were obedient he promised pleasures in Paradise beyond all the heart could conceive; but the disobedient he threatened with condign punishment and hell-fire. Circulars written in this sense were despatched far and wide, and the Emirs were enjoined to allow only those to remain in their districts whose services were absolutely necessary for the cultivation of the lands, but that all others must forthwith immigrate to him and range themselves under his banners.[24]

To lead the army of 3,000 men that would harass the rear of the Hicks column, the Mahdi despatched Muhammad 'Osmán Abú-Girja and 'Abd-al-Halím Musá'id as generals, with 'Umar the son of Ilyás Umm Bireir to help them stir up the local tribes.[25] Their orders were strict: do not confront the much larger government army but shadow it, picking off any stragglers. Above all, they were commanded, fill in as many wells as possible between Dueim and Rahad. 'If you find the chance and killing the enemy of God is possible,' the Mahdi wrote to his generals, 'then I have no objection – providing that you are motivated not by the sordid booty of this world but by God and pursuance of the afterlife'.[26] Along with their orders, the umará' were sent 2,000 copies of a fiery proclamation from the Mahdi. These, he instructed, were to be placed on the government army's route to give them one last chance to surrender.

> To those among the army who have brains and will listen to the Mahdi,
>
> It is well known to the intelligent man that this affair is in God's hands. Neither artillery nor rifles nor rockets can share that role. . . . You should not be deceived by your arms or the sheer numbers with which you propose to frighten us, us the soldiers of Allah. . . . If your eyes are no more blinded and you believe in God, his Prophet, the afterlife and in our Mahdía, then you will come and surrender to us. He who surrenders will be spared. But if you refuse to do so and cling to denial and reliance on your guns and powder, we have been assured by the Prophet himself that you will be killed just like those who went before you.[27]

At the small village of Abú-Gewi, the Mahdist generals rendezvoused with Sheikh 'Asákir of the Jimi', who was evidently still serving both sides in hopes of emerging from the war in the favour of the victor, come what may.[28]

۞ ۞ ۞

From the moment of departure from Dueim to the first night's camp at Shat, nothing went right for General Hicks. Two incidents illustrated the continuing bickering between the force commanders, their incompetence to mount a coordinated march and their naivety. The arrival of the army at Shat on 27 September was a shambles; thousands of troops milling in total disorder, their officers unable to maintain any semblance of discipline. The regiments were split apart, the whole force stretched out over nearly three miles. 'All through Friday night', wrote 'Abbás Bey in his campaign journal, 'it was impossible for any soldiers to know his companion, or the Beluk to find its Battalion, because of the miserable state of disorder into which the army had fallen – in addition to the horrible noise of camels, horses and mules numbering about 7,000'.[29] The incident prompted renewed arguments among the senior officers. Brigadier Hussein Mazhar, whose loyalties had always been to the ousted General Suleimán Niyázi rather than to the foreigner Hicks, promptly went to Governor-General 'Alá al-Dín to insist that he, Hussein Mazhar, replace Hicks as Commander-in-Chief. 'Abbás Bey, liaising diplomatically between the rival Pashas, succeeded in calming tempers, blaming the fiasco on mistakes committed by the translators. But it was a telling example of mutual mistrust and resentment that would be repeated many times in the coming weeks.

The very next day, Hicks' trust was betrayed in another, perhaps more predictable, way. On the eve of the march, on the recommendation of the interpreter Major Evans (who liked to think of himself as the force's Intelligence Officer), the General had welcomed a deserter from the Mahdist ranks, a veteran from 'Ali Bey Lutfi's failed attempt to retake Obeid. The soldier had been given promotion, two months' pay and two new uniforms. Sent out to take charge of grazing the camels, the duplicitous veteran stole a camel and made off for the Ansár force shadowing the army's march, taking his Remington rifle and ten dozen bullets. 'No doubt,' reflected 'Abbás Bey ruefully and accurately, 'he is a clever scout who will communicate to Muhammad Ahmad all our news, proving his statements by the money, clothes and the firearm which he has stolen'.[30] Hicks was even more distressed when he learned from Major Evans that the spy had succeeded in spreading tales of the Mahdi's miraculous powers among the rank and file.

Evans told me afterwards that he had heard the man telling several of the army that 3 men had attempted to murder the Mahdi by stabbing him, but 'their knives would not enter his body'. So much for my 'intelligence' officer – not *intelligent*. He [the spy] was allowed to preach this to an ignorant mussalman soldiery for 4 days.[31]

And so the doomed expedition staggered on into the wilderness. As the terrain changed, they began to encounter dense forests of mimosa trees, spiny thickets of thorn-bushes and plains of tall impenetrable grass, arresting their progress still more. Hicks' confident itinerary, which anticipated marches of up to twenty-five miles in a single day, was abandoned; such distances were taking up to three days. A day's march rarely lasted more than four hours and extensive rests were required for the troops to regain their strength and morale. From the beginning, the fifteen guides were suspected of harbouring loyalties to the Mahdi. One group, all from the northern Mahas clan, were put in chains on the second day after failing to locate a well-watered route and were subsequently escorted by twenty-five armed horsemen during the day and kept 'tied up by their necks' at night to prevent them from slipping off to join Abú-Girja's force.[32] The first water crisis came early, on 10 October.

We all expected to reach Akila on this day, so much so, that the men had only taken sufficient water for one day. The guides did not know the direct route, but led us very crookedly, and finally we were worn out and in a pitiful state of thirst . . . and our energies were broken down after the heat and fatigue endured on this crooked march. The men's water bottles were empty, and they now began to wander about in the hope of finding water, parties of fives and tens leaving the square, without regard to the danger, so that the force was now scattered over about 2,000 metres. Hicks Pasha shouted to the officers to keep order and asked them to bring their men back, lest they should fall an easy prey to the enemy, but they would not listen.

The Governor-General then proceeded on horseback along the sides of the square and from left to right, urging the officers to keep order and the men to be obedient. . . . All the Staff were in a state of fury. . . . Alas for an army which cannot keep order after 12 hours lack of water. . . . Parties of Muhammad Ahmad's followers were tracking us from behind, but they did not exceed 300 footmen and 80 cavalry. . . . These followed hardly half an hour behind, carrying off what we dropped and killing any weak man left on the road.[33]

Mid-October brought a brief morale-boosting reprieve from the rigours of the trek. On the eve of the *'Eid al-Adha*, known to the Egyptian officers by its Turkish name as the 'Kurban [Great] Bairam', the troops beat off a determined attack on their overnight zaríba by a concentration of Mahdist fighters.[34] Disciplined and sustained fire from behind the thorn-fence drove off the rebels with heavy losses and brought the men cheering to their feet. The Governor-General was moved to order a 21-gun salute in honour of their bravery. A two-day rest followed, during which 'Alá-al-Dín hosted a reception for senior staff. 'Everyone cheered the Khedive', noted the Governor-General's Secretary sardonically, 'and we all felt very sanguine as to our ultimate victory.'[35] General Hicks, remembering his propaganda offensive in that summer's Jazíra campaign, decided to send out another quasi-Mahdist proclamation to the local chiefs and sheikhs.

No doubt you have heard of the victorious army that has come to destroy the rebels, and is now in the midst of your country. For your own well-being, we offer you this advice: Be obedient and loyal to the Government, and for the welfare of your country hasten to meet us with all your followers, then the blessing of God and his Prophet be upon you. The disobedient and the rebellious among you shall reap the fruit of their actions and no blame shall rest on us.[36]

After the momentary cheer of the 'Eid, the next fortnight was a litany of woes. The Mahdist fighters prowling the surrounding countryside became ever bolder and the skirmishes more frequent. Hicks argued constantly with Hussein Mazhar. The Egyptian officers were openly disrespectful and disobedient, their resentment perhaps fuelled by the knowledge that their families, in contrast to those of the European officers, would receive a miserably inadequate pension in the event of their death.[37] As for the rank and file, it was Frank Power who observed subsequently that 'as each Egyptian soldier has at least two wives and a mud-hovel full of children, about 25,000 fellaheen widows and 300,000 poor brown children are penniless in Lower Egypt'.[38] The Krupp artillery pieces were unreliable and often failed to fire because the officer in charge, Wahbi Bey, had neglected to service them adequately. Camels, mules and men continued to die. There was never enough water and often, drawn straight from pools on the ground, it was muddy. On 20 October, Colonel Farquhar, Hicks' Chief of Staff, succeeded in destroying the morale of the whole army by rejecting the advice of the guides and insisting on following his compass bearing, right through a maze of trees, brush and reeds. Observing the sorry mess from a nearly hilltop, the Governor-General and 'Abbás Bey were horrified to see that the army was strung out over more than three miles. 'Is this what they call the skill of the English?' 'Abbás asked sourly that evening. 'All ranks from the Governor-General downwards felt very much discouraged by this march, and the men began to say that the English General would never have led them through this jungle with high grass all round unless he wanted them to be all annihilated. I thank God the enemy had not fired the grass or the result would have been terrible.'[39]

On 24 October, the army reached Rahad, an important staging post and watering-point on a large swampy stream variously known as the Khor Abú-Habl ('Father of Fertility') or simply, for its bountiful supply, the Khor al-Níl. Muhammad Bey's slave-boy described Rahad as 'a large swamp with pools of water . . . on elevated ground, and rocks and hills around'.[40] It was here that General Hicks had hoped to meet Adam of Tagali with reinforcements from the hills. Despite a six-day wait, relatively secure behind a robust zaríba and deep trench, the promised allies never appeared. Mahdist riflemen sniped continually at the Egyptian troops from the surrounding woods and grasslands. One bullet zipped through the canvas of Hicks' tent and buried itself into the wooden seat on which he was sitting.[41] Morale was further affected

1. Memorial shrine at the Mahdi's birthplace on Jazírat Labab near Dongola. (*Author*)

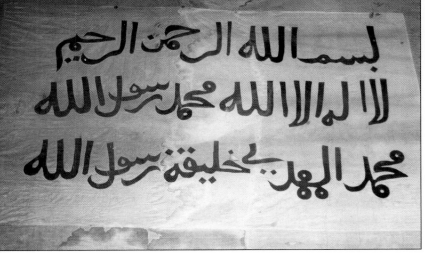

بسم الله الرحمن الرحيم
لا إله إلا الله محمد رسول الله
محمد المهدي خليفة رسول الله

2. Ansár banner, bearing the words 'In the name of God, the compassionate, the merciful | There is no God but Allah; Muhammad is the messenger of God | Muhammad al-Mahdi is the successor of God's messenger'. (*Author*)

3. Stylised pit commemorating the place where the Mahdi prayed, inside a small mosque on Jazíra Aba, central Sudan. (*Author*)

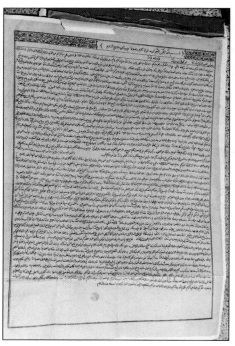

4. Proclamation of the Mahdi in the Beit Khalífa museum, Omdurman. (*Author*)

5. Extract from the Mahdi's Rátib, a collection of prayers and quotations from the Qorán, printed shortly after the Mahdi's death, 1885. *(Reproduced by permission of the University of Durham)*

بسم الله الرحمن الرحيم

الحمد لله الذي خلق السموات والأرض وجعل الظلمات والنور ثم الذين كفروا بربهم يعدلون
هو الذي خلقكم من طين ثم قضى اجلاً واجل مسمى عنده ثم انتم تمترون ٭ وهو الله في السموات
وفي الأرض يعلم سركم وجهركم ويعلم ما تكسبون ٭ وما تكون في شأن وما تتلو منه
من قرآن ولا تعملون من عمل الا كنا عليكم شهوداً اذ تفيضون فيه وما يعزب عن ربك من مثقال
ذرة في الأرض ولا في السماء ولا اصغر من ذلك ولا اكبر الا في كتاب مبين ٭ اللهم يا مذكورا

6. The Saráya, residence of the Governor-General in Khartoum. The inset shows Awad-al-Karím Ahmad Abú-Sin, chief of the Shukría. (The Graphic, *3 May 1884*)

7. Governor-General Charles Gordon, captioned as 'Pacificator of the Soudan'. (*The Graphic, 26 January 1884*)

8. Colonel J.D.H. Stewart, intelligence officer and Gordon's aide-de-camp. (*Courtesy of the National Portrait Gallery, London*)

9. Colonel William Hicks (front row, second right), in Cairo with members of his doomed Soudan Field Force, as well as General Valentine Baker (seated, next to Hicks), 1883. (*Courtesy of the Director, National Army Museum, London*)

10. Remains of earth ramparts used by the Ansár in the defence of Omdurman in 1898. (*Author*)

11. Memorial to the members of the 21st Lancers killed in the Battle of Karari outside Omdurman on 2 September 1898, protected by a steel fence. (*Author*)

12. Ansár fighters wearing the *jibba*, the traditional patched smock of the Mahdist movement, after their defeat at Karari, 1898. (*Reproduced by permission of the University of Durham*)

3. Osmán Digna, the general who led the Mahdi's campaign in the eastern Red Sea Hills, photographed after the Ansár defeat at Karari, 1898. (*Reproduced by permission of the University of Durham*)

14. The bodies of the Khalífa and senior commanders at Umm Dibeikarát, 1899. (*Reproduced by permission of the University of Durham*)

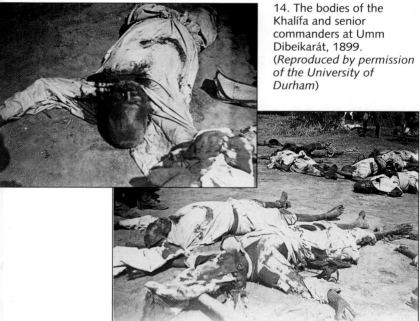

15. The destruction of the Mahdi's tomb in Omdurman inflicted by British shellfire, 1898. (*Reproduced by permission of the University of Durham*)

16. The Mahdi's tomb today, receiving a fresh coat of silver paint. (*Author*)

by the recent discovery of the Mahdi's latest proclamation. Hundreds of copies had been pinned to the trees on the way into Rahad by Abú-Girja's men. Hicks had as many as possible gathered and burnt but the damage had already been done. Colonel Farquhar wrote in his diary: 'I spoke to Mr. O'Donovan to-day, and asked him where he thought we should be eight days hence. "In Kingdom-Come", was his reply.'[42]

&#9753; &#9753; &#9753;

With his enemy encamped at Rahad, the Mahdist amír, 'Abd-al-Halím Musá'id, rode excitedly for Obeid to seek fresh instructions from his master at the Mahdi's camp outside the city walls. 'Abd-al-Halím was so convinced that the government force was weak and demoralised that he begged to be allowed to spring the trap at Rahad itself. But the Mahdi commanded him only to return immediately, followed by all available men and boys of fighting age. The final battle would be planned with greater cunning and involve all the manpower at the Mahdi's disposal. Muhammad Ahmad himself continued to receive twice-daily updates on the deteriorating condition of the government army. Not only had 'Abd-al-Halím Musá'id and Abú-Girja's men been reporting on the desultory progress of the army, picking off stragglers and counting the corpses of the pack animals that died along the way, but also more direct information had come from the heart of the camp. An officer in the 3rd Battalion, 'Abd-al-Rahmán Bey Bannaga, whose father was an influential Mahdist supporter in Obeid, had been sneaking out of the army camp at night and briefing Ansár fighters loyal to Ilyás Umm Bireir.[43] Bannaga's servants, too, had been carrying messages to the Mahdists at regular intervals and had even smuggled Ansár spies into the square.[44] There were also further desertions. Gustav Klootz, a German valet serving first Baron von Seckendorf then O'Donovan of the *Daily News*, escaped at Rahad. Fr Joseph Ohrwalder, still a prisoner at the Ansár camp, translated for Klootz when he was interrogated by the Mahdi. Klootz, wearing canvas clothes and a 'dirty tarbush', confirmed that morale among the Egyptian officers was at its nadir. He did, however, warn that Hicks' fire-power was sufficiently dangerous that the Mahdi should expect to lose a large number of his own army. Ohrwalder noted the pious riposte of Ahmad Suleimán, the head of the Beit al-Mál who accompanied the Mahdi to the interrogation: 'Death will be our reward.'[45]

The Mahdi committed his forces to the final attack on Thursday, 1 November. Even as Hicks and 'Alá-al-Dín goaded their weary and thirsty men on from Rahad to Alloba, Muhammad Ahmad moved on camel-back with his main force to Abú-Safíya. The following day, New Year's Day in the Islamic calendar, he moved cautiously forward to Fartangúl.[46] Aware that Hicks would try for Birka, the next substantial supply of water just thirty-five miles short of Obeid, the Mahdi sent a large force to cut them off before occupying the well-watered campsite himself. Despite their overwhelming numerical superiority, many of the Ansár were nervous about the Egyptians' fire-power and began to fret that Hicks would reach Obeid, where the Mahdist families and camp followers had been left, after all. Anxious that his men were becoming dangerously demoralised, Muhammad Ahmad tried a pep talk in parables.

> First, he spat into the palm of his hand and asked them what it was. They answered that it was spittle. The Mahdi commented: 'We are like the ground and the Turks are like the spittle'. Secondly, he asked where a bird in flight would descend. They replied: 'On the ground'. The Mahdi commented: 'The Turks are like the birds and we are like the ground'.[47]

The southern Jihádía, under the banners of Hamdán Abú-Anja, moved rapidly forward to join 'Abd-al-Halím Musá'id's force as it tracked the government army. During the day's march and each night as the government soldiers camped, Abú-Anja's riflemen poured sustained Remington fire into their ranks. Sleep was impossible. Every Egyptian soldier hugged the ground for fear of the incessant bullets. 'So fierce was the fire', one of the Ansár recalled later, 'that all the bark was stripped from the trees and they gleamed white as if washed with soap'.[48] On Saturday morning, impelled by sheer desperation, the huge but impotent army was again roused into marching formation. In a purely defensive posture now, the whole force was organised in a massive square; one battalion forming each side, Shaigía cavalry on each flank, with the field-guns, camels, stores and camp-followers sheltering in the middle. The army struggled to maintain its formation as it passed through the trees and thickets. Muhammad Bey's slave-boy found the experience terrifying.

> Presently all around we saw Arabs innumerable; the whole world surrounded us, and [flags] were waving and spears gleaming in the sunshine above the bush. Our square was halted, and we opened fire, killing a great many, but we too lost many. There were too many bushes for the Krupps to do execution, but the machine guns were at work day and night. Next morning when we marched I saw Arabs lying in six heaps, slain by these guns. . . . At first the Egyptians lay down to hide, but General Hicks ordered his English Officers to go round and make them stand up; some of the English were killed when doing this, and Hicks took out his pocket-book and wrote down their names and the time of day that they were killed and the manner.[49]

Sunday 4 November was a desolate time, the eve of destruction: Privation, terror and death on one side, triumph on the other. 'These are bad times,' wrote Major Artur Herlth in his diary; 'we are in a forest, and everyone very depressed. The general orders the band to play, hoping that the music may enliven us a little; but the bands soon stop, for the bullets are flying from all directions, and camels, mules, and men, keep dropping down.'[50] The army had entered the most inhospitable territory imaginable, a region known to the people of Kordofan as 'Sheikán', named after the densely clustered thorn bushes that stabbed the passing troops with hard, three-inch-long spines.[51] To cope with this difficult terrain, Hicks now adopted a more flexible formation. The army was broken up into three separate squares, formed in a triangle with the guns and supplies, as before, in the middle. Hicks, 'Alá-al-Dín and their senior staff rode line abreast in front with four Krupps guns. The remaining cavalry brought up the rear.[52] But again, the Mahdi's spies were able to anticipate Hick's destination: Fula al-Masarín, another good water supply. Again, the Ansár beat him to it. While the Mahdi and his followers enjoyed clean water, Hicks, his men and his equally parched beasts were forced to make rudimentary camp in the middle of the thorn forest.

The Mahdi paraded his forces under their divisional banners and prayed with them before the final attack. After the prayer was concluded, the Mahdi drew his sword and pointed it at the army. 'Allahu akbar!' he cried, three times.[53] Then, turning to the Ansár fighters, he said: 'You will kill this expedition in less than half an hour . . . because the angels and all the jinns will fight for you. . . . And be afraid of neither their numbers nor of their guns and arms, because their souls are already caught in our hands.'[54] The onslaught was utterly terrifying for the government troops. As Abú-Anja's riflemen fell back, thousands upon thousands of spearmen rushed up to replace them. The Mahdi's main army, led by two umará', 'Abd-al-Rahmán al-Nujúmi and Ibráhím al-Haj al-Turjumáwi, and two khulafá', 'Abdulláhi and 'Ali wad Helu, attacked from the front, sprinting through the woods directly at the massed ranks of Khartoum's best army, wholly fearless. From behind came the Baggára tribesmen with swords and spears who had been tracking them for nearly a month. And now from inside the government formation came an entirely unexpected assault, sowing chaos and confusion at the heart of the column. Rebel fighters had hidden themselves in shallow holes with wooden roofs. As the officers and the first square passed over, they leapt out and began stabbing from behind.[55]

It was now noon. Just about this time, a rush terrible and sudden, sweeping like the torrent from the mountain, was made. The Arabs burst upon our front force in overwhelming numbers. It was swept away like chaff before the wind. Seeing this, the other sides of the square turned inwards, and commenced a death-dealing fusillade both on the Arabs pouring into the square and on each other crossways. A terrible slaughter commenced.

Hicks Pasha and the very few English officers left with him, seeing all hope of restoring order gone, spurred their horses and sprang out of the confused mess of wounded, dead, and dying. These officers fired away their revolvers, clearing a space for themselves, till all their ammunition was expended. They killed many. They had got clean outside. Then they took to their swords and fought till they fell.[56]

The destruction of the government army was accomplished with terrible swiftness. The battalions were slaughtered in their squares and the bodies of as many as seven thousand soldiers were left to the vultures and animals of the wilderness. The Ansár who were killed, certainly numbering several hundred, were buried with honours before the day was out. Some time later, a government prisoner from the southern front was taken to see for himself the fate that had befallen the mighty army of Hicks Pasha.

There I saw the skeletons of the troops laid side by side with skeletons of camels, horses, donkeys, etc. all amongst a large zariba – made as to prevent the tribes from robbing the army's stores until the Mahdi's emirs carried them to Obeid – in three lumps forming a triangle – and very few skeletons between. I saw also outside the zariba at different distances up to a mile at all sides skeletons of men, apparently of those who fled away out of the squares and were overtaken by the rebels.[57]

There was a strange footnote to this gruesome episode. One of the late Governor-General's brothers arrived from Cairo the following February, expressing the desire to travel west to the battlefield at 'Sheikán'. There he hoped to pick his brother's bones out from those of Hicks and the rest of the staff and give them honourable burial. 'I have asked him if he has another brother to go prospecting after *his* bones in a few weeks,' wrote Frank Power sardonically; 'he is evidently an utter idiot'.[58]

# FIFTEEN

## 'In God's Fist'
## Darfur, Red Sea Hills and Bahr
## al-Ghazál, 1882–1884

The Mahdi's wider campaign to wrest Sudan from Egyptian control had begun in earnest in the western province of Darfur in the summer of 1882. Immediately after the Ansár victory over Yúsuf al-Shalláli at the end of May, Muhammad Ahmad sent a personal envoy to Darfur to raise rebellion in one of the government's most recently acquired and most remote outposts.[1] As in Kordofan, there were tribal and political divisions to exploit and the resentment of the disaffected and powerless to be seized upon. The influential Rizeigát tribe of southeastern Darfur was split between two mutually hostile chiefs, Madibbu 'Ali and 'Ujeil wad al-Jangáwi. Forced into a subordinate position, Madibbu 'Ali joined the Mahdi at Jebel Gadír. His immediate reward for making the hijra to the Nuba Mountains was to be sent back home, charged with leading the Darfur revolution.[2]

The man in command of government forces in Darfur was an Austrian aristocrat and part-time soldier, Rudolf Slatin, who had served under Colonel Gordon in the late 1870s and who had been promoted to the provincial governorship by Gordon's successor, Ra'úf Pasha, in 1881.[3] To combat the rising tribes, he had fewer than 5,000 men, concentrated at the capital, Fasher, as well as Dara and Shakka.[4] In the early stages of the uprising, news of the Mahdi's activities had only filtered through to the west as 'disquieting rumours'. But in Darfur itself, Madibbu 'Ali's message quickly spread among the Rizeigát, the Habbanía and the Málía in the southern districts around Shakka. The early seizure of the telegraph station at Foga by the Ansár cut Slatin's communications with Khartoum, compelling him to send messages via Obeid 'concealed in hollowed-out lance-staves, between the soles of boots or sandals, or sewn into the bearer's clothing'.[5] Slatin determined to build a small fort at Shakka to hold back Madibbu's marauding fighters and in October 1882 he mounted an expedition to establish a strong outpost. Behind him at Dara, Slatin left his Deputy Governor, Muhammad Khálid, whose nickname was 'Zugul' ('the Liar').[6] Slatin's force consisted of 6,000 spearmen, recruited from pro-government tribes, 550 Egyptian Army regulars armed with Remingtons and 1,300 bazingers with their double-barrelled guns.[7] Advancing into Rizeigát territory, a landscape obscured by dense bush and forests, the square and its flanking cavalry units were ambushed at Umm Waragat. Rudolf Slatin later described a scene of intense confusion.

Within the square the Arabs who had already penetrated, although suffering heavily from the fire from my own small party, were creating frightful havoc amongst the almost defenceless Bazingers, who, armed only with muzzle-loaders, could do nothing, whilst the regulars – so sudden had been the rush – had not even time to draw their bayonets; eventually, however, those who had entered were all killed. The flank guards, taken in front and rear, suffered even more heavily than the square, and, breaking up entirely, they fled in all directions, hundreds being killed by the Rizighat horsemen concealed in the forest.[8]

Of the original 8,500-strong force, just 900 fighting men survived. Slatin had lost at a stroke all his best officers and tribal advisers. After a long but courageous retreat to Dara, Slatin was forced to dig in, not just for the winter but well into the spring and summer of 1883. He smuggled out desperate letters to his colleague the Governor of Bahr al-Ghazál, Frank Lupton, asking for men, ammunition, supplies, anything. But no help came from the south. Instead came letters from Madibbu 'Ali, reporting the Mahdi's siege and capture of Obeid and urging surrender. Outside Dara's strong stone fortifications, all Darfur seized the opportunity to rise against the government. Inside the massive walls of the square fortress, Slatin focused on strengthening his defences and laid in extra stocks of corn, sensibly anticipating a siege. There was already a tower at each corner of the fort and a deep trench around the walls. Inside were the government magazines and barracks, while the townspeople themselves lived in 'straggling lanes of huts, irregularly built, to the south and east of the citadel'.[9]

The Governor's difficulties were compounded by two betrayals. His senior Egyptian officers at Fasher had received word from home about the revolution led by Ahmed 'Arábi and now reasoned that, if 'Arábi ruled Egypt, he must rule Egypt's Sudanese territories as well. That meant they no longer had to obey the orders of the inexperienced, non-military and, above all, non-Muslim foreigner placed as their superior. The message was spelled out to Slatin in person by a trusted officer who relayed to him the conviction of the entire battalion that, in a war of religion, a Christian would 'never be able to gain a victory, and that in every battle . . . [would] suffer great losses'. Rudolf Slatin then took the extraordinary step of converting to Islam. Asked whether he did this from true conviction or pragmatism, his answer to the friendly officer was quite clear.

'Mohammed Effendi,' said I, 'you are an intelligent and well-educated man; here conviction has nothing to do with the case. In this life one has often to do things which are contrary to one's persuasions, either by compulsion or from some other cause. I shall be quite content if the soldiers believe me and abandon their silly superstitions. Whether others believe me or not is a matter of indifference to me.'[10]

Slatin's recital of the shahada in front of all his officers and troops, and his expedient adoption of the Muslim name, 'Abd-al-

Gádir Salátín, may have done the trick in the short term, had it not been for the second betrayal.[11] Slatin's deputy, Muhammad Khálid, was among the wealthiest individuals in Darfur and, as a government employee, commanded the loyalty of a large body of subordinates in the garrisons. But he was also a close relative of the Mahdi, having married Butúl, the daughter of the Mahdi's eldest brother, Muhammad.[12] Slatin resolved to put his sworn allegiance to the test by sending him to Obeid on a fact-finding mission, while his closest family was detained pending his return. Muhammad Khálid arrived in the Kordofan capital in September and promptly threw in his lot with his wife's uncle. Just six days after the defeat of the Hicks expedition on 5 November, one of the Mahdi's first moves was to appoint 'al-Zugul' his supreme commander, *amír 'umúm*, for the western province. Two days later, the renegade official set out from Obeid to defeat his former superior, escorted personally to the outskirts of Obeid by the Mahdi and his three Khulafá' and armed with his letter of appointment.[13] With such a letter and with Darfur in such ferment, no more than a small force was thought necessary to accompany him. The letter, however, was as much a cautionary rebuke to the messenger as to the people of the west; the Mahdi knew of his relative's record as a dishonest merchant and government stooge and, as with the traders of Obeid súq, made it clear that back-sliding would not be tolerated.

You have sworn allegiance on the basis of following the Book, the traditions and the way of the Prophet. So fear God and fear his watchful eye! Do not embark on any project before you know God's ruling on it. Strip your heart of love for this world. . . . You and your companions must adhere to fairness in deeds and in words. You must show mercy and compassion to the weak and the poor, especially to the followers of our Mahdía. Avoid envy, arrogance and pride – banish them from your heart. God willing, through your repentance you may amend your past behaviour and become a model of good. . . . But you and your friends must not, after this time, revert to your old ways. God himself has changed you. Perform your prayers, make your zakát payments, enjoin what is good, prohibit what is forbidden and uphold the Sharí'a. As the Book says:

'When you speak, speak justly, even if a close relative is concerned. Fulfil the covenant of God; so he commands you, so you may remember. In truth, this is my way, which leads straight: follow it!'[14]

Mindful of these chastening instructions, Muhammad Khálid made rapid progress. Ansár under Ibráhím al-Milíh, a junior amír originally from Kordofan, already besieged the garrison at Umm Shanga. Rather than surrender to the rapacious Baggára, the soldiers at Umm Shanga held out until Muhammad Khálid's arrival; they knew him and trusted him to treat them rather more leniently. Muhammad Khálid then set his sights on Dara, where his relatives were still held hostage and where Slatin, his condition worsened by defections and a grave shortage of rifle ammunition, was failing to contain fresh outbreaks of insurgency. Desperately playing for time and pinning his hopes on the Hicks expedition, the Governor tried one last delaying tactic. With the rebels now gathered around Dara 'in considerable strength', he proposed to surrender – but only to an envoy sent personally by the Mahdi at Obeid. Towards the end of November, however, confirmation reached Dara that Hicks was dead and all hope of relief dead with him. With the full agreement of his senior officers, Slatin accepted the inevitable and on 23 December rode out to surrender to Muhammad Khálid in person at an agreed rendezvous.

At midnight, accompanied by my kavasses, and a few Arab chiefs who remained faithful to the last, I quitted Dara.[15] During my service in Darfur I had had many disagreeable experiences, but this journey was quite the hardest. Not a word passed. We were all fully occupied with our miserable thoughts. . . . I sent an orderly ahead to see if Zogal had arrived, and he soon returned, stating that he had been there since yesterday, and was waiting for me. . . . I advanced to salute him; he pressed me to his heart, and assured me of his entire friendliness, begged me to be seated, and then handed to me the Mahdi's letter.[16]

The garrison at the provincial capital, Fasher, held out for another fortnight, their resolve stiffened by accounts of the looting of Dara, in which the homes of all wealthy merchants and government supporters were ransacked for cash and their owners tortured for information on hidden treasure. As at Obeid, the loot was all destined for the Mahdi's swelling Beit al-Mál. Fasher's Egyptian commanding officer, Sa'íd Juma, bravely defended the town, which had its own square, mud-brick fort, surrounded by a fifteen-foot ditch and fitted with artillery in four small corner towers. His garrison, as elsewhere, had their families with them and 'sufficient provisions for a siege of years' but the placing of Fasher's wells outside the walls of the fort was a strategic disaster. When the Ansár began filling in the wells as they had done in Kordofan, both soldiers and civilians inside the walls became as desperate as 'thirsty camels'.[17] After little more than a week of siege, surrender was inevitable. On 15 January 1884, Sa'íd Juma swore allegiance to the Mahdist cause, joining Yúsuf Mansúr of the Obeid garrison in commanding the Ansár artillery contingent.[18]

🕎 🕎 🕎

The war in the eastern provinces was dominated by the towering figure of 'Osmán Abú-Bakr Digna, whose personal courage, military abilities and natural leadership made him an essential part of the Mahdist hierarchy, a valued amír right up to and beyond the disaster at Karari.[19] 'Osmán Digna's family was an intriguing blend of local and outsider. While his father was descended from a Kurdish family in what is now southeastern Turkey, his mother was of the Hadendawa clan of the Red Sea hills Beja tribe. Like so many before him, he joined the Mahdi partly because of similar religious inclinations and partly out of bitterness against the government, born of a family grievance that was specific to the slave trade. The Digna clan had been highly active in shipping slaves from Suakin over to the Arabian peninsula. The port's government officials, who by 1877 had been formally charged with eradicating the trafficking of humans, were usually content (for a small consideration) to look the other way. That year, however, the British Consul at Jedda became outraged at the sheer scale of the Digna operation. 'Osmán, his brothers and cousins were all arrested, the entire family's possessions were confiscated and their business summarily ejected from Jedda.[20] In the religious context of the Red Sea region, 'Osmán Digna also found himself opposed to the authorities because the Majdhúbía brotherhood to which he belonged was a weaker local rival to the pro-government Khatmía taríqa. The head of the Majdhúbía, Sheikh al-Táhir al-Tayyib, a man of great prestige in the Red Sea districts, had been exchanging correspondence with Muhammad Ahmad since before his declaration as Mahdi at Jazíra Aba.[21]

Reports of the Mahdi's early successes reached 'Osmán Digna at Berber, adopted as a temporary home after his expulsion from both Jedda and Suakin. Travelling to Obeid in the aftermath of the city's surrender, he must have made a rapid impression on the Mahdi, or perhaps his Majdhúbía credentials gave him immediate access to the inner circle. Certainly his role was to be vital. As well as raising rebellion in the east and preventing nearly 9,000 government soldiers along the Red Sea coast being redeployed elsewhere, the Mahdi wanted to cut the Suakin–Berber corridor, along which reinforcements of artillery, horses, men and ammunition from Egypt could be expected to pass.[22] On 8 May 1883, 'Osmán Digna left Obeid for the east, recognised as the Mahdi's amír for the Red Sea coast and armed with a formidable letter of introduction. This proclamation, copied hundreds of times and disseminated as a mass circulation propaganda tool, was among the most important of all the Mahdi's manshúrát. In it, Muhammad Ahmad rehearsed in detail, with many quotations from the Qorán, his own claim to the status of Mahdi and the invalidity of the rule of the 'Turks', before going on to exhort the people of the region around Suakin to follow 'Osmán Digna in the jihad.

I have sent to you Sheikh 'Osmán Digna to help you uphold religion and fight the infidels. I have made him a blessed amír over you and over all the nomadic peoples and natives of Suakin province, so that he may lead and guide you, uphold the faith and revive the Sunna of the Lord of the Prophets and Apostles. Listen to him and obey both his commands and prohibitions! Stand by him. Support and swear allegiance to him. He who swears allegiance to Sheikh 'Osmán swears allegiance to me. He who is martyred while with him is deemed to have been martyred while with me. His companions are my companions and enjoy the same privileges. . . .

If my ultimatum is given to the people of Suakin and its surrounding area and they all surrender, then thank Allah and praise him . . . If the natives surrender and the Turks disobey, then you must all rise together and fight as one, causing them to perish, for the sake of making God's religion victorious and his sublime world supreme. . . . All those who agree with Sheikh 'Osmán Abú-Bakr should join him; leave Suakin and go to the place outside the town which he chooses for you. Beware and be alert! Tighten the siege and intensify your raids against them. Cut off their supplies completely until God destroys them as he did their fellows. This is because they are people decreed by God to be driven out and tortured. They are in God's fist. He is taking them by the forelock. So do not fear them; they are doomed to perish, God willing! Soon, Allah will transfer to you their land, their homes and their property. He will give you victory over them, for as he said:

'The fellowship of God must surely triumph.'[23]

Do not fear the power that stems from their apparent strength; it is not an inner strength. Do not fear their visible numbers; all power is with Allah:

'How often, by God's will, has a small force defeated a large army? All is with those who persevere steadfastly.'[24]

Observe honesty, loyalty; follow the example of the Prophet. Choose the side of God![25]

The response to 'Osmán Digna's call to arms, as he distributed copies of the Mahdi's proclamations and letters, was swift and emphatic. Sheikh al-Táhir al-Tayyib of the Majdhúbía, already a convert to the cause, humbled himself before the Mahdi's amír. Reading the letter, he 'kissed it, and, after raising it to his head and eyes, retired into an inner chamber [where] he discarded the clothes of silk and satin with which he had previously been clad, and, to the amazement of his little circle of worshippers, returned garbed in a simple white garment of the common herdsman'.[26] The fact that the large Hadendawa clan were adherents of his taríqa offered 'Osmán Digna 'a ready-made revolutionary army'.[27] The Hadendawa were extremely tough fighters, wearing long, straight swords in tooled leather scabbards, short daggers strapped to their arms, round leather shields and short stabbing spears. As the Mahdist quartermasters equipped each regional force with Hicks' Remingtons, bundles of rifles quietly smuggled along the territory's trading routes, so the Hadendawa learned to use the weapons of the new age.[28] With their frizzy hair teased into a striking crest and glued with tallow into tufts and trailing plaits, these were the brave men that would become known to the British as 'fuzzy-wuzzies'. In addition, 'Osmán Digna succeeded in raising the Erkowit and other local tribes under his revolutionary banner. But it was Sheikh al-Táhir al-Tayyib's open declaration for the Mahdi that most dismayed government officers like William Hicks in Khartoum.

A very influential and holy Sheik, a man who can raise 20 to 30,000 followers, has in a most unexpected and unaccountable way joined the rebels about Souakin. He has lived always in Souakin and is well known to Ala el-Din Pasha who tells me he is quite astonished at the news. The Sheik and he have often conversed about the Mahdi and he professed utter disbelief in him, and has always been friendly to the Govt.; besides he is a man of education and intelligence and must know that eventually the rebellion must be crushed.[29]

The Mahdist propaganda distributed by 'Osmán Digna and his new followers raised great alarm among senior members of the Khatmía. If local government officials at Suakin and Sinkát, a key point on the trade route from Berber to the sea, had been unaware of this new groundswell of discontent and potential instability, Muhammad 'Osmán al-Mirghani, the Khatmía leader, was only too happy to share with them his concerns. The new Governor of Suakin was Lieutenant-Colonel Muhammad Tawfíq, appointed by the Khedive in February and regarded as 'a cultured man and a good sportsman with the rifle'.[30] In early August 1883, he marched from Suakin to Sinkát, trusting in a small contingent of police to secure 'Osmán Digna's arrest. But the amír, arriving from his tribal hometown at Erkowit, had already joined forces with Sheikh al-Táhir on the outskirts of the town. After a tentative truce, during which the government forces hastily attempted to throw up some rudimentary defences to protect the garrison, hostilities commenced in earnest. It was, however, a most unpropitious beginning to the Ansár eastern campaign. Attacking from the shelter of a deep khor to the west of the barracks, the rebels managed to breach the newly erected barricades and penetrated as far as the government barracks; but 'Osmán Digna sustained a serious wound and was carried away into the hills, followed swiftly by his demoralised fighters.

A full month later, an emboldened Muhammad Tawfíq was ready to give chase but it rapidly became clear that the rebels were impossible to catch out in the open. The eastern campaign evolved into a succession of hit-and-run raids by 'Osmán Digna's guerrilla fighters, descending from their bases in the Red Sea Hills to harry the government's outposts. The Mahdists were greatly assisted by the appointment of elderly and incompetent officers such as General Suleiman Niyázi, transferred east out of Hicks' way, and General Mahmúd Táhir, sacked as Governor of Kordofan in 1878 but reinstated after a period in disgrace.[31] One of the most striking differences between the eastern and western campaigns was the involvement of the British in the Red Sea region. Egypt's British occupiers, now dictating both domestic and foreign policy, may not have been much interested in the fate of Sudan as such but the stability of Sudanese ports on the Red Sea were vital for the security of vessels entering and leaving the Suez Canal. The issue became of still greater interest to London and Cairo when the British Consul in

Suakin, Commander Lynedoch Moncrieff of the Royal Navy, was killed on 4 November near Tokar during an attempt to lift the siege of the town by 'Osmán Digna's forces.[32] This became known in Ansár circles as the first Battle of the Coast; to the British (owing to a linguistic misunderstanding) it was the first Battle of El-Teb.[33] In response, General Valentine Baker was charged with recruiting 3,600 Egyptian soldiers, now labelled 'gendarmes' although they wore the same uniforms and bore the same weapons as they had before Tel al-Kabír. These men were of no higher standard than the conscripts who had been sent to march and die with General Hicks. One Canadian officer sneeringly labelled them 'a rubbishy lot of worthless ex-soldiers'.[34] Once shipped south to Trinkitat and marched inland during the first week of February 1884, their performance in battle was abysmal. Baker's force of more than 3,600 men was cut to pieces, two thirds of them slaughtered. Baker himself managed to cut his way through the Ansár foot soldiers to Trinkitat.[35] British journalists accompanying the expedition watched in dismay.

There was no sign of discipline or steadiness; it was a mere armed mob tramping along. I was convinced that they would break at the first charge. As the [Ansár] cavalry rode wildly in, the order was given for the infantry to form square – a manoeuvre in which they had been daily drilled for weeks. At this crisis, however, the dull, half-disciplined mass failed to accomplish it. Three sides were formed after a fashion, but on the fourth side two companies of the Alexandria Regiment, seeing the enemy coming on leaping and brandishing their spears, stood like a panic-stricken flock of sheep, and nothing could get them to move into their place.

Into the gap thus left in the square the enemy poured, and at once all became panic and confusion. . . . The miserable Egyptian soldiers refused even to defend themselves, but throwing away their rifles, flung themselves on the ground and grovelled there, screaming for mercy. No mercy was given, the Arab spearmen pouncing upon them and driving their spears through their necks or bodies.[36]

His forces rampaging through the Red Sea Hills, pinning the government garrisons and their British allies down in fewer and fewer bases, 'Osmán Digna fought on to fulfil his master's mission. His was among the most lavish of the Ansár banners, its heavy material stitched with flowing script in thick silver thread. The Qorán's 'Verse of the Throne' – 'Who is there that can intercede in his presence excepts as he allows?' – is regarded by Muslims as particularly valuable because the one who recites it is relieved from dangerous spots. For the Egyptians on the Red Sea coast, its sighting was an omen of despair.[37]

ψ ψ ψ

The southern provinces of Bahr al-Ghazál and Equatoria fell to the Mahdi in a much more straightforward way. Despite the great distance from the centre of government power at Khartoum, the people of Bahr al-Ghazál were close to Jebel Gadír, where the Mahdi had established his first headquarters and which was still the spiritual heart of the rebellion. The provincial Governor, Frank Lupton, was another European, a British appointee of two years' standing and still under thirty at the time of the Mahdist uprising.[38] Lupton's problems had been inherited from his predecessor, Romolo Gessi, one of the most zealous campaigners to end the slave trade. That campaign, spearheaded by first Sir Samuel Baker then Colonel Charles Gordon, had provoked turmoil in the southern provinces, where scattered government garrisons were unable to exercise the kind of control that al-Zubeir had wielded. Al-Zubeir's old headquarters, in the far west of the region, was now used as the provincial capital and was known by various names. Officials labelled it, simply and bureaucratically, *Markaz al-Mudíría*, the 'Centre of Government', but most knew it by the names of its former rulers: Deim al-Zubeir or, for the son killed by Gessi, Deim Suleimán.[39] To reach it, government steamers had to travel for days up the White Nile, passing Fashoda on the right bank and turning into the swampy hinterland to the first important trading post and garrison at Mashra' al-Req.[40] From here, the lines of supply and communication stretched west towards Deim Zubeir and the Bahr al-'Arab, so named because to cross it meant passing into Baggára territory. From these regions of western Bahr al-Ghazál a circle of government-controlled trade routes could be completed by taking tracks north through forest and savannah into south-western Darfur.

Over the previous five years, Governor-General Gordon and Governor Gessi had done their best to undermine the power and influence of the jallába, whose families had migrated down across the lucrative central and southern trading territories, motivating and arming instead the southern tribes, especially the Dinka.[41] Dismayed with their relegation in status and wealth, many influential Danágla and Ja'aliyín figures in the province heard with great pleasure the reports that the Mahdi had been made manifest and was summoning the people to revolution. There was a rush north to Jebel Gadír as the disaffected jallába hastened to pledge their allegiance and stake a claim in what promised to be a new order. In making the hijra, they were joined by several Dinka chiefs, who were impressed by both the Mahdi's religious qualities and his military victories against the Egyptians (even if many southern tribesmen were not convinced that he had a divine right to rule over *them*).[42] The distance they had to travel was far less than Muhammad Ahmad and his followers had achieved during their hijra the previous year, although the difficulties involved traversing many miles of swampy terrain and, of course, the Gazelle River itself. When the masháyikh returned to Bahr al-Ghazál, the Mahdi sent with them loyal ideologues, to read the Mahdi's proclamations to the tribesmen in the scattered communities of Liffi, al-Dembu and Jur Ghattas, to explain his doctrines in detail and to persuade them to embrace jihad.

The first flare-up came on 16 August 1882 at Tel Gowna, the main town in Liffi district near the River of the Arabs.[43] There had been early skirmishes in the spring, in which rebellious tribes had attacked small government contingents. Then, during the early summer and after several months of calm, word came from the north-east of the destruction of the Shalláli force in the Nuba

Mountains. Just a few weeks later, from the north-west this time, reports filtered through of Madibbu 'Ali's uprising among the Rizeigát of south-western Darfur. A tribal chieftain in the Tel Gowna region, Yango, promptly gathered his supporters and slaughtered a small contingent of government troops. Yango was one of the Dinka chiefs who had been used by Romolo Gessi to 'fight with and arrest the Jelabba who were driving slaves' for al-Zubeir. Gessi himself had earlier described a meeting with Yango on an occasion when the chief had survived a counter-raid by the slave-traders and Tel Gowna had been 'liberated from the scourge'. 'The Sheikh Yango received me with all honour,' wrote Gessi, 'dressed in his suit of ceremony, which consisted of a long silk garment richly embroidered with gold . . . like a bishop in pontificals'.[44] But four years was a long time in southern tribal politics and Yango had himself made the pilgrimage to the Mahdi at Jebel Gadír. Now, Lupton gave chase with a substantial force of four detachments of regulars and 600 bazingers but was frustrated by the same heavy seasonal rains that had impeded Brigadier Muhammad Sa'íd's pursuit of the Ansár the previous year. 'The country by this time was overflowed with water and the road was impassable,' wrote Lt-Col Mahmúd 'Abdallah, a government officer involved in the abortive pursuit. Yango had made good his escape, joining Madibbo 'Ali in Darfur. Tel Gowna was deserted. For months, fortunes in the campaign in the west of Bahr al-Ghazál swung to and fro, as Yango received more help from the Rizeigát and as Mahmúd 'Abdallah built up his own force. By the end of the year, two solid government victories had driven the rebels back into southern Darfur, at the cost of hundreds of casualties and still more prisoners.[45] But, after a convincing victory on 28 December, the commander fell ill, his collapse triggered as much by his men's behaviour towards captured camp followers as by illness. 'Our Bazinger soldiers killed many of the children as to leave women of their choice unbothered by the children of other men,' he remembered in later years; 'I was very badly affected to see that and in consequence of this I became sick and had to leave the force in this place'.[46]

The next explosion came in the east of the province in February 1883, when a troop of around sixty bazingers escorting slaves and ivory to Mashra' al-Req was ambushed by Dinka tribesmen and annihilated. Lupton's Egyptian deputy, the Mudír of Deim Suleimán, Lieutenant-Colonel Sá'ti Bey Abú-al-Qásim, led a successful counter-attack but by then the government was struggling to contain an uprising that challenged its limited manpower on many fronts. After a long summer of inconclusive and attritional skirmishes, in which the government army sustained losses it could not afford, the tide of conflict turned in the favour of the Ansár. Their morale high, the rebels attacked government contingents in ever-increasing numbers, so furiously that in one particularly fierce engagement 'they, never caring for the troops' fire, trod upon their dead brothers, picked out the zaríba thorns with their hands and entered inside the zaríba and killed nearly all soldiers and officers. . . . Very few officers escaped and had it not been dark (as the attack was made near sunset) they would have been overtaken and killed.'[47]

When Lupton marched from the capital with all his remaining men to rescue the survivors of that battle, he was shocked and dismayed to see such heavy casualties. But even with this force, 800 regulars and 1,500 bazingers, Lupton was unable to quell even this localised part of the rebellion. After repelling a second attack and inflicting heavy losses, the army was so low on ammunition that Lupton had to order a furtive evacuation, creeping back to base under cover of darkness. On 7 September, he charged Lt-Col Sá'ti Abú-al-Qásim with a difficult and dangerous mission, to travel through rebel-infested territory to Khartoum and return with desperately needed ammunition. The fact that Lt-Col Abú-al-Qásim did not return was one of the turning points of the Bahr al-Ghazál campaign.[48] More significant, though, was the arrival in late November of Karamallah al-Sheikh Muhammad, another prominent Dongláwi who had gone over to the Mahdist cause. Karamallah had travelled to Obeid to meet Muhammad Ahmad and had taken part in the annihilation of the Hicks expedition at Sheikán. Like Muhammad Khálid in the west and

'Osmán Digna in the east, he had been rewarded with the title of amír, in his case of Bahr al-Ghazál.[49] With the last government army destroyed, the Mahdi could now afford to send substantial forces with Karamallah. He allocated 1,500 men from Obeid itself and another 3,500 were recruited by Karamallah en route. Backed by the ever-present propaganda campaign of Mahdist letters and proclamations, the Ansár swallowed up the garrisons of Bahr al-Ghazál one by one. Seven of the eight sub-district administrators, including Hassan Agha at Liffi, were Danágla. News of the Hicks defeat had 'spread terror in the whole Mudirieh' and Lupton was alone in offering more than token resistance.[50] At least – as two British anti-slavery campaigners had discovered while touring the district the previous year – he had a reasonably well-fortified base from which to stand up to Karamallah's forces.

> The stockade of Dem Suleiman is not constructed in the usual manner; trees and logs of wood were sunk into the ground, and were often fifteen or twenty feet high, but the crevices were not filled up. At each corner of the oblong stockade well-built platforms were constructed for cannon, so that all the approaches could be swept by their fire, and rocket-tubes were placed one on each side near the gates.[51]

Unfortunately for Lupton, he had just 1,200 regular army troopers to man those guns, rockets and walls – and all of them openly declared that they would rather surrender than die fighting for the government. As Karamallah closed in, Lupton wrote increasingly desperate letters to his colleague further south, the Governor of Equatoria (just as he himself had received begging letters from Slatin). Dr Emin Pasha was a Muslim convert of German origin, a thin, bespectacled man who spoke fluent Arabic and Turkish as well as a clutch of European languages.[52] Dr Emin had served the Egyptian administration since 1876, originally as chief medical officer then – following promotion by Governor-General Gordon in March 1878 – as Governor of this exceptionally isolated posting. But Dr Emin had no ammunition to spare, having himself received nothing from

Khartoum since 'Abd-al-Qádir Hilmi sent fifteen cases of bullets on 16 March 1883.[53] Lupton's letters make desperate reading.

> The Mahdi's Army is now encamped six hours' march from here. Two dervishes have arrived here and want me to hand over the mudiria to them. I will fight to the last. . . . I will, I hope, from my fort, be able to turn them out again. They will come to you at once if I lose the day, so look out. Perhaps this is my last letter to you. My position is desperate, as my own men have gone over to them in numbers. I am now known by the name of Abdallah. I win the day or die, so goodbye. . . . If steamers come to you, write to my friends and let them know I died game.[54]

Faced with treason among the ranks of his senior officers and Danágla district officials – and the failure of his expedient conversion *à la* Slatin – Lupton swore that he would stand by the guns with his wife Zenuba, a pretty young woman from Shendi, and his young daughter Fánna and fight to the end. If necessary, he told his officers, somewhat hysterically, he would kill both wife and daughter before shooting himself. Finally dissuaded by his subordinates, Lupton agreed to surrender the town to the amír Karamallah. As with all previous conquests, the price of survival was an oath of allegiance to the cause and, on 28 April 1884, Frank Lupton, now known as the amír 'Abdallah, became a prisoner of the Mahdi.[55] As Karamallah paused to consolidate his grip on the province, he wrote to the Mahdi at Obeid asking whether the Danágla who had made the hijra and supported the uprising qualified for compensation from the Beit al-Mál for their financial suffering under the Gessi and Lupton administrations. Muhammad Ahmad assured his amír that money would be forthcoming (upon production of proper paperwork); he also clarified a few points about correct Islamic punishments and spelled out in detail the precise wording of the ba'ya to be administered to all prisoners.[56] The uprising had swallowed up almost the entire southern region. Dr Emin was the only remaining obstacle to victory in the south, committed to holding out 'until help may reach us or until we perish'.[57]

# SIXTEEN

# 'The Place of a Native'
# *Khartoum, London and Cairo,*
# *1883–1884*

By mid-November 1883, the jihad in the south, west and north was going well but the only strategic target that really mattered to the Mahdi was Khartoum itself, seat of the hated 'Turks' and their puppets, the contemptible 'ulamá'. The capital, modernist and secular, was to Muhammad Ahmad the epitome of evil, a haven for the godless, for those who placed the profits of this world above the merits of the next, for the bloated officers and officials from Egypt who filled their bellies and their purses from the sweat of Sudanese, for the despised sanjaks who took the Egyptian's silver in addition to pursuing their own tribal vendettas and skimming their own profits from the working man's tribute. Above all, the continued existence of the town represented a challenge to his own status as the Mahdi. Certainly, not everyone in the town rejected his calling. Many secretly supported him but for various practical reasons had not been able to cast aside their businesses, homes and families and travel, as his da'wa had enjoined, to Jebel Gadír or now to Kordofan. But had he not pledged to pray in the mosque at Khartoum on his way to unifying the Umma across the whole Muslim world? Khartoum must fall, as surely as Cairo, Damascus and Jerusalem must follow, to the forces of rightful Islam. Khartoum had to be destroyed. Surely it was now ripe for the taking. Its mighty army was destroyed; its outposts either already looted and burning or so demoralised as to pose no danger; its administrators rendered rudderless by the death of Governor-General 'Alá-al-Dín Siddíq. A new capital would take its place, from which the people of Sudan could be guided along the stony road to the Mahdi's puritanical perfect state. The staid, sedentary merchants and farmers of the riverain clans would be no harder to tame than the wild and wayward tribes of the outlying provinces. Khartoum must be destroyed! So, just four days after the demolition of the Hicks force, the Mahdi dictated a long letter to his father-in-law, Muhammad al-Tayib ibn al-Basír, who had already served him so loyally in the Jazíra campaigns of 1882–3. Amid the thorn-bushes of Sheikán, Muhammad Ahmad boasted, 'we killed them easily . . . in less than half an hour. Praise God who has cut down the oppressors of the people.' Now, he wrote, it was time to gather the Haláwiyín alongside their allies from the Blue Nile region and push north for the capital. Indeed, the letter suggests, in the Mahdi's habitually censorious tone, there had already been too long a delay.

There have been numerous proclamations from me, exciting and upholding and enforcing jihad as urged by God and his Prophet. As I ordered you to carry on the jihad by besieging Khartoum, you may not depart from this command – for you know that relaxing one's efforts in matters of religion is not permissible. . . . The Qorán is full of passages commanding the jihad and blaming those who abandon it. . . . May your resolution be strengthened and may you obey God and his Prophet!

On the arrival of this letter, rouse up all the Muslims who are with you, join together, rise up and besiege Khartoum. Block the roads to it in all directions. Embarrass the Turks in the city, those infidels, and all who are united with them. Let them see your courage and valour before God, until they listen to Allah's commands or are destroyed as those before them tasted the punishment for their deeds. Their firepower will not avail them as God's command has gone forth. Be zealous in the good fight and there is no doubt that we shall be victorious over them by God.[1]

In Khartoum itself, confirmation of the Hicks disaster, after weeks of rumour and counter-rumour, brought panic. A formal state of emergency was declared. No one was allowed to be in the streets after nine o'clock at night and, in a bid to prevent further demoralisation, anyone heard discussing the disaster in Kordofan was liable to a sound beating or summary imprisonment.[2] Hussein Yusri, a Syrian, was appointed acting Governor-General and Colonel de Coëtlogon, invalided out of the doomed Obeid campaign, assumed interim command of the town's defences.[3] In addition to the garrison itself, these men had in their care as many as 15,000 civilians directly or indirectly connected to the government: Egyptian government employees, wives and children of civilians and soldiers, as well as the Europeans who had made Khartoum their home. Frank Power allowed readers of *The Times* no room to harbour doubt about the gravity of the situation. 'We have . . . only 2,000 men to defend nearly four miles of lines,' he telegraphed on 25 November. 'It is perfectly useless to attempt to hold this place, where the population is a slumbering volcano. The land line of retreat is closed, the river line may be stopped tomorrow.'[4] It was hardly surprising that those who could afford to leave did so. An exodus of foreigners and the well connected poured from Khartoum. Some consolation to the anxious residents came on 26 December, when the Fashoda garrison arrived on a steamer and 30 barges: 2,000 soldiers fleeing their post in the face of insurmountable opposition and inevitable defeat. Others came in from southern stations. Colonel de Coëtlogon, though, wanted more and he wanted out. On 7 January 1884, he telegraphed to the Khedive a strongly worded appeal that orders be sent for the immediate evacuation of the Sennar garrison to Khartoum, to be swiftly followed by the retreat of 'the united Egyptian garrisons' to Berber. As many as a third of the soldiers under his command, he asserted, were quite unreliable; it would be impossible to use them even to suppress the disloyal population of Khartoum, let alone hold the town when the entire surrounding countryside was up in arms.[5]

Cairo continued to stall. The Khedive Tawfíq was determined to salvage part of his southern dominion. Instead of sending soldiers up-river, Tawfíq lamely suggested that local tribes be solicited for assistance. This, as Frank Power observed in a letter home to Ireland, was 'really rich, as the Khedive knows very well that there is not a Sheik in the Soudan who would, or dare, help us; and the fact of our sending to a tribe for help would confess our weakness and bring it down on us like a hundred of bricks'. As if this revelation of political naiveté were not enough, the khedivial message went on to ask whether the garrison had actually closed the town gates. 'As if the place had walls,' scoffed Power; 'it is an open town, with garden, fields, &c., and not a bit of defence round it till Col de C. commenced the ditch, and yet they try to hamper our movements by trying to command us from Cairo'.[6] Nevertheless, there was some good news. The Egyptian government not only offered to pay transport costs for fugitives from the European community in Khartoum who could not afford it themselves, but pledged to the garrison that was *not* permitted to leave to pay all outstanding salary arrears. In the cases of some soldiers who had been in remote postings, these dated back a full eight months. On 16 January, Cairo ordered the garrisons at Sennar, in Bahr al-Ghazál and at Gondokoro in Equatoria to fall back on Khartoum, bringing with them their civil servants, camp followers and any civilians who might wish to flee too. The order, of course, was much too late. Frank Lupton in Bahr al-Ghazál was on the verge of surrender, Dr Emin was beyond contact and Sennar was under tight siege – but would hold out with extraordinary bravery and stoicism until the following October. No more soldiers would come up from the south, either to buttress Khartoum or to pursue their own escape route from the conflict.[7] By 22 January, the capital's garrison stood at 6,100 men. Unless the political decision could be taken to withdraw them swiftly, those men would have to stand, fight and probably die. The Egyptian Ministry of War was certainly pessimistic about their chances. On 11 January, ministry officials had drawn up a statement to the effect that there were '21,866 Egyptian troops [a wildly optimistic figure, given the many reverses of recent months] and 84 guns in the Soudan provinces, between Dongola and Gondokoro'.

The removal of the supplies of ammunition stored at Kassala to Khartoum will require 4,000 camels, or 6,660 if the supplies of war material on the Abyssinian frontier are also to be withdrawn. The report goes on to state that a march from Berber to Wadi Halfa, through the desert, is a physical impossibility, and the homeward journey will therefore have to be made by river. Such a journey would occupy three months, and would require 1,300 boats.[8]

Khartoum was not yet surrounded; the river route to Berber still lay open and the Mahdi had not yet committed his full forces to the capture of the main prize. Escape was still possible – if only someone could be found to take the job in hand.

♆ ♆ ♆

The annihilation of the Hicks mission not only destroyed the Khartoum government's last hope of retaking Kordofan, it also convinced the Gladstone administration in London that Sudan was not worth the outlay in blood or money and certainly not worth risking troops from the British Empire. 'We cannot lend English or Indian troops,' the Foreign Secretary, Lord Granville, wrote to Sir Evelyn Baring in Cairo. 'Do not encourage British officers to volunteer. It would not be for the advantage of Egypt to invite British troops into the Soudan. If consulted, recommend abandonment of the Soudan, *within certain limits*,' the peremptory telegram concluded, somewhat vaguely.[9] The Gladstone government prepared urgent briefing papers, furnishing ministers with arguments to rebut any criticism of its tacit endorsement of the Hicks mission. These arguments sought to pin the blame squarely on the Prime Minister of Egypt, Sharíf Pasha, who 'considered that it was desirable to crush the Mahdi, and not leave him permanently installed at Obeid, and able at any moment to pounce down on Khartoum'. 'Up to the time of the last expedition from Duem,' the briefing paper continued, 'Hicks had defeated the Mahdi in every encounter. Even if Hicks' defeat could have been foreseen, it was not possible to foresee a defeat of so overwhelming a character, followed by such far reaching consequences.' (Colonel Stewart would likely have disagreed.) Ministers were also advised on what to say when it came to defending Britain's new Sudan policy – evacuation.

The arguments here are:
1. That the Soudan could not be held without the assistance of England, and that it is not a British interest to hold the Soudan.
2. That the Egyptian Government is bad, and also a foreign Government.
3. That the cost of the Soudan was one of the causes which ruined the Egyptian Treasury.[10]

The British conclusion that Sudan must be abandoned was as pragmatic as it was self-interested. The bulk of the territory was already aflame or in Ansár hands. Fast-riding Mahdist scouts made sure that news of the Hicks defeat spread rapidly, encouraging rebels where the government had succeeded in holding them down and prompting fresh uprisings to emerge in new areas. In Cairo, the British authorities were no more enthusiastic about involvement than after Tel al-Kabír. Egypt's new political and military masters reflected that they would never be able to focus on reshaping the country's finances, army and civil administration if they had to worry about a campaign to retake and hold the vast territories to the south of what they called 'Egypt proper'. But it was also the unanimous opinion of those commanders and administrators that the fall of Khartoum to the Mahdi's forces (in the words of the new British Agent-General in Egypt, Sir Evelyn Baring, 'a not improbable eventuality') would jeopardise Egypt to the extent that British forces should remain in Egypt at full strength for the time being.[11] But what of Sudan? Given that London would not send British or Indian Army troops to buttress the Khartoum garrison or even to help evacuate it, the only remaining option was to abandon the entire territory. 'Excepting for securing the safe retreat of garrisons still holding their positions in Sudan,' wrote the Foreign Secretary, 'HMG [Her Majesty's Government] cannot agree to increasing the burden on the Egyptian revenues by expenditure for operations which, even if successful, and this is not probable, would be of doubtful advantage to Egypt'.

> HMG recommend the Ministers of the Khedive to come to an early decision to abandon all territory south of Assuan, or, at least, of Wady Halfa. They will be prepared to assist in maintaining order in Egypt Proper, and in defending it, as well as the ports in the Red Sea.[12]

The same telegram also indicated that London would raise no objection to the deployment of Turkish troops, provided that they were paid for by the Sultan in Constantinople and came nowhere near Egypt. But the British knew perfectly well that the Sultan could not afford to fit out and send a force on the scale needed to restore Sudan to Ottoman control. The best he could do was send troops, ammunition and stores down to the Arabian side of the Red Sea to contain any possible spread of Mahdist loyalty.[13] So, as the New Year arrived, Sir Evelyn Baring arranged a brisk audience with Khedive Tawfíq on 6 January to ensure that the puppet leader would toe the line.[14] The Egyptian cabinet of Prime Minister Sharíf Pasha was much harder to convince. The very next day, the ministers resigned en bloc with a sharply worded statement.

> The Queen's Government have demanded that we should abandon Sudan, but we have no right to take that step, since Sudan is a possession of the Ottoman Porte, entrusted to our charge. The Queen's Government state that Egypt should follow their counsels without discussion, but this declaration violates the Organic Rescript of 28th August 1878, which declares that the Khedive governs with, and through his Ministers. We resign our posts because we are prevented from governing in accordance with the constitution.[15]

The ministers' action was entirely correct, in that abandoning Sudan was a direct violation of the rights of the Khedive's own master, the Sultan in Constantinople. Tawfíq's own firman of investiture had specifically stated that 'the Khedive shall not, under any pretext or motive, abandon to others, in whole or in part, the privileges accorded to Egypt, and which are emanations of the rights and natural prerogatives of my imperial government, nor shall he abandon any part of the territory'.[16] But Sultan Abdülhamit was left to fulminate in vain; his proxy Tawfíq had become the proxy of the British.

Many thousands of words have been written about Colonel Charles Gordon, the man picked to identify the best way of extracting the Egyptian garrisons marooned in Sudan, whose impetuous but usually honourable actions in the field led, ultimately, to long-term British involvement in exactly the country they had hoped to avoid. All the major decisions leading to Gordon's appointment were taken in less than three weeks of January 1884. Throughout those hectic days of deliberation, answers to the crucial central questions – what might be done to salvage a respectable exit strategy and should the man in charge be simply an adviser or should he be entrusted with executive powers – became increasingly blurred. From the perspective of the Gladstone government, the logic was straightforward enough. Colonel Gordon was a man of great personal experience in Sudan; the policy of abandonment had already been decided upon; so who better to recommend a method of evacuation? One potential snag foreseen by the British government was that it would be difficult to disown or reject any advice presented by its new envoy that did not match its own desired outcome. Better, then, to maintain an arm's-length relationship. 'Must we not be very careful in any instruction we give', wrote Gladstone to Lord Granville on 16 January, 'that he does not sight the centre of gravity as to political and military responsibility for that country? In brief, if he reports what should be done, he should not be the judge who should do it, nor ought he to commit us on that point by advice officially given.' It seems extraordinary that these hopes were expressed just a week after a crucial newspaper article in which Gordon had set out his own opinions on the Sudan question. Interviewed by the editor of the *Pall Mall Gazette*, Gordon had suggested that Cairo should appoint a new Governor-General with full powers to 'relieve the garrisons and quell the revolt'. During this landmark interview, Gordon made a prescient declaration.

> You have 6,000 men in Khartoum. What are you going to do with them? You have garrisons in Darfur, in Bahr Gazelle, and Gondokoro. Are they to be sacrificed? . . . How will you move your 6,000 men from Khartoum – to say nothing of other places – and all the Europeans in that city, through the desert to Wadi Halfa? Where are you going to get the camels to take them away? Will the Mahdi supply them? . . . Whatever you may decide about evacuation, you cannot evacuate, because your army cannot be moved. You must either surrender absolutely to the Mahdi, or defend Khartoum at all hazards. The latter is the only course which ought to be entertained. There is no serious difficulty about it.[17]

The *Gazette* itself heartily concurred and spearheaded a press campaign supporting 'Chinese Gordon for Sudan', quickly whipping up support among the public and parliamentarians for the appointment. The *Gazette*'s front-page editorial called for Gordon to be sent 'with full powers to Khartoum, to assume absolute control for the territory, to treat with the Mahdi, to relieve the garrisons, and to do what he can to save what can be saved from the wreck in the Soudan'.[18] It already seemed unlikely that this man would take to heart the politically expedient priorities of his masters as ardently as they hoped.

Even if the various strands of debate had been resolved unequivocally and early – the question of Gordon's advisory or executive authority, the question of retreat or reinforcement, the question of whether the British or Egyptian government should have oversight of the mission – there were important drawbacks to Gordon's appointment itself. He was touted as an expert on Sudan, but his experiences and knowledge were in reality far out of date. He grossly underestimated the religious quality of the Mahdi's uprising against the 'Turks', even if he sympathised with the grievances of the ordinary people against their corrupt Egyptian and Ottoman administrators and was 'proud of their prowess'.[19] The areas where he had had particular expertise, the south and west, had already fallen or were as good as lost. Nor was Gordon as universally beloved by Sudanese people, supposedly for his eradication of the slave trade, as his supporters in the press and parliament argued. In fact, the jallába, who had profited most from the trade and many of whom had had their businesses destroyed, still remembered him with loathing. Most had gone over to the Mahdi with enthusiasm. The southern bazinger troops who had served him so loyally in Equatoria had either been killed in the succession of government defeats since August 1881 or had been conscripted into the Mahdi's own army. A few hundred still resisted with Dr Emin, but too far away to be of any use. The Baggára of Kordofan, too, had found a charismatic new leader who might be more severe on looting than they had hoped but had certainly freed them from the tiresome tributes, taxes and other depredations of the Ottoman authorities and their despised sanjaks. Another problem was that Gordon spoke little more than a smattering of colloquial and wholly grammar-free Arabic. He dealt with the Khedive and other Egyptian court officials in French and, for the rest, had to depend on translators. Then there was Gordon's personality. Here was a man well known for acting on whim and intuition rather than on hard facts or logical deductions, notorious for his quick temper and rapid personal judgements and famous as much for the tenacity with which he clung to his beliefs as for the rapidity with which those beliefs changed. To take on the Sudanese assignment, he had to renege on a commitment to serve King Leopold of Belgium in the Congo, a vast territory whose colonial administrators needed 'a person of merit, rank and devotion' to help them.[20] 'The contradictions in his disposition . . . render him an enigma even to his intimate friends,' wrote one colleague, while another officer who had worked with Gordon in Equatoria was even more damning.

> At times he is condescending, affable, and cordial; again, he storms at everybody, is rough, crusty, and unapproachable. His plans are changed even during their execution, and his actions only proceed in a straight line when carried along by his enthusiasm.[21]

Finally, his loyalty to government had to be regarded as temporary at best. Gladstone and his colleagues would have done well to scan more closely Gordon's own earlier reflections on the priorities of a European entering service with a foreign government.

> As to his *façon d'agir* [behaviour], I maintain the foreigner should, for the time, actively abandon his relations with his native land: he should resist his own Government, and those of other powers, and keep intact the sovereignty of the Oriental state whose bread he eats; he should put himself into the place of a native when he has to advise the Sultan, Ameer or Khedive.[22]

After a hasty departure from England, his influential friends hustling around the gentlemen's clubs to scrounge 300 pounds in gold coins as travelling money for the departing emissary, Gordon fizzed with impatience on the long train and boat journey south.[23] As he travelled south, he peppered London with telegrams, proposing radical and often contradictory solutions to the crisis into which he was stepping.[24] 'The Soudan is a useless possession,' he wrote to a friend, seized by melancholy and pessimism aboard the steamer *Tanjore* between Brindisi and Port Said; 'ever was so, and ever will be so. No one who has ever lived in the Soudan can escape the reflection, what a useless possession is this land.'[25]

Gordon's stopover in Cairo in late January 1884 was not initially planned. He had hoped to go directly by sea to Suakin, still a bastion of British-supported Egyptian authority, surrounded by the Hadendawa forces of 'Osmán Digna, and thence to Khartoum. He was, after all, far from assured of a hearty welcome in the Egyptian capital. He despised Khedive Tawfíq as a stooge whose appointment had ended his own earlier stint as Governor-General in Khartoum; this was a grievance nursed for five long years. Among resident British officials, too, Sir Evelyn Baring had resolutely opposed Gordon's reinstatement as Governor-General. In private, Baring was profoundly anxious that Gordon's mercurial personality made him a risky prospect, though he diplomatically restricted his public arguments to the sensible assertion that putting a Christian in command in Khartoum at a time when the momentum behind an Islamic revolution was well-nigh unstoppable was hardly the most effective way of securing the continuing support of those tribes that continued to oppose the Mahdi. Now, Gordon's final instructions from Lord Granville at the Foreign Office in London dictated that he was to report to the British Agent in Cairo and, in a splendidly vague rider that opened the door to unlimited unforeseen possibilities, 'perform such other duties as may be entrusted to him by the Egyptian Government through Sir Evelyn Baring'.[26] Baring had been horrified by Gordon's comments to the *Pall Mall Gazette* on 9 January and hoped at this late stage to hammer into Gordon's head the basic principle of withdrawing Sudan garrisons with as little loss of life as possible. Baring had been receiving increasingly desperate telegrams from his agent in Khartoum, Frank Power, correspondent for *The Times* and, since 14 December, Baring's appointee as honorary British Consul. Irrepressibly self-satisfied and enjoying a comfortable life in General Hicks' luxurious quarters in the Saráya, Power wrote home to Ireland of his conviction that Gordon's mission to evacuate Sudan garrisons would be premised on his own wise counsel. 'It was solely on my confidential, and I hope conscientious, reports England has recognised the fact that the holding of Khartoum is *bosh*,' he wrote; 'I believe when Gordon comes he will sit upon me for this; but I have facts on my side'.[27]

So Gordon in Cairo was a man who felt himself among, if not exactly enemies, certainly not supporters. Nevertheless, with the exception of a few minor incidents of defiance and rudeness (such as his petulant refusal to dress for dinner at the residence of his host, General Sir Evelyn Wood, who had been delegated to travel to Port Said and 'induce him to go up the Nile after paying his respects to His Highness the Khedive') the formalities passed off smoothly enough.[28] During an audience with the Khedive Tawfíq, Gordon secured his second formal appointment as Governor-General of Sudan. 'Tewfik gave me the Firman on the same sofa as Ismail gave me [the] same Firman as Gnr. Gnl,' Gordon wrote to a young army protégé that evening; 'I was as civil as I could be to Tewfik'.[29] But there was also a second firman, to be kept secret for the time being, which set out a twofold mission: Evacuate the Egyptian soldiers, officials and families and oversee the establishment of some kind of purely Sudanese governing structure, using traditional rulers and tribal elders, that might continue to administer those parts of the country not yet seized by the Mahdi. This last element was an initiative from the British in Cairo and yet another embellishment of Gladstone's basic advisory mission.

You are aware that the object of your arrival here and of your mission to the Soudan is to carry into execution the evacuation of those territories, and to withdraw our troops, civil officials, and such of those inhabitants, together with their belongings, as may wish to leave for Egypt. We trust that your Excellency will adopt the most effective measures for the accomplishment of your mission in this respect, and that, after completing the evacuation, you will take the necessary steps for establishing an organised Government in the different provinces of the Soudan, for the maintenance of order, and the cessation of all disasters and incitement to revolt.[30]

There were two other important meetings, the first with Cairo's movers and shakers: Baring himself, the Sirdar Sir Evelyn Wood, his ADC General Reginald Wingate and the new Egyptian Prime Minister, Nubar Pasha Boghos.[31] After discussing key elements of the mission, including an initial budget of 100,000 Egyptian

pounds, the assembled dignitaries agreed to reconvene the next day
with the man who had dominated Gordon's waking thoughts
during his earlier attachment in Sudan: Zubeir Rahmatallah
Mansúr. Zubeir had been helping the British in Egypt enrol new
recruits for the ongoing attempts to counter 'Osmán Digna's
uprising in the Suakin region. Just four days before the meeting
with Gordon on 26 January, Zubeir had returned from Suez,
where he had been supervising the embarkation of those reluctant
recruits for their Red Sea passage. Indeed, Zubeir had been hoping
to take ship for Suakin himself. There had been many in Cairo
who believed that he would be a much more plausible candidate
than Gordon to assume the position of a Governor-General
specifically charged with confronting the Mahdi. He was a
Muslim, a member of the influential and widespread Ja'aliyín
tribe, a man who still commanded a considerable following in the
south and centre of Sudan and a man who had attracted the
attention of Muhammad Ahmad's own lieutenant, the Khalífa
'Abdulláhi, as a possible Mahdi. But those in Cairo who advocated
the Zubeir solution underestimated the power of the anti-slavery
lobby in Britain. No sooner had the idea been mooted in London
than the Anti-Slavery Society mounted a demonstration, on 4
December 1883, to denounce his possible employment in
Khartoum. The politicians were immediately cowed. In one
communication with Cairo, Lord Granville simply said that to
promote Zubeir was 'inexpedient', though this was a diplomatic
way of obscuring the reality that the Gladstone government was
simply too weak to force the issue in the House of Commons.[32]

The Cairo meeting at Sir Evelyn Wood's house, where Gordon
was staying, began with an ugly row, sparked by Zubeir's trenchant
airing of his many grievances against Gordon. His son, Suleimán,
had been killed by Romolo Gessi in Bahr al-Ghazál, his own
property had been plundered or confiscated at Gordon's personal
orders after a court martial in 1879 and he was now massively in
debt.[33] Yet, despite this often furious and always tense exchange, the
two men emerged with greater mutual respect. Only days earlier,
Gordon had advocated Zubeir's constant surveillance 'by a

The Governor's Cottage in Cyprus, where Zubeir Rahma was exiled by the British. (The Graphic, *27 July 1885*)

European to prevent his sending emissaries or letters to Soudan' and his exile to Cyprus.[34] Now he determined to push for Zubeir's immediate return to Khartoum, where he would form a new government.[35] 'All the followers of the Mahdi would, I believe, leave the Mahdi on Zebeyr's approach,' he wrote to Baring; 'for the Mahdi's chiefs are the ex-chiefs of Zebeyr'. But Gordon was wrong about Zubeir. Charged with sending messages to Khartoum in later months, Zubeir instead directed his messengers to the Mahdi at Obeid. His betrayal, once discovered, was rewarded by immediate exile to Cyprus.[36]

His unexpected meetings concluded, his ambitions greatly modified from the original outlines of a non-binding report, Gordon caught the train south on 26 January 1884 to continue his long journey, 'precious tired of long wearisome talks'.[37] He had exactly one year to live.

As a deliberate counter-balance to Gordon's mercurial personality, Colonel Stewart, the intelligent and, above all, steady officer whose impressive and meticulously researched report had done so much to inform serious debate on the Sudanese question, was sent as aide-de-camp. Also in the party was Ibrahím Fawzi Pasha, a former Governor of Equatoria who had been reprieved during Gordon's earlier tenure at the Saráya from a death sentence for administrative misconduct. Fawzi had been languishing in Cairo since the failure of the 'Arábi revolution, which he had served as Chief of Police in the capital. He may have been *persona non grata* in Cairo but Gordon, to his credit, was often ready to give an officer a second chance.[38] But even these two experienced campaigners could not restrain Gordon from making up for his forced inactivity on the long journey south by river and rail, via Korosko and Abú-Hamed, by firing off more telegrams and letters.[39] To Baring, Gordon wrote so many and such mutually contradictory messages that the Agent in Cairo passed them on to London with the caveat that 'his general ideas are excellent, but that undue importance should not be attached to his words'! Gordon again demanded the presence of Zubeir, 'this remarkable man'.[40] And to the Mahdi himself, Gordon dictated and had translated an extraordinary offer, one that revealed the extent to which he failed to understand Muhammad Ahmad. In his capacity as Wáli of Sudan, Gordon conferred upon the Mahdi the position of Sultan of Kordofan and requested a face-to-face meeting to discuss various issues, including the war, the release of Christian prisoners, the reconstruction of the destroyed telegraph network and the reopening of a secure pilgrimage route from Darfur to the Red Sea coast. 'Know, respected sir, that that I would like to be in your presence on terms of the utmost affection and cordiality,' Gordon concluded. 'My intentions are nothing but good.' In a package with the letter went a scarlet cloak and a tarboush – perhaps, besides the hated kourbash, the most readily identifiable symbol of Ottoman occupation.[41]

Two days after this demonstration of colossal misjudgement, Gordon committed a worse blunder, graver because he had himself anticipated how seriously it would be taken. In his interview with the *Pall Mall Gazette*, he had commented on 'the impolicy of announcing our intention to evacuate Khartoum'. 'The moment it is known we have given up the game,' he had told the paper, 'every man will go over to the Mahdi. All men worship the rising sun.'[42] Yet, on his arrival at Berber, one of the very few remaining garrisons held by the government, the new Governor-General made the drastic error of revealing the secret khedivial firman to the local governor, Hussein Pasha Khalífa, as well as the town's leading officials, merchants and 'ulamá'.[43] These loyalists were, of course, utterly dismayed that they would, all too soon, be abandoned to their fate. It was only to be expected that those who had risked everything to stand against the Mahdi and those who yet remained undecided now asked themselves what they might have to gain by supporting another foreign Pasha who was planning to abandon them anyway.

# SEVENTEEN

# *The Siege of Khartoum*
# *Khartoum, 1884*

The Mahdi reacted with stern dignity to Gordon's letter offering him the Sultanate of Kordofan. Had his enemies so misunderstood him that they thought that he could be bought off with a meaningless title, granted rights over a territory that he already controlled? What kind of man could make such a peremptory offer, tantamount to an order, when he came backed by no army, just a small contingent of officers and civil servants? Muhammad Ahmad certainly knew of Charles Gordon, even if he had never moved in his circles, and he respected him, a Christian, more than his Egyptian or Ottoman predecessors. To a Muslim of the Mahdi's thinking, a Christian of equal commitment deserved the respect that he could not accord to the less-than-perfect Muslims he was pledged to overthrow, even if, as a Christian, a personal friendship was impossible. So Muhammad Ahmad embarked on a long campaign, pursued over nearly ten months, to persuade Gordon to return home with honour rather than waste his life in the defence of the indefensible. The Mahdi's reply to Gordon's letter, like that addressed to General Shalláli in the wilds of the Nuba Mountains two years earlier, was a point-by-point rebuttal of what Muhammad Ahmad saw as basic misunderstandings inherent in the British officer's argument. It began with the very pointed description of Gordon as 'the *'Azíz* of Britain and the Khedive', a point probably lost on the Governor-General but which likened him to the senior court official in ancient

222

Egypt who had purchased and adopted Joseph. The 'Azíz was doubtless a kind and just figure but in the service of an unjust administration.[1] 'What are *you*', the Mahdi was asking Gordon, 'doing serving *these* people?'

I wrote to the Hikimdária at Khartoum from Jazíra Aba about my call to the truth and about my Mahdía being from God and his messenger. I am not a trickster, nor do I aspire to seats of power, to money or prestige. I am a servant of God; I value humility and hate pride, the boasting of sultans and their deviation from the truth, driven by their love of prestige, power and dynasties. . . .

How can it be that one who does not follow the path of the Prophet wishes to open the way to visit his grave? Purify yourself, firstly by entering his faith then by showing mercy to God's creatures by following his path . . . for God says:

'Oh you who believe, take not Jews or Christians to be your friends and protectors. They are only friends and protectors to each other. He among you who turns to them is like them. In truth, God does not guide an unjust people. Your only real friends are Allah, his messenger and the community of believers, those who pray and give to charity regularly and bow humbly in worship.'[2] . . .

So turn your back on your non-Muslim faith and turn instead to Allah and his messenger, looking forward to the life hereafter, and then I will take you as my friend and brother . . . You should know that the *Hizballah*, the party of God, can reach and remove the spurious power with which you claim sovereignty over God's worshippers and his land. . . . As for the Christians and those who have converted to Islam whom you have asked me to release, I desire for them – as I desire for you and all God's creatures – the right course, piety and the benefits of the eternal abode.

I am the Expected Mahdi and I do not boast! I am the successor of God's Prophet and have no need of any sultanate, of Kordofan or anywhere else. . . .

For now, as your intentions are good, I hope God will reward you and guide you to the right path. As I have explained, I have no desire for the pleasures or ornaments of this life, so I return them to you, together with the kind of attire that we desire for ourselves and our companions who seek the after-life. . . . Let me repeat what Suleimán said to [the ambassadors sent by] Bilqís.[3]

'Would you give me wealth in abundance? What God had given me is better than what he has given you. Indeed, it is you that rejoices in your gift. Return and be sure that we shall come with such armies as they may never hope to meet. We shall expel them in disgrace and they will feel humbled.'[4]

If you surrender to me, I will educate you and show you a light to give serenity to your heart and take away your greed for the trappings of this life. Then, if I see improvement and piety in you, I shall award *you* a rank, as I did with Muhammad Khálid Zogal, the former Mudír of Dara.[5]

PS. Enclosed is the dress of ascetics and men of true happiness, who reject lustful desires in their pursuit of high ideals – a jibba, an under-shirt, trousers, a turban, a straw skull-cap, a belt and prayer-beads. Revert to Allah and seek what he offers and you will not find it hard to wear these clothes![6]

The multitude of fighters, supporters, camp followers and prisoners surrounding the Mahdi had by now forced him to move his headquarters out of Obeid itself, south-east towards the more plentiful water supply that had eluded Hicks. The meagre wells of Obeid, barely enough to sustain the town as an effective provincial capital under the old order, were nowhere near enough to keep the Ansár hordes alive. Water was more readily available from the pools and khayrán around Birka and Rahad. It was at Rahad that Rudolf Slatin met Muhammad Ahmad, in the middle of a camp that was 'a perfect sea of straw huts, or tokuls, stretching as far as the eye could reach'. The settlement became known as *Buqá' al-Mahdi*, 'the Mahdi's resting-place'.[7] Muhammad Ahmad's own quarters consisted of 'several large straw huts fenced off by a thorn zariba'.[8] Swelling the enormous camp, new recruits poured in from the Jazíra and from Berber in the north. Chief Adam Umm Dabbalu, too, finally came down from the Nuba Mountains with 'all the notables of Jabal Tagali in submission and obedience'.[9] Adam must have known that, after resisting the Mahdi's call for so long and after daring to ambush and capture Muhammad Ahmad's wives and children, he was in real trouble. Sure enough, when Fr Joseph Ohrwalder saw the chief at Rahad, he was 'mounted on a mule, and his feet heavily chained'.[10]

A market was opened and provisions were cheap. Various Arab tribes . . . streamed hither with their flocks and herds, and soon the camp extended greatly. Sherif Mahmud, whom the Mahdi had left behind in El Obeid, was instructed to send all the people on from there.[11] The Mahdi set up his abode between two large trees, and the Khalifas lived around him. . . . At prayer-time thousands upon thousands of Dervishes ranged themselves in well-ordered lines behind the Mahdi, and the shout of 'Allahu Akbar' resounded through the air. Often the singers of the Mahdi's praises would go on till long after midnight, and thus did he continue to inspire his gigantic audience.[12]

At Rahad, Muhammad Ahmad waited, receiving reports from his umará' in the various theatres of conflict, and watched, as his army grew still more immense. From this base, his most senior generals – Muhammad 'Osmán Abú-Girja, 'Abd-al-Rahmán wad al-Nujúmi and Hamdán Abú-Anja – were appointed to oversee the siege and capture of Khartoum, a reward for their loyal and consistently high-quality service over the previous years. First, though, they had other missions to accomplish. Abú-Girja was despatched to quell the persistent irritation caused by Salih al-Mak, the Shaigi commander in the Jazíra who had succeeded in delaying Muhammad al-Tayib al-Basír and his followers from advancing on Khartoum from the south. Abú-Girja was kept busy with this campaign until the end of March, finally forcing Salih al-Mak's surrender near Massalamía. As for al-Nujúmi and Abú-Anja, they were charged with the final subjugation of the Nuba Mountains, especially Jebel Dayír; this was a protracted campaign that would keep them out of the action around the capital until the early autumn of 1884.[13]

☙ ☙ ☙

In Khartoum itself, Gordon arrived on 18 February 1884 to find the town isolated but not yet under siege. He and Stewart had been ferried up from Berber on the *Ismailia*, escorted by the *Abbas*. Their arrival at the dock in front of the Saráya was greeted by a thunderous artillery salute from Omdurman Fort and the cheers of Khartoum's garrison commanders, merchants and excited townspeople. At a ceremony in the Residence, the firman from the Khedive that confirmed his reappointment (not the one that spoke of abandonment) was read out in public. When Gordon himself spoke, his anxiety to assuage the concerns of his audience prompted him to preface his remarks with a barefaced lie. His words were later recalled in an official report by a committee of eight officers and officials under the chairmanship of Muhammad Nushi Pasha, who would witness the siege and capture of Khartoum.

This Firman which you have just heard is to appoint me as Governor-General of the Soudan, to examine its difficult state and to beg of God almighty to help us all, and to guide us to the right way of reform. I would have been able to bring with me a large number of troops but my confidence in you, and my previous good conduct in the Soudan, which I do not think you will deny, have made me content with the troops which are here.[14]

He went on to promise a clean sheet for anyone who owed back-taxes; from 1884 onwards, he added, taxes would be cut by 50 per cent.[15] The ledgers and registers containing names and records would be torched, as would the whips and bastinado rods with which the taxes were customarily gathered. Most importantly, renewed ownership and trading of slaves would be permitted. 'I know that the hardship which opposition to the slave traffic has caused you is very great,' he told his astonished audience. 'Today I desire you to recommence with perfect freedom the traffic in slaves, and I have given orders that public criers shall make this known to all, that they may dispose of their domestics as they may see proper, and no one in the future shall interfere with the commerce.'[16] This announcement may have been a pragmatic and decisive measure to win over the population of Khartoum but it caused a storm in Europe. The implacable enemy of slavery, allowing it to carry on under his very nose! Coming so soon after Gordon's public championing of Zubeir as the salvation of Sudan, it badly damaged Gordon's credibility, with consequent adverse effects on the support base that may have called more resoundingly for his rescue.

Determined to set his own stamp on the town's administration, Gordon immediately set about appointing senior officials. To oversee the day-to-day running of Khartoum, he decided to summon 'Awad al-Karím Abú-Sinn, the Shukría chief who had supported Giegler's Jazíra campaign in 1882, to be Mudír.[17] But the Dár Shukría was overrun by Mahdist fighters and Abú-Sinn was far from convinced that Gordon had the charisma or the resources to challenge the Mahdi. When he declined to come to Khartoum, Gordon had to settle for 'Ali Músa Bey, a former Governor of Bahr al-Ghazál.[18] The Governor-General then established parallel civil and military committees to administer justice from the Mudíría, a substantial brick-built complex on the riverbank immediately to the west of the Saráya. Among the civilian notables were Sheikh al-Amín al-Darír, the head of the Khartoum 'ulamá', and Sheikh 'Abd-al-Gádir, the Qádi of Kalakla village to the south of Khartoum. To preside over the six-man Court Martial, meanwhile, Gordon picked Colonel Faraj Muhammad al-Zeini, a distinguished Egyptian army officer with more than thirty years' experience.[19] Gordon then turned to the question of how best to deploy fewer than 9,000 men – regulars, bashi-bazouks, other militiamen and volunteers – along nearly fifteen miles of mostly rudimentary ditch-and-rampart fortifications.[20] In anticipation of an Ansár attack from the west, the garrison at Omdurman Fort was reinforced. A proper hospital for Egyptian troops was opened and the town's stores searched and thoroughly inventoried. There was found to be plenty of durra, rice and hard biscuit, though next to no wheat. Plenty of Remingtons and ammunition had been stored in their packing cases, alongside even larger quantities of unusable shells and bullets for the antiquated firearms that still lurked in the darker corners of the store.[21] Gordon also continued the work of shepherding Europeans, as well as Egyptian soldiers and civilians, out of the city and downstream to safety in Egypt, where a special unit of local infantry were seconded to refugee reception duties. 'These poor wretches . . . had lost everything they had got in the world,' wrote one observer; 'an enormous number of people passed through . . . before Khartoum having become thoroughly invested, no more could leave, and all further escape was impossible'.[22] Gordon and his senior colleagues then turned their attention to the town's defences, begun in the days of 'Abd-al-Qádir Hilmi and since embellished by subsequent administrations. Frank Power described the latest refinements.

> We have paved the bottom of the ditch and side of the fortification with spear-heads and have for 100 yards the ground in front strewn with iron 'crows' feet', things that have three short spikes up however they are thrown, and then beyond, for 500 yards, broken bottles (you know the Mahdi's men are all in their bare feet); at intervals we have put tin biscuit-boxes full of powder, nails and bullets, at two feet under ground, with electric wires to them, so Messieurs the rebels will have a *mauvais quart d'heure* before they get to the ditch.[23]

The Mahdi's firm but dignified rejection of his offer of the Sultanate of Darfur and request for the liberation of the Christian prisoners angered Gordon. And when he opened the parcel brought by his messengers on 22 March, containing Muhammad Ahmad's counter-offer of the battered jibba, straw skullcap and other accoutrements, he was furious. Any man with a sense of humour might have muttered a wry 'Touché'. The dour and frustrated Gordon, however, kicked the gift across his well-appointed room on the upper floor of the Residence, before dictating a terse reply to the man he labelled a pretender, a *Mutamahdi*. 'I have received your pallidly styled and meaningless letter, which shows your evil designs and the wickedness in your heart,' he wrote.

> Very soon you will be tested by armies beyond your abilities. You will be the one who has to account to God for the bloodshed. It is you who are responsible for all those whom you have misguided, whose children you have orphaned and whose homes you have destroyed. There was no requirement for me to address an ungrateful, dishonest man like you but I was clinging to the hope that God would reveal your ambitions to be degenerate and that you would accept the sultanate.
>
> I am ready for you. I have men here with me who will cut off your breath.[34]

Pinned to this grumpy riposte, Gordon sent a copy of another fatwa from the 'ulamá' of Khartoum rehearsing all the orthodox legal reasons for the rejection of Muhammad Ahmad's claim to be the true Mahdi.

☙ ☙ ☙

The beginning of the siege of Khartoum – a bitter 320-day imprisonment for the inhabitants, garrison and commander-in-chief – came an hour after sunrise on 13 March 1884. Sheikh Muhammad Badr al-'Ubeid, a leading faqí in the Blue Nile region, had moved up the east bank of the river from al-Ailafún with as many as 30,000 men. With this advance force came Muhammad wad al-Basír, the Mahdi's brother-in-law, rallying the Haláwiyín, and Sheikh Mustafa al-Amín, heading up the west flank to besiege the government fort at Omdurman. Sheikh al-'Ubeid had in 1882 been peripherally involved in the clashes between the Halawiyín and the Shaigi commander Salih Pasha al-Mak.[25] Now, with an advance contingent of about 5,000 Ansár, he had manoeuvred around the capital's eastern and northern outposts and engaged the government garrison of 500 Shaigía bashi-bazouks stationed at Halfáya, on the east bank of the river a few miles downstream from Khartoum, to prevent the steamer-route to Berber from being cut off. Sheikh al-'Ubeid's sudden appearance on the scene caused a great deal of bewilderment in Khartoum. Both Gordon and Stewart were confused by the similarity of the sheikh's name and that of the Kordofan capital, Obeid, and for a while were perplexed by the town's 'wandering' into the vicinity of the capital.[26] This first encounter was brutal and protracted; eventually, giving up the fight as lost after a five-hour battle, half the government soldiers retreated and fought their way back to the river crossing. Their colleagues who had brought their families with them to the Halfáya outpost were compelled to surrender, with wives and children, to the gleeful Mahdists. Gordon, watching the first of many defeats and failed sorties by telescope from the roof of the Residence, swiftly sent steamers to retrieve the remnants of the garrison before they could be slaughtered on the sandy riverbank.

Gordon's attempt to retake Halfáya on 16 March was an unmitigated disaster, caused by the unexpected treachery of two leading officers, Generals Hassan Ibráhím Shalláli and Sa'íd Hussein al-Jimi'ábi.[27] The report of Muhammad Nushi's committee subsequently described a series of events so perfidious that the subsequent trial and execution of the two Egyptian officers for treason was inevitable. At first the sortie was a great success, the rebels driven back by the 4,000-strong government relief force, advancing in square formation with artillery support. The renegade officers first tried to sabotage the mission by ordering their own guns to cease firing. When the artillery lieutenant refused, Hassan Shalláli beheaded him with his own sabre. When the bugler, too, refused to blow the retreat, Sa'íd al-Jimi'ábi cut *his* head off. Driving the men back against their will, the two generals succeeded in turning certain victory into defeat, with the loss of artillery, camels, ammunition and water supplies. Their treachery was clearly prearranged; both officers reportedly held their tarboushes in their mouths so as to be readily identifiable in the mêlée of battle.[28] Neither, however, managed to escape to the Mahdist forces and both were tried by Gordon's Court Martial, found guilty of treason and shot.

After this first series of skirmishes involving minor Ansár commanders, the arrival of Muhammad 'Osmán Abú-Girja in April signalled the beginning of a serious reorganisation of the Mahdist forces.[29] The campaign against Salih al-Mak and his sanjaks in the Jazíra had not taken long. Having bravely sworn that they would 'prefer to be transferred from the backs of their horses to the bottom of their tombs', the Shaigía militiamen had tossed their weapons and ammunition into the river before wisely surrendering in the face of vast opposition. Now, around Khartoum, Abú-Girja commanded all the various junior umará' who were already deployed: Muhammad al-Tayib al-Basír, positioned to the south of al-Jireif village outside Khartoum, and Sheikh al-'Ubeid to the north. They had their own divisional flags but all were brought together under one command banner.[30] In his capacity as Ansár Commander of the River District, Abú-Girja wrote to Gordon to give him another chance to surrender and save the lives of his garrison. But the new commander's first engagements, launched from camps at Jireif and Burri, resulted in complete failure. A bashi-bazouk officer, 'Abdallah Agha Muhammad, succinctly described the first four-day skirmish: 'We fought them on land and from the steamers on the river . . . until we killed most of them and routed them. We made booty of their weapons, ammunition, rockets, grain, possessions and so forth and burnt their camp.'[31] Worse was to follow during the summer. On 27 July, Gordon launched a well-organised counter-attack from Burri Fort.[32] Four armoured steamers – the *Bordein*, *Tel el Hoween*, *El Mansureh* and *Abbas* – moved upstream, providing cover for a substantial force of 800 regulars and Shaigía militiamen who advanced in squares along the riverbank. With the steamers standing to off the heaviest concentrations of Ansár fighters, laying heavy covering fire with cannon, rockets and massed rifles, the land force was able to make ground swiftly. The brief expedition caused huge losses among Abú-Girja's forces. The amír's own brothers, Nasr and Mustafa, were among the many dead. Colonel Muhammad

'Ali Hussein, responsible for Gordon's first successful counter-strike, was promoted to Brigadier.[33] A swift follow-up sortie to the north drove Sheikh al-'Ubeid's men back from Halfáya, a second success that brought more supplies of food into the town and granted some respite during the hottest summer months. Less successful was a steamer expedition led by Lt-Col Sá'ti Abú-al-Qásim to quell Ansár activity and steal grain at Gateina up the White Nile. Sá'ti Bey, who had survived the perilous journey from Frank Lupton's headquarters in Bahr al-Ghazál but had been trapped inside the ring of siege, was killed along with all his men. Frank Power was withering in his scorn for the Egyptian troops who were so inadequate to the task.

> One Arab horseman is enough to put 200 of our men to flight. The day Saati Bey was killed 8 men with spears charged 200 of our men armed with Remingtons. The soldiers fled at once leaving Saati and his Vakeel to be killed.[34] A black officer cut down 3 of the Arabs and the other five chased our men. A horseman coming up rode thro' the flying mass cutting down seven. Col Stewart, who was unarmed, got off by a fluke, the Arabs not having seen him. With such men as these we can do nothing.[35]

Despite this minor victory, the heavier defeat inflicted by Gordon's amphibious sortie compelled Abú-Girja to retreat up-river to Wad Shukralla to lick his wounds and compose a letter reporting the larger setbacks to his senior general, 'Abd-al-Rahmán wad al-Nujúmi. When he in turn promptly passed on the dismal news to the Mahdi at Rahad, the response was uncharacteristically sympathetic, even gentle. Instead of berating Abú-Girja for incurring such heavy losses, Muhammad Ahmad, who had himself lost all three brothers in military engagements, offered his consolations. 'Do not grieve at what has happened,' he wrote; 'when God wishes to single out the bad from the good, he places the bad upon the bad and piles it up together, and thrusts it all at last within our grasp'.[36]

Ansár reinforcements were not long in coming. After subduing the last recalcitrant elements at Jebel Dayír in the Nuba Mountains, 'Abd-al-Rahmán al-Nujúmi and Hamdán Abú-Anja left Rahad on 25 June. Their march was stately enough; the army did not rendezvous with Abú-Girja's men until late August and even then they remained well away from the guns of Khartoum for another month.[37] Then al-Nujúmi, appointed by the Mahdi to be the *amír umará'*, overall Commander-in-Chief, made his dispositions. After his reverse at Halfáya, Sheikh al-'Ubeid had fallen back with his forces on the 'fly-infested' village of Umm Dubbán but was still able to secure a hold on the northern bank of the Blue Nile, opposite Gordon's Residence; here he was supported by divisions under the flags of 'Abdallah wad Jubára and Abú-Bakr wad 'Amr. 'Abdallah al-Núr, an 'Arakiyín tribal chief and veteran of the Kordofan campaign, was stationed just to the east of Burri Fort.[38] 'Abd-al-Gádir Mudarra watched the gates at Báb Massallamía, on the south-east corner of the town, while al-Nujúmi himself made camp at al-Gúz, facing Kalakla Gate and guarding the southern flank. Abú-Girja's men now returned to take up positions on the White Nile. Khartoum was completely surrounded by rebel encampments and hastily dug trenches and parapets. Most were within rifle range of the government garrison. All were well within range of Gordon's Krupp artillery. One account described how the besieging Ansár forces near Burri Fort were so close that they could 'see the glow of the enemy's cigarettes and hear their conversation'. They could only leave their trenches to get water at night, for fear of being fired upon from government positions.[39] So dangerous was it at Burri, with armoured government steamers making forays up-river and shells exploding around them, that the Ansár camp was labelled *Dár al-Akhira*, the 'Last Home' before paradise.[40]

# EIGHTEEN

# 'The Torture of Defeat'
## Khartoum, 1884

The arrival of 'Abd-al-Rahmán al-Nujúmi and Hamdán Abú-Anja in support of Muhammad 'Osmán Abú-Girja and Sheikh al-'Ubeid put an end to Gordon's last chance of evacuating Khartoum. Stripped of obfuscations and digressions, that had been his specific responsibility. With the Ansár beaten back around Khartoum and with the Nile waters rising abnormally early, the early summer of 1884 was his final opportunity for escape. Had he taken the decision to leave, it is likely that a great number of his still substantial garrison and their families could have made the arduous journey to safety – either north to Berber or south-east to the Abyssinian frontier. Well armed and supported by the small flotilla of gunboats, such a force would very likely have been able to fight its way through to freedom. It would have been difficult, it would have been terrifying but it would have been possible. Those who were forced to remain would inevitably have been compelled to surrender and pledge allegiance to the Mahdi and his cause. But at least they would have lived. The Mahdi was a man of his word and did not habitually massacre either soldiers or civilians who yielded to him. Muhammad Ahmad's seizure of Khartoum would not have been averted but the slaughter of so many in the town would.

Instead, Gordon resolved to stay and fight.[1] Despite all the evidence to the contrary, including the repeated declarations by the Gladstone administration's most senior figures, the Governor-General refused to accept that London would not send a relief force. In April, he wrote to Baring in Cairo, who had passed on London's latest refusal to send a British force. 'I do not see the fun of being caught here to walk about the streets for years as a dervish with sandaled feet; not that, D.V., I will ever be taken alive.[2] It would be the climax of meanness, after I had borrowed money from the people here . . . to go and abandon them . . . and I feel sure that, whatever you may feel diplomatically, I have your support – and that of any man professing himself a gentleman – in private.'[3] By June, in the hopes that some kind of expedition was already afoot, he smuggled out a terse message via the government garrison at Dongola. 'Khartoum and Sanaar in perfect security,' he wrote. 'Give [the messenger] all the news as to the direction of the relieving force and their numbers. As far as Khartoum, there are in it 8,000 men and the Nile is rising rapidly.'[4] Much later in the year, as the siege reached its most intense levels, the Governor-General would write even more unequivocally. 'I want to get out of the affair, but with decency. . . . Put yourself in my position if you say "*rapid retreat, and leave Senaar to its fate*". I will say, "*No, I would sooner die first*", and will resign my commission, for I could not do it.'[5] That stubbornness or bravery resulted in his complete isolation before the end of May. 'Osmán Digna and his Hadendawa roamed the east, cutting the direct land route to the Red Sea. Muhammad Ahmad's new armies, hurrying forward from Rahad, cut off the western and southern approaches. And the final escape route to the north – the way Gordon had come in – was cut off in mid-May when the Mahdi's former teacher, Muhammad 'al-Kheir' 'Abdallah Khojáli, succeeded in capturing Berber, the vital junction between the Nile and the desert road from the Red Sea. Since leaving Obeid on 31 March, Muhammad al-Kheir had progressed north via al-Metamma, Shendi and al-Damer, cutting the government telegraph line en route and gathering tribesmen loyal to the al-Majdhúb clan, which had been softened up by repeated letters from the Mahdi.[6] Faced with siege, the Governor of Berber, Hussein Khalífa, ordered the garrison to dig still deeper trenches and to reinforce its gun emplacements.[7] It took time, but the end came as surely as it had at Obeid, Fasher and so many other garrison towns.

Following the tradition established by his former pupil and current master, Muhammad al-Kheir unleashed the Ansár in the early hours of Monday, 18 May.[8] Storming the trenches, they penetrated the town rapidly. The Governor and some of his Jihádía survived, bringing with them an immense treasury of more than 60,000 pounds, but in a repeat of earlier incidents, the victory became an opportunity to settle tribal scores and the Majádhib slaughtered as many 'Abábda as they could lay their hands on.[9]

Penned inside the town during the long, hot summer, Gordon took increasingly desperate measures to preserve an illusion of normality. He ordered the military band at the Saráya to put on public concerts of cheerful music every Friday and Sunday after sunset. When Ramadan arrived at the end of June, he persuaded the 'ulamá' to issue a ruling that fasting was not obligatory in time of war. The people and garrison may have already been effectively fasting, such were the shortages, but to stand guard in a Khartoum summer without drinking was unbearable torture. Money was becoming ever scarcer; those who had it were hoarding it. To boost morale among the soldiers, he had special 'Siege of Khartoum' medals struck and awarded to those who showed particular gallantry.[10] When the officers of the 1st Battalion complained that their uniforms were getting too shabby, Gordon distributed the spare uniforms left behind by the officers of the Hicks expedition. Gordon ordered 50,000 Egyptian pounds' worth of new banknotes to be printed; this enabled him to pay the arrears for the soldiers who had come in from Kordofan, Darfur and Bahr al-Ghazál.[11] Above all, the Governor-General sought to preserve the illusion that rescue was imminent. 'Yesterday,' he would announce, untruthfully, 'I received a mail in which I am informed that 30,000 English soldiers are coming via Dongola to relieve us; also 30,000 are coming via Taka . . . Besides, 30,000 Turkish soldiers are coming from Suakin via Berber, also 30,000 men under the leadership of Mohd. Osman El Mirghani who is coming via Rifa'a.'[12]

All the time, the Mahdi's generals were sending him letters pointing out the futility of his resistance and urging surrender. 'Do not let disinformation and fancy talk dissuade you from taking my advice,' wrote Ilyás Umm Bireir that summer. 'Otherwise, be sure that you will perish. Allah will make you taste the torture of defeat at the hands of the Mahdi in this life and the defeat of torture in the life hereafter. You will fall into humiliation and your punishment will be most severe. Learn the lessons of those who perished before you!'[13] And from the Mahdi himself – relayed by his commanders, 'Abd-al-Rahmán al-Nujúmi and 'Abdallah al-Núr – Gordon received a stark warning of the Ansár's commitment to the jihad.

> Time has now been prolonged, and he has become aware of your firm resolve not to obey and submit. He has now appointed us . . . and he has supplied us with trusty men from among his companions – men who love death as you love life, and who count, in fighting you, on the great reward. Death is dearer to them than their wives or the very best of their possessions . . . The desire of the Mahdi is for your good. . . . Notwithstanding all this you have remained stubborn, and turned your back to counsel in your greed for transitory power, from which you must soon be removed.[14]

Gordon also had to contend with counter-propaganda from within. Among the most articulate was written by Ahmad al-Awwám al-Husseini, an Egyptian clerk who had served as a secretary in Colonel 'Arábi's Ministry of War.[15] Exiled to Khartoum after the overthrow of 'Arábi's revolution, Awwám transferred his loyalties to the Mahdi. In July, at the height of the siege, he published a long treatise in praise of the Mahdía as a struggle for the cause of Islam against a government that had betrayed the Umma. The polemic was disarmingly titled 'Awwám's Advice to the Educated and Common People'. Stating that the war had so far lasted 'in blazing flame' for three years and three days (since the first skirmish at Jazíra Aba), Awwám railed against the 'Turkish–Egyptian government that has turned this country to ruin and sacrificed souls by kindling the flames of war and thundering her rifle-shots among her subjects, the true believers'.[16] He accused Sultan Abdülhamit II in Constantinople and the Khedive Tawfíq in

Cairo of committing 'an awful crime and an indelible sin' in renouncing Sudan to the British – and accused Gordon himself of turning 'so many hypocrites to his own ends, including the chief of Sudanese 'ulamá', that blind man . . . who endeavoured most energetically to belie Mahdism by sending letters and advice to all Sudanese'.[17]

Ahmad Awwám also demanded, rhetorically, to know why the 'ulamá' in Egypt who had endorsed the 'Arábi revolution would not ratify Muhammad Ahmad's rebellion. Was it not, after all, against the same khedivial administration, buttressed by Europeans and exercising its rule in even more oppressive ways? Awwám specifically questioned the fatwa passed the previous November by the 'ulamá' of al-Azhar in response to a legal question from Governor-General 'Alá-al-Dín Siddíq. What, the Hikimdár had asked, was the opinion of the 'ulamá' about a man who had 'declared disobedience against the Emir of the Believers, the Sultan of the Muslims, who had declared himself Imam and Khalífa, who had fought the armies of the Khedive and killed Muslims . . . pretending that the Prophet Muhammad appeared to him in vision, telling him that he was the Awaited Mahdi'?[18] Appended to the question as evidence was the Mahdi's proclamation of 18 May 1883 to the people of Suakin, in which Muhammad Ahmad had set out his claim to a prophetic mandate and supremacy over even the Sultan in Constantinople. The fatwa from al-Azhar had been brief and unequivocal. The 'ulamá' could not forgive such flagrant opposition to their own spiritual and temporal commander in Constantinople. 'He whose actions are as described should be denied and fought until he finds a path back from his ignorance.'[19]

Awwám denounced the ruling as politically expedient and 'feeble'.[20] He was a dangerous personality to have spreading pro-Mahdist propaganda inside a besieged city where morale was already low but, astonishingly, he was employed as a translator by Colonel Stewart and the Governor-General himself. Translating his ideological beliefs into disruptive action, Awwám lost no time in sabotaging not just Gordon's correspondence by mistranslating and fabricating letters but also the town's main arsenal. On 29 September, someone tried to set fire to the ammunition supply; Ahmad al-Awwám was arrested and, under pressure from a delegation of Khartoum dignitaries, a reluctant Gordon had the intriguer hanged.[21]

As well as Gordon's increasingly desperate attempts to browbeat, cajole or shame London into sending reinforcements, the 'ulamá' in Khartoum had tried too. In August, they sent a telegram to the Khedive, thanking him for sending Gordon, who had 'bestowed all kinds of favours and . . . brought order out of chaos'. More importantly at the time of writing, the Governor-General had just beaten back the most serious offensive yet by Muhammad 'Osmán Abú-Girja at Burri and Khartoum still felt 'fortified like an impregnable rock'. But reading between the lines of this ostensibly obedient and optimistic note, the subtext was clear and the 'ulamá' concluded by begging Tawfíq to 'remove our present disturbances'. The letter took a full month to arrive in Cairo; Tawfíq's response of 21 September – addressed not just to the 'ulamá' but to the Qádi, as well as Khartoum's military officers and civilian administrators – was far from reassuring.

> We regret the condition you are in by reason of the impossibility of sending reinforcements and help up till now on account of circumstances. But we are very glad because you are still safe, and the city is kept by your energy and bravery. God willing, reinforcements will soon reach you, and you shall be rewarded. We hope you will exercise all diligence in upholding the honour of the Government. The difficulties are being overcome and the time of relief is at hand by the grace of God.[22]

With the telegraph lines cut on all sides, the only way in which Gordon could make contact with Cairo and London was through hand-delivered messages. Given enough time, local messengers could make their way through enemy territory but what more credible messenger could there be, when it came to convincing his reluctant superiors that reinforcements must be sent to Khartoum, than Colonel Stewart? Gordon resolved to send his trusted deputy downstream, to run the gauntlet of Mahdist guns and rifles through hundreds of miles of rebel-held territory, to Dongola and freedom in Egypt. Stewart would travel on the *Abbas*, the smallest steamer whose shallow draft would maximise the chances of getting through the Nile's troublesome cataracts. Stewart left Khartoum on 10 September, bearing an immeasurably valuable collection of papers, effectively the history of the siege thus far, chronicling every aspect of the life of the city since Gordon's arrival, every emotional twist and mercurial turn in the Governor-General's own strategic thinking. These, Gordon believed, would prove to Baring and thus to Gladstone's reluctant cabinet that the military relief of Khartoum was the only way that its inhabitants could be brought out alive. With Colonel Stewart travelled Frank Power, the honorary British Consul, whose instructions since January had been 'to leave . . . as soon as he considers it dangerous to remain'.[23] Also on the *Abbas* were the French Consul, Monsieur H. Herbin, and nineteen Greek merchants similarly fleeing Khartoum.[24] Against all odds, they managed to pass through the fusillades of Ansár bullets, spears and shells at Berber – only to run aground in shallow water between Abú-Hamed and Merowe. Stewart's poignant last letter to Gordon was written shortly before Berber, after 'several vicissitudes' during the first four days of the journey. He described how the *Abbas* and her escort ships, the *Safia* and the *El Mansureh*, had been fired upon at Metamma, at Shendi and all points between. With the exception of isolated Shaigía villages, he wrote, 'we found both banks of the river openly hostile'. En route, they had stopped to destroy *ságiya* water wheels, damaging the local farmers' livelihoods and profiting from the rough timber for fuel for the steamers. The letter concluded with a movingly humble expression of loyalty to a man that Stewart must have believed he was leaving to his death.

You may depend upon it that I shall do everything in my power to assist you. Thanking you for the very great kindness with which you have over-looked my short-comings, and praying that

the blessing of the Almighty may abide with you,
I remain, my dear General,
Yours very truly, D.H. Stewart[25]

For his part, Monsieur Herbin contributed a short note expressing his own gratitude to Gordon for securing his escape from Khartoum. 'I will never forget', he wrote, 'the charming welcome that the Consul of France found at the "O Komudar"'.[26] Within days, Stewart, Power and Herbin were all dead. Their vessels aground, they were lured by Manásír tribesmen and slaughtered at Wadi Gamr. Gordon's last messages would never reach London; on the contrary, they would be carried straight to the Mahdi, along with his 'Cypher O' codebooks.[27]

☙ ☙ ☙

As the autumnal rainy season drew to a close, the Mahdi's reinforcements continued to gather in immense numbers at Rahad, his field headquarters forty miles south of Obeid. Muhammad Ahmad was conducting a campaign on many fronts but his information on the latest developments was sketchy at best. By way of updates, he told his followers of continuing visitations by the Prophet that spoke of victory achieved and victory to come. Unfortunately, these prophetic advisories were not always accurate. On Friday 22 May, for example, the Mahdi said he had been told that Sennar was been penetrated by rebel forces from the west and had fallen; at the same time, he said, a 'great army of light' was advancing to destroy advancing British forces north of Dongola. Neither claim was true.[28] But now his chance for a truly sweeping victory had come. On his orders, the army now split into three parts, travelling along different routes to envelop Omdurman and Khartoum, facing each other across the river, in a blanket attack from the west. The war-drums were beaten and the great horn blown and the massed armies began to move, their banners fluttering in the hot breeze. Those tribes with desert experience and sturdy camel transport headed north, via Khursi, Helba and

Tur'a al-Khudra. Most of the Baggára clans opted for the familiar southern route, tracing the steps of the Hicks expedition in reverse, along the now plentiful watercourses to the White Nile. The entourage of the Mahdi and his three khulafá', surrounded by more than 300 mulázimín bodyguards and the standard-bearers of his leading umará', followed the most direct path, via Tayára, Abú-Rukba, Shat and Dueim.[29] Those who could find and afford it rode, on camel, horse, mule or ox; those who could not walked. The Mahdi himself walked until his feet blistered; after that, he took to his fine camel, his feet resting on the shoulders of a bodyguard on each side of the beast. Even divided in three, such a vast army on the move – tens of thousands of Ansár fighters accompanied by families and slaves – was like a swarm of locusts. Apart from driving a huge herd of several thousand cattle, they lived off the land, as the Mahdi had specifically ordered them not to bother about food rations; God would feed those whose intentions were pure and whose sincerity was genuine as they went along, he said. As well as snaring wild guinea fowl on the march, the Ansár felt free to help themselves at roadside homes along the way. Anyone who was not on the march, they argued, must be a backslider from the jihad and therefore an enemy of the Mahdi. The army was also welcomed at improvised markets by jallába selling cheap meat, dates, salt and onions. Nomad tribesmen of the Hamr Baggára helped find water on night expeditions. But to arrive late at a watering hole was to face a muddy green swamp where a multitude of men and animals had drunk, washed and made their toilet. When the weary and half-starved soldiers finally reached the Nile at Dueim, those from Kordofan and further west who had never seen a river, let alone the majestic Nile, clustered in their thousands on the bank to watch the birds and crocodiles. When two government paddle-steamers, the *Bordein* and the *Husseinieh*, hove into view, sent by Gordon to reconnoitre the movements of the Ansár, the Baggára (who had never seen such a machine before) dived in and tried to hold it back with their bare hands; the gigantic paddles trod several underwater, drowning them in the river they had struggled so hard to reach.[30]

The journey took many weeks; the longest of several rest stops came late, at Tur'a al-Khudra, when the Mahdi paused for several days to celebrate the 'Eid al-Adha.[31] Among his baggage, strapped to the back of a sturdy camel, was a robust wooden *minbar*, a portable pulpit on which the imam could elevate himself above the masses at prayer. 'At the Feast of Bairam', recalled Slatin, who had been brought with the army as a prisoner, 'the Mahdi repeated prayers in an unusually loud voice, and when he read the "Khutba" he wept long and bitterly.[32] . . . It had the desired effect on the fanatical crowds who had flocked to his banners from the river tribes, and who were roused by this touching sermon to the highest pitch of enthusiasm.'[33] Three weeks later, on the first day of the Muslim New Year, Muhammad Ahmad's vast force moved into sight of Omdurman, camping at Abú-Sa'ad.[34] The arrival of 60,000 Ansár reinforcements made the outcome of the siege inevitable, boosting the morale of the besiegers, a crushing blow to the besieged.

Shortly before his arrival at Omdurman, Muhammad Ahmad had written again to Gordon from Kawa, near his old home of Jazíra Aba. The tone of the letter was one of unconcealed satisfaction; it must have made for excruciating reading. The Mahdi confirmed Gordon's worst fears: The *Abbas* had been captured near Berber; Stewart, Power and Herbin were all dead; and all Gordon's communications with Cairo and London had fallen into rebel hands. Even mourning the loss of his friend and colleagues must have been overshadowed by Gordon's terrible realisation that his entire strategy was laid bare in comprehensive detail, any doubts clarified by the code books that were in the package too. This was a huge coup for the Mahdi. 'We never miss any of your news,' he gloated, 'nor what is in your innermost thoughts and about the strength and support – not of God – on which you rely. We have now understood it all.' Muhammad Ahmad knew exactly how much food and ammunition Khartoum had in stock. He knew the deployments, the armaments, even the ammunition supplies of General Faraj al-Zeini's battalions in the five forts surrounding the town, as well as those deployed on each of the armoured steamers. He knew the names and ranks of all the capital's leading 'ulamá', merchants, officers and bureaucrats. He knew of the special siege medals struck by Gordon. He knew of the Governor-General's desire to see Zubeir installed as ruler in Khartoum. Above all, Muhammad Ahmad now knew for certain that Gordon had been sent to oversee the abandonment of Sudan, had turned his back on that mission and had himself been abandoned by Cairo and London. The package of papers that Stewart had been charged to carry safely to Egypt proved to be, in the Mahdi's possession, a more lethal weapon than anything in Gordon's own arsenal. After listing his enormous scoop in crushing detail, the Mahdi concluded by repeating his stick-and-carrot formula.

> As to your expecting reinforcements, reliance for succour on others than God will bring you nothing but destruction. . . . Nevertheless, if you become a Muslim and surrender to God's order and that of his Prophet and believe in me as the Mahdi, send me a message, after laying down your arms and giving up all thought of fighting, so that I may send you safe conduct . . . If not, you will have to face war from Allah and his messenger.[35]

The serried ranks of the Ansár, under the banners of Hamdán Abú-Anja and the Khalífa 'Abdulláhi, thronged around Omdurman Fort, digging deep trenches and throwing up earth ramparts.[36] As well as sniping from government troops in the fort, the Mahdists had to beware of artillery shells from Gordon's guns at the fort on the Moghran, a spit of land on the east side of the White Nile at its junction with the Blue. On 18 November, the Mahdi wrote a personal letter to the fort commander, Brigadier Farajallah Rághib, one of the highest-ranking Sudanese soldiers serving Governor-General Gordon. Farajallah had served at Fashoda garrison during the 1870s and had known and respected Muhammad Ahmad during his years at Jazíra Aba, before his manifestation as the Mahdi.[37] 'Do not think', the letter read, 'that if you surrender we will come for your property or possessions. On the contrary, you will be promoted and stand among the ranks of our beloved companions. I believe my warnings have already reached you; there is no need to elaborate – still, you should know that whoever disbelieves in me will be tormented in this world and the next. . . . You yourself have witnessed my victories when I was still weak, with few men. Now I have the weapons and ammunition of Ráshid Bey, of al-Shalláli, of Hicks and the garrisons of Darfur and Bahr al-Ghazál!'[38]

For Brigadier Farajallah and his 240 subordinates inside Omdurman Fort, the evidence of incessant fire from the captured Krupp artillery pieces, Nordenfeldt machine-guns and Remington rifles in the Ansár trenches during the next several weeks was ample proof of the Mahdi's claim. Despite his best efforts, Gordon was unable to maintain a supply line for reinforcements, ammunition or food. There was no bridge across the river, communication was reduced to flag signals and any steamer that tried to cross came under constant bombardment. On 5 January 1885, Omdurman negotiated a dignified surrender to Hamdán Abú-Anja. The Mahdi (still based at Abú-Sa'ad) kept his promise to the fort commander; Farajallah Rághib adopted the jibba and turban and became an amír. Muhammad Ahmad now had possession of the entire west bank; his fighters, troops released from their siege positions around Omdurman, went to join their colleagues who were subjecting Khartoum itself to constant fire from long-range guns positioned at all points of the compass.

On the east side of the town, Ansár under the banners of 'Abdulláhi wad al-Núr, a Mahdist agent from Kordofan, faced frequent sorties from Burri Fort and Massallamía Gate. Wad al-Núr himself, according to his followers, demonstrated personal bravery to the point of 'boiling and foaming as though possessed, and we attacked the enemy until they fell back before us towards their fortifications'.[39] Each attack from Burri village was met by a counter-attack from Burri Fort and vice versa. The government had the advantage of their steamers, launching sorties by land and water, while the Ansár had the greater advantages of more artillery, more men, unlimited time and the freedom to come and go from the front line almost at will. One contemporary description of the siege indicated that the number of Ansár around Khartoum fluctuated as the months passed, 'sinking sometimes to seven or eight thousand, and again rising to forty and fifty thousand, according to the seasons and the requirements of agricultural pursuits, as no impediment was ever placed in the way of their going off, sometimes for weeks together – the fellaheen to look after their crops and harvests, the Bedouins to graze their camels, and their flocks and herds'.[40] So the Mahdi could keep his men resupplied from the surrounding countryside but, inside Khartoum, both soldiers and civilians were dying of malnutrition. Gordon kept the best of his supplies for his garrison, obsessively monitoring his dwindling stocks of durra and wheat, but as a fighting force the men were dangerously weakened. Khartoum was a tiny island in a sea of Mahdist rebels.

ψ ψ ψ

Almost from the day that Gordon had travelled to Khartoum, the army men in Cairo and London had been pestering the politicians to endorse a support expedition. General Sir Evelyn Wood wrote to Gordon in April that he 'would give anything to be allowed to go up . . . by river with British and Egyptian troops when the Nile rises, but I fear I may not be so fortunate as to get the chance'.[41] Lord Wolseley – ennobled by a grateful government for the victory at Tel al-Kabír – was back in London as Adjutant-General, charged with reshaping and modernising the entire British Army and 'in the habit', as he put it later, 'of framing military projects for the consideration of Ministers'.[42] He, too, was anxious to get military action in Sudan underway. With considerable prescience, he wrote to Lord Hartington at the War Office recommending immediate preparations for an exclusively British expedition to Khartoum. 'This feeling that something should be done, like a rolling snowball, will go on increasing until the Government will be forced to adopt measures to save the Khartoum garrison,' he observed, 'but if nothing is done that place will be besieged, and we shall be, in my humble opinion, faced with a war on a large scale'.[43] Frank Power's despatches to *The Times* came as a regular reminder of the difficulties facing the residents of Khartoum. 'We are daily expecting British troops,' he wrote on 1 April. 'We cannot bring ourselves to believe that we are to be abandoned by the Government.'[44] The *Pall Mall Gazette*, which had championed Gordon's original mission, now lamented that the Gladstone government was prepared to 'let Gordon be speared with the garrisons he was meant to save!'

One option was to force a way through from the Red Sea via Berber. But the Egyptians and their British allies were finding it impossible to make any headway against 'Osmán Digna's guerrilla forces, who had not only staged damaging hit-and-run raids but had proven themselves more than competent to meet government troops in set-piece battles. The period of February and March 1884 was, however, effectively the first phase of Britain's first Sudan campaign, in which greater efforts and more troops were invested and the name of Suakin became almost as familiar to readers of English newspapers as Khartoum. The rout and destruction of Valentine Baker's expedition on 4 February and the consequent seizure of both Tokar and Sinkát by the Mahdists prompted the despatch of General Sir Gerald Graham at the head of a force of more than 3,000 men, all British Army.[45]

> Our government then resolved to send troops to Suakin for a serious contest against Osman Digna, one of our main objects being to counteract the evil effect, on the minds of Mohammedan subjects in India, of repeated defeats inflicted by Arabs, not indeed upon British forces, but on armies led by British officers. The rumour was arising in the bazaars of the East that the arms of Britain were being beaten from our hands by soldiers fighting under the banner of Islam.[46]

Graham's initial brief was for punitive action and revenge was indeed achieved on 29 February. Advancing from Trinkitat over ground still covered with the rotting, vulture-pecked remains of Baker's Egyptian conscripts and any equipment that 'Osmán Digna's men had not managed to haul off the field of victory, Graham inflicted heavy losses on the Mahdists on the same battlefield. A 6,000-strong Ansár force – Hadendawa, Arteiga and other clans under the banners of the generals 'Abdallah Hasid and 'Osmán Digna's nephew, Madani 'Ali – had taken up well-prepared positions in and around 'El Teb' village. They had at least six artillery pieces and their riflemen were well protected in deep trenches and foxholes. But after several hours of intense fighting, the Mahdist were forced to withdraw, leaving 2,100 dead and as many wounded.[47] General Graham had lost only 34 killed and 155 wounded. An apparently spontaneous decision to execute wounded Ansár fighters was prompted by the suicidal bravery of the Hadendawa and was only inadvertently revealed to the public back in Britain when an artist for the *Illustrated London News* sent home a sketch of the battle which included a note for the Fleet Street engravers: 'Shooting wounded Rebels in the trenches'.[48] Returning to Suakin, Graham sent the motley crew of Egyptian survivors home, beefed up the resident garrison and established a solidly British base of operations that would resist all Mahdist attempts to capture it.

General Graham achieved a second victory on 13 March at al-Tamainaib, this time against a larger force of around 10,000 Ansár under 'Osmán Digna's cousin, Mahsúd Músa.[49] But the Hadendawa continued to show their fierce determination, breaching one of the British squares before being driven back and off the battlefield.[50] Despite inflicting these reverses on the Mahdi's eastern front, however, General Graham was never given the reinforcements that might have enabled him to move forward and consolidate advanced positions in the huge territory between these coastal villages and Berber. On 28 March, he was ordered to sail for Egypt, leaving two British battalions to maintain the security of the Suakin garrison. There would be no relief of Khartoum from the Red Sea.[51]

As spring dragged into summer, Gladstone continued to examine, with little enthusiasm, the various proposals put forward by the military for a relief expedition. Despite increasingly strident public opinion, mobilised by the press in support of the isolated Gordon, he stalled any revision of his hands-off policy. It was not until the end of July that his hand was forced by Lord Hartington at the War Office. Agreeing with Wolseley's angry insistence that an expedition had to be sent and soon, Hartington threatened to resign from the cabinet. 'It is a question of personal honour and good faith,' he told his colleagues.[52] On 5 August, the Prime Minister told the House of Commons that he would be ready to approve funding to the tune of £300,000 for 'operations for the relief of General Gordon should they become necessary'. The resulting expeditionary force (effectively phase two of Britain's first Sudan campaign) placed 10,500 British troops, from Britain, Egypt, India and elsewhere, under the command of General Wolseley. Having champed at the bit since the spring, Lord Wolseley put his plans swiftly into action, rushing to Egypt on 9 September and, hurriedly but efficiently, assembling his main force at Wadi Halfa on Egypt's southern border. Wolseley was set on the Nile route from the beginning, having mounted two successful river campaigns earlier in his career. In 1870, he had transported 1,400 men over 600 gruelling miles through the Canadian wilderness along the turbulent Red River to prevent the USA gaining control of Canadian territory. Later, in 1874, Wolseley had navigated the Volta during the second Ashanti War, when Britain faced rebellion in what was then the Gold Coast of West Africa. Now, Wolseley ensured that his own preference would be chosen over the alternative – a railway from the Egyptian border directly to Abú-Hamed, proposed in a secret memorandum – by the simple expedient of forming an evaluating committee and staffing it with three Red River veterans loyal to him.[53] His tactics, however, were a variation on the advice already given by Sudan veteran, Sir Samuel Baker, who had proposed a force of 9,000 men, to be carried south in a substantial flotilla of 30 steamers, 10 steam launches and as many as 100 well-built Egyptian sailing boats.[54]

With General Wood in command of the line of communications and supply, the army beat its way up-river, using brute force to negotiate the cataracts of enormous black boulders stretching fully eighty miles south of Wadi Halfa.[55] Local labourers were commandeered for the job of pulling the steamers against the strong current through the narrow channels, as many as 6,000 'darkies' being available to pull on the steel hawsers.[56] Wolseley, again remembering his Red River campaign into the wilds of

Manitoba, had decided to use shallow-draft whaling boats. He even hired 386 Canadian *voyageurs*, expert watermen mostly from the lumber industry, to help navigate the Nile's turbulent waters (despite the ridicule of London papers like the *Army and Navy Gazette*, which denounced 'that monstrous armada of boats, that unfloatable flotilla for the Nile').[57] To motivate his troops, he offered a prize of £100 to the first battalion to reach Korti with the smallest loss of supplies.[58]

It was a desperate race against time, the generals frustrated by the dearth of accurate information on the situation inside Khartoum but certain that the garrison's food and ammunition must be running out. By the time spies and messengers made their way through Ansár-held territory to Dongola – one of a handful of settlements still in government hands – secret messages were often weeks or months out of date.[59] Delays in receiving accurate news were compounded by mistakes made in Khartoum during the encoding process, making the numerical sequences undecipherable.[60] Most frustrating for Wolseley, Gordon's decision to entrust his 'Cypher O' codebook to Stewart meant that he could no longer interpret Wolseley's messages. Wolseley (who noted in his diary 'that any man could have been so idiotic is to me a puzzle') was forced to invent complicated new ciphers based on rules set out in his *Soldier's Pocket-Book for Field Service*.[61] In one, the key to a transposition code was the name of Gordon's maternal grandfather (Samuel); in another, the key to transposition was an equation, $A^2 \times B^2 + C$, in which A represented the number of guns in the Battery of the Right Attack on Gordon's Hill at Sebastopol; B was the day of the month when Gordon himself was born; and C was the number of letters in the surname of the General who commanded at Shanghai in 1862 when Gordon was in China. Wolseley concluded: 'I don't believe the Mahdi with all his powers of divination, not anyone but a well-educated Englishman could have made much out of such a puzzle.'[62]

As for Gordon himself, he had learned that a rescue mission was at last afoot on 18 September, a fortnight after Stewart's departure. A message had been smuggled through from Major Herbert

Kitchener at Debba, listing the generals steering the campaign under Wolseley's overall command and relaying news from the British Chargé d'Affaires in Cairo, Edwin Egerton.[63] 'Tell Gordon steamers are being passed over second cataract, and that we wish to be informed through Dongola exactly when he expects to be in difficulties as to provisions and ammunition.' When would he expect to be in difficulties? To Gordon on his lonely rooftop, knowing the rescue effort could not possibly cut through rebel-held territory before his 'difficulties' were ended yet pointing his telescope ever north for a glimpse of a British flag, this must have seemed a tragicomic message. As he wrote in his diary that evening, 'It is as if a man on the bank, having seen his friend in [the] river already bobbed down two or three times, hails, "I say, old fellow, let us know when we are to throw you the life buoy".'[64] Nevertheless, on 27 September he sent Muhammad Nushi with the *Tel el Hoween*, the *Safia* and the *El Mansureh* to fight through to Metamma and wait for Wolseley.[65] He could not have guessed that they would have to wait four full months.

Through October and November, Wolseley's Nile Expedition picked its way up-river, making painfully slow progress. Below Dongola, the entire territory was rife with marauding squads of Mahdist fighters. To follow the river from Wolseley's new camp at Korti would mean tracing the long stretch to the east before turning south again at Abú-Hamed, a route that included three more cataracts. So the General resolved to split his force, sending a River Column under Major-General William Earle the long way round with the steamers and whalers, while simultaneously pushing a Desert Column of just over 1,000 men south-east across the Bayúda Desert to Metamma. It was 200 miles of open country, mostly featureless wastes, flat and sandy, pockmarked with small, craggy hills; en route were two significant wells, at Jakdúl and Abú-Tulayh.[66] Under General Sir Herbert Stewart, advance units of the Desert Column moved out on camel-back from Korti on 30 December.[67] Progressing rapidly across the wilderness, Stewart established another staging post at Jakdúl oasis, bringing forward another 2,000 men.[68] By 14 January 1885, Stewart was again moving forward at a brisk pace; unimpeded, he would have reached Metamma. But the Ansár were waiting in large numbers at Abú-Tulayh and a fight could not be avoided.

The new master of Berber, Muhammad al-Kheir 'Abdallah al-Khojáli, had learned swiftly of the British troops moving in his direction. After sending a report to the Mahdi (who was still at Abú-Sa'ad, south of Omdurman) and receiving his instructions, the amír of the north despatched a formidable army of Ja'aliyín, Danágla, Abábda and Bisharín under the banner of 'Abd-al-Májid Muhammad to Abú-Tulayh to contest the desert crossing.[69] From the vast army laying siege to Khartoum, Muhammad Ahmad split off a second force, under Músa wad Helu, the brother of the Mahdi's second Khalífa.[70] On the morning of 17 January, the two forces met north-west of the oasis. Enveloping the British square with simultaneous attacks from the east and the north, as many as 10,000 Ansár charged, screaming invocations and God's name. It was a furious battle, pitching the naked blades and almost unbelievable commitment of the Mahdists against the rigid discipline and superior fire-power of the British. One elderly sheikh, apparently impervious to the blizzard of bullets, managed to penetrate the square at a full gallop, rein in his horse, plant his standard and begin to read Qoránic verses from a scrolled parchment. He was shot where he stood.[71] 'Despite the large distance between them and the unbelievers, the unbelievers poured deadly fire, and the Martin [sic] rifles had a great effect,' the official Mahdist history recorded. 'The Companions reached the unbelievers only after many of them had died as martyrs.'[72] The attack of the Ansár, great holes blown in their ranks, whole phalanxes obliterated, faltered and stopped. They retreated in dignified silence, leaving more than a thousand lying dead in great piles. But the fight had achieved much for the Mahdi by delaying the British, who staggered on towards the river at Metamma. Confronted again by a lesser force near the qubba of a saint's tomb outside the little town on 19 January, Stewart was forced to fight again. Again, discipline and cool application of fire under great pressure saw off the rebels – but not before General Stewart was

General Wolseley, 'in a reverie on board the Ferouz', in southern Egypt during the attempt to rescue Gordon. (The Graphic, *15 November 1884*)

fatally wounded. Sir Charles Wilson took over command of the Desert Column and, reaching the Nile at last, encountered Nushi Pasha and the steamers sent by Gordon. The intrepid contingent from Khartoum had endured four months of constant attacks and hard foraging for food during their patient wait at Metamma. The *El Mansureh* had been sunk by Ansár artillery but in late December the *Bordein* had joined them, limping north from Khartoum with Gordon's last packet of mail. But instead of pressing on immediately for Khartoum, Wilson delayed, resting his battle-wearied men for three whole days. It was not until the morning of 24 January that he resolved to make the final push to Khartoum, accompanied by just a small contingent of British, Egyptian and Sudanese soldiers on board the *Bordein* and the *Tel el Hoween*.

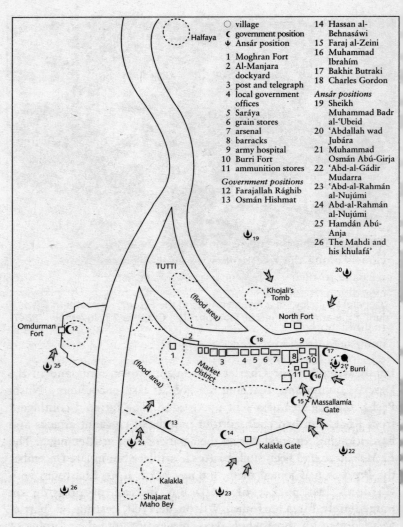

Khartoum under siege, 1884–5.

# NINETEEN

# *Victory*
# *Khartoum, 1885*

The Mahdi's northern generals sent messengers south, flogging their camels along the riverbank from Metamma, bringing an urgent message to their master encamped outside Khartoum: The British expeditionary force was coming. They had succeeded in delaying the foreigners but, with heavy losses already sustained, could not hope to hold both Desert and River Columns for long. The Mahdi's immediate decision to end the prolonged agony of Khartoum and seize the town by force was taken in consultation with his council of closest advisers. The decision was buttressed by information from deserters and spies fleeing Khartoum that people in the town had begun to drop dead in the streets from malnutrition. By the end of December, Gordon had sent the town's poorest inhabitants – those unable to afford the wildly inflated prices demanded for the remaining provisions – out to the Mahdi. The garrison's own rations had been severely cut back. By early January, all the provisions in the government stores and elsewhere had been consumed. The troops were reduced to eating 'the flesh of hateful animals', including donkeys, horses, mules and dogs.[1] In this hour of their need and despair, the Mahdi judged his time had come.

Muhammad Ahmad had tried persistently to coax Charles Gordon into surrendering the town without unnecessary bloodshed. In the last of nine letters written to the Governor-General, the Mahdi appealed to Gordon to accept a guarantee of safe passage.

We have been told by God's Apostle . . . of the imminent destruction of all those in Khartoum, save those who believe and surrender: them God will save. We do not wish you to perish with those doomed to perish because we have frequently heard good of you. Yet often as we have written to you about your regeneration and felicity, you have not returned to us an answer that will lead to your good . . . We have repeatedly written to you urging you to return to your own country where your virtue will achieve the highest honour. In order that you should not abandon hope of God's mercy, I say to you that God has said: 'Kill not thyself for God is merciful to thee.'[2] Peace be upon you.[3]

As he had against Shalláli at Jebel Gadír, as he had against Hicks among the thorn-bushes of Sheikán, the Mahdi resolved to launch his final assault at first light. And so, late at night on 25 January he crossed to the eastern bank of the White Nile, still some way south of the sleeping town, having ordered all his umará' to gather in wad al-Nujúmi's camp to hear his eve-of-battle briefing.[4] Addressing his disordered but enormously numerous forces from the saddle of his fine camel, Muhammad Ahmad told them of his latest prophetic vision, in which he had been ordered to kill the people of Khartoum. He warned the Ansár that they should take particular care crossing the town's ditch-and-rampart defences and keep a wary eye out for the crippling spiked caltrops, strewn on all fronts to pierce their feet. 'Do you wish with all your hearts to fight for God?' he screamed. 'Yes!' they responded in a shout that must have sent somnolent Egyptian sentries scrambling for their rifles. 'Even if two thirds of you were lost?' 'Yes!'[5]

Then he said, 'Swear allegiance to me unto death!' and was silent for a moment, when the whole army with one voice shouted three times, 'We swear allegiance to you unto death!' Then he said, 'If God grants you the victory, Gordon is not to be killed . . . and Fakī al-Amīn al-Darīr is not to be killed.' . . . Then he said, 'If a man throws down his arms, do not kill him, and if a man bars his house against you, do not kill him.' . . .

Then we swore the accustomed oath: 'We swear by God and his Prophet, and we swear by you, that we will not worship any but God, that we will not steal, that we will not commit adultery, that we will not disobey your lawful commands, that we will not flee from the Holy War.' And finally some words which at the time I did not fully understand, though I did later – 'We swear to renounce the world and to choose the next.' Then the flags were unfurled, and we were on our way to the fortress.[6]

The Mahdi then pointed his drawn sword towards the town and cried 'Allahu akbar!' – 'God is great!' – unleashing his army before himself re-crossing the river to his camp south of Omdurman. Most of the town's exhausted garrison and starved civilians still slept, expecting only to be awoken by the imam's call to the dawn prayer. A few weary sentinels on the southern fringes fingered their Remington rifles nervously, troubled by the yelling from the south and by furtive movements in the grey half-light. The Ansár crept forward on their bellies, slowly making ground until – at a signal – they charged on two fronts. Wad al-Nujúmi led from the south-west, with the Baggára, the Dighaim and the Kinána. Abú-Girja moved in from the east and south-east with the tribes of the Blue Nile and the Jazíra. Swords and spears in their tens of thousands flashed as the sun came up. Among the hordes, the riflemen of the Jihádia maintained a solid broadside against the government positions. Artillery pieces opened up from their trenches between the Mahdist infantry and the villages of Burri and Kalakla, throwing shells screaming into the streets of Khartoum. Gordon's perimeter screen of caltrops and makeshift biscuit-tin land-mines caused death and injury but on a scale that was utterly dwarfed by the hordes rushing forward to claim either victory or death – both equally prized. The bashi-bazouks facing al-Nujúmi's men, frail and utterly demoralised, cracked immediately, running for the town centre or for the desert. Those who stayed to fight died where they stood. The Ansár war cries echoed against the brick walls of the town. 'Allahu akbar', they echoed their leader, asserting 'Lá illah ill'Allah' and pledging to die 'fí sabíl Allah'.

Some also screamed for revenge for their dead flag-commander 'Abdallah wad al-Núr.

In the south-western sector, 'Abd-al-Qádir Hilmi's defensive moat had filled with White Nile water but then emptied again as the Nile had receded and drained away. When the attacking Mahdists reached the ditch, they found it full of watery mud but passable. Some Ansár sank in up to their knees, those tearing forward after them left with little option but to clamber or leapfrog over the trapped fighters, forcing them further down until the mud came up to their waists. More and more fighters stuck in the mud, but the lighter and more nimble sprang over their heads and out on to the dry mud on the Khartoum side of the ditch.[7] Seeing their defences so easily breached, most government soldiers bolted. The 1st and 2nd Companies of the 4th Battalion stood their ground and were cut to pieces.[8] There were tales of courage and of cowardice. The 1st Battalion fought heroically until overwhelmed. Colonel Hassan al-Behnasáwi of the Egyptian 5th Brigade, watching the debacle from the fort at Kalakla Gate, stripped off his uniform and fled into the desert. At Massallamía Gate, the officer in command of all five forts, General Faraj al-Zeini, did the same; the difference was that he left the gate *open* behind him when he escaped, thus exposing himself to accusations of treachery as well as cowardice. Into the gateway poured the Baggára tribesmen, given easy access to the remaining soldiers of the 2nd Battalion and a direct route to attack Burri Fort from the inside. At Burri itself, the 3rd Battalion regulars and bashi-bazouks under Bakhít Bey Butraki put up a brave fight but fell almost to the last man. Back on the western flank, the commanding officer at the Moghran Fort ran up the white flag of surrender. Ignoring it completely, the battle-maddened Baggára attacked anyway, killing every member of the small garrison. On Tuti Island, north of the town proper, the station garrison was similarly overwhelmed by boatloads of fighters charging forward under the banner of Sheikh al-'Ubeid.

With the outer ring of soldiery slaughtered or fled, Khartoum was now completely at the mercy of the invaders. They showed none. It was a long, hot day of relentless killing. Many thousands in Khartoum were beheaded, speared, stabbed and shot. 'The Arabs who were fighting at the White Nile now turned with fury to the town and then they behaved in a savage manner,' wrote Nushi Pasha's investigating committee. 'Any number of men were killed, any kind of immorality was exercised and they behaved in a manner as if they had no mercy in their bosom – may the curse of God and man fall upon them . . . The whole town was now filled with screams and shouts. The Arabs killed every person they met in their way. They also attacked the natives in their houses and slaughtered them and ransacked the houses.'[9] Rape was widespread. 'After the conquest of Khartoum', wrote Yúsuf Mikhail, 'all the people and, in particular, the Danágla, were not only plundering money, slaves, and treasures, but also began to lay their hands on decent women of the Ja'aliyín, Shaigía and a few of the Egyptians and other tribes – because they considered themselves to be Ashráf. They disgraced the women . . . then they evacuated the people of Khartoum and drove them outside the town . . . opposite Kalakla village. They lived there a month – the earth was their bed and the sky was their cover.'[10] Some officers, rather than see their wives and children fall into the hands of the Ansár, shot their families before turning their guns on themselves. As the court biographer, Ismail 'Abd-al-Gádir, later reported, the Mahdi did not order a stop to the killing until 5 p.m.[11]

> The slaughter continued from dawn until about forenoon, when the ground became red with the blood of people and the streets were filled with corpses. . . . Gordon was killed in his palace, his head was cut off and hung in the market as a punishment for him and a lesson to others. A party of pashas, governors, consuls . . . merchants and notables of the town also perished.[12]

Gordon himself could still have survived if he had resolved to flee the Saráya before sunrise. The steamer Ismailia had been prepared, its flanks protected with bolted-on boilerplates, its guns equipped with ammunition, the boiler protected by stacked logs. He was, however, determined to share the fate of the people whom he governed. For months, he had stood on the roof of the Saráya, his telescope trained to the north, always hoping for an eleventh-hour rescue, but his hopes had been ill founded. Gathering the small contingent of soldiers permanently based at the Residence, he now organised a fierce but brief defence of the building, firing from the roof and windows at the Ansár who advanced in the early morning twilight, yelling his name 'like wolves' and completely ignoring the Mahdi's explicit call for Gordon's life to be spared.[13] As Gordon descended the stone outer staircase on the western side of the building, he ran out of pistol ammunition. Ibráhím Sabir, a clerk from Obeid serving under the flag of ʿAbd-al-Rahmán al-Nujúmi, was among the first attackers to penetrate the main entrance in the west wing of the Saráya.

> There was scarcely light to see, but we could dimly discern a figure standing on the steps leading up to a roof and gazing intently at the troops who were rushing into the town. Mursal [Hamúda, the contingent's standard-bearer] had a gun as well as his flag and he fired at the standing figure, thinking it was a Turk. The man was hit and fell down. His body rolled down the stairs to the ground, staining the steps with blood. It was now lighter and onlookers shouted that the dead man was Gordon Pasha. A man called Babikr Koko . . . came riding up on a horse and asked me if I knew Gordon. I said I did and that Gordon was a man of slight build and had whiskers with a clean-shaven chin. Babikr rolled over the corpse and I said 'It is Gordon'. He was wearing a black coat and trousers with a tarboush on his head.[14] Babikr searched the body and took a watch and other articles. Mursal's shot had entered Gordon's chest. Babikr then cut off the head with his sword and put it in a leather bag which hung from his horse and rode away.[15]

Formal identification of the severed head was made by Rudolf Slatin, still imprisoned at the Mahdi's camp near Omdurman. A southern soldier – formerly a member of Ahmed Dafaʿallah's bodyguard in Kordofan but now in the service of the Khalífa

'Abdulláhi – unwrapped a bloody cloth with an arrogant gesture to reveal the head to Slatin. 'His blue eyes were half-opened,' the Austrian recalled in later years; 'the mouth was perfectly natural; the hair of his head and his short whiskers were almost quite white'.[16]

The aftermath of the Mahdi's victory at Khartoum was almost as brutal as the fighting itself. After ordering the cease-fire so late, there were few male prisoners of fighting age. Those survivors who might be reasonably assumed to be harbouring personal wealth were tortured to reveal any secret hiding places. There were rich pickings to be had, especially in the merchant quarter in the north-western part of town. Despite the bloodlust of the Baggára, however, wad al-Nujúmi and the Mahdi's other generals were aware that as many civilians as possible should be saved, especially the bureaucrats, officials and artisans who would be useful to the administration and commerce of the Mahdía.[17] But the hated 'sanjaks', the Shaigía who had collaborated with the Ottoman occupiers for decades, were accorded particularly savage treatment. The Shaigía were exempted from the general post-cease-fire amnesty and, when found alive, were subjected to vengeful torments, especially by the Danágla. One technique used by the Shaigía to control the Danágla in northern areas had traditionally been to tie the hands of a Dongoláwi behind his back using just the long leaves of an onion. As well as illustrating the Shaigía's contempt for their tribal rivals, it ensured that the detainee could barely move a muscle, for if the onion leaves were to be broken, a savage beating would result. Now, in Khartoum, the Danágla took their revenge, using this time a cigarette paper rolled over the thumbs of a Shaigi prisoner. Few, however, submitted to the insult; most broke the paper with defiance and braced themselves for more 'cruel treatment'.[18]

While many tribesmen still hoped to secure some loot for themselves, discipline had improved to the extent that a vast amount of cash, gold, jewellery and other luxury items was promptly transferred to the new premises of the Beit al-Mál, under the ever-watchful eye of Ahmad Suleimán and his two assistants. Babikr Bedri described finding women's gold ornaments down a well in a private house belonging to an Egyptian merchant. 'We got them out,' he wrote later, 'and wrapped them in a towel and took them to the public treasury. I tell you truly that we thought no more of this jewellery than we did of the corpses which we passed on our way to the treasury, and it did not occur to either of us that what we were carrying would give each of us riches for life if we were to steal it. Think of the power of those teachings which could thus control a young man like me.'[19] The treasury had been set up in the house of the Mufti Shákir al-Ghazi, a prominent member of the Khartoum 'ulamá', commandeered for the purpose. By the time the Mahdi made his own triumphal entry into Khartoum – as late as Friday 6 February – the accumulated loot had reached enormous proportions.[20]

When the ferry arrived he waded ashore like the rest, and mounted a black horse with a decorated saddle and bridle. We followed behind him until we reached the public treasury . . . When the Mahdi dismounted at the door and entered, I was close behind him . . . They opened for him the room where all the gold was kept, and there it was – jewellery and guineas and ingots. But as soon as the door was opened, and all the gold glowed at us, the Mahdi, with whom be God's peace, turned his back on it with the quickness of lightning, and left. I stood where I was, and thought about the gold, and remembered the line of al-Būsīrī – 'They tried to tempt him with the hills of gold' – and I said to myself, 'Here indeed is disdain for the things of this world'.[21]

The Mahdi himself had personal business to attend to. That same evening, he visited his mother's grave at a cemetery near the Kalakla Gate. It had been several years since he had last travelled to the spot. He also had to decide where best to make his new headquarters – the real capital of his new state. Initially at least, Muhammad Ahmad alternated between Khartoum and Omdurman, where the open spaces to the north of the village were spacious enough to contain his vast army camp. When he was not with his troops in his habitually modest accommodation, he took over the Khartoum home of Abú-Bakr al-Jarkúk, a wealthy merchant who had been killed during the sack of the town. Discovering one morning the plight of the thousands of women and children still incarcerated in miserable conditions in a zaríba on the southern fringes of the town, Muhammad Ahmad ordered Ahmad Suleimán to find them all suitable homes by sunset. 'If a woman is known to anyone, or knows him, let her go to him,' he prescribed; 'as for the young ones whom nobody knows and who know no one, let them be married.'[22] It was all part of the service for the Beit al-Mál, which (in addition to its treasury responsibilities) served as a welfare office for any Ansár whose livelihoods had been lost in the name of the cause and 'a communal form of financial aid to all those who required it'.[23] The Mahdi himself took many of the captives into his crowded compound, including Amina, daughter of the late Abú-Bakr al-Jarkúk, Fátima, daughter of another prominent Egyptian merchant, and Zeinab, daughter of Colonel Hassan al-Behnasáwi, the coward of Kalakla Gate.[24] To the surviving head of the al-Jarkúk family, Ahmad Muhammad, the Mahdi wrote a letter that, conciliatory as it was, might have proved disappointing to a young man hoping to regain the family fortune.

> My beloved, your request for my pardon and your request for the return of your loved ones to you so you may look after them are both approved. Ahmad Suleimán will be looking into making you and your families comfortable. As for those luxuries and worldly goods that you had earlier, they would bring you nothing but evil consequences and lasting sorrow. Allah has relieved you from all that by bringing you to me and letting you join our ranks. God be praised for rescuing you from darkness![25]

⚜ ⚜ ⚜

News of the fall of Khartoum sent a convulsion through British society. Sir Charles Wilson's token force aboard the *Bordein* and the *Tel el Hoween* – 20 red-coated men of the Royal Sussex Regiment and 240 Egyptian and Sudanese troopers – arrived at

Tuti Island early on 28 January. At the junction of the two Niles, Ansár fire became intense and the plumes of smoke still rising from Khartoum made it all too clear what had just happened. 'Never in history was there such a race,' General Wolseley reflected much later, rueing the only failure of his career; 'about 1,800 miles up the Nile from the sea, when we lost at the post by a neck'.[26] At the time, he was traumatised.

> Oh my dear child, I am in despair. News just in that Khartoum was taken by treachery on 26th January. My steamers reached Khartoum on 28th instant just in time to see it occupied by the enemy & have a very heavy fire opened upon them from Mahdi's Batteries. I have telegraphed home for fresh instructions, for now I have no '*mission*' left to carry out, and to begin a campaign at this season of the year with British troops in the Soudan, would in my private opinion be simply madness. . . . Poor Gordon! For his sake I hope he is dead. . . . I should think this blow will kill poor old Gladstone. He alone is to blame. Had he been a statesman, this misfortune could never have fallen upon us. . . . [The Mahdi] has won, and we all look very foolish.[27]

Major Kitchener, who would lead a merciless campaign of vengeance for the murdered Charles Gordon, was in no doubt about who was the true hero, even in defeat. 'The memorable siege of Khartoum lasted 317 days,' he wrote, 'and it is not too much to say that such a noble resistance was due to the indomitable resolution and resource of one Englishman.[28] Never was a garrison so nearly rescued, never was a Commander so sincerely lamented.'[29] The press in London took up that lament. Even the jocular magazine *Punch* was not immune to the prevailing emotion, featuring an illustration of a grief-stricken Britannia, her arm held across her eyes to ward off the sight of the Mahdist hordes pressing into the grounds of the Saráya, and a poem bewailing, with patriotic filigree, 'delay's stern Nemesis'.

> Too late! Too late! Loud through the desert sounds
> That piteous cry and to the farthest bounds
> Of England's Empire echoes. There she stands,
> BRITANNIA, stricken 'midst the Libyan sands [*sic*]
> With bitter disappointment's venomed dart,
> Wrath in her soul and anguish at her heart.
> Too late! . . . Where
> Is our lost lion? See his desert lair
> Bristles with hostile spears. At Khartoum's gate
> Brave GORDON greets us not! Too late! Too late![30]

The Mahdi was undisputed master of a vast terrain, from the Red Sea Hills to the plains of Darfur, from the swamps and jungles of the Bahr al-Ghazál to Dongola. Wolseley's forces were compelled to fall back. Sir Charles Wilson barely survived the retreat from Khartoum, both his steamers grounding en route and his small force having to be rescued by colleagues from the Desert Column, which in turn had to fight off innumerable raids as it marched back across the wasteland to Korti. As for the River Column, it had made frustrating progress through the cataracts between Korti and Abú-Hamed. The capture of Khartoum by the Mahdi, relayed to Major-General William Earle by telegraph on 4 February, only underlined that sense of frustration and futility. A pointless and irrelevant final encounter at Kirbekán on 10 February with around 2,000 Ansár from Berber provided a pyrrhic victory; large numbers of Mahdists were killed but so was General Earle. After briefly occupying Abú-Hamed and surveying the wreck of Colonel Stewart's steamer, the *Abbas*, the River Column was also ordered back to base. Britain's first Sudan Campaign, running to a cost of more than seven million pounds, had ended in failure.[31] It was time to fall back on Egypt. Only Suakin now flew the Union Jack alongside the crescent and star of the khedivial banner. In a defiant last bark before conceding the inevitable, Lord Wolseley had issued a proclamation on 28 February at Korti.

We invite you to come to us and aid us in exterminating the monster Mahomet Ahmed whom the British Government will never rest till it has exterminated. He alone is growing rich and fat while you the deluded people who are following him are poor, badly clothed, half starved and enduring many and great hardships. If you come to us you will receive 2½ piastres a day, you will be clothed fed and well treated . . . All slaves who join us from the enemy will also be enrolled at the same rate of pay as above and when peace is restored to the land they will be allowed to choose whether to return to their homes as free men, or else to continue to serve the Government as soldiers.[32]

# TWENTY

# 'The Last Grave of Mahdism'
## Omdurman and Umm Dibeikarát,
## 1885–1899

The Mahdi wasted little time resting on the laurels of victory. The capture of Khartoum had cemented his position as the supreme figure in undisputed command of a vast territory but there were still a few minor problems. The Khalífa 'Abdulláhi, delegated with responsibility for all military arrangements, saw to a brisk series of mopping up campaigns. The continually troublesome clans of the Nuba Mountains had again to be brought to heel; Hamdán Abú-Anja took care of that operation. Now the only settlements that remained in the possession of government garrisons were Sennar, Kassala and Suakin. One of the Mahdi's uncles, Muhammad 'Abd-al-Karím, was despatched at the head of a substantial force to intensify the siege of Sennar, whose garrison held out stubbornly until 19 August despite desperate conditions in the town.[1] 'Osmán Digna's men in the east were ordered to take care of Kassala although, as in many previous sieges, the defenders considered it wiser to surrender to an envoy sent personally by the Mahdi from Omdurman rather than a known and feared local adversary.[2] Suakin, buttressed by the British Army, was a tough nut to crack but was soon forced into a purely defensive posture. In the third phase of British involvement, the months between March and May saw one last serious expedition. The plan was to commit 13,500 troops, including an Indian Brigade of 2,000 men, to an advance on Berber by the desert route.[3] General Graham took on 'Osmán Digna's Hadendawa and Bisharín in two long engagements at Hashin and Tofrik on 21 and 22 March; like the fight at Kirbekán the previous month, these were bloody but pointless encounters. With Khartoum lost and Gordon presumed dead, Graham's commanders had lost their will to fight in Sudan. Wolseley came to Suakin in person in May to tell his forces that the campaign was to be abandoned; Suakin itself would be held but by a much reduced garrison, supplied from the sea. 'Taken altogether,' Wolseley noted later, 'our operations in the Suakin neighbourhood were neither decisive nor marked by any special military genius'.[4]

Meanwhile letters and proclamations poured forth from the Mahdi's own secretariat. In the five months after the fall of Khartoum, more than 300 letters passed on Muhammad Ahmad's instructions to his generals, his administrators, his treasurers and judges. Founded on the core values that he had consistently espoused – especially public morality and social order – the Mahdist state was already taking shape. The social strictures laid out in his commandments of previous years all still applied. Prayers were mandatory, not just the five daily prostrations but also the communal gathering on Friday and the twice-daily recitation of the Rátib. For the tens of thousands of adherents now gathered at Omdurman, a vast space was needed for collective prayers; instead of a mosque, a huge space was roofed over with 'enormous mats, held up on innumerable forked sticks, which gave it the appearance of a forest'.[5] Nor were the religious obligations of asceticism, prayer and self-discipline set aside just because victory had been achieved. The jihad in Sudan might have been won, the Mahdi argued in his sermons, but each individual still had a personal, moral jihad to wage.

Three problems at the heart of the new administration suggested early on that the Mahdi would struggle to establish the pure, utopian, neo-Ansár community of his dreams. On the one hand, the practicalities of government dictated that officials of the despised Turkía (mainly literate Ashráf and Copts) had to be assimilated into the workings of the Mahdía. Not only that but the equipment and machinery of government had to be used too and the printing press, weapons workshops, boatyards, accountancy offices and miscellaneous civil service offices of a functioning state bureaucracy were all inherited and used – a solid manifestation of the 'innovations' so long decried by Muhammad Ahmad.[6] A further problem in building the community in a new capital was disease. The rapidly erected shanties that housed the Mahdi's myriad fighters also bred germs. Smallpox, dysentery and other fevers spread through the ranks, driving many to flee the unwholesome spot for the open spaces of Kordofan and Darfur.[7] The third impediment to a smooth social order was the rapid disintegration in relations between the Khalífa 'Abdulláhi and the Mahdi's own clansmen among the riverside tribes. It was only natural that they, as blood relatives, should expect at least an equal share in the real power of the new state. They were rapidly disabused of this heady notion. After the capture of Obeid in January 1883, the Mahdi had given due warning that 'Abdulláhi was to be obeyed in everything; a message that had been reaffirmed by his recognition in July 1884 as the Mahdi's *wazír*, minister and right-hand man.[8] Now his pre-eminence over the other khulafá' was institutionalised. 'He who does not love the Khalífat al-Siddíq ['Abdulláhi]', the Mahdi wrote to his uncle at Obeid, 'will not be benefited or revived by the conversation of the Mahdi, even as cut herbs are not revived by the rain.'[9] Large numbers of Ta'íshi tribesmen began to settle in camps on the western fringes of Omdurman, feeding the anxieties of the Ashráf. As for the wider population, they were growing accustomed to the methods of the new administration. The Khalífa 'Abdulláhi was still in charge of tax collecting; his Baggára agents dispersed to ensure that the Beit al-Mál was continually replenished – largely in kind rather than cash. And as the Mahdi's new judiciary set about recasting the legal system on the basis of the Qorán, the Sunna and Muhammad Ahmad's own proclamations, decisions were constantly delayed while cases were referred up to the 'Successor of the Prophet' himself for arbitration. Not all the state's newly empowered officials were popular. Many of them had successfully parleyed local influence into a national position. A ribald poem about Muhammad al-Tayib al-Basír, the leading amír of the Jazíra region, bemoaned the jumped-up nobodies who were profiting from the Mahdi's victory.

> It is all very well for that Mahdi to swagger about in glory;
> But how come even wad al-Basír can make life so hard for us?[10]

As his domestic political arrangements proceeded apace, the Mahdi began planning the next stage of his jihad, the conquest of Egypt. To pray in Cairo was his pledge – perhaps at the new Muhammad 'Ali mosque in the ancient citadel, perhaps at the mosque of al-Azhar itself, home of his orthodox adversaries, or maybe at the 1,200-year-old mosque of 'Amr ibn al-'As, nestled among the Christian churches of the Old City.[11] He also wanted to spread his da'wa into new territories and expand his following in the north-west African Maghreb and, to the south, in Abyssinia. That spring, he had received a letter from the Moroccan community in Egypt, asking him to honour one of their number, Muhammad al-Gháli, with the Mahdi's personal endorsement as Governor of Fez. Al-Gháli and his compatriots would then return to their homeland to spread the Mahdía across northern Africa. Under a covering letter which skated over the specific question of appointing Muhammad al-Gháli (merely entrusting the decision to 'worthy leaders who serve as examples in the Faith' in Fez itself), Muhammad Ahmad sent a long message rehearsing the details of his claim to be the Awaited Mahdi and demanding their adherence to the call.[12] Addressed to 'the families of Fez' and the town's actual Governor, al-Hassan Muhammad 'Abd-al-Rahmán, the letter is replete with Qoránic quotations and contains a ringing declaration: 'Know that shortly, insha'Allah, I shall come with the party of God to Egypt, for the affair of Sudan is finished.'[13]

That ominous message was followed up by a succession of letters to the government, 'ulamá' and people of Egypt.[14] The letters were to be copied in huge numbers, carried north by trusted agents and distributed in a massive propaganda drive. In his letter to the Khedive Tawfíq, Muhammad Ahmad rehearsed his own divine credentials and his victorious campaign thus far, warned the Egyptian ruler against the 'evil 'ulamá'' of al-Azhar and chastised him for succumbing to the domination of the perfidious British. The Mahdi's language was strikingly different in this letter; far from deriding the Khedive as an infidel or a 'Turk', he addressed him respectfully and admonished him (with plentiful Qoránic quotations) for taking unbelievers as friends.

> I do not desire power, prestige or material possessions. If you accept my guidance and revert to Allah sincerely, I will offer you the safe conduct of God, his Prophet and his Mahdi. We will be on hand for the sake of religion, to expel the enemies of Allah from the land of the Muslims and eradicate them to the last man if they do not surrender or revert to God.[15]

Then disaster struck. On 16 June, the Mahdi fell ill with a 'severe fever' and was confined to his quarters in Omdurman, a modest shed made from the boards of General Hicks' stable.[16] The speed and severity of the onset led many to suspect poison, but Rudolf Slatin, now in the Khalífa 'Abdulláhi's service and well placed to observe at close hand, believed the cause of this sudden and acute illness to be typhus fever, an ailment caused by exposure to rat fleas.[17] The historian Na'úm Shuqair, who spoke to many who were also in Omdurman, believed it to have been meningitis.[18] Certainly the unhygienic conditions prevalent in Omdurman might have prompted the aggressive symptoms, the extremely high temperature, the rash, abdominal pains and vomiting. Muhammad Ahmad's family did their best to bring him out of his fever, while his devoted followers anxiously milled around outside the compound, asking each other why their master no longer appeared for Ramadan's communal prayers. To calm them, Khalífa 'Abdulláhi ordered them to recite the Verse of Purity from the Qorán, four short verses usually declaimed at times of distress.

Say: He is Allah, the one and only; God the eternal and absolute. He neither begets nor is begotten and there is none like him.[19]

Despite his illness – and despite a proclamation beseeching his officials and followers to let him concentrate on prayer during Ramadan – Muhammad Ahmad attempted to continue the business of ruling.[20] Even as his symptoms worsened, he dictated letters to his favourite lieutenants in the field, including 'Osmán Digna and Muhammad al-Tayyib al-Basír.[21] But as the weekend of 20–21 June passed, Muhammad Ahmad's condition deteriorated rapidly and it became clear to even the Mahdi's most ardent followers – who simply could not comprehend that he might be taken from them before his mission was complete – that the Mahdi was dying. In the corner of his room crouched the huddled and grieving figure of his principal wife, Aisha Umm al-Mu'minín. Around his angareb stood the three khulafá' – 'Abdulláhi, 'Ali wad Helu and Muhammad Sharíf – as well as a handful of followers loyal to both the Mahdi and 'Abdulláhi, including al-Makki Ismail al-Wali (who had been with Muhammad Ahmad since his earliest tour of Kordofan) and Muhammad wad Bushára.[22]

From time to time he lost consciousness, and, feeling that his end was drawing near, he said, in a low voice, to those around him, 'Khalifa Abdullahi es Sadik has been appointed by the Prophet as my successor. He is of me and I am of him; as you have obeyed me, and have carried out my orders, so you should deal with him. May God have mercy upon me!' Then, gathering up all his strength, with one final effort he repeated a few times the Mohammedan creed ('La Illaha illallah, Mohammed Rasul Allah'), crossed his hands over his chest, stretched out his limbs, and passed away.[23]

So, on Monday, 22 June 1885, the life of the Mahdi came to a shockingly abrupt end.[24] It was, in the obedient but accurate words of the court biographer Ismail 'Abd-al-Gádir, the 'greatest of calamities'.[25] In less than four years, his Islamic revolution had swept away six decades of Egyptian colonial rule. Starting with a tiny core of adherents to a minority Sufi sect, he had gathered Sudan's squabbling tribes under the black, red and green banners of their generals and deployed them to devastating effect. Even setting aside his claim to be the Mahdi, it was triumph enough that the son of a boat-builder from a small island in the northern Nile had, by dint of sheer self-belief and overwhelming charisma, become the ruler of a nation of millions. The people were stunned. Could the Mahdi just *die*? What about the promises of conquests to come? And for the Mahdi's senior followers there was a more critical decision to address, even as the Mahdi's body still lay on his deathbed: Who was to lead after the death of the leader? 'Abdulláhi, as 'Khalífat al-Siddiq', had had the repeated and unequivocal personal endorsement of the Mahdi as his heir apparent. But the Ashráf wanted to see the young Khalífa Muhammad Sharíf honoured quickly as his kinsman's successor, avoiding a power vacuum and avoiding the prospect of the Baggára shaping the future of the new nation. A short but intense debate ensued, concluded only by the recognition by three key Ashráf figures – the Khalífa 'Ali wad Helu, al-Makki Ismail al-Wali and the Mahdi's father-in-law Ahmad Sharfi – that 'Abdulláhi's right to succeed was unarguable.[26] With their loyalty duly sworn over the body of Muhammad Ahmad, the hasty funeral took place. As the Mahdi's weeping family washed and wrapped his body in linen shrouds, the three khulafá' – for now, brothers united by grief – turned their hands to grave-digging, cutting down into the ochre soil beneath the angareb where Muhammad Ahmad had spent his last days. The business of the committal was brief, prayers muttered, hands raised. Then immediately 'Abdulláhi turned his energies to shoring up an irresistible power-base. Ordering servants to move the Mahdi's pulpit out into the doorway of the small mosque, he mounted and faced the crowd.

'Friends of the Mahdi,' he shouted, 'God's will cannot be changed. The Mahdi has left us, and has entered into heaven, where everlasting joys await him. It is for us to obey his precepts, and to support one another, just as the stones and walls of a house go to make a building.[27] . . . You are the friends of the Mahdi, and I am his Khalífa. Swear that you will be faithful to me.' . . . As only a certain number could take the oath of allegiance at one time, those who had finished made way for others, and the crowd was so enormous that many were in danger of being trodden to death. The ceremony went on till nightfall.[28]

Draping his late master's colours around his own shoulders, the Khalífa adopted a terse motto – *al-dín mansúr* – designed to suggest that individual ambitions be subordinated to the success of the movement.[29] His religious arguments for the ruthlessly swift succession were articulated in a proclamation addressed to the people of Egypt but no doubt circulated as widely at home. 'Do not trouble yourself over the cessation of that divine assistance with the passing of the Mahdi,' he wrote,

for between the Mahdi and his ancestor, the elect Prophet, is a close similarity. When the Prophet passed away, the assistance remained with his noble Companions until the Faith of God was confirmed and its compass extended, as you know. The passing of the Mahdi to the world to come before the conquests of Mecca, Constantinople, and other cities . . . does not impugn his being the Mahdi of the end of the age, of whose manifestation the Prophet gave the Muslim community good tidings. . . . It is known that in his time [the Prophet] conquered only Mecca and Khaybar; the rest of the conquest being by the hands of the caliphs after him. Likewise his successor, the Mahdi, came and all the conquests of countries attributed to him in the hadíth must certainly be by the hands of his successors and companions, since they are his heirs who undertake the affair after him.

The reign of the Khalífa 'Abdulláhi lasted fourteen years, a period in which maintenance of his personal power consumed as much energy as the pursuit of his former mentor's mission of international jihad. The legacy of the Mahdi was almost forgotten in the paranoia of the autocrat. What had begun as a grand dream, a movement of Islamic revivalism of sweeping ambition, dwindled rapidly into the mere consolidation of an impoverished political state. The sense of surging confidence among the Ansár, fuelled by the Mahdi's own extraordinary charisma and self-belief, was replaced by mutual mistrust and resentment, the very ordinary symptoms of a classic power struggle. In June 1885, it had been possible to believe that anything could be achieved in the way of nation building; by the autumn, Muhammad Ahmad's entire project was on the verge of disintegration. The heart had gone out of the movement and the ascent to supreme power of 'Abdulláhi Muhammad al-Ta'íshi destroyed collective morale. The clans and tribes that had been brought together in the common struggle split apart again. From a genuine theocracy, headed by an inspirational leader and with administrative, military, financial and legal systems modelled on strict Islamic precedents, the new nation became the fiefdom of one clan and one individual, who cited Mahdist endorsements and precedents to buttress his own rule.

Almost immediately, 'Abdulláhi set about removing influential figures, in Omdurman and in the provinces, whose loyalty to the Mahdi might possibly be transferred to his rival, Muhammad Sharíf. The assistance of Hamdán Abú-Anja, one of the few non-Ashráf generals and the commander of the feared and highly mobile Jihádía, was invaluable. As the years passed, many were forced out of positions they held on Muhammad Ahmad's personal appointment and often imprisoned or executed. Muhammad Ahmad's wives and children – especially his sons – were kept under close watch; they could not be touched but their movements and activities could be controlled. The Mahdi's cousin, Muhammad Khálid, was recalled from Darfur before being banished to the swamps of Equatoria. The Mahdi's former teacher, Muhammad al-Kheir 'Abdallah al-Khojali, was sacked as governor of Dongola and Berber; his job went to an

'Abdulláhi loyalist. The Mahdi's uncle, Mahmúd 'Abd-al-Gádir, was killed in pursuit of a large contingent of mutinous jihádía, who had headed for the Nuba hills themselves, hoping to establish a private fiefdom far from the censorious strictures of the Mahdía. Even the Khalífa Muhammad Sharíf himself was stripped of his banners, the emblems of his status as the Mahdi's chosen lieutenant. Only 'Osmán Digna in the east and Karamallah al-Sheikh Muhammad in Bahr al-Ghazál survived unscathed, too far from the centre of power to be a threat.[30]

Had it come to a full-scale fight, the Danágla and their allies among the jallába would have simply been no match for the Khalífa. With his brother Yaqúb in command of legions of Baggára and with Abú-Anja's fearless southern gunmen in support, 'Abdulláhi was invincible, especially as he had seized control of the entire arsenal of artillery and rifles. Stripped of actual power, the Ashráf attempted at least to regain some of their material influence. All the traditional jallába livelihoods, especially trading on the river, were heavily taxed by the Beit al-Mál. Their vessels had been commandeered by the state and large quantities of tribal lands had been confiscated. The Mahdi's own sons, reduced to minor roles despite their sworn loyalty to the Khalífa, were denied their due allowances from the state treasury.[31] In late 1891, the simmering resentment boiled over into a brief exchange of fire between Ashráf rebels and 'Abdulláhi's bodyguard, the feared mulázimín.[32] 'Abdulláhi pledged to pardon the dissidents but then, deploying a well-timed prophetic vision as a device to cloak an abrupt volte-face, ordered the arrest and deportation of seven influential conspirators. The seven, including the veteran head of the Beit al-Mál, Ahmad Suleimán, and the Mahdi's uncle, Muhammad 'Abd-al-Karím (who had served 'Abdulláhi so well in pressing the siege of Sennar), were executed at Fashoda by Zaki Tamal, one of Abú-Anja's clansmen. But there were limits to the purging of the Ashráf. In seeking a replacement treasurer, 'Abdulláhi could find no one among his own Ta'íshi clan with the qualifications or literacy to handle the vast amount of bookkeeping, paperwork and other administrative chores.[33]

ψ ψ ψ

'Abdulláhi's decision to evacuate and destroy Khartoum may have followed from his anxiety about the security of Ashráf personalities living in comfort in the town, while the Ta'íshi made do with rudimentary accommodation in and around Omdurman.[34] He would also have heard his late master quote the Qorán in his last sermon at the Khartoum mosque: 'And you dwelt in the homes of men who wronged their own souls, despite being clearly shown how we dealt with them . . . The plots they hatched were mighty indeed – but they were made in God's sight, even if they were strong enough to move mountains.'[35] So, just over a month after the death of the Mahdi, his successor ordered the entire population of Khartoum to move. He gave them just four days to do it. 'Let no one among you delay,' read his proclamation, 'even one employed by the arsenal or the dockyard or the Beit al-Mál or wherever else'.

Anyone found lagging behind will be reported to 'Abd-al-Halím Musá'id, and upon his notification that person will be forcibly uprooted. If anyone interferes with the execution of this order, he will be reported to me, that I might punish both the one who delays and the one who interferes. Peace!'[36]

In fact, it took 'Abdulláhi another year to enforce the total abandonment of Khartoum. By September 1886, the factories, workshops, armouries and boatyards had all been replicated or physically removed to Omdurman. New market premises had to be built for the merchants, though their homes never attained the same luxury. The buildings of imperial Khartoum were demolished for their bricks and timber, of far better quality than anything now available in the alleys of Omdurman. The capital, defeated and degraded, became a town of ghosts, its dismal lanes blocked with rubble.

Despite the constant preoccupation with maintaining this iron grip on power, the Khalífa pressed on with sporadic efforts to extend the frontiers of the fledgling state. His generals mounted a successful assault on Abyssinia in 1889, routing the forces of King John at al-Gallábát and fatally wounding the king himself.[37]

Celebrations, however, were short-lived. European powers were moving decisively to claim as much of Africa as they could lay hands on and Italy swiftly attacked from the old Egyptian port at Massawa. By 1890, control was wrested from the Mahdists and by 1894 the Italians were on the outskirts of Kassala. Pursuit of the Mahdi's jihad in Egypt, meanwhile, was still less glorious. After chasing the British out of the northern territories in 1885, 'Abd-al-Rahmán al-Nujúmi had camped, first at Berber then at Dongola, awaiting instructions. But the Khalífa at Omdurman was too worried about al-Nujúmi's loyalties to allow him to launch an attack on the British forces watching Egypt's southern border. Instead, he sent his cousin, Yúnis al-Dikkeim, to assume command as the army languished at Dongola, wracked with smallpox.[38] There were frequent desertions as the soldiers, sick at heart to see their beloved general humiliated by this representative of the new Ta'íshi autocracy, abandoned the service of this new kind of Mahdía. And the soldiers were slowly starving. When the Mahdi had initially sent them north in pursuit of the Desert Column in early 1885, he had specifically ordered them not to take large stocks of food. 'Follow God's way, lame and halt,' he had urged, 'and care not for the vanity of preparation and of supplies, for that can lead only to delay'.[39] A region of limited resources could not at the best of times support an army of more than 5,000 men and at least as many camp followers – and the years 1888–9 were not the best of times. Famine wracked the entire territory; the rivers ran low and the crops failed.[40] Sheer need drove the army north into Egyptian territory and towards the waiting British, even as al-Nujúmi's soldiers continued to melt away into the desert to escape the imminent disaster. Not a single Egyptian came forward to greet their Mahdist liberators. 'Twenty-seven days without the taste of bread had left my body very weak', recalled Babikr Bedri. 'Yet if they had brought me a Koran I would have sworn upon it that we would still conquer Egypt. What a spirit was this! Say that it was due to faith or recklessness or to madness – as you like; but you cannot deny that it was there.'[41]

The end of Mahdist aspirations in Egypt came with merciless finality on 3 August 1889 as General Francis Grenfell, one of

Wolseley's protégés, dealt al-Nujúmi a crushing defeat near the village of Túshki on the west bank of the Nile. The amír's body was brought to be identified by Ansár prisoners. 'There was dust in his fine beard as though he had just returned from reviewing his army,' remembered one veteran, 'and there was no sign about him of the ugliness of death'.[42] Unlike the survivors of Túshki, the Khalífa did not weep when he heard the news that 'Abd-al-Rahmán al-Nujúmi, one of the Mahdi's oldest and closest followers, had been killed. After all, few of his own loyalists had died, merely a few thousand potentially troublesome rivals. It was a time of famine, illness and paranoia. And when news finally reached Omdurman that an Anglo-Egyptian army was advancing from the north, few were surprised. The Khalífa 'Abdulláhi's own son, Osmán 'Sheikh al-Dín', warned his father not to underestimate the determination of the 'Christians' to have their revenge.

> You know well enough that the English have an axe to grind with you; they want to avenge the death of Hicks, of Gordon, and of all the Englishmen who were killed in the Sudan. The Egyptians too want to avenge the death of their Turkish and Egyptian armies and the loss of the lands they once ruled. Now they are coming to avenge themselves and to reconquer the country.[43]

☙ ☙ ☙

Fourteen years was a long time for the British government and people to mull over the failure to rescue Charles Gordon. Certainly he was not forgotten. In the popular imagination, fed by the popular press, the image of a British hero abandoned by a perfidious government and speared to death by the barbarian hordes was more dramatic than the rather more prosaic picture of an eccentric mercenary soldier and administrator, hired by the Egyptian government to salvage some dignity from the wreck of a doomed colony. For many, it was simply unfinished business. The eminent Egyptologist, E.A. Wallis Budge, wrote that he hoped to see 'that villain the Khalifa . . . being tarred & feathered, & cut up piece-meal & so on'.[44] But the 1890s was a decade of consolidation of British military and civilian control over Egypt (and a time when the War Office and Treasury in London were absorbed with other colonial conflicts demanding their attention, from Ashanti on the West African Gold Coast to New Zealand, from Abyssinia to Afghanistan). Yet it was the British military command in Cairo – many of whom had been involved in the campaign of 1883–5 which had failed to relieve the siege of Khartoum – that was always more enthusiastic about another attempt at the subjugation of Sudan than were the politicians back in London. Indeed, it was a military officer who played a crucial part in stirring up British public opinion to the extent that a fully-fledged campaign to 'avenge Gordon' received huge support. The memoirs of both Rudolf Slatin and Fr Joseph Ohrwalder were ghost-written by Major F.R. Wingate, a senior figure in British military intelligence in Cairo whose own history of Muhammad Ahmad's uprising had sold well and caused much discussion in the salons of London.[45]

After the planning, the intelligence gathering and the patient troop build-up, the re-invasion of Sudan in the late 1890s was a ruthless and inexorable campaign, one that crushed the forces (though not the nationalist aspirations) of Sudan. Despite the construction of 760 miles of railway across utterly barren terrain, the laying of 2,000 miles of telegraph cables, the haulage of six gunboats through the Nile's vicious cataracts and the deployment of 20,000 men (7,500 of them British, 12,500 Egyptian), Britain's second Sudan campaign was much less expensive than the first, costing nearly two-and-a-half million pounds, of which the bulk was paid by the Government of Egypt.[46] It was a meticulously phased operation, in which General Herbert Kitchener steered his army south, mile by careful mile, never outreaching his supply line, inexorably eating into the Khalífa's territory. The conquest of Dongola was achieved by September 1896; it took another full year for Kitchener's Egyptian brigades to occupy Berber. The spring of 1898 saw the campaign on the Atbara and the year drew to a close with the carnage of Karari.

Yet if the Khalífa knew he was defeated, he refused to surrender. Whatever his methods of government, no one could doubt his courage. Even after the disaster in the Karari hills he was ready to fight to the end; but his followers 'took him away by force', first south via Dueim to Shat and into the wilds of Kordofan. Even there, though, 'Abdulláhi's core support had melted away and the party of refugees made their weary way up into the Nuba Mountains before regrouping with Ansár soldiers in the area.[47] As British and Egyptian troops fanned out across Sudanese provinces to crush remaining Mahdist resistance during 1899, the mission to catch the Khalífa was entrusted to Wingate, now a colonel and commanding officer in the White Nile sector, who led a 'flying column' of 3,700 mainly Egyptian soldiers into eastern Kordofan. Two main Ansár forces remained intact west of the river; the first, under the Khalífa himself, stood near Jadíd, in the northern Nuba hills; a second force under his loyal amír Ahmad Fadíl Muhammad was deployed nearby.[48] The Ansár launched their first attack but were repelled with heavy losses by the massed fire-power of the disciplined Egyptians and pursued through thick bush and into a grassy plain. The final action came at Umm Dibeikarát, where at last the Khalífa 'Abdulláhi was brought to bay, his escape routes blocked either by 'waterless and densely wooded districts' or by carefully deployed Egyptian units.[49] At the Khalífa's side to the last were his bravest and most loyal followers, many of them Ta'íshi Baggára, like 'Abdulláhi's two surviving brothers and Ahmad Fadíl, but also dignitaries from among the Ashráf: the Khalífa 'Ali wad Helu and the Mahdi's eighteen-year-old son Siddiq. Wingate resolved to strike at dawn on Friday, 24 November but was pre-empted by the Khalífa, whose forces made the last screaming charge of that era shortly before first light. The storm of bullets and shrapnel from the British artillery, Maxims and rifles blasted great gaps in the Ansár attack and the fight was quickly over. The cease-fire was blown at 6.25 a.m., after a little more than an hour of fighting. Recognising that the day was lost and rejecting the option of surrender, 'Abdulláhi and his comrades dismounted, unrolled their sheepskins, knelt in prayer and awaited their fate.[51] When British officers moved through the battlefield later that morning, after accepting the surrender of thousands of Ansár survivors, they found an extraordinary sight.

I went back to see the Khalifa. In front of him lay the riflemen of his bodyguard, in a double line, evidently killed to a man in their places shooting, each man had shot and shot till he died. . . . The Khalifa was a little behind them, with that grand old fighting Dervish Ahmed Fadil by his side, and nearly all the great Emirs in a group round him. The Khalifa had quite a nice face, a stoutish built, powerful, elderly gentleman, with a slight grey beard, rather fair than dark for a Begara . . . with good aquiline features, a rather broadish face, not a bit the cruel tyrant one expected. The faithful Ahmed Fadil . . . had a very pleasing face, broad and straight forward, with blue grey eyes. Next then was 'Ali wad Helu, the third Khalifa, the leader in all the Dervish atrocities when raiding. He looked it every inch of him. A little wiry man, covered with hair all over, the wickedest, cruellest face I ever saw. He was snarling just like a wolf as he lay there dead, with all his teeth showing.[52]

The Mahdi's revolution had been launched on the eve of a new Islamic century. Now, on the threshold of a new Christian century, it was blown away by the discipline and fire-power of a better army. It was not, however, utterly extinguished. The Mahdi's posthumous son, al-Sayyid 'Abd-al-Rahmán, would fan the embers, keeping the clan alive as a cohesive force despite the constant watchfulness of Britain's colonial officers, spreading his father's word, publishing a new edition of his Rátib. In the twentieth century, the Ansár would be reborn as a potent political and commercial force, with their spiritual home as before at Jazíra Aba. But the days of a purely Mahdist state died that day at Umm Dibeikarát.

Thus the last grave of Mahdism lies not far from its cradle on Abba Island, in a beautiful spot near a large sheet of water girdled round with trees.[53]

# Chronology

| AD | AH | Event |
|---|---|---|
| 1844 | 1260 | |
| 12 August | 27th Rajab | Birth of Muhammad Ahmad at Labab Island |
| 1849 | 1265 | |
| ? | ? | Muhammad Ahmad's family moves to Karari, near Omdurman (aged 5) |
| 2 August | 13th Ramadan | Egypt: Death of Wáli Muhammad ʿAli and accession of ʿAbbás Hilmi |
| ? | ? | Muhammad Ahmad studies under Sharaf al-Dín Abú-al-Sádiq in Khartoum |
| ? | ? | Muhammad Ahmad studies under Mahbúb al-Habáshi in Khartoum |
| ? | ? | Muhammad Ahmad studies under Mahmúd al-Mubárak in Burri village |
| 13 November | 27th Dhú al-Hijja | ʿAbd-al-Latíf Sharkas becomes Governor-General of Sudan's northern, eastern and central regions |
| 1852 | 1268 | |
| 14 January | 22nd Rabíʿ I | Rustum Sharkas becomes Governor-General |
| 4 July | 16th Ramadan | Ismail al-Hajji Abú-Jabal becomes Governor-General |
| 1853 | 1269 | |
| 24 April | 15th Rajab | Salím al-Gazáli becomes Governor-General |
| 1854 | 1270 | |
| 13 July | 17th Shawwál | Egypt: Death of Wáli ʿAbbás Hilmi and accession of Muhammad Saʿíd |
| 22 July | 26th Shawwál | ʿAli Sirri Arnavut becomes Governor-General |
| | 1271 | |
| 29 November | 8th Rabíʿ I | ʿAli Sharkas becomes Governor-General |

| AD | AH | Event |
|---|---|---|
| 1855 | 1272 | |
| 24 November | 14th Rabí' I | Prince 'Abd-al-Halím of Egypt becomes Governor-General |
| 1861 | 1277 | |
| ? | ? | Muhammad Ahmad becomes Sammánía novice under Muhammad al-Sharíf Núr al-Dá'im (aged 17) |
| ? | ? | Muhammad Ahmad studies under Sheikh Al-Amín al-Suwayli in the Jazíra |
| 1862 | 1279 | |
| 27 December | 5th Rajab | Músa Hamdi Sharkas becomes Governor-General |
| 1863 | | |
| ? | ? | Muhammad Ahmad studies under Muhammad al-Dikkeir 'Abdallah Khojali at Berber (aged 19) |
| 18 January | 27th Rajab | Egypt: Death of Muhammad Sa'íd and accession of Ismail Ibrahím |
| 1865 | 1282 | |
| 19 June | 25th Muharram | Ja'far Sádiq Sharkas becomes Governor-General |
| 1866 | | |
| 9 January | 21st Sha'bán | Ja'far Mazhar becomes Governor-General |
| ? | ? | Muhammad Ahmad marries Fátima bint al-Hajj (aged 22) |
| 1868 | 1284 | |
| ? | ? | Muhammad Ahmad becomes a sheikh of the Sammánía order |
| 1869 | 1285 | |
| 29 January | 16th Shawwál | Bahr al-Ghazál Province comes under Egyptian rule |
| 1870 | 1286 | |
| ? | ? | Muhammad Ahmad moves to Jazíra Aba |
| ? | ? | Muhammad Ahmad marries Fátima bint Ahmad Sharfi (aged 26) |

# CHRONOLOGY

| AD | AH | *Event* |
|---|---|---|
| **1871** | **1288** | |
| 26 May | 6th Rabíʿ I | Equatoria Province comes under Egyptian rule |
| **1873** | **1290** | |
| 2 December | 11th Shawwál | Ismail Ayúb becomes Governor-General |
| **1874** | **1291** | |
| 24 October | 13th Ramadan | Darfur Province comes under Egyptian rule |
| **1876** | **1293** | |
| 25 December | 9th Dhú al-Hijja | Egypt: British and French Ministers appointed |
| **1877** | **1294** | |
| 18 February | 4th Safar | Charles Gordon becomes Governor-General |
| 4 August | 24th Rajab | Anti-Slavery Convention signed by Britain and Egypt |
| **1878** | **1295** | |
| ? | ? | Split with Muhammad al-Sharíf Núr al-Dáʿim; joins al-Quráshi wad al-Zain |
| ? | ? | Muhammad Ahmad marries al-Niʿma bint al-Quráshi (aged 34) |
| 25 July | 25th Rajab | Sheikh al-Quráshi dies; Muhammad Ahmad inherits leadership of order |
| **1879** | **1296** | |
| 7 April | 15th Rabíʿ II | Egypt: Khedive Ismail dismisses European Ministers |
| 26 June | 6th Rajab | Egypt: Sultan deposes Ismail and Tawfiq is appointed Khedive |
| **1880** | **1297** | |
| March | | Muhammad ʿAbd-al-Raʾúf becomes Governor-General |
| December | Dhú al-Hijja | Muhammad Ahmad meets ʿAbdulláhi al-Taʿíshi at al-Massallamía |
| ? | ? | Muhammad Ahmad's first tour of Kordofan and Nuba Mountains |
| **1881** | **1298** | |
| 15 January | 14th Safar | Egypt: Ahmad ʿArábi leads army mutiny |
| March | Rabíʿ II | Muhammad Ahmad's private declaration as Mahdi |

285

| AD | AH | Event |
|---|---|---|
| 29 June | 1st Sha'bán | Muhammad Ahmad's public declaration as Mahdi |
| ? | ? | Mahdi's second tour of Kordofan and Nuba Mountains |
| July–August | Ramadan | Mahdi writes to Governor-General Muhammad 'Abd-al-Ra'úf |
| ? | ? | Appointment of three khulafá' |
| 7 August | 11th Ramadan | Muhammad Abú-al-Su'úd meets the Mahdi |
| 12–13 August | 16th–17th Ramadan | Battle at Jazíra Aba |
| 13 August | 17th Ramadan | Hijra to Jebel Gadír begins |
| 30 August | 30th Dhú al-Qaida 1299 | Hijra ends at Jebel Gadír |
| 8 December | 16th Muharram | Defeat of Ráshid Bey Ayman, Governor of Fashoda |
| 1882 | | |
| 5 February | 16th Rabí' I | Egypt: Ahmad 'Arábi appointed Minister of War |
| 16 February | 27th Rabí' I | 'Abd-al-Qádir Hilmi appointed Governor-General; Carl Giegler serves in interim |
| 4 March | 13th Rabí' II | Muhammad Ra'úf departs from Khartoum |
| 15 March | 25th Rabí' II | Government force under Yúsuf Hassan al-Shalláli sets out from Khartoum |
| 30 March | 10th Jumáda I | Government force defeated at al-Massallamía |
| 5 April | 16th Jumáda I | Siege of Sennár begins |
| 3 May | 15th Jumáda II | Government force under Giegler victorious at Abú-Haráz |
| 4 May | 16th Jumáda II | Shalláli force sets out from Fashoda |
| 11 May | 23rd Jumáda II | 'Abd-al-Qádir Hilmi arrives in Khartoum |
| 22 May | 4th Rajab | Mahdi writes to Shalláli at Jebel Fungur |
| 30 May | 12th Rajab | Shalláli force routed by Mahdists near Jebel Gadír |
| 11 June | 24th Rajab | Egypt: Riot in Alexandria |
| 15 June | 28th Rajab | Mahdi sends Madibbu 'Ali to lead uprising in Darfur |

# CHRONOLOGY

| AD | AH | Event |
|---|---|---|
| 30 June | 14th Sha'bán | 'Abd-al-Qádir Hilmi begins fortifications around Khartoum |
| 9 July | 23rd Sha'bán | Madibbu 'Ali destroys Shakka garrison at al-Allali |
| 11 July | 25th Sha'bán | Egypt: British naval bombardment of Alexandria |
| 28 August | 14th Shawwál | Mahdi advances on Obeid |
| 30 August | 16th Shawwál | Mahdi writes to Muhammad Sa'íd, Governor of Kordofán |
| 8 September | 24th Shawwál | 'Friday Battle' at Obeid |
| 13 September | 30th Shawwál | Battle of Tel al-Kabír |
| 14 September | 1st Dhú al-Qaida | Christian missionaries captured at Dillinj |
| 15 September | 2nd Dhú al-Qaida | Egypt: British troops occupy Cairo and arrest Ahmad 'Arábi |
| | **1300** | |
| 14 November | 3rd Muharram | Detachment of 1,000 reinforcements leave Suez for Suakin |
| 15 November | 4th Muharram | 'Abd-al-Qádir Hilmi begins ditch on south side of Khartoum |
| 12 December | 1st Safar | Detachment of 5,000 reinforcements leave Cairo |
| 16 December | 5th Safar | Lt-Col Stewart arrives in Khartoum |
| **1883** | | |
| 6 January | 26th Safar | Surrender of Bara to the Mahdists |
| 19 January | 10th Rabí' I | Mahdists capture Obeid |
| 15 February | 7th Rabí' II | Egypt: Last detachment of General Hicks' force leaves Cairo for Suakin |
| 16 February | 8th Rabí' II | 'Alá-al-Dín Siddíq appointed Governor-General |
| 21 February | 13th Rabí' II | 'Alá-al-Dín Siddíq and Suleimán Niyázi arrive to replace 'Abd-al-Qádir Hilmi |
| 4 March | 24th Rabí' II | General Hicks arrives in Khartoum |
| 8 March | 28th Rabí' II | Lt-Col Stewart leaves Khartoum |
| 26 March | 16th Jumáda I | 'Ala-al-Dín installed as Governor-General |
| 8 May | 1st Rajab | 'Osmán Digna appointed amír to lead uprising in Red Sea region |
| 9 July | 4th Ramadan | Egypt: Cholera epidemic |

| AD | AH | *Event* |
|---|---|---|
| 5 August | 1st Shawwál | First attack on Sinkat; 'Osmán Digna wounded |
| 9 September | 7th Dhú al-Qaida | General Hicks leaves Khartoum for Dueim |
| 20 September | 18th Dhú al-Qaida | General Hicks joins Governor-General 'Ala-al-Dín at Dueim |
| 24 September | 22nd Dhú al-Qaida | General Hicks begins five-week march into Kordofan |
| | 1301 | |
| 4 November | 4th Muharram | Death of General Hicks, 'Ala-al-Dín and their army at Sheikán |
| 5 November | 5th Muharram | 1st Battle of the Red Sea Coast |
| 19 November | 19th Muharram | Egypt: Sir Evelyn Baring, Consul-General in Cairo, advocates abandoning Sudan |
| 16 December | 16th Safar | Hussein Yusri Sirri becomes acting Governor-General |
| 1884 | | |
| 15 January | 16th Rabí' I | Surrender of Fasher to the Mahdists |
| 24 January | 25th Rabí' I | Charles Gordon appointed Governor-General in Cairo |
| 4 February | 6th Rabí' II | Rout of Valentine Baker's force near Trinkitat (2nd Battle of the Coast) |
| 8 February | 10th Rabí' II | Mahdists capture Tukar |
| 18 February | 20th Rabí' II | Charles Gordon arrives in Khartoum |
| 29 February | 2nd Jumáda I | General Graham defeats Ansár in 3rd Battle of the Coast ('el-Teb') |
| 5 March | 7th Jumáda I | Mahdi rejects Gordon's offer to become Sultan of Kordofan |
| | | British government refuses to allow Zubeir Pasha to work with Gordon |
| 13 March | 15th Jumáda I | Siege of Khartoum begins |
| | | Surrender of Bahr al-Ghazál to amír Karamallah |
| | | General Graham defeats Ansár at Tamainaib ('Tamai') |
| 31 March | 3rd Jumáda II | Muhammad al-Kheir appointed amír of Berber region |
| 1 April | 4th Jumáda II | Muhammad Khálid appointed amír of Darfur region |
| | | Muhammad 'Osmán Abu-Garja |

| AD | AH | Event |
|---|---|---|
| | | appointed amír of Nile region, in charge of siege of Khartoum |
| 3 June | 9th Sha'bán | Emin Pasha retreats before advance of amír Karamallah |
| 18 May | 22nd Rajab | Mahdists under Muhammad al-Kheir capture Berber |
| 5 August | 13th Shawwál | Gladstone approves budget for Relief Force |
| 26 August | 5th Dhú al-Qaida | Sir Garnet Wolseley appointed to command Relief Force |
| 18 September | 19th Dhú al-Qaida | Lt-Col Stewart and companions killed after wreck of the *Abbas* |
| 27 September | 7th Dhú al-Hijja | Gordon sends four steamers to await Relief Force |
| 1885 | 1302 | |
| 5 January | 18th Rabí' I | Surrender of Omdurman Fort to Hamdán Abú-Anja |
| 8 January | 21st Rabí' I | *Bordein* and *Tel el Hoween* sent to relieve Khartoum |
| 17 January | 30th Rabí' I | Desert Column defeats Ansár at Abú-Tulayh oasis ('Abu Klea') |
| 19 January | 2nd Rabí' II | Desert Column defeats Ansár near Berber ('Abu Kru'); General Stewart is killed |
| 24 January | 7th Rabí' II | Sir Charles Wilson sends two steamers towards Khartoum |
| 26 January | 9th Rabí' II | Capture of Khartoum and death of Charles Gordon |
| 28 January | 11th Rabí' II | Sir Charles Wilson, with small force, reaches Khartoum too late |
| 17 June | 4th Ramadan | Mahdi falls ill in Omdurman |
| 22 June | 9th Ramadan | Death of the Mahdi |
| 19 August | 8th Dhú al-Qaida | Surrender of Sennar to the Mahdists |
| 30 September | 21st Dhú al-Hijja | Surrender of Kassala to the Mahdists |
| 1886 | 1303 | |
| 26 January | 20th Rabí' II | Last British troops evacuate Suakin |
| 7 May | 2nd Sha'bán | Last British troops evacuate Wadi Halfa and Korosko |

# *Appendix*

# *Ottoman, Egyptian and Sudanese Officials During the Lifetime of the Mahdi*

| | | | | | |
|---|---|---|---|---|---|
| † | British | †† | German | ††† | Italian |
| * | French | ** | Austrian | *** | American |
| ‡ | Prussian | ‡‡ | Swiss | | |

## *Constantinople*

### SULTAN OF THE OTTOMAN EMPIRE

| | |
|---|---|
| Abdülmecit I | 1 July 1839–25 June 1861 |
| Abdülaziz I | 25 June 1861–30 May 1876 |
| Mehmet Murat V | 30 May–31 August 1876 |
| Abdülhamit II | 31 August 1876–27 April 1909 |

## *Cairo*

### WÁLI OR KHEDIVE

| | |
|---|---|
| Muhammad 'Ali | 9 July 1805–2 August 1849 |
| 'Abbás Hilmi | 2 August 1849–13 July 1854 |
| Muhammad Sa'íd | 13 July 1854–18 January 1863 |
| Ismail Ibrahím | 18 January 1863–26 June 1879 |
| Muhammad Tawfíq | 26 June 1879–7 January 1892 |

## *Khartoum*

### GOVERNOR-GENERAL (POSITION ESTABLISHED IN MARCH 1826)

| | |
|---|---|
| Ahmad al-Kawalili | 18 March 1844–14 December 1845 |

| | |
|---|---|
| Khálid Khusraw al-Stanali | 14 December 1845–12 November 1849 |
| 'Abd-al-Latíf 'Abdallah Sharkas | 13 November 1849–14 January 1852 |
| Rustum Sharkas | 14 January–28 May 1852 |
| Ismail al-Hajji Abú-Jabal | 4 July 1852–20 April 1853 |
| Salím Sá'ib al-Ghazairli | 24 April 1853–22 July 1854 |
| 'Ali Sirri Arnavut | 22 July–29 November 1854 |
| 'Ali Sharkas | 29 November 1854–24 November 1855 |
| Prince M. 'Abd-al-Halím | 24 November 1855–28 December 1856 |

There followed a gap in succession, during which time Arakil al-Armani (28 January 1857–13 November 1858), Músa Hamdi Sharkas (13 November 1858–13 February 1859) and Hassan 'Ali Arnavut (13 February 1859–1 July 1861) were in turn appointed 'Múdir of Khartoum and its dependencies', while the territory as a whole was ruled from Cairo.

| | |
|---|---|
| Músa Hamdi Sharkas | 27 December 1862–19 June 1865 |
| Ja'far Sádiq Sharkas | 19 June 1865–9 January 1866 |
| Ja'far Mazhar | 9 January 1866–30 September 1871 |

There followed another gap in succession, during which time overall rule again passed to Cairo. Various provincial officials were appointed and Ahmad Mumtáz (30 September 1871–October 1872) and Edhem al-Arifi al-Atqalawi (October 1872–2 December 1873) were in turn appointed 'Múdir of Southern Sudan, Sennar and Khartoum'.

| | |
|---|---|
| Ismail Ayúb | 2 December 1873–17 February 1877 |
| Charles Gordon† | 18 February 1877–8 December 1879 |
| Muhammad 'Abd-al-Ra'úf | March 1880–15 February 1882 |
| Carl Giegler†† | 16 February–11 May 1882 (acting) |
| 'Abd-al-Qádir Hilmi | 11 May 1882–16 February 1883 |
| 'Ala-al-Dín Siddíq | 16 February 1883–5 November 1883 |
| Hussein Yusri Sirri | 16 December 1883–18 February 1884 (acting) |
| Charles Gordon | 18 February 1884–26 January 1885 |

*Sudan Provinces*

## GOVERNOR OF BAHR AL-GHAZÁL (UNDER EGYPTIAN RULE FROM 29 JANUARY 1869)

| | |
|---|---|
| Muhammad al-Hiláli | 29 January 1869–1872 (as Názir) |
| Al-Zubeir Rahma Mansúr | 1872–March 1878 |
| Idris wad Daftardar | March–June 1878 |
| Muhammad Sa'ti | June 1878–1879 |
| Romolo Gessi††† | 1879–September 1880 |
| 'Ali Músa | September 1880–December 1881 |
| Frank Lupton† | December 1881–28 April 1884 |

## GOVERNOR OF BERBER

| | |
|---|---|
| Muhammad al-Amín | 1843–6 |
| Hassan Hosni | 1846–51 |
| 'Ali Hasíb | 1851–4 |
| Hilmi | 1854–7 |
| Ibrahím Abú-Fileija | 1857 |
| Mahmúd | 1857–9 |
| 'Abdallah al-Wanli | 1859–62 |
| Ibrahím | 1862–5 |
| 'Umar | 1865–7 |
| 'Ali 'Uweida | 1867 |
| Ahmad Rámi | 1867–9 |
| Hussein Khalífa | 1869–73 (with Dongola) |
| 'Ali Sharíf | 1874–5 |
| Mustafa Murád | 1875–8 |
| Muhammad Sa'íd Wahbi | 1878 |
| Ibrahím al-Sabbán | 1878–9 |
| Muhammad Ma'ni | 1879–81 |
| Firhád Muhhíb | 1882 |
| 'Abd-al-Rahmán Fá'iz | 1882–3 |
| Hussein Khalífa | 1883–4 |

## GOVERNOR OF DARFUR (UNDER EGYPTIAN RULE FROM 24 OCTOBER 1874)

| | |
|---|---|
| Hassan Hilmi | 1874–79 |
| Charles-Frédéric Rosset* | 1879 |

| | |
|---|---|
| Giacomo Messedaglia††† | 1879–80 |
| 'Ali Sharíf | 1880–1 |
| Rudolf Slatin** | November 1881–December 1883 |

## GOVERNOR OF DONGOLA

| | |
|---|---|
| Hassan Rifa'at | 1843–6 |
| Hassan Hosni | 1846–51 |
| Khurshid | 1851–2 |
| Hussein | 1852 |
| Mahmúd | 1857–9 |
| 'Abdallah al-Wanli | 1859–62 |
| 'Osmán | 1866–70 |
| Hussein Khalífa | 1869–73 (with Berber) |
| Almás Muhammad | 1873–9 |
| Sír Mustafa Yawar | 1879–85 |
| Muhammad Jawdat | 1885 |

## GOVERNOR OF EQUATORIA (UNDER EGYPTIAN RULE FROM 26 MAY 1871)

| | |
|---|---|
| Samuel Baker† | 26 May 1871–3 |
| Muhammad 'Abd-al-Ra'úf | 1873–4 |
| Charles Gordon | 1874–6 |
| Henry Prout*** | 1876–7 |
| Alexander Mason*** | 1877–August 1877 |
| Ibráhím Fawzi | August 1877–1878 |
| Muhammad Emin‡ | 1878–89 (Edouard Schnitzer) |

## GOVERNOR OF KORDOFAN (UNDER EGYPTIAN RULE FROM 16 AUGUST 1821)

| | |
|---|---|
| Mustafa Kiridli | 1843–8 |
| Músa Hamdi | 1848 and 1850 |
| 'Abd-al-Qádir | 1851–3 |
| Muhammad al-Amín | 1854–8 |
| Hassan 'Ali Arnavut | 1858–63 |
| Muhammad Hílmi | 1863–5 |
| Hassan Hilmi al-Juwaisar | 1866–7 |
| 'Abd-al-Wahhab | 1871–4 |

| | |
|---|---|
| Muhammad Sa'íd Wahbi | 1874 |
| Hassan Hilmi al-Juwaisar | 1874 |
| Mahmúd Táhir | 1875–8 |
| Ilyás Umm Bireir | 1878 |
| Muhammad Sa'íd Wahbi | 1879–19 January 1883 |

## GOVERNOR OF RED SEA DISTRICT (BEFORE 1873, PART OF JEDDA PROVINCE)

| | |
|---|---|
| Johann Munzinger‡‡ | 1873–5 |
| Rashíd Rajab | 1875 |
| 'Ali al-Rida al-Tubji | 1880–1 |
| 'Alá-al-Dín Siddíq | 1882–3 |
| Rashíd Kámil | 1883 |
| Suleimán Niyázi | 1883 |
| Hussein Wasif | 1883–4 |
| Sir William Hewett† | 1884 |
| Sir Cromer Ashburnham† | 1884 |
| Sir Herbert Chermside† | 1884–6 |

# Glossary

| | |
|---|---|
| abú | father of |
| agha | honorific for junior officers, below Bey (q.v.) |
| agsám | provincial sub-districts; s. gism |
| ahl | family, people |
| alai | infantry regiment |
| 'alim | Islamic scholar or jurist, pl. 'ulamá' |
| 'Allahu akbar' | 'God is great' |
| amín | Mahdist official; commissioner; pl. umana' |
| amír | Mahdist general; pl. umará' |
| Amír al-Sharq | eastern commander, i.e. 'Osmán Digna |
| angareb | bedstead of wood and rope or woven palm-leaves |
| Ansár | supporters of the Mahdi, named after the followers of the Prophet Muhammad in Medina |
| aragi | date liquor |
| Arnaut | Albanian |
| arrági | knee-length man's buttonless smock |
| ashráf | blessed descendents of the Prophet Muhammad; sing. sharíf |
| awlád | boys, sons of; s. walad |
| al-Azhar | Sunni Muslim mosque and university in Cairo |
| | |
| báb | gate, door; pl. abwáb |
| Baggára | nomadic tribe of central, western and southern Sudan, sub-divided into many clans |
| baraka | holiness (of a Sufi saint) |
| bashi-bazouk | irregular troops, often from Shaigía tribe |
| bay'a | oath of allegiance |
| bazingers | southern Sudanese troops, often former slavers |
| beit | house; pl. buyút |
| Beit al-Mál | Mahdist treasury ('House of Property') |
| bey | honorific for middle-ranking officers, below Pasha (q.v.) |
| bimbáshi | Major or Lieutenant-Colonel; commander of 1,000 men, i.e. one battalion |
| bint | girl, daughter of; pl. banát |
| buluk | company of 200 men |

| | |
|---|---|
| courbash | hippopotamus-hide whip |
| daftardár | keeper of fiscal or tax registers |
| Danágla | natives of Dongola region; s. Dongoláwi |
| dár | tribal homeland, e.g. Dár Shaigía |
| dár al-harb | 'domain of war', i.e., in Mahdist rhetoric, places still to be subjugated |
| dár al-Islam | 'domain of Islam', i.e. under the Mahdi's sway |
| darb al-arba'ín | trade route from Darfur to Assyút in Egypt, the forty days' road; pl. durúb |
| da'wa | call, invitation, summons by the Mahdi |
| deim | market settlement; pl. diyúm |
| dhikr | prayers and supplications to God, especially in a Sufi sect |
| diwán | reception area or sitting room; council meeting |
| diyúm | market settlements; s. deim |
| Dongoláwi | native of Dongola region; pl. Danágla |
| effendi | honorific for junior officers and administrators, below Bey (q.v.) |
| 'Eid al-Adha | festival of the Sacrifice, ending the month of pilgrimage to Mecca |
| 'Eid al-Fitr | festival ending Ramadan |
| fantass | wheeled metal water-bowser (colloquial) |
| faqí | traditional Sudanese Islamic holy man; pl. fuqara' |
| faríq | Lieutenant- or Major-General in Egyptian army |
| fatwa | Islamic legal ruling |
| fellahín | Egyptian rural labourers and farmers; s. fellah |
| fiqh | study of Islamic law |
| 'fí sabíl Allah' | 'in God's cause' |
| fúl | field beans |
| fuqara' | traditional Sudanese Islamic holy men; s. faqí |
| geiger | defensive trench-and-rampart combination |
| ghaníma | booty |
| ghár | cave or pit |
| ghazwa | raid, incursion |
| gism | provincial sub-district; pl. agsám |
| gyássa | twin-masted wooden sailing boat |
| Hadendawa | clan of the Beja tribe in eastern Red Sea Hills (known by British as 'fuzzy-wuzzies') |

| | |
|---|---|
| háfiz | student who has memorised the entire Qorán |
| Hajj | Muslim pilgrimage to Mecca and Madina |
| hajji/hajjía | man or woman who has made the pilgrimage |
| Haláwiyín | tribe of the Jazíra region |
| harám | taboo, forbidden (adj.) |
| Hikimdár | Governor-General of Sudan |
| hijra | flight by the Prophet Muhammad and followers to Medina (622 AD); imitated by the Mahdi (1881) |
| hilál | crescent moon |
| hosh | courtyard; pl. heishán |
| huwár | disciple, student; pl. hiyrán |
| | |
| ibn | son of |
| Imám | prayer leader; head of mosque |
| insha'Allah | God willing |
| Ismailía | Sufi sect, dominant in central Sudan |
| | |
| jallába | merchants, often of the Ja'aliyín and Danágla tribes; s. jallábi |
| jazíra | island or peninsula; Sudanese region between the Blue and White Niles |
| jellabía | ankle-length man's shirt |
| jibba | patched smock; uniform of the Ansár |
| jihad | holy war |
| jihádía | corps of southern soldiers or slaves trained as riflemen; 'holy warriors' |
| | |
| karáma | miracle; pl. karámát |
| Kawali/Kawalili | Greek |
| khalífa | deputy or successor, pl. khulafá' |
| khalwa | Qoránic school, attached to a mosque |
| Khatmía | Sufi sect, dominant in eastern Sudan |
| Khedive | title of Viceroy of Egypt after c. 1850, first formally conferred upon Ismail Ibrahím and heirs on 7 July 1867 |
| khor | seasonal watercourse, replenished by annual rains; pl. khayrán |
| Krupps | artillery (after manufacturer) |
| Kurjí | Georgian |
| | |
| 'lá illah ill'Allah | 'there is no God but Allah' |
| liwa | brigade; abbreviated form of Brigadier-General |

| | |
|---|---|
| madháhib | schools of Islamic law |
| Mahdi | divinely guided one who will restore true Islam |
| Mahdía | period of rule by the Mahdi and his successor the Khalífa (1885–99) |
| Majdhúbía | Sufi sect, prevalent in eastern regions |
| mamúr | provincial official |
| manshúr | proclamation (pl. manshúrát) |
| marísa | beer made from fermented sorghum |
| masháyikh | holy men; teachers; s. sheikh |
| minbar | pulpit |
| mír | commander |
| míralai | commander of infantry regiment, i.e. Colonel |
| mírliwa (also liwa) | brigade commander, i.e. Brigadier-General |
| mudír | provincial governor |
| mudíría | governorate or governor's office |
| mulázimín | corps of bodyguards to the Mahdi and the Khalífa |
| muqaddam | subordinate officer in Mahdist army |
| muríd | disciple, follower |
| murkab | passenger boat on the Nile (p. marákib) |
| mutamahdi | false Mahdi |
| mu'uminín | the (Muslim) faithful |
| | |
| nasráni | Christian |
| názir | administrative title given to tribal chiefs |
| noggára | wooden war-drum |
| Nordenfeldt | five-barrelled machine-gun (after manufacturer) |
| nugúr | wooden sailing boat |
| | |
| pasha | honorific for senior civil or military figure in Egypt, above Bey (q.v.) |
| | |
| qádi | Muslim judge |
| | |
| Rátib | collection of devotional prayers and quotations from the Qorán |
| razzia | slave-raid, corrution of ghazwa (q.v.) |
| Rizeigát | sub-clan of the Baggára (q.v.) |
| | |
| ságiya | waterwheel |
| Sammánía | Sufi sect, with three branches |
| sanjak | commander of irregular cavalry squadron of Shaigía (q.v.); used generically for the tribe |

# GLOSSARY

| | |
|---|---|
| saráya | government house; palace (used of Governor-General's official residence) |
| shádúf | lever-and-bucket device to raise water from the Nile |
| sharíf | blessed descendent of the Prophet Muhammad; pl. ashráf |
| shahada | declaration of Muslim belief: *Lá illah ill'Allah (wa) Muhammad rasúl Allah* ('There is no God but Allah and Muhammad is the Messenger of Allah') |
| Shaigía | tribe from region north of Khartoum; loyal to Egyptian government against Mahdía |
| sharí'a | Islamic law |
| Sharkas | Circassian |
| sheiba | wooden yoke to punish runaway slaves |
| sheikh | holy man; leader of a Sufi order; tribal elder; pl. masháyikh |
| Shukría | Sudanese tribe of Blue Nile region |
| sirdar | Commander-in-Chief of the Egyptian army |
| Sirri | Syrian |
| sirwál | men's baggy trousers, tied around the waist |
| Stanali | native of Constantinople |
| súq | market; pl. aswáq |
| sunut | Sudanese tree, *acacia nilotica* |
| | |
| takbír | prayer asserting God's greatness: *Allahu akbar* |
| tálib | student in a Qoránic school; pl. tuláb |
| tarboush | tall felt hat like a cone with flattened top |
| taríqa | Sufi order or brotherhood; pl. turuq |
| tawhíd | theology of Allah's oneness |
| Tijánía | Sufi sect |
| Turkía | period of rule by Ottoman invaders (1820–85) |
| turuq | Sufi brotherhoods; s. taríqa |
| | |
| 'ulamá' | Islamic scholars or jurists, s. 'alim |
| umana' | Mahdist commissioners, s. amín |
| umará | Mahdist generals; s. amír |
| Umm al-Mu'uminín | 'Mother of the Faithful', honorific of the Mahdi's wife Aisha bint Ahmad Sharfi |
| umma | community of Muslims |
| | |
| wad | son of; abbreviation of walad (q.v.) |
| wakíl | deputy or agent |

| | |
|---|---|
| walad | boy; son of; pl. awlád |
| wazír | minister, vizier |
| yuzbáshi | Captain (commander of 100 men) |
| zakát | Islamic charitable donations; effectively a tax |
| zaríba | protective thorn fence; pl. zará'ib |
| zuhur | revelation, manifestation |

# Notes

## Introduction

1 Col. C. Chaillé Long, *The Three Prophets: Chinese Gordon, Mohammed-Ahmed (El Maahdi), Arabi Pasha* (New York, 1884), p. 60.

2 Major Gaetano Casati, *Ten Years in Equatoria and the Return with Emin Pasha*, tr. Mrs J. Randolph Clay (2 vols, London, 1891), vol. 2, p. 2.

3 Muhammad Ibráhím Abú-Salím, *Al-athár al-kámila lil-Imám al-Mahdi*, vol. 1 (Khartoum, Khartoum University Press, 1990), pp. 175–8.

4 John Ralph Willis, 'Jihād Fī Sabīl Allāh – Its Doctrinal Basis in Islam and Some Aspects of its Evolution in Nineteenth-Century West Africa', *The Journal of African History*, vol. VIII (Cambridge, 1967), p. 395.

5 L. Carl Brown, 'The Sudanese Mahdiya', in Robert L. Rotberg and Ali A. Mazrui (eds), *Protest and Power in Black Africa* (New York, Oxford University Press, 1970), p. 147.

6 The *Sunna* and the *Hadíth*; Abú-Salím, *Al-athár al-kámila*, vol. 1, pp. 162–4, is an early example of the Mahdi urging followers to follow these examples; Dr Fisal Muhammad Musa, 'Judiciary and the Nile Fleet in the Mahadya State in Sudan', lecture given at 5th International Conference on Sudan Studies at Durham University, 1999; online at www.dur.ac.uk/justin.willis/judiciary.htm; Aharon Layish, 'The Legal Methodology of the Mahdi', *Sudanic Africa*, vol. 8 (1997), pp. 37–66; available online at www.hf.uib.no/smi/sa/08/8Layish.pdf.

7 The Qorán, Súra Yúnis (10/4).

8 Abú-Salím, *Al-athár al-kamila*, vol. 1, pp. 359–60.

9 Ibn, 'son of', is not normally used in Sudanese names but the Mahdi used it to sign his own letters and proclamations; the more common word used was *walad* ('boy', hence 'son of'), often abbreviated to *wad*.

10 Brown, 'Sudanese Mahdiya', p. 145.

11 Heather Sharkey, 'A Jihad of the Pen: Mahdiya History and Historiography', (unpublished) draft lecture, 18 November 1993.

12 Ismail 'Abd-al-Gádir al-Kordofáni, *Kitáb sa'ádat al-mustahdi bi-sírát al-Imám al-Mahdi* ('Book of Bliss of Him who Seeks Guidance by the Life of al-Imám al-Mahdi'), ed. Muhammad Ibrahím Abú-Salím

(Oxford, Clarendon Press, 1972), pp. 73–5; Haim Shaked, *The Life of the Sudanese Mahdi* (New Jersey, Transaction Press, 1978), provides a condensed translation and commentary; Sudan Archive at Durham University (SAD), 99/6, is the original MS; SAD, 247/4, an anonymous translation. Ismail 'Abd-al-Gádir was educated at al-Azhar mosque in Cairo for more than sixteen years and became Mufti of Obeid; he crossed to the Mahdi's side shortly before the capture of the city; his Síra was completed on 7 November 1888.

13  Sudan Library at the University of Khartoum (SLUK), MS 'Abd-al-Rahmán Hussain al-Jabri, 'Al-nafahat al-wardía wal-shajarat al-Mahdía'; Muhamed O. Beshir, 'Abdel Rahman ibn Hussein el Jabri and His Book "History of the Mahdi"', *Sudan Notes and Records (SNR)*: 44 (1963), 136–9; Gabriel Warburg, *Islam, Sectarianism and Politics in Sudan* (London, Hurst, 2003), p. 37; al-Jabri was a Yemeni who converted to the Mahdist cause and was commissioned by the Mahdi's posthumous son 'Abd-al-Rahmán to research a history of the Mahdía.

14  Sub-titled *Al-Sawarim al-Hindía* ('The Indian Swords').

15  Al-Sádiq al-Mahdi, *Yas'alúnaka 'an al-Mahdía* ('You will Ask about the Mahdía')(Beirut, 1976); al-Sádiq al-Mahdi, *Al-Jazíra Aba wa-dawraha fí nahdat al-Sudán* (Khartoum, 1981); the author is Muhammad Ahmad's successor as Imám of the Mahdist community.

16  Thomas Keneally, *Bettany's Book* (London, Sceptre, 2001), p. 85.

17  Henryk Sienkiewicz, *In Desert and Wilderness* (Edinburgh, Polish Book Depot, 1945), p. 101; tr. Max Drezmal from *W pustyni i w puszczy* (Warsaw, 1912).

18  The film *The Four Feathers* (directed by Zoltan Korda) is a pale shadow of A.E.W. Mason's emotionally sensitive and less jingoistic 1902 novel, but it features stunning images of lost landscapes such as the Sudanese port city, Suakin, and the Nile cataracts in Nubia.

19  Rudolf Carl Slatin, *Fire and Sword in the Sudan: A Personal Narrative of Fighting and Serving the Dervishes, 1879–1895* (London, Edward Arnold, 1892); ghost written by F.R. Wingate; subsequently translated as *Feuer und Schwert im Sudan, Meine Kämpfe mit den Derwischen, meine Befangenschaft und Flucht, 1879–1895* (Lepizig, 1896). Slatin served as Governor of Darfur before being captured by the Mahdi's forces; Fr Joseph Ohrwalder, *Ten Years' Captivity in the Mahdi's Camp, 1882–1892* (London, Darf, 1986), rewritten by F.R. Wingate from original MSS and Ohrwalder's letters; Ohrwalder, a missionary, was captured by the Mahdists at Dillinj in the Nuba Mountains.

20  F.R. Wingate, *Mahdiism and the Egyptian Sudan* (London, Macmillan, 1891).

21 P.M. Holt, *The Source-Materials of Sudanese Mahdia*, St Antony's Papers (Oxford, Oxford University Press, 1958), pp. 109–13.

22 Wingate, *Mahdiism*, pp. 466–7.

23 Richard Bermann, *The Mahdi of Allah: The Story of the Dervish Mohammed Ahmed* (New York, Macmillan, 1932), p. 28, tr. Robin John from *Die Derwischtrommel: Das Leben des Erwarteten Mahdi* ('The Dervish Drum: The Life of the Expected Mahdi'), written under pseudonym Arnold Höllriegel (Berlin, 1931).

24 P.M. Holt, *The Mahdist State in the Sudan, 1881–1898*, 2nd edition (Oxford, Clarendon Press, 1970).

25 Muhammad Sa'íd al-Gaddal, *Lawha li-tha'ir Sudáni: al-Imam al-Mahdi Muhammad Ahmad b. 'Abdallah (1844–1885)* ('A Portrait of a Sudanese Revolutionary: The Imám Muhammad Ahmad ibn 'Abdallah al-Mahdi (1884–1885)') (Khartoum, Khartoum University Press, 1985); Dr al-Gaddal's own leftist politics undermined the credibility of the book in the eyes of some Sudanese academics, while those on the left have criticised the *Portrait* for a deficiency of serious Marxist critique.

26 Muhammad Ibráhím Abú-Salím, *Al-athár al-kámila lil-Imám al-Mahdi*, 7 vols (Khartoum, Khartoum University Press, 1990–4); the Mahdi's writings have been divided by some into categories: proclamations (*manshúrát*), warnings (*indharát*), visions (*hadhrát*) and legal rulings (*akhám*).

27 He served as Prime Minister of Sudan twice, 1964–5 and 1986–9 (on the latter occasion he was overthrown in a *coup d'état*).

*Prologue. 'Leaves after a Storm'*

1 The Qorán, Súrat al-Tauba (9/41), enjoins Muslims to 'struggle . . . in the cause of God'.

2 The Mahdi had named his followers the 'Ansár', after the supporters of the Prophet Muhammad in 622 AD; see chapter 8, note 1.

3 Lieutenant R.S. Grenfell, Sergeants F. Allen, E. Carter and A. Grantham, Corporals F. Elliott, J. Borthwick, J. Wood, J.S. Cattercook, C. Wright and J. Weller, Privates H. Hunt, T. Hannah, A. Roberts, F. Rawle, C. Hatter, T. Miles, F. Morhall, F. Kelly, W. Oldbury, W. Etherington, H. Bradshaw and W. Hadley.

4 The campaign had begun on 16 March 1986; during the advance on Khartoum, via Dongola, Abu Hamed and Berber, principal battles included Firket (7 June 1986), Abu Hamed (7 August 1896), Harir (19 September 1896), Atbara (8 April 1898); Donald Featherstone, *Omdurman 1898: Kitchener's Victory in the Sudan* (Oxford, Osprey, 1993).

5 'Ismat Hasan Zulfo, *Karari*, tr. Peter Clark (London, Frederick Warne, 1980), pp. 151–4; SOAS, PP MS 07/3/3/'Personalia'/d, MS J.A. Reid, 'Story of a Mahdist Amir', dated 30 August 1926; the account is of 'Isa wad al-Zein, a junior amír from the Khalífa's Ta'íshi clan, who had arrived in Omdurman from Obeid along with 800 riflemen and 500 cavalry as last-minute reinforcements.

6 J.A. Reid, 'The Mahdi's Emirs', *SNR*, 20 (1937), 308–9.

7 NAM, 6604–44, MS letter from Colonel William S. Sparkes (1862–1906) to Mrs Turnure, pp. 2–3, dated 13 September 1989; the title Sirdar was borrowed from the Indian Army (from the Urdu *sardā r*, 'head man').

8 Philip Ziegler, *Omdurman* (London, Collins, 1973); Winston Churchill, *The River War*, abridged edition (London, Prion Books, 2000), pp. 191–218; Randolph Churchill, *Winston S. Churchill* (5 vols, London, 1966), vol. 1: *Youth 1874–1900*, pp. 408–19.

9 SLUK, 89CV/261015, MS Lt-Col F.C.C. Balfour, 'Fiki 'Ali', unpublished article dated 1951.

10 SAD, 403/2, pp. 14–20, MSS Papers of (later, Major-General Sir) George Franks, letter to T.J. Franks, dated 5 September 1898.

11 F.R. Wingate, 'Note on the Dervish Wounded at Omdurman', in *Egypt No. 1 (1899)* (London, HMSO, 1899), p. 2; memo dated 3 March 1899.

12 Winston Churchill, *The River War* (2 vols, London, Longmans, 1899), vol. 2, pp. 198–9.

13 SAD, 267/1/387, MSS Wingate Papers, 'General Order of the Day', dated 2 September 1898.

14 Account of Ronald Meiklejohn of the Royal Warwickshire Regt. in *Omdurman Diaries 1898: Eyewitness Accounts of the Legendary Campaign*, ed. John Meredith (London, Leo Cooper, 1998), p. 188.

15 Lt-Col Andrew Haggard, *Under Crescent and Star* (London, William Blackwood, 1896), 2nd edn, pp. 181–3. The battle of Tamai (in the Red Sea Hills) took place on 13 March 1884.

16 Churchill, *The River War*, vol. 2, pp. 195–7.

17 Author's italics; Maj-Gen Lord Kitchener to Lord Cromer, in *Egypt No. 1 (1899)*, p. 1.

18 Babikr Bedri, *The Memoirs of Babikr Bedri*, ed. and tr. Yusuf Bedri and Peter Hogg (2 vols, London, Ithaca Press, 1980), vol. 2, p. 80.

19 SAD, 430/6, p. 4, MS Arabic letter to Kitchener (dated 2 October 1898 and signed by sixty-seven influential figures in the town, including the Mahdi's former tutor, Sheikh Muhammad Sharíf Núr al-Dá'im and the leader of the Khatmía sect, al-Sayyid Ahmad al-Mirghani); pp. 5–6, tr. Na'úm Shuqair.

20  Zulfo, *Karari*, p. 235.

21  Letter from Col. (later General Sir) Archibald Hunter, in *Omdurman 1898: The Eye-Witnesses Speak*, ed. Peter Harrington and Frederic Sharf (London, Greenhill, 1998), p. 158.

22  NAM, Col. William Sparkes, pp. 2–3.

23  Churchill, *The River War*, vol. 2, p. 212.

24  *Omdurman 1898*, p. 158.

25  Many towns and villages in northern Sudan were submerged when the Aswan High Dam was built in the 1960s.

*1. The Boat-Builder's Son*

1  27 Rajab 1260; P.M. Holt, *The Mahdist State in the Sudan, 1881–1898*, 2nd edn (Oxford, Clarendon Press, 1970), p. 45.

2  Sudanese names usually follow the pattern of the individual's name followed by the father's name; Muhammad Ahmad, however, is effectively a 'double-barrelled' first name.

3  Al-Mahdi, *Al-Jazíra Aba*, p. 3.

4  Al-Gaddal, *Lawha*, p. 27; NRO, INTEL 2/43/357, 'The Family Tree of the Mahdi' (Intelligence Department report, Khartoum, 25 November 1924); Graham and Ismay Thomas, *Sayed Abd El Rahman Al Mahdi, A Pictorial Biography, 1885–1959* (London, 1986).

5  Pl. *Danágla*.

6  Ernst Dietrich, 'Muhammad Ahmad b. 'Abdallah', *The Encyclopaedia of Islam*, various editors, vol. 3 (Leiden 1936), pp. 680–1; William Adams, *Nubia: Corridor to Africa* (Princeton, Allen Lane, 1977), pp. 44–63.

7  Holt, *Mahdist State*, p. 26; 'Ali was married to the Prophet's daughter Fátima.

8  Sing. *sharíf*.

9  Abú-Salím, *Al-athár al-kámila*, vol. 1, p. 53; letter dated 10 August 1877 (3 Sha'bán 1294); SAD, 100/10/1, original MS; the document concerns the legal transfer of a slave woman.

10  Ibid., p. 339; letter dated 12 May 1883 (5 Rajab 1300).

11  'Abd-al-Gádir, *Sírát al-Imám al-Mahdi*, pp. 74–5; Shaked, *Life*, p. 56; Bermann, *The Mahdi*, p. 52.

12  'Abd-al-Gádir, *Sírát al-Imám al-Mahdi*, pp. 80–1; Shaked, *Life*, pp. 56–9. The book was completed in Omdurman in 1888 under the watchful eye of Muhammad Ahmad's successor, the Khalífa 'Abdulláhi, who subsequently ordered the manuscript to be destroyed. In SAD, 260/2/1–6, 'Memorandum to Director of Military Intelligence on Ismail 'Abd-al-Gádir and his biography of the Mahdi',

Na'úm Shuqair describes how he arranged for a single copy of the work to be smuggled out of Sudan. Shuqair describes it as 'an excellent account' by 'the most learned man in Sudan'.

13  Beshir, 'el Jabri', pp. 136–9.

14  Interview with Muhammad Hassan Ihímir, Jazíra Aba, January 2003.

15  NRO, INTEL 9/1/1, a British intelligence file dated 12 May 1926, contains notes on the author and his work; it includes details of al-Jabri's interrogation by British intelligence and his deportation to Abyssinia as an undesirable activist 'engaged on Mahdist propaganda'.

16  J.S. Trimingham, *Islam in Sudan* (London, Frank Cass, 1965), pp. 126–39; the biographies of 260 saints who lived between 1500 and 1800 are given in the *Tabaqát* of Wad Daif Allah; see 'Tabaqāt Wad Dayf Allah: Studies in the Lives of the Scholars and Saints', S. Hillelson, *SNR*, 44 (1963): 136–9.

17  Dongola is still the capital of Sudan's Northern State.

18  Úrdí is the arabicised form of the Turkish *ordu*, 'camp' or 'army' (from which the phrase 'the Golden Horde' is derived); Karl Richard Lepsius, *Denkmäler aus Ägypten und Aethiopien* (12 vols, Berlin, 1849–59), p. 233.

19  El-Sayed el-Bushra, 'Towns in the Sudan in the Eighteenth and Early Nineteenth Centuries', *SNR*, 52 (1971): pp. 63–70.

20  Louis-Maurice Adolphe Linant de Bellefonds, *Journal d'un voyage à Méroé dans les années 1821 et 1822* ('Diary of a Journey to Merowe in the Years 1821 and 1822'), ed. Margaret Shinnie (Khartoum, Sudan Antiquities Service, 1958), p. 25; also Marcel Kurz and Pascale Linant de Bellefonds, 'Linant de Bellefonds: Travels in Egypt, Sudan and Arabia Petraea (1818–1828)', in *Travellers in Egypt*, eds Paul and Janet Starkey (London, Tauris Parke, 2001), pp. 61–9.

21  Bayard Taylor, *A Journey to Central Africa* (New York, 1854), pp. 454–6.

22  Ibid., p. 452.

23  Alan Palmer, *The Decline and Fall of the Ottoman Empire* (London, John Murray, 1992), p. 33.

24  1769–1849; Muhammad 'Ali, whose title was *Wali* of Egypt, was an Albanian from Kavalla in what is now north-eastern Greece.

25  Khaled Fahmy, *All the Pasha's Men: Mehmed 'Ali, His Army and the Making of Modern Egypt* (Cairo, American University of Cairo Press, 2002), pp. 82–4; 'Abd-al-Rahmán al-Jabarti, *'Ajá'ib al-Athár fí'l-Tarájim wa'l-Akhbár* (4 vols, Cairo, 1880), vol. 4, pp. 127–32. The fate of the Mamluks is narrated in detail in A.E. Robinson, 'The Mamelukes in Sudan', *SNR*, 5 (1922): 88–94.

26  In Turkish, *nizam-i ceded*; Fahmy, *Pasha's Men*, pp. 79–82.

27  1795–1822; Ismail Kámil was murdered by a Sudanese tribal monarch, Mek Nimr Muhammad Nimr, at Shendi; Hill, *Biographical Dictionary*, pp. 185–6.

28  *Amír al-mu'minín*; Gabriel Warburg, *Historical Discord in the Nile Valley* (London, Hurst, 1992), p. 19.

29  Richard Hill, 'Rulers of Sudan 1820–1885', *SNR*, 32 (1951): 89.

30  AH 1265; al-Mahdi, *Al-Jazíra Aba*, p. 3.

31  Bahr al-Ghazál came under formal Egyptian rule in January 1869, Equatoria in May 1871.

32  Sunut is *acacia arabica*; Linant de Bellefonds, *Journal*, p. 24.

33  Al-Mahdi, *Al-Jazíra Aba*, p. 4; while 'Abdallah is traditionally believed to have reached Karari before dying, this account is likely to be the most carefully corroborated.


## 2. The Shadow of the Saráya

1  The Qorán, Súrat al-'Aráf (7/200–1).

2  Originally 'seclusion' or 'solitude' (in the Sufi context, living alone with God), khalwa also means 'religious assembly area'; Ahmed Uthman Ibrahim, 'Some Aspects of the Ideology of the Mahdiya', *SNR*, 60 (1979): p. 33, discusses the use of the term in the context of progressive stages of Sufi meditation.

3  The Qorán, Súrat al-'Aráf (7/204–6).

4  Khalwa students are known variously as *hiyrán* (s. *huwár*) or *tuláb* (s. *tálib*).

5  Pl. fuqara'.

6  Al-Mahdi, *Al-Jazíra Aba*, p. 4; SLUK, 8CB 291059; Viviane Yagi, 'Le Kalifa 'Abdullahi: sa vie et sa politique' ('The Khalífa 'Abdulláhi: His Life and His Politics') (unpublished PhD thesis, Université Paul Valery, Montpellier, 1990), p. 70; pl. of sheikh is *masháyikh*.

7  Interview with Muhammad Hassan Ihímir, Jazíra Aba, January 2003.

8  Zulfo, *Karari*, p. 10: 'The story of the early days of Islam was a tale of military glory, so the student also studied, willy nilly, military history.'

9  Prayer (*salát*) is one of the essential elements of Islam, enjoined by The Qorán in Súrat al-Bagara (2/239–9), Súrat al-Nisa' (4/43), Súrat Húd (11/114), Súrat Bani Israel (17/78) and Súrat Qáf (50/39–40); the five daily prayers are *fajr* (pre-sunrise), *zuhur* (noon), *asr* (mid-afternoon), *maghrib* (early evening) and *'asha* (suppertime); see S. Hillelson, 'Tabaqát Wad Dayf Allah, *SNR*, 44 (1963): 208.

10  A large bed of this kind (an *angareb*), said to be from Muhammad Ahmad's first khalwa, is in the Beit Khalífa museum in Omdurman.

11 Bedri, *Memoirs*, p. 7, describes the author's own education at a khalwa near Wad Medani under the septuagenarian faqí Ahmad Hamid. Despite many hardships, including beatings, Bedri affectionately recalled: 'In spite of the intensity of his work, Faki Ahmad used to read the Koran every night, and he was a searcher after religious knowledge until the day of his death.' Bedri was later the patron of girls' education in the modern Sudan.

12 SAD, 721/1/56, Brownell MSS, 10 March 1862, describes Omdurman as still 'a little village'.

13 Many historians ascribe the founding of Omdurman to one Sheikh Hamad wad Mariam in the late seventeenth century; F. Rehfisch, 'A Sketch of the Early History of Omdurman', *SNR*, 45 (1964): 35–47; also Robert Kramer, 'Holy City on the Nile: Omdurman, 1885–1898' (unpublished PhD thesis, Northwestern, 1991), pp. 43–4.

14 The title Bey was a grade below that of Pasha; Hill, *Biographical Dictionary*, pp. 227–8; Richard Hill, *Egypt in the Sudan* (Oxford, 1959), p. 64; also K.D.D. Henderson, Sudan Republic (London, 1965), pp. 30–5.

15 In modern times, *khartúm* is extended to mean 'hose' or even 'fire-hydrant'.

16 Brun Rollet, *Le Nil Blanc et le Soudan* ('The White Nile and Sudan') (Paris, 1855), cited in C.E.J. Walkley, 'The Story of Khartoum', *SNR*, 18 (1935): 221–41 and 19 (1936): 71–92; also R.C. Stevenson, 'Old Khartoum, 1821–1885', SNR, 47 (1966): 1–38.

17 P.M. Holt, *Sudan of the Three Niles: The Funj Chronicle 910–1288/1504–1871* (Leiden, Brill, 1992), pp. vii–viii and 131; H.A. MacMichael, 'Notes on Old Khartoum', *SNR*, 6 (1923): 110–11. The mosque (rebuilt in 1837 and since renamed in honour of its latest benefactor, King Farúq of Egypt) still stands at the crossroads of Liberation Street and Republic Street in north-western Khartoum.

18 Albanians; the ruling class in Khartoum included representatives of races and nations from across the Ottoman Empire.

19 Walkley, 'Story of Khartoum', pp. 230–1.

20 Jean-Pierre Greenlaw, *The Coral Buildings of Suakin* (London, Oriel Press, 1976); Walkley, 'Story of Khartoum', p. 231.

21 Peter Rowley-Conwy, John Rowley-Conwy and Deborah Rowley-Conwy, 'A Honeymoon in Egypt and Sudan: Charlotte Rowley, 1835–1836', in Paul and Janet Starkey, *Travellers*, p. 116; the author, visiting the harem of Governor-General 'Ali Khúrshíd, found 'one lawful Wife . . . an ugly Lady of high rank, whom he married for her money' and forty-six concubines.

22 H.S. Job, 'The Coinage of the Mahdi and the Khalífa', *SNR*, 3/i (1920): 165–78; Warburg, *Islam*, p. 52.

23 Three carriages, stripped of their fittings and shrouded in dust, are on display in the Beit Khalífa museum in Omdurman.

24 Taylor, *Journey*, pp. 269–77.

25 From the Turkish (originally Persian) *hükümdar*, 'monarch'; Richard Hill, 'Rulers of the Sudan 1820–1885', *SNR*, 32 (1951): 85–95; A.E. Robinson, 'The Rulers of Sudan since the Turkish Occupation until the Evacuation by Order of the Khedive', *Journal of African Studies* (1924); NRO, INTEL 1/1/7 and 5/1/7 'Copy of List of Names of Hakimdars and Mudirs of Sudan . . . supplied by the Egyptian Daftarkhana (Citadel Archives) to the Ministry of the Interior on 28 April 1901' and 'Names of Hakimdars, Mudirs and Governors of Sudan from 1878 to 1882'.

26 Hill, *Biographical Dictionary*, pp. 10–11, notes that 'Abd-al-Latíf 'suspected most Europeans of being liars and evil-doers'; the Governor-General's origins in the Caucasus were indicated by the cognomen 'Sharkas' (from the Turkish *çerkes*).

27 Hill, *Egypt in the Sudan*, p. 87.

28 Taylor, *Journey*, p. 285.

29 Letter from Muhammad 'Ali Pasha to the commander of Egyptian forces in Sudan, dated 23 September 1825; quoted in Holt and Daly, *History*, p. 39.

30 Holt, *Three Niles*, p. 105, and William Shipley-Conwy, in Paul and Janet Starkey, *Travellers*, p. 113, describe slave-raids by Governor-General 'Ali Khúrshíd in 1835; also Frédéric Cailliaud, *Voyage à Méroé, au Fleuve Blanc, au-delà de Fâzoql* ('Journey to Merowe on the White Nile and From There to Fazoghli') (2 vols, Paris, 1826), vol. 2, pp. 313–16, cited in Fahmy, *Pasha's Men*, p. 211.

31 Gabriel Barr, 'Slavery in Nineteenth Century Egypt', *Journal of African History, Vol. VIII, Nos. 1, 2 & 3*, ed. R.A. Oliver and J.D. Fage (Cambridge, 1967): 417–41.

32 Bernard Lewis, *Race and Slavery in the Middle East: An Historical Inquiry* (Oxford, 1990), pp. 62–71; also Ira Lapidus, 'Sultanates and Gunpowder Empires', *The Oxford History of Islam*, ed. Professor John Esposito (Oxford, Oxford University Press, 1999), pp. 376–7; the Ottoman Empire had used slaves to form infantry units, the janissaries (*yeni ceri*: Turkish for 'new troops').

33 Romolo Gessi, *Seven Years in the Soudan: Being a Record of Explorations, Adventures, and Campaigns Against the Arab Slave Hunters*, tr. Lily Wolffsohn and Bettina Woodward (London, Sampson Low Marston & Co., 1892), p. 2.

34  SAD, 605/6/4–12, A.N. Gibson MSS; correspondence between Muhammad Shinnáwi, chief merchant at Suakin, and 'Abd-al-Wahid 'Abd-al-Rahmán Siddiq, in 1789, itemising slaves' names and prices in gold ounces.

35  Yagi, 'Le Kalifa 'Abdullahi', p. 42.

36  Abú-Salím, *Al-athár al-kámila*, vol. 1, p. 53; dated 10 August 1877 (3 Sha'bán 1294); SAD, 100/10/1, MS.

37  The Qorán, Súrat al-Nisá' (4/92), Súrat al-Núr (24/32 and 33), Súrat al-Mujádila (58/3) and Súrat al-Baqara (2/178); Vincent Cornell, 'Fruit of the Tree of Knowledge; The Relationship Between Faith and Practice in Islam', in *The Oxford History of Islam*, p. 92.


## 3. The Handclasp

1  AH 1277; al-Mahdi, *Al-Jazíra Aba*, p. 4.

2  Muhammad Ibrahím Abú-Salím, *Al-Harakat al-Fikría fí'l-Mahdía* ('The Intellectual Movement During the Mahdía') (Khartoum University Press, 1970), p. 63.

3  Ibn Taimía (1268–1328); in 1258, invading Mongol armies had overthrown the capital of the Abbasid Empire; Ibn Hanbal (780–855); his followers founded the most conservative of the four major legal schools (*madháhib*) in Sunni Islam (Hanbali, Hanafi, Sháfi'i and Máliki); most Sudanese teachers taught Islamic law according to the Máliki school.

4  1165–1240; raised in the Moorish culture of Andalusian Spain, Ibn 'Arabi travelled extensively in the Islamic world; among his most important works are *Fusús al-Hikám* ('Settings of the Wisdoms') and *Futúhát al-Makkía* ('Meccan Illuminations'); online at http://www.ibnarabisociety.org/IbnArabi.html.

5  The term Sufi comes from *súf*, 'wool'; sect leaders used fleeces as mats for prayer and meditation; Ohrwalder, *Ten Years*, p. 109: 'When the Mahdi came to the place where the sheepskin was stretched out on the ground . . . he conducted prayers.'

6  Layish, 'Legal Methodology', p. 44.

7  Hillelson, 'Tabaqát', pp. 200–1.

8  Literally, 'path'; pl. *turuq*.

9  Hill, *Biographical Dictionary*, p. 274; because of internal splits caused by personality differences and clashes over ethnic and regional loyalties, Sheikh Núr al-Dá'im's was one of three rival Sammánía factions; the other faction leaders were al-Quráshi wad al-Zein and Ahmad Basír; 'Ali Saleh Karrar, *The Sufi Brotherhoods in Sudan* (London, 1992), pp. 47–8.

10  Quoted in Karrar, *Sufi Brotherhoods*, p. 2. It is also said that 'He who studies without a sheikh can never become a true 'alím'; see Hillelson, 'Tabaqāt', p. 197.

11  This 'connection in series' is known as *salsala*.

12  The Qorán, Súrat al-Fatih (48/10); also Constance Padwick, *Muslim Devotions: A Study of Prayer-Manuals in Common Use* (Oxford, Oneworld, 1961), pp. xxiv–xxv.

13  Maxime Rodinson, *Muhammad*, tr. Anne Carter (New York, New Press, 1980), pp. 69–70.

14  Interview with Muhammad Hassan Ihímir, Jazíra Aba, January 2003. The Qorán says these *tahajud* austerities are performed 'in the small watches of the morning' and 'at the retreat of the stars'; The Qorán, Súrat Bani Isrá'íl (17/79) and Súrat al-Túr (52/49); see also Súrat al-Muzzammil (73/1–4).

15  Na'úm Shuqair, *Taríkh al-Súdán al-qadím wa al-hadíth wa jughrafíyátuhu* ('The History, Traditions and Geography of Sudan') (3 vols, Cairo 1903), vol. 3, p. 324; Bermann, *Mahdi of Allah*, pp. 116–17. The sheikh's poem is written in a dense, highly stylised and archaic Arabic; each line of the original ends with a rolling '-r'.

16  The *shahada* or 'testimonial': *Lá illah ill'Allah (wa) Muhammad rasúl Allah*.

17  Christopher Spring and Julie Hudson, *North African Textiles* (London, British Museum Press, 1995), pp. 99–105; also Trimingham, *Islam*, p. 181.

18  From the verbal root *raqqa'a*, 'to repair'; battered examples of the muraqqa'a can be seen in the British Museum in London and the Beit Khalífa Museum in Omdurman; Karrar, *Sufi Brotherhoods*, p. 135, notes that turuq such as the Khatmía and the Qádiría spurned such ostentatious trappings of poverty and prided themselves on being respectably turned out.

19  In A. Yúsuf 'Ali, *The Holy Qurán* (Brentwood, Amana Corp., 1983), p. 61, the commentator notes that, in Sufi devotions, 'zikr represents both a solemn ritual and a spiritual state of mind or heart, in which the devotee seeks to realise the presence of God. Thus there is a zikr of the mind and zikr of the heart. For beginners the one may lead to the other, but in many cases the two may be simultaneous.'

20  The Qorán, Súrat al-Baggara (2/152 and 200); Súrat al-Al Imrán (3/41).

21  William Chittick, 'Sufi Thought and Practice', *Oxford Encylopaedia of the Modern Islamic World*, ed. John Esposito (Oxford, Oxford University Press, 1995), pp. 102–9.

22  Padwick, *Muslim Devotions*, pp. 13–20.

23  Ibid., p. 17.

24  SAD, 721/1/58, Brownell MS, 12 March 1862.

25  Al-Mahdi, *Al-Jazíra Aba*, p. 3; Holt, *Mahdist State*, p. 45.

26  Hill, *Biographical Dictionary*, p. 260.

27  A.B. Theobald, *The Mahdīya, A History of the Anglo-Egyptian Sudan, 1881–1899* (London, Longmans, Green & Co., 1951), p. 27.

28  Hill, *Biographical Dictionary*, p. 168; Musa, 'Judiciary and the Nile Fleet'; al-Hussein Zahrá was later appointed the Mahdi's amír of Kassala and wrote a legal treatise on the Mahdía; Ibrahim Fawzi, *Al-Sudán bein yedí Gordon wa Kitchener* ('Sudan Between the Hands of Gordon and Kitchener') (2 vols, Cairo, 1901), vol. 1, pp. 238–9, says that al-Dikkeir had to receive remedial education from Sheikh al-Hussein Zahrá because his own pupils found him so unsatisfactory; this account, by a government employee, is likely to be propaganda aimed at denigrating the Mahdi's tutor.

29  Al-Gaddal, *Lawha*, p. 37; Holt, *Mahdist State*, p. 45.

30  Bedri, *Memoirs*, pp. 11–12, describes a visit by Ja'far Mazhar to Muhammad al-Izayriq's subsidised mosque at Wad Medani; also Hill, *Egypt in the Sudan*, pp. 113–18; Hill, *Biographical Dictionary*, pp. 189–90; John Udal, 'Ja'afar Pasha Mazhar: A Worthy Governor-General, 1865–1871', paper presented to 5th International Conference on Sudan Studies at Durham University, 30 August–1 September 2000; online at www.dur.ac.uk/justin.willis/udal.htm.

31  Brown, 'Sudanese Mahdiya', p. 157.

32  Sing. *'alim; al-Jámi'a* al-Azhar, 'the radiant mosque', was founded in 972 AD; Veronica Seton-Williams and Peter Stocks, *Blue Guide: Egypt* (2nd edn, London, A. & C. Black, 1988), pp. 256–63.

33  The way of life prescribed for Muslims to follow in obedience to the will of God; the University of Southern California in Los Angeles enables the Internet user to search for quotations from the Hadíth: http://www.usc.edu/dept/MSA/reference/searchhadith.html.

34  Albert Hourani, *A History of the Arab Peoples* (New York, Warner Books, 1991), pp. 223–4 and pp. 158–62.

35  Three scholars representing the schools of law prevailing in the Ottoman Empire, Egypt and Sudan accompanied the invading Egyptian army in 1820: Muhammad al-Asyúti (Hanafi school), Ahmad al-Baqli (Sháfi'i) and Ahmad al-Saláwi (Máliki); Karrar, *Sufi Brotherhoods*, p. 11; see also Muhammad Mahmoud, 'Sufism and Islamism in Sudan', *African Islam and Islam in Africa*, eds David Westerlund and Eva Evers Rosander (London, Hurst, 1997), p. 170; and Shuqair, *Taríkh*, pp. 3–4.

36  Hill, *Biographical Dictionary*, p. 260; he inherited the leadership of the

tariqa from his father, its founder, Muhammad 'Osmán al-Mirghani. The name is taken from the phrase *khatm al-turuq*, 'seal of the paths'. Also Neil McHugh, *Holymen of the Blue Nile: The Making of an Arab-Islamic Community in the Nilotic Sudan, 1500–1850* (Evanston, Ill., Northwestern, 1994); reviewed by Heather Sharkey in *Sudanic Africa*, 5 (1994), pp. 266–9; online at www.hf.uib.no/smi/sa/05/5Holymen.pdf.

37  Karrar, *Sufi Brotherhoods*, p. 63, details the history and practices of the Khatmía.

38  Hill, *Biographical Dictionary*, pp. 390, 15.

39  Or, variously, *aragi*, the potent Sudanese date liquor; interviews with Sheikh al-Núr 'Abd-al-Mahmúd, Muhammad Hassan Ihímir, and 'Abd-al-Rahmán Birrah, Jazíra Aba, January 2003; the third incident is related in al-Gaddal, *Lawha*, p. 42; also al-Mahdi, *Al-Jazíra Aba*, p. 4.

40  Islam permits a man to marry four wives, although the Prophet Muhammad himself is believed to have had more. By the end of the Mahdi's life, he had had at least five wives (though no more than four at any one time) and sixty-five concubines; Kramer, 'Holy City', pp. 269–72; also SAD, 106/2, 'Dervish Who's Who' MS, anonymous and undated (but believed to be c. 1920s) list of the Mahdi's surviving relatives.

41  Al-Mahdi, *Al-Jazíra Aba*, p. 4.

42  Zeinab, married to the Khalífa Muhammad Sharíf; Umm Kalthúm, to the Khalífa 'Abdulláhi; Núr al-Shám, to the Khalífa 'Ali wad Helu; and Nafisa, to al-Sayyid Hámid (son of Muhammad Ahmad's older brother, Hámid).

43  Abú-Salím, *Al-athár al-kámila*, vol. 1, pp. 47–52.

44  'Ali Mubárak, *Al-Khitat al-Tawfiqía al-Jadída* (Cairo, 1887–8), cited in Michael Reimer, 'Views of al-Azhar in the Nineteenth Century: Gabriel Charmes and 'Ali Pasha Mubarak', Paul and Janet Starkey, *Travellers*, pp. 269–75.

45  Richard Dekmejian and Margaret Wyszomirski, 'Charismatic Leadership in Islam: The Mahdi of Sudan', *Comparative Studies in Sociology and History*, 4 (2) (1972): 203–4; SLUK, 8CM/226349 MS.

46  Jamál al-Dín al-Afghání (1838–97); Muhammad Abdúh (1849–1905).

## 4. The Voice of the People

1  From the verbal root *ghára*, 'sink' or 'collapse'. A note in the Beit Khalífa museum in Omdurman explains that 'worshipping in the seclusion inside the cave was . . . a common practice among all sheikhs of Sufi sects, particularly his teachers of the Sammánía sect'.

The Mahdi's successor, the Khalífa 'Abdulláhi, had as his 'cave' a small cell attached to the living-area of his house.

2　Formerly the palace of the Mahdi's posthumous son, al-Sayyid 'Abd-al-Rahmán al-Mahdi, an important figure in the Mahdist revival during the British occupation.

3　'Mek' is assumed to be a colloquial abbreviation of the Arabic for king, *malik*.

4　Súrat al-Nisá' (4/3).

5　Rodinson, *Muhammad*, pp. 54–5; on one occasion, the Prophet married a woman from each of two rival clans as a way of persuading them to settle their feud.

6　She was also known as Umm al-Mu'minín or Umm al-Fuqará', 'Mother of the Holy Men'; both her sons were killed as young men, Mohammed at Karari and al-Bushra by the British at al-Shukába; NRO, INTEL 1/43/357, 'Family Tree of the Mahdi'. The honorific is still used today; al-Sayyida Sára, wife of al-Sádiq al-Mahdi, is known as Umm al-Mu'minín.

7　She bore him three children: Batúl (who married Muhammad Khálid 'Zugul', the Mahdi's amír in Darfur), 'Abd-al-Wáli and Zahra.

8　The Swedish National Library website illustrates the different styles of Arabic calligraphy; online at www.kb.se/HS/islam/eng/kalligrafi.htm.

9　Fashoda was an important garrison town upstream; Jazíra Aba fell under the jurisdiction of its military, civil and judicial authorities; despite being a state-appointed official, the Qádi appears to have been a member of the Sammánía brotherhood.

10　Abú-Salím, *Al-athár al-kámila*, vol. 1, pp. 58–60; the letter has been dated to between 1878 and 1881 (AH 1295–8).

11　SAD, 228/15/31, Ohrwalder MSS.

12　Abú-Salím, *Al-athár al-kámila*, vol. 1, p. 57.

13　Ibid., vol. 1, pp. 47–52, between 1875–7 (AH 1292–5). This manshúr was one of the last to be signed 'Muhammad Ahmad'; the second part of his double-barrelled name was subsequently dropped away to match more closely the name of the Prophet Muhammad, in compliance with a tradition that the Mahdi would bear the Prophet's name and the Mahdi's father the Prophet's father's name ('Abdallah). Some Mahdists insist, however, that Muhammad Ahmad was effectively 'two names in one'.

14　Shuqair, *Taríkh*, vol. 3, pp. 116–18; endorsed by Holt, *Mahdist State*, pp. 46–7.

15　The Sudanese phrase is *al-huwár ghalab sheikhu*, 'the student outstripped his sheikh'.

16　*Tatabuq ismein fí ism*; see note 13 above.

17   Interview with Muhammad Hassan Ihímir, Jazíra Aba, January 2003.

18   Theobald, *Mahdíya*, p. 28.

19   Holt, *Mahdist State*, p. 48; Slatin, *Fire and Sword*, pp. 124–5, quotes the Arabic proverb: '*Ed Dongolawi Shaitan mugalled bigild el insan*'; Bermann, *Mahdi of Allah*, p. 47: 'Miserable Dongolawi! A traitor! O Mussulmans, he is splitting the firm staff of Islam! O Believers, how true is the saying, "A man from Dongola is the Shaitan in human shape".'

20   Abú-Salím, *Al-athár al-kámila*, vol. 1, pp. 54–5.

21   Hill, *Biographical Dictionary*, p. 312.

22   SAD, 777/14, Peter Acland MSS, p. 42.

23   Al-Ni'ma bore him a son, 'Ali, one of only two who survived the Mahdía.

24   The Arabic word *'asabíya* (from the same root as 'neural network') conveys a sense of *esprit de corps* bordering on the fanatical.

25   A Sudanese proverb reflects on the phenomenon of the itinerant preacher arriving with his entourage to request food and lodging: *Minshán 'ain nakram alf 'ain*, 'For the sake of one eye a thousand eyes are honoured'; H.C. Jackson, 'Sudan Proverbs', *SNR*, 2 (1919): 105–11.

26   Richard Hill, *On the Frontiers of Islam* (Oxford, Oxford University Press, 1970), pp. 43–50; gum arabic was a valuable product of the grey-barked *acacia fistula* and the red-barked *acacia spirocarpa*, especially in Kordofan.

27   Slatin, *Fire and Sword*, pp. 90–1.

28   Cornelia May Speedy, *My Wanderings in the Sudan* (London, R. Bentley & Son, 1884), pp. 168–71.

29   From Turkish *başıbozuk*, mercenaries notorious for their brutality, and *sanjaq*, 'flag', coming to mean 'squadron commander'; the term Sanjak is still used, as a term of abuse, for Shaigía.

30   Ahmed Al-Shahi, 'The Distinctiveness of the Shaygiya', *Sudan: History, Identity, Ideology*, various edns (Reading, Ithaca, 1991), pp. 107–19; W. Nicholls, *The Shaiḱíya: An Account of the Shaiḱíya Tribes and of the History of Dongola Province from the XIVth to the XIXth Century* (Dublin, 1913), pp. 28–42; Henderson, *Sudan Republic*, p. 31; SAD, 113/3/282–6, Shuqair MS, includes a hand-drawn map of *Dár Shaigía* (the tribal homeland), between Debba and the Fourth Cataract of the Nile; the Shaigía were (and still remain) devoted followers of the Khatmía sect.

31   Lieutenant-Colonel J. Donald H. Stewart, *Report on the Soudan, Egypt No. 11 (1883)* (London, HMSO, 1883), p. 13.

32   S.M. Nur, 'A Critical Edition of the Memoirs of Yúsif Mikhail',

(unpublished PhD thesis, School of Oriental and African Studies, University of London), pp. 13–14; SOAS, LP962.403/332255, Nur MS; SOAS LP962.403/332259, unpublished tr. P.M. Holt (London, 1954), p. 48. Yúsuf Mikhail, a Coptic Christian, was the son of an Egyptian clerk who had migrated to Kordofan in the wake of the conquest of Sudan. There were many Coptic families in Kordofan, especially among the administration's clerical staff; provincial accounts were closed each year in the month of Tút, the Coptic equivalent of October; SAD, 404/10/8, James Macphail MSS; Yúsuf Mikhail exaggerates the usual proverb, *zolein fí turba wa lá riyál fí tulba*, 'Better two in a grave than a penny on demand'.

33  A quarter of a tenth.

34  January 1864 diary of Belgian aristocrat and cartographer resident in Khartoum, Eugène Edouard Jacques Marie de Pruyssenaere de la Wostyne; Eugène de Pruyssenaere, *Reisen und Forshungen im Gebiete des Weissen und Blauen Nil* (Gotha, 1876), contains useful maps; British Library, MSS PP3946/2.

35  Ismail ruled from 18 January 1863 to 26 June 1879, when he was deposed by his European creditors; he had been given the title Khedive (from Persian *ḳadīv*, 'prince') by Sultan Abdülaziz in Constantinople; Hill, *Biographical Dictionary*, pp. 68–9.

36  Abbas Ibrahim Muhammad 'Ali, *The Slave Trade and Slavery in Sudan 1820–1881* (Khartoum, Khartoum University Press, 1972), pp. 42–51; Brian Thompson, *Imperial Vanities* (London, HarperCollins, 2002), pp. 116–34; Col Sir C.M. Watson, 'The Campaign of Gordon's Steamers', *SNR* 12/ii (1929): 121, lists the six steamers as the *Tel el-Hoween*, the *Bordein*, the *Safia*, the *Mansureh*, the *Shebeen* and the *Imbaba*.

37  Gessi, *Seven Years*, p. 4.

38  The decree, dated 16 February 1874 (2 Muharram 1291), is written in the French of the europhile Egyptian court; NRO, CAIRINT 1/3/8, decree MS.

39  Charles Chenevix Trench, *Charley Gordon: An Eminent Victorian Reassessed* (London, Allen Lane, 1978), pp. 66–160, is a comprehensive account of his efforts.

40  These included the Frenchman Linant de Bellefonds (who was killed in a skirmish with slavers), the American Colonel Challié-Long, a provincial administrator named Muhammad Ra'úf (later to be Governor-General of Sudan) and Baker's former arch-enemy, the slaver Mohammed Bey Abú-al-Su'úd.

41  Revd C.T. Wilson and R.W. Felkin, *Uganda and the Egyptian Sudan* (2 vols, London, Sampson Low, 1882), vol. 1, p. 194.

42  The word 'razzia' was a crude Anglicisation of *ghazwa*, 'raid' or 'incursion'.

43  Hill, *Biographical Dictionary*, pp. 390–1; NRO, INTEL 1/15/74, MS 'Account of the Actions of Zubeir Pasha', pamphlet by Gen Gordon, printed in Khartoum, August 1879.

44  Suleimán was executed by Gordon's man in the south, Romolo Gessi.

45  Merchants, mainly of the Ja'aliyín tribe, who often rose to influential positions.

46  Núr, 'Yūsif Mikhail', p. 17; Holt translation, pp. 56–7.

47  *The Times*, 28 April 1879, p. 13.

48  Chenevix Trench, *Charley Gordon*, p. 125.

49  Gordon was Governor-General from 18 February 1877 to 8 December 1879.

50  Report on examination by the Surgeon to Her Majesty's Consulate in Alexandria, 11 January 1880; British Library (BL), Add. MS 52395B, f. 45.

51  Interview with Sheikh al-Núr 'Abd-al-Mahmúd, Jazíra Aba, January 2003.


## 5. 'A New Dhikr'

1  25 July 1878 (25 Rajab 1295); evidence of Sheikh 'Abd-al-Mahmúd Núr-al-Dá'im, an eye-witness, cited in Yagi, 'Le Kalifa 'Abdullahi', p. 71 fn and Holt, *Mahdist State*, p. 50 fn.

2  Slatin, *Fire and Sword*, p. 126.

3  SAD, 228/15/31, Ohrwalder MSS.

4  In February 1870, at which time Muhammad Ahmad had only been there for two years.

5  Casati, *Ten Years in Equatoria*, vol. 1, pp. 33–4; Holt, *Mahdist State*, p. 46; also Carl Giegler, *Sudan Memoirs of Carl Christian Giegler Pasha, 1873–83*, ed. Richard Hill (Oxford, Oxford University Press, 1984), p. 155 fn.

6  *Fí taqwím al-dín*.

7  Abú-Salím, *Al-athár al-kámila*, vol. 1, pp. 68–70; letter to 'Abd-al-Fatáh 'Abdallah, written between 31 September and 7 October (3–27 Dhú al-Qaida 1297).

8  Every mention of the Prophet Muhammad in every letter or proclamation is followed by the formula *Salla Allah aleyhi wa-sallam*, 'may God's blessings and peace be on him'.

9  The Qorán, Súrat al-Tauba (9/119).

10  Ramadan 1297 (8 August–6 September 1880); Shawwál (6 September–6 October 1880).

11  Abú-Salím, *Al-athár al-kámila*, vol. 1, pp. 63–4; letter to Hájja Amna, the daughter of a traditional faqí, Muhammad Núr, dated 20 June 1880 (12 Rajab 1297).

12  Abú-Dom lies about halfway between Jazíra Aba and Jebel Gadír, the destination of Muhammad Ahmad's subsequent migration with his followers.

13  Abú-Salím, *Al-athár al-kámila*, vol. 1, pp. 65–6; letter to Sheikh Suleimán Kámil, dated 22 June 1880 (14 Rajab 1297).

14  He became the Mahdi's amír in the Jazíra region; Hill, *Biographical Dictionary*, p. 275.

15  Kramer, 'Holy City', p. 272.

16  Described variously as *al-sábiqún min ashábihi* and *akbar al-mahdía*.

17  Many thousands of Fuláni from Hausaland (in what is now northern Nigeria) have settled in Sudan, their transit camps evolving into permanent communities; see C. Bawa Yamba, *Permanent Pilgrims: The Role of Pilgrimage in the Lives of West African Muslims in Sudan* (Washington, Smithsonian, 1995).

18  Shuqair, *Taríkh*, vol. 3, p. 139; also Mahmoud, 'Sufism and Islamism', p. 175; a briefer and less elaborate variant on this wording is given by Muhammad Ahmad in a letter dated 18 October 1882 (5 Dhú al-Hijja 1299); Abú-Salím, *Al-athár al-kámila*, vol. p. 192.

19  Translated from Babikr Bedri, *Táríkh Hayáti*, pp. 26–7; Bedri, *Memoirs*, p. 13, has a freer but more poetic translation.

20  Al-Mahdi, *Al-Jazíra Aba*, p. 5, says the meeting was scheduled for Ramadan 1298 (July–August 1881) but that date is not consistent with the letters quoted above.

21  The Qorán, Súrat al-Saf (61/14); Muhammad Ahmad would have known that the verse continues: 'We gave power against their enemies to those who believed and they became the ones that prevailed.'

22  Abú-Salím, *Al-athár al-kámila*, vol. 1, p. 67, dated 9 October 1880 (4 Dhú al-Qaida 1297).

23  Ibid., pp. 71–2, written between 5 October and 4 November 1880 (during the month of Dhú al-Qaida 1297).

24  The Qorán, Súrat al-Qári'a (101/1–5), about Judgement Day: 'The day of calamity, what is it? And what will explain to you what it is? It is a day on which men will be like moths scattered about and the mountains will be as insubstantial as carded wool.'

25  Bedri, *Memoirs*, p. 19.

26  Hill, *Biographical Dictionary*, p. 271; the Egyptian rank was *liwa*, 'flag commander'.

27  SAD, 404/10/8, James Macphail MSS.

28 Hill, *Biographical Dictionary*, pp. 31 and 180; Ilyás' daughter was married to al-Zubeir Rahma; *The Times*, 7 January 1884, p. 10.

29 Nur, 'Yūsif Mikhail', p. 15; Holt translation, p. 53.

30 'How Ilyās Pasha outwitted the Danāqla', in S. Hillelson, *Sudan Arabic Texts*, Cambridge University Press, 1935, pp. 24–7.

31 Slatin, *Fire and Sword*, pp. 144–5; Hill, *Biographical Dictionary*, p. 228.

32 Nur, 'Yūsif Mikhail', pp. 20–2; Holt translation, pp. 63–7.

33 Baggára clans include the Rizeigát, the Ta'ísha, the Homr, the Habbanía, the Jawama'a and the Jimi'.

34 H.C. Jackson, 'Sudan Proverbs', pp. 105–11.

35 In Nur, 'Yūsif Mikhail', p. 6 (Holt translation, p. 30), the author describes how he wrote out petitions on behalf of a large number of illiterate 'nomad Arabs' complaining against official corruption.

36 'Abd-al-Gádir, *Sírát al-Imám al-Mahdi*, pp. 113–14; Shaked, *Life*, pp. 71–2.

37 Hill, *Biographical Dictionary*, p. 25.

38 Janet Ewald, *Soldiers, Traders, and Slaves: State Formation and Economic Transformation in the Greater Nile Valley, 1700–1885* (Wisconsin, University of Wisconsin Press, 1990), pp. 118–21; King Adam would later pay the ultimate price for refusing to give the Mahdi his whole-hearted support.

## 6. 'From the Mouths of Babes'

1 I.e. around eighteen months after Sheikh al-Quráshi's death; he himself is said by Mahdist followers to have predicted that the Mahdi would help construct his tomb.

2 Hill, *Biographical Dictionary*, pp. 5–6; J.A. Reid, 'Some Notes on the Khalífa 'Abdullahi', *SNR*, 21 (1938): 207–12.

3 R. Salmon, 'The Story of Sheikh Abdullahi Ahmed Abu Galaha, A Sudanese Vicar of Bray', *SNR*, 21 (1938): 85.

4 Slatin, *Fire and Sword*, pp. 126–30; Theobald, *Mahdíya*, pp. 29–30.

5 Yagi, 'Le Kalifa 'Abdullahi', p. 60, says 'Abdulláhi was born in AH 1258 (1841) at Rihayd al-Birdi Abu Roq in southern Darfúr; his mother was Umm Na'im bint al-Hassan of the Ta'íshi clan of the Baggára.

6 Leadership of the order had passed from father to son since the days of Muhammad al-Qutbi al-Wawi of Tunis.

7 Yaqúb (later to be an influential general), Yúsuf and Sammáni; Yagi, 'Le Kalifa 'Abdullahi', p. 66.

8 Holt, *Mahdist State*, pp. 51–2.

9 'Abdulláhi is widely believed to have written to Zubeir asking if he was the Mahdi; Zubeir replied that he was not. Yagi, 'Le Kalifa 'Abdullahi', p. 67, denonunced 'this forged history' as an attempt 'to discredit the Khalífa by portraying him as some kind of quack, a peddler of magic charms, incapable of discerning who was the real Mahdi'.

10 Al-Mahdi, *Al-Jazíra Aba*, p. 6.

11 Nur, 'Yūsif Mikhail', p. 22; Holt translation, p. 68.

12 Professor Wilfred Madelung, 'Al-Mahdi', *The Encyclopaedia of Islam New Edition*, various eds (8 vols, Leiden, 1985), vol. 5, pp. 1230–8, is an authoritative analysis of Mahdist traditions; also Holt, *Mahdist State*, pp. 22–31. The Mahdist tradition remained strongest among Shí'a sects, where the belief in a divinely appointed guide, concealed until just before the end of time, was central; for Sunnis, the community itself, with its collective capacity for reform and learning, was believed to be infallible, so there was less doctrinal necessity for an eschatological redeemer-figure.

13 The title was assigned to Muhammad ibn al-Hanafíya, the son of the Khalífa 'Ali, in AH 66.

14 *Sunan Abu-Dawud* (partial), book 36, number 4272, narrated by Abu-Sa'íd al-Khudri; see www.usc.edu/dept/MSA/fundamentals/hadithsunnah/abudawud/036.sat.html#036.4271; this text was no doubt consciously copied by Ismail 'Abd-al-Gádir, in his own description of Muhammad Ahmad al-Mahdi, though the biographer also adopted other elements of *Sunan Abu-Dawud* to modify the figure of seven years to five (i.e. between 1881 and 1885); see Shaked, *Life*, p. 57.

15 Ibn Khaldún was a North African scholar, universally recognised as the founding father of the philosophy of Islamic history and sociology.

16 'Abd-al-Rahmán Wali al-Dín ibn Khaldun, *The Muqaddimah: An Introduction to History*, tr. Franz Rosenthal (3 vols, New York, Pantheon, 1958), vol. 2, p. 156.

17 1785–1883.

18 Founded by Muhammad ibn 'Abd-al-Wahhab (1703–92); like Muhammad Ahmad, he was influenced by Ibn Taimía. He insisted that every idea added to Islam after the third century of the Muslim era (about 950 AD) was false and should be eliminated.

19 Knut Vikør, *Sufi and Scholar on the Desert Edge: Muhammad b. 'Ali al-Sanúsi, 1797–1859* (London, Hurst, 1995).

20 1754–1817; Mervyn Hiskett, *The Sword of Truth: The Life and Times of the Shehu Usman Dan Fodio* (New York, Oxford University Press, 1973); Murray Last, *The Sokoto Caliphate* (London, Longmans, 1967).

21 Usman Muhammad Bugaje, 'The Jihad of Shaykh Usman Dan Fodio and its Impact Beyond the Sokoto Caliphate', paper read at a symposium in honour of Usman dan Fodio at the International University of Africa in Khartoum, 19–21 November 1995; online at www.ballina.com/~ubugaje/beyond.html.

22 Usman Muhammad Bugaje, 'Shaykh Uthman ibn Fodio and the Revival of Islam in Hausaland', *Al-Mizan*, 2/1; online at www.ummah.org.uk/kcl/files/Fodio.htm.

23 Mahmoud, 'Sufism and Islamism', pp. 171–2; also Hiskett, *Sword of Truth*, p. 66.

24 Holt, *Mahdist State*, p. 113.

25 Interview with 'Abd-al-Rahmán Birrah, Jazíra Aba, January 2003.

26 *Al-hawátif al-rabbánía*; 'Abd-al-Gádir, *Sírát al-Imám al-Mahdi*, p. 88; Shaked, *Life*, p. 63.

27 The recipient is described as *ná'ib*, a 'deputy' in the movement; this informal rank would be replaced by the khulafá' and umará'.

28 This dogmatic statement became the basis for the Mahdi's claim that those who opposed him were infidels, liable to the 'penance of the dissenters' (*takfír al-mukhálafín*).

29 Ahmad al-Tayib wad al-Bashír, who introduced the Sammánía taríqa into Sudan.

30 Abú-Salím, *Al-athár al-kámila*, vol. 1, p. 76–81; Muhammad Ahmad wrote that he saw this vision on 1 July 1881 (4 Sha'bán 1298), three days after his public declaration as the Mahdi; also Wingate, *Mahdiism*, pp. 40–1.

31 *Sahíh Bukhári* 8/73/217 (on the authority of Abú-Huraira).

32 Rabí' II 1298; Holt, *Mahdist State*, p. 53; also Shuqair, *Taríkh*, vol. 3, p. 120. Heather Sharkey, 'Ahmad Zayni Dahlán's al-Futuhát al-Islámía: A Contemporary View of Sudanese Mahdi', *Sudanic Africa*, 5 (1994): 67–75 (online at http://www.hf.uib.no/smi/sa/05/5Sharkey.pdf) the author cites oral testimony gathered among Haláwiyín tribespeople in the Jazíra region that Muhammad Ahmad had been confiding his Mahdiship to close friends 'for some time' before this.

33 Slatin, *Fire and Sword*, p. 131.

34 *al-shurút wa al-awsáf*.

35 The Qorán, *Súrat al-Baqara* (2.106) states the principle known as abrogation (*naskh*): 'None of our revelations do we abrogate, but we substitute something better or similar. Do you not know that God has power over all things?'

36 Abú-Salím, *Al-athár al-kámila*, vol. 1, pp. 334–9; letter written on 12 May 1883.

37 Ibid., vol. 4, p. 274; letter to a senior amír, Muhammad 'Osmán Abú-

Girja, dated between 31 December 1884 and 9 January 1885 (12 to 23 Rabí' I 1302).

38  Nur, 'Yúsif Mikhail', pp. 25–6; Holt translation, pp. 72–4.

39  Hill, Biographical Dictionary, p. 34; Holt, Mahdist State, p. 108.

40  Nur, 'Yúsif Mikhail', p. 25; Holt translation, pp. 72–4.

41  1 Sha'bán 1298; Holt, Mahdist State, p. 54.

42  P.M. Holt, 'The Place in History of Sudanese Mahdía', SNR, 40 (1959): 107–12.

43  Slatin, Fire and Sword, p. 138 says these appointments were not made until after the first clash with government forces on 12 August 1881 (16 Ramadan 1298); Ohrwalder, Ten Years, pp. 14–16, says it followed the hijra to Kordofan; the official history of Ismail 'Abd-al-Gádir, however, places the Khulafá' on the scene between the manifestation of the Mahdi and his first meeting with government representatives in early Ramadan.

44  With the title 'Khalífat Abú-Bakr al-Siddíq'.

45  His honorific was 'Khalífat Omar al-Farúq'; Ohrwalder, Ten Years, pp. 14–15; Hill, Biographical Dictionary, p. 47; SAD, 403/2, George Franks MS, p. 37 (dated 28 November 1899).

46  He was accorded the title 'Khalífat 'Ali al-Karrár'; Hill, Biographical Dictionary, p. 273; Ohrwalder, Ten Years, p. 41, estimates the Khalífa Sharíf's age as 'twelve or thirteen' in early 1883.

47  Reid, 'Mahdi's Emirs', pp. 310–11; Hill, Biographical Dictionary, p. 17.

48  He would have had the title 'Khalífat 'Osmán'; Hill, Biographical Dictionary, p. 249; he was the son of the sect's founding father.

49  The Qorán, Súrat al-Nahl (16/41).

50  Abú-Salím, Al-athár al-kámila, vol. 1, pp. 334–9; Holt, Mahdist State, pp. 112–13; this letter, dated 12 May 1883 (5 Rajab 1300), quotes commentaries by Mohi-al-Dín ibn 'Arabi and Ahmad wad Idris.

51  Muhammad Ibrahím Abú-Salím and Knut Vikør, 'The Man Who Believed in the Mahdi', Sudanic Africa, 2 (1991): 29–52; the title of the article refers to Yúsuf Ahmad Muhammad 'Awad al-Síd, who attempted to use the quoted correspondence to prove that al-Sanúsi had endorsed the Mahdi.

52  Bermann, Mahdi of Allah, pp. 161–71; Wingate, Mahdiism, p. 89.

53  The Times, 31 January 1884, p. 5 (datelined Algiers).

54  'Abd-al-Gádir, Sírát al-Imám al-Mahdi, pp. 85–6; Shaked, Life, pp. 60–1.

55  Bedri, Memoirs, p. 12.

# NOTES

## 7. The Sword of the Prophet

1 22 March 1880; *The Times*, 23 March 1880, p. 11; NRO, INTEL 5/1/7 MS; Hill, *Biographical Dictionary*, p. 270.

2 Sir Ronald Wingate, *Wingate of Sudan: The Life and Times of General Sir Reginald Wingate, Maker of the Anglo-Egyptian Sudan* (London, John Murray, 1955), pp. 15–28, is a concise and impartial analysis of Egypt's financial crisis.

3 Stephen Cave, 'The Financial Condition of Egypt', *Parliamentary Papers LXXXIII* (London, HMSO, 1876), p. 99; on one loan of three millions pounds, repaid by Egypt between 1869–74, the report calculates a compound interest rate of 26.9 per cent; the report for 1876 includes two revealing sums: £31,713,987 in 'Loans' in the Receipts column; £34,898,962 in 'Interests and sinking funds' in the Expenditure column.

4 Alexander Broadley, *How We Defended Arabi and his Friends: A Story of Egypt and the Egyptians* (London, Chapman and Hall, 1884), p. 169.

5 Muhammad Tawfíq (30 April 1852–7 January 1892) was the great-grandson of Muhammad 'Ali Pasha.

6 *The Times*, 9 January 1880, p. 3.

7 Hill, *Biographical Dictionary*, pp. 183–4.

8 *The Times*, 16 January 1880, p. 5; 27 January 1880, p. 5.

9 Shuqair, *Taríkh*, vol. 3, pp. 324–5; Slatin, *Fire and Sword*, p. 135; also Holt, *Mahdist State*, p. 55. In 1882, Sheikh Núr al-Dá'im was commissioned by a subsequent Governor-General to write a long poem denouncing the Mahdi.

10 Abú-Salím, *Al-athár al-kámila*, vol. 1, pp. 82–3.

11 The telegraph, invented in 1830s, enabled the government to send signals along a network of wires stretching from Egypt up the Nile to Khartoum; additional branch-wires extended east, south and west; *The Times*, 6 February 1885, p. 6, has a detailed map of the network; lines in 1882–3 were listed in Stewart, *Report on the Soudan*, p. 8: '1. Cairo-Dongola-Berber-Khartoum; 2. Khartoum-Abu-Ghurrad-Kordofan-Foggia; 3. Khartoum-Abu Harez-Messelemia-Senaar-Fazoglou; 4. Messelemia-Kaua; 5. Abu Harez-Guedaref-Kassala-Sennehyt-Massowah; 6. Kassala-Geuz Redjeb-Berber; 7. Souakin-Kassala; 8. Guedaref-Doka-Gallabat; 9. Guedaref-Guiré, on the Setit River'.

12 The Qorán, Súra Muhammad (47/7).

13 Abú-Salím, *Al-athár al-kámila*, vol. 1, pp. 94–5; also quoted in Shuqair, *Taríkh*, vol. 3, pp. 127–8; 'Abd-al-Gádir, *Sírát al-Imám al-Mahdi*, pp. 119–20; Shaked, *Life*, pp. 75–6.

14  Hill, *Biographical Dictionary*, pp. 274–5.

15  Giegler, *Sudan Memoirs*, p. 174.

16  11 Ramadan 1299.

17  'Abd-al-Gádir, *Sírát al-Imám al-Mahdi*, pp. 117–19; Shaked, *Life*, p. 75; al-Mahdi, *Al-Jazíra Aba*, p. 5; Zulfo, *Karari*, p. 1.

18  Telegram sent on 12 August 1881; Giegler, *Sudan Memoirs*, pp. 169–70; Hill, *Biographical Dictionary*, p. 136.

19  In the Turkish of the occupation army, a *buluk*; see Douglas Johnson, 'The Egyptian Army 1880–1900', in *Savage and Soldier*, VIII/1.

20  The *Ismailia*, a 250-ton paddle steamer, had been imported in pieces and reassembled in Khartoum in 1875 on the orders of Charles Gordon; Richard Hill, 'A Register of Named Power-Driven River and Marine Harbour Craft Commissioned in Sudan 1856–1964', *SNR*, 51 (1970): 141; Watson, 'Gordon's Steamers', p. 122.

21  Cpt J.J. Leverson, 'Insurrection of the False Prophet 1881–83' (4 vols, Cairo, 1883–4), vol. 1 (23 November 1883), p. 3, NRO, CAIRINT 1/3/13 MS; 'Abd-al-Gádir, *Sírát al-Imám al-Mahdi*, p. 124, confirms their arrival at Jazíra Aba on 12 August (16 Ramadan).

22  The figure was calculated to emulate the 313 men fielded by the Prophet Muhammad at the battle of Badr in March 624 (AH 2).

23  'Abd-al-Gádir, *Sírát al-Imám al-Mahdi*, p. 126; Shaked, *Life*, p. 79.

24  Another Turkish rank: *Saghkolaghasi*.

25  *Salát al-khawf*.

26  'Abd-al-Gádir, *Sírát al-Imám al-Mahdi*, pp. 129–32; Shaked, *Life*, pp. 80–1.

27  Poem by al-Sayyid Mukhtár, quoted in al-Mahdi, *Al-Jazíra Aba*, p. 6.

28  *The Times*, 23 August 1881, p. 3.

## 8. Hijra to Jebel Massa

1  The Prophet reached Medina on 28 June 622 (12 Rabí' I); Fred Donner, 'Muhammad and the Caliphate', *Oxford History of Islam*, p. 9.

2  Musa, 'Judiciary', p. 7.

3  Slatin, *Fire and Sword*, pp. 138–9.

4  'Abd-al-Gádir, *Sírát al-Imám al-Mahdi*, p. 141, includes a minutely detailed itinerary of the hijra, down to the most obscure village and, as important, watering stop; Shaked, *Life*, p. 85; Abú-Salím, *Al-athár al-kámila*, vol. 1, p. 79 fn notes the attention to detail in planning the hijra, even to the extent of ordering prayers and incantations for each stage of the trek.

5  Ewald, *Soldiers, Traders, and Slaves*, pp. 120–1.

6  Abú-Salím, *Al-athár al-kámila*, vol. 1, pp. 96–100; letter to Dafa'allah Bigwi written between 28 August and 25 September 1881 (during the month of Shawwál).

7  Slatin, *Fire and Sword*, pp. 139–40.

8  The fight happened on 24 October 1881 (30 Dhú al-Qaida 1298); 'Abd-al-Gádir, *Sírát al-Imám al-Mahdi*, pp. 146–8; Shaked, *Life*, pp. 87–9; Holt, *Mahdist State*, p. 56.

9  An al-Azhar-educated scholar and jurist who joined the Mahdi at Obeid, Muhammad al-Badawi was the son of an influential holy man in the hills near Tagali; Ewald, *Soldiers, Traders, and Slaves*, p. 120; Hill, *Biographical Dictionary*, p. 253.

10  Abú-Salím, *Al-athár al-kámila*, vol. 2, pp. 310–11; NRO, CAIRINT 11/1/3, MS; dated 17 April 1884 (20 Jumáda II 1301).

11  *The Times*, 24 August 1881, p. 5 (dateline Alexandria); in Nur, 'Yūsif Mikhail', p. 26 (Holt translation, p. 75), the author notes that the government treated the threat posed by the Mahdi 'as if he were a mosquito in a sycamore tree'.

12  The Qádi was the senior Islamic judge; telegram from Ra'úf to the Khedive on 15 October 1881, 'Abdín Palace Archives, Cairo, cited in Mekki Shibeika, *The Independent Sudan* (New York, Oxford University Press, 1959), p. 43.

13  Hill, 'River and Marine Harbour Craft', *SNR*, 51 (1970): 131–46 and 53 (1972): 204–14; Watson, 'Gordon's Steamers', p. 123.

14  Giegler, *Sudan Memoirs*, p. 170.

15  NRO, CAIRINT 1/10/52, MS report of Bimbashi 'Abdallah Agha Muhammad; SOAS, PP MS 7/1/xiii, p. 1, MS translation by P.M. Holt. The khayrán (correct plural of khor) of Kordofan were used by nomadic tribes as natural corridors for annual migration; rain water was often retained long after the rainy season in wells beneath the khor.

16  Shibeika, *Independent Sudan*, pp. 46–7.

17  Giegler, *Sudan Memoirs*, p. 177.

18  Hill, *Biographical Dictionary*, pp. 314–15.

19  'Abd-al-Gádir, *Sírát al-Imám al-Mahdi*, p. 149; Shaked, *Life*, p. 90.

20  'Girl', i.e. 'daughter of'; the woman's name, 'Winner', would have been seen as a good omen.

21  16 Muharram 1299.

22  'Abd-al-Gádir, *Sírát al-Imám al-Mahdi*, p. 154; Shaked, *Life*, p. 92.

23  Yaqúb Muhammad al-Ta'íshi, younger brother of the Khalífa 'Abdulláhi, had joined the Mahdi during the hijra with a substantial force of clansmen.

24  Hill, *Biographical Dictionary*, p. 62.

25  Abú-Salím, *Al-athár al-kámila*, vol. 1, pp. 131–2; SAD, 100/1/20, MS of letter, dated 25 June 1882 (8 Sha'bán 1299).

26  Ohrwalder, *Ten Years*, p. 19.

27  Abú-Salím, *Al-athár al-kámila*, vol. 1, pp. 76–81; also Wingate, *Mahdiism*, p. 41. The phrase used in the letter is 'blue patch' (*ruq'a zarqá*); in colloquial Sudanese Arabic, however, this is another way of saying 'black'. In subsequent years, the jibba evolved into a highly stylised, finely tailored and appliquéd garment; there are some fine examples of late-Mahdía jibbas (taken during Belgian military expeditions against Mahdist territory in the mid-1890s) in the Royal Museum for Central Africa near Brussels.

28  Muhammad Ahmad ibn 'Abdallah al-Mahdi, *Rátib al-Imám al-Mahdi* (Khartoum, 1885), printed on government presses after the capture of Khartoum; Beit Khalífa Museum, Omdurman; SAD, 97/1; Middle East Centre, Oxford University, DT 108.05.MI (same text, interspersed with invocations such as *máshá'allah* and *lá hawl walá* in red ink); Muhammad Ibráhím Abú-Salím, *Al-athár al-kámila lil-Imám al-Mahdi* (7 vols, Khartoum University Press, Khartoum, 1993), vol. 6. The Rátib is still carried by Mahdist followers today.

29  SAD, 97/1, p. 9, MS dated 27 Ramadan 1302; SAD, 247/1, pp. 6–7, MS of translation, dated 2 April 1890 (28 Sha'bán 1307).

30  The Qorán, Súrat al-Falaq (113/1–5) and Súrat al-Nás (114/1–6); 'Ali, *Holy Qurán*, pp. 1808–10, notes in his commentary that blowing upon knots was 'a favourite form of witchcraft practised by perverted women' and, of the 'Whisperer', that 'evil insinuates itself in all sorts of insidious ways from within so as to sap man's will'.

31  Wingate, *Mahdiism*, p. 42; Abú-Salím, *Al-athár al-kámila*, vol. 4, pp. 41–2; letter to 'Abdallah al-Núr written on 17 November 1884 (28 Muharram 1302).

32  NRO, CAIRINT 11/11/8, MS of another short edict (undated), which says that, as 'smoking Persian tobacco is worse than drinking alcohol', the punishment should be 100 lashes.

33  Abú-Salím, *Al-athár al-kámila*, vol. 1, pp. 301–8; Kramer, 'Holy City', pp. 145–8.

34  Musa, 'Judiciary', p. 4.

35  Fawzi, *Al-Sudán*, vol. 1, pp. 92–3.

36  'Abd-al-Gádir, *Sírat al-Imám al-Mahdi*, p. 144; Shaked, *Life*, p. 87.

37  Fawzi, *Al-Sudán*, vol. 1, pp. 92–3; Warburg, *Islam*, p. 39.

38  As note 27 (above), the word 'blue' is used to describe the black battle-flag of the Khalífa 'Abdulláhi (*al-ráya al-zarqa*).

39 There is a fine example of a war-drum in the Beit Khalífa museum in Omdurman, complete with Qoránic inscription etched into the brass.

40 The Qorán, Súrat al-Anfál (8/60).

41 The muqaddam was a rank below the amír, equivalent to a major or lieutenant-colonel.

42 Abú-Salím, *Al-athár al-kámila*, vol. 1, pp. 288–9, dated 21 April 1883 (13 Jumáda II 1300).

43 The Nordenfeldt was a five-barrellèd gun which used a crank mechanism to fire salvos.

44 Christopher Spring, *African Arms and Armour* (London, British Museum, 1993), pp. 31–46.

45 Col the Hon John Colborne, *With Hicks Pasha in the Soudan: Being an Account of the Sennar Campaign in 1883* (London, 1884), pp. 142–4, describes an encounter with a sheikh of the Halawiyín Baggára: 'Whether original or a copy, it was undoubtedly the dress of the Crusaders. The hauberk of mail was fastened around the body . . . and formed a complete covering from head to foot. The long two-handed double-edged sword was worn between the leg and the saddle . . . [It] came from the Saracens, who stripped it from the bodies of slain or captured knights . . . I asked him where he had got his armour. He replied that it had been in his family 310 years.'

## 9. *Jihad*

1 Telegram from Ra'úf to the Khedive on 17 December 1881, in Shibeika, *Independent Sudan*, p. 49.

2 *The Times*, 20 December 1881, p. 5.

3 Hill, *Biographical Dictionary*, pp. 13–14; NRO, INTEL 1/1/7, 'Rulers of Sudan' and 'List of Names of Hakimdar'; his rank was, at the time of his appointment, *Faríq*; Shuqair, *Taríkh*, vol. 3, p. 659, has a contemporary (1903) photograph of Hilmi Pasha, a dignified elderly man in state uniform, tarboosh and white walrus moustache.

4 Hill, *Biographical Dictionary*, p. 136.

5 Giegler, *Sudan Memoirs*, p. 184.

6 Sennar is depicted in *The Graphic*, 3 May 1884, p. 428, as a ramshackle assortment of small houses and huts, with a rudimentary mud-brick mosque.

7 Hill, *Biographical Dictionary*, p. 35.

8 A Shaigi from Merowe in the north and one of the government's most distinguished officers; Hill, *Biographical Dictionary*, pp. 328–9.

9 Giegler, *Sudan Memoirs*, pp. 192–3.

10 He held a government post as *názir*, provincial administrative

director; Hill, *Biographical Dictionary*, pp. 63–4; SAD, 777/14/1–44, Peter Acland MSS include an article on the history of the Shukría and a map showing the tribal homeland between the Blue Nile and the River Atbara.

11 Giegler, *Sudan Memoirs*, pp. 197–8.

12 Bedri, *Memoirs*, p. 15; this letter has not survived. Both recipients subsequently died in prison during the rule of the Mahdi's successor, the Khalífa 'Abdulláhi.

13 Hill, *Biographical Dictionary*, p. 386; Theobald, *Mahdīya*, pp. 36–7.

14 Quoted in letter to *The Times* from C.H. Allen of the British and Foreign Anti-Slavery Society, 15 July 1882, p. 6; Mr Berghoff was killed in the subsequent battle against the Ansár.

15 Nur, 'Yūsif Mikhail', p. 35; Holt translation, p. 95.

16 Wingate, *Mahdiism*, pp. 18–19, says 6,000; Slatin, *Fire and Sword*, pp. 141–4, and Ohrwalder, *Ten Years*, pp.10–11, say 4,000; Shuqair, *Taríkh*, vol. 3, pp. 135–8, says 13 companies (2,600 men) and 1,500 irregulars; Mekki Shibeika, *British Policy in Sudan, 1882–1902* (London, Geoffrey Cumberlege, 1952), p. 39, says 13 companies and 2,500 irregulars.

17 'Abd-al-Gádir, *Sírát al-Imám al-Mahdi*, pp. 154 and 159–60; Shaked, *Life*, pp. 92 and 94.

18 The Qorán, Súrat al-Má'ida (5/33).

19 Ibid., Súra Húd (11/27).

20 Ibid., Súrat al-'An'ám (6/7).

21 Abú-Salím, *Al-athár al-kámila*, vol. 1, pp. 121–8, dated 4 Rajab 1299; also quoted in Nur, 'Yūsif Mikhail', pp. 27–31; Holt translation, pp. 78–88; Shuqair, *Taríkh*, vol. 3, pp. 133–7; and 'Abd-al-Gádir, *Sírát al-Imám al-Mahdi*, pp. 160–8.

22 12 Rajab 1299.

23 Holt, *Mahdist State*, p. 58, fn 2. A subsequent proclamation orders that the legal ordinances of the Mahdía begin on this date; see Abú-Salím, *Al-athár al-kámila*, vol. 1, pp. 301–8. Coins struck later during the Mahdía took this point as the new 'year one'; Job, 'Coinage', pp. 165–78.

24 'Abd-al-Gádir, *Sírát al-Imám al-Mahdi*, p. 178; Shaked, *Life*, p. 99.

25 SAD, 403/2, George Franks MSS p. 5; letter dated 9 April 1898. Lyddite was a high explosive made from crystalline picric acid, which exploded in a yellow puff.

26 'House of property'; 'Abd-al-Gádir, *Sírát al-Imám al-Mahdi*, p. 178; Shaked, *Life*, p. 99; Holt, *Mahdist State*, pp. 125–6.

27 SAD, 867/7, F.R. Wingate MS; 'Chronological Events in Sudan for the Years 1881–1889', Sudan Government, Intelligence Office, Cairo, p. 18.

28  He would serve again as acting Governor-General in Khartoum the following year.

29  Shibeika, *Independent Sudan*, p. 59.

30  The five forts were: Makram/Moghran (north-west); North (on the north side of the Blue Nile, opposite the palace); Burri (north-east); Kalakla (south); and Messalamieh (south-east).

31  Leverson, 'Insurrection', vol. 1, p. 7; also Wingate, 'Chronological Events', p. 19.

32  Leverson, 'Insurrection', vol. 1, p. 8.

33  Al-Mahdi, *Yas'alúnaka*, pp. 145–53.

34  Undated proclamation by the Mahdi, cited in Wingate, *Mahdiism*, p. 38.

35  Holt, *Three Niles*, p. xviii; Hill, *Biographical Dictionary*, p. 55.

36  Shuqair, *Taríkh*, vol. 3, pp. 375–91; after the capture of Khartoum in January 1885, Shákir al-Ghazi's home was commandeered for use as the Mahdist treasury.

37  Warburg, *Islam*, p. 36.

38  Titled in Arabic *Hudi al-mustahdi ila al-Mahdi wa al-Mutamahdi*; see also BL, Add. MS. 52395B, pp. 51–6, 'Proclamation des Docteurs de la loi Musulmane à Khartoum contre Mohamed Ahmed, soi-disant Mahdi' ('Proclamation of the Doctors of Islamic Law in Khartoum against Muhammad Ahmad the Self-Proclaimed Mahdi'), tr. 27 May 1885.

39  Titled in Arabic *Risálat al-mufti Shákir al-Ghazi fí batlán da'wa Muhammad Ahmad al-Mahdi*.

40  Titled in Arabic *al-Nasíhat al'áma li-ahl al-Sudan 'an mukhálifat al-hukum wa al-khurúj 'an tá'at al-Imám*.

41  Holt, *Mahdist State*, pp. 107–9.

42  Egmont Hake, *The Journals of Major-Gen. C.G. Gordon at Kartoum* (London, Kegan, Paul, Trench & Co., 1885), pp. 410–20, includes the translation of a letter from the 'ulamá' to 'Abd-al-Rahmán al-Nujúmi during the siege of Khartoum, dated 14 September 1884.

43  *The Graphic*, London, 19 April 1884, p. 377 and 9 February 1884, p. 124.

44  I.e. 1878, the year of Muhammad Ahmad's split from Sheikh Núr al-Dá'im's branch of the taríqa.

45  A reference to 'Abdulláhi al-Ta'íshi.

46  Shuqair, *Taríkh*, vol. 3, pp. 324–5.

47  Telegram from 'Abd-al-Qádir Pasha to the Khedive on 12 July 1882, in Shibeika, *Independent Sudan*, p. 61.

48  Fawzi, *Al-Sudán*, vol. 1, pp. 92–3.

49  Salmon, 'Vicar of Bray', p. 86.

## 10. 'Star with a Tail'

1 Shuqair, *Taríkh*, vol. 3, p. 159, estimates the Mahdi's core fighting force at this time as 50,000 men, although it would be greatly swollen by new recruits in Kordofan.

2 Salmon, 'Vicar of Bray', p. 87.

3 Banner captured from Mahdist forces at the Battle of Atbara (8 April 1898), displayed in the Beit Khalífa museum, Omdurman.

4 Dillinj fell to an Ansár force under the leadership of 'Umar, son of Mek Adam of Tagali; Shuqair, *Taríkh*, vol. 3, pp. 152–4.

5 Ohrwalder, *Ten Years*, pp. 40–1; SAD, 228/16/30–1, MSS.

6 Hill, *Biographical Dictionary*, p. 271.

7 The Qorán, Súrat Húd (11/113).

8 Proclamation dated 16 Shawwál 1299; Abú-Salím, *Al-athár al-kámila*, vol. 1, pp. 175–8; 'Abd-al-Gádir, *Sírát al-Imám al-Mahdi*, p. 203, fn 1.

9 Hill, *Biographical Dictionary*, p. 7.

10 NRO, CAIRINT 1/10/51, MS report of unnamed government officer; SOAS, PP MS 7/1/xviii, pp. 4–5, translation by P.M. Holt.

11 Wilson and Felkin, *Egyptian Sudan*, vol. 1, p. 311; passing through Obeid in 1880, the authors noted that, because of acute water shortages, the authorities were debating moving the seat of provincial government to Bara, where there was 'plenty of good water'.

12 SAD 404/10/1–5, James Macphail MSS, include the account of an anonymous clerk in Obeid's Mudíría, the Governor's Office; SAD, 404/10/9, MS unpublished translation by Richard Hill.

13 SAD 404/10/6, MS; Henderson, *Sudan Republic*, p. 37.

14 24 Shawwál 1299.

15 'Abd-al-Gádir, *Sírát al-Imám al-Mahdi*, pp. 209–11; Shaked, *Life*, p. 112–14.

16 Nur, 'Yúsif Mikhail', pp. 45–6; Holt translation, pp. 117–19.

17 Shuqair, *Taríkh*, vol. 3, p. 160; Ohrwalder, *Ten Years*, p. 239; Nur, 'Yúsif Mikhail', p. 48 (P.M. Holt translation, p. 123), rather hysterically puts the number at 70,000.

18 Muhammad was subsequently referred to in Mahdist literature as *al-Shahíd*, 'the martyr'.

19 Holt, *Mahdist State*, pp. 61–5.

20 'Abd-al-Gádir, *Sírát al-Imám al-Mahdi*, p. 188; Shaked, *Life*, p. 103 (his italics).

21 Leverson, 'Insurrection', vol. 1, p. 7.

22 NRO, CAIRINT 1/10/51, MS; SOAS PP MS 7/1/xviii, p. 8, Holt translation.

23 Hill, *Biographical Dictionary*, p. 49; 'Ali Lutfi's Egyptian army rank

was *Qá'immaqám*; his nickname may simply have been a reference to a particularly bow-legged gait.

24 Yúsuf Mikhail's memoirs were written at the behest of Edward Aglen, a British colonial officer at Obeid in January 1933; the 'slight, white haired and frail' Yúsuf Mikhail and his wife were then in prison for illicitly distilling *aragi*, the potent Sudanese date liquor.

25 *Historical Dictionary of Sudan*, ed. Richard Lobban, Robert Kramer and Carolyn Fluehr-Lobban, 3rd edn (Maryland, Rowman & Littlefield, 2002), p. 180; Slatin, *Fire and Sword*, p. 174. The comet, known to astronomers as 'C/1882 R1' or the 'Great September Comet', was visible to the naked eye in various parts of the world for 135 days.

26 Wingate, *Mahdiism*, pp. 54–5, quoting an anonymous officer.

27 Ohrwalder, *Ten Years*, p. 53.

28 Account of an army bugler (from Rizeigát clan at Shakka), in A.C. Hope, 'The Adventurous Life of Faraj Sadik', *SNR* 32/i (1951), pp. 154–8.

29 NRO, CAIRINT 1/10/51, MS; SOAS PP MS 7/1/xviii, p. 9, Holt translation.

30 Shibeika, *Independent Sudan*, p. 86.

31 Holt, *Mahdist State*, pp. 68–9.

32 Hicks, *Road to Shaykan*, p. 24.

33 Dated 15 January 1883 (6 Rábíʿ I 1300); Abú-Salím, *Al-athár al-kámila*, vol. 1, p. 236.

34 10 Rábíʿ I 1300.

35 'Al-Shámi' means someone from Damascus; Abú-Salím, *Al-athár al-kámila*, vol. 1, p. 438.

36 Hill, *Biographical Dictionary*, pp. 147–8.

37 Ibid., p. 51 ('Ali Sharíf, previously Governor of Darfur and of Kordofan) and pp. 279–80 (Muhammad Yassín).

38 Nur, 'Yūsif Mikhail', p. 54; Holt translation, pp. 134–5.

39 Leverson, 'Insurrection', vol. 1, p. 14.

40 Another account says that he and another prisoner were 'made to work as slaves to common Arabs; after being maltreated and beaten for one month they were beaten to death'; PRO FO 78/3680, MS Baring letter to Granville, citing testimony of Haj Mahmúd Maligi.

41 Shuqair, *Taríkh*, vol. 3, p. 168; Holt, *Mahdist State*, p. 65; Ohrwalder, *Ten Years*, p. 59.

42 Salmon, 'Vicar of Bray', p. 87.

43 *The Times*, 20 February 1883, p. 5; Lieutenant-Colonel J. Donald H. Stewart of the 11th Hussars was appointed while serving in Egypt to write a report on Sudanese rebellion. He reached Khartoum in December

1882, while Obeid was still besieged, and travelled widely before completing his detailed *Report on the Soudan* the following year; SAD, 218/4/122–43, MS copy; Hill, *Biographical Dictionary*, pp. 345–6.

11. *'The Rapacious Grasp of Foreigners'*

1   Stewart, *Report on the Soudan*, pp. 16–21.
2   Cave, 'Financial Condition'.
3   Egyptian National Party manifesto, 1879, quoted in Robin Brooke-Smith, *Documents and Debates: The Scramble for Africa* (Basingstoke, Macmillan Education, 1987), p. 9.
4   Henry Stanley, *In Darkest Africa: Or the Quest, Rescue and Retreat of Emin, Governor of Equatoria* (2 vols, London, Sampson Low, 1890), p. 55, has a contemporary portrait of the Khedive Tawfíq, showing him as a solid man of large features with an elegantly trimmed beard, wearing a tarboush and splendidly brocaded uniform.
5   Juan Cole, *Colonialism and Revolution in the Middle East: Social and Cultural Origins of Egypt's 'Arábi Movement* (Princeton, Princeton University Press, 1993), p. 235.
6   Hill, *Biographical Dictionary*, pp. 40–1.
7   During the 1870s, 'Arábi also attended meetings of the Society of the Lovers of Knowledge, founded by Yaqub Sannu', who was subsequently exiled for his criticism of the Khedive Ismail in his satirical newspaper *Abú Nadhára Zarqa* ('Mr Dark Glasses'); Cole, *Egypt's 'Arábi Movement*, pp. 94 and 137.
8   Theobald, *Mahdíya*, pp. 48–50.
9   Public Record Office, Kew (PRO), Foreign Office file (FO) 78/3326, MS Memorandum from Auckland Colvin, a British national involved in supervision of Egypt's debt-servicing, dated 2 November 1881, quoted in Cole, *'Arábi Movement*, p. 237.
10  SAD, 113/3/246, MS 'Chronological Table of Recent Events in Egypt and Sudan'.
11  *Misr li'l Misriyín*.
12  *Levant Herald*, 27 February 1882, p. 4.
13  Telegram dated 16 June 1882, quoted in Shibeika, *Independent Sudan*, p. 60.
14  Telegram quoted in Abdel-Moneim Omar, *The Soudan Question Based on British Documents* (Cairo, Misr Press, 1952), p. 3.
15  Letter to 'Arábi from Muhamed Zaffer, the Sultan's closest spiritual adviser, dated 22 February 1882 (4 Rabí' II 1299), quoted in Broadley, *Arabi and His Friends*, pp. 166–9.
16  *Mír-liwa*.

17  Broadley, *Arabi and His Friends*, p. 171.

18  Richard Shannon, *Gladstone: Heroic Minister 1865–1898* (London, Hamish Hamilton, 1999), p. 301; letter from Gladstone to Sir William Gregory, who, by contrast, believed 'Arábi to be 'the purest and noblest oriental I have ever met'.

19  *Illustrated London News*, 3 June 1882, p. 538.

20  Sir Edward Malet, *Egypt 1879–83* (London, John Murray, 1909), p. 404.

21  Long, *Three Prophets*, p. 138.

22  Earl of Cromer, *Modern Egypt* (2 vols, London, Macmillan, 1908), vol. 1, pp. 288–9.

23  *The Times*, 12 July 1882, p. 5.

24  'Allah yunasrak yá 'Arábi!'

25  Broadley, *Arabi and His Friends*, p. 174.

26  4 June 1833 to 26 March 1913; until the 'Arábi revolution, he had been serving as Adjutant-General, in command of reforming the British army, after distinguished service in the Crimea (where he had been blinded in the right eye), India, China and Canada; Hill, *Biographical Dictionary*, p. 387. *The Egyptian Gazette*, 18 August 1882, p. 3, reports the total strength of the campaign army as 15,239 men, 15 squadrons of cavalry, 18 batteries of artillery, as well as telegraph units, field hospitals, etc.

27  'Expeditionary Force in Egypt', *Army List, Sept.–Oct.* (London, HMSO, 1882), pp. 34a–c; also known as the 'Ashanti Ring' after an earlier campaign in West Africa.

28  Joseph Lehmann, *All Sir Garnet: A Life of Field Marshal Lord Wolseley* (London, Jonathan Cape, 1964), pp. 320–9.

29  Handwritten letter from Balmoral, dated 30 October 1882; facsimile in 'Illustrated Interview No. XI: Lord Wolseley' in *The Strand Magazine: An Illustrated Monthly, January to June* (London, 1892), vol. 3, p. 447.

30  William Hicks, *The Road to Shaykan: Letters of General William Hicks Pasha, Written During the Sennar and Kordofan Campaigns, 1883*, ed. M.W. Daly (University of Durham, 1983), p. 25.

31  'Ulamá' practising in the Sháfi'i and Máliki legal traditions (prevalent in Egypt) were subordinated to those in the Hanafi (Ottoman) tradition.

32  Cole, *Egypt's 'Arábi Movement*, pp. 36–7 and 104–5.

33  In legal language, an *istifhám*.

34  Broadley, *Arabi and His Friends*, pp. 175–6.

35  The Qorán, Súrat al-Má'ida (5/51).

36  Ibid., Súrat al-Nisá' (4/138–9); Broadley, *Arabi and His Friends*, pp. 176–7.

37  Muhammad ibn Muhammad Muqaybil al-Máliki al-Ash'ari al-Hasani, *Nasíhat al-umma fí shurút 'aqd al-dhimma* ('Advice to the Community on Conditions for Dealing with Foreigners') (Khartoum, 1882); Royal Library, Windsor Castle (RLWC), RCIN 1005006. The book contains a hand-written dedication by General Wolseley to Queen Victoria.

38  Muhammad Isa Waley, 'Islamic manuscripts in the British Royal Collection: A concise catalogue', *Manuscripts of the Middle East 6 (1992)* (Leiden, 1994), p. 8.

39  Broadley, *Arabi and his Friends*, pp. 495–6.

40  Ibid., p. 496.

41  House of Lords, 3 January 1883.

42  Major-General Sir Evelyn Wood VC, 1838–1919; Hill, *Biographical Dictionary*, pp. 381–2.

43  Lord Dufferin had been Governor-General of Canada (1872–8).

44  1841–1917; Hill, *Biographical Dictionary*, pp. 72–3.

45  Gladstone's diary, 15 November 1883, quoted in Shannon, *Gladstone*, p. 318.

46  John Morley, *The Life of William Ewart Gladstone* (3 vols, London, Macmillan, 1903), vol. 3 (1880–98), p. 146 fn; entry dated 2 November 1882.

47  Telegram from Khartoum to Cairo dated 18 September 1882, cited in Shibeika, *Independent Sudan*, p. 61.

48  PRO, FO 78/3442, MS letter from Malet to Lord Granville (British Foreign Secretary), dated 26 October 1882.

49  Evelyn Wood, *From Midshipman to Field Marshal* (2 vols, London, Methuen, 1906), vol. 2, p. 161; Ayúb had flirted with Ahmad 'Arábi's cause but returned to the Khedive's side before conflict erupted; in 1883, he was appointed Minister of the Interior in Egypt.

50  PRO, FO 78/3443, MS telegram from Malet to Granville, dated 1 November 1882; Hill, *Biographical Dictionary*, pp. 43–4.

51  NRO, INTEL 1/1/10; 'Alá-al-Dín was replaced the same day as Governor of the Eastern Sudan by Rashíd Kámil Pasha.

52  SAD, 867/7/25, MS Wingate, 'Chronological Events'.

53  Telegram from Khedive, cited in Shibeika, *Independent Sudan*, p. 73.

## 12. A New Order

1  Abú-Salím, *Al-athár al-kámila*, vol. 5, p. 458; the Ka'ba at Mecca is called *Beit Allah al-harám*, 'the sacred house of God', while Yathrib, the name that predated the hijra of the Prophet, is used for Medina; for Cairo, Muhammad Ahmad uses the ancient name Misr (which has

come to mean Egypt) rather than al-Qáhira; also Holt, *Mahdist State*, p. 112; F.R. Wingate, *Mahdiism*, pp. 40–1.

2 Al-Kúfa was the rallying point for the faction led by the Prophet's grandson, al-Hussein, in the power struggle between the House of Hashim (based in the holy cities of Arabia) and the House of Umayya (based in Damascus) over the Muslim caliphate; al-Hussein was subsequently killed on 9 October 680 (10 Muharram 61) and became a martyr of the Shí'a cause.

3 Holt, *Mahdist State*, pp. 73–4.

4 Konya is an important centre of Sufi worship in Turkey, home of the 'whirling dervishes'.

5 H. Ganem, 'Europe's Stake in Sudan', *The Fortnightly Review* (CCIX, new series, 1 May 1884), pp. 645–54, in SLUK 8CM/645.

6 *The Times*, 3 January 1884, p. 5.

7 Shuqair, *Taríkh*, vol. 3, p. 261.

8 Long, *Three Prophets*, p. 5.

9 *The Times*, 29 November 1883, p. 5; marabout is the term used in Francophone North and West Africa for a Muslim holy man (from the Arabic *murábit*, 'holy man').

10 Abú-Salím, *Al-athár al-kámila*, vol. 1, pp. 334–9; dated 12 May 1883 (5 Rajab 1300); Holt, *Mahdist State*, p. 113.

11 Abú-Salím, *Al-athár al-kámila*, vol. 2, pp. 302–8, dated 16 April 1884 (19 Jumáda II 1301); this letter accompanied the letter to Muhammad al-Sanúsi (above). The Mahdi's first letter to Sultan Muhammad Yúsuf has not survived.

12 Ibid., vol. 2, p. 309, also dated 16 April 1884.

13 Ibid., vol. 1, pp. 212–15, dated only AH 1299, so some time before December 1882; Holt, *Mahdist State*, p. 114.

14 The Qorán, Súrat al-Ra'ad (13/17).

15 Abú-Salím, *Al-athár al-kámila*, vol. 1, pp. 216–20; other letters from the Mahdi to Hayatu ibn Sa'íd are in vol. 1, pp. 363–6 (dated 6 August 1883) and vol. 2, pp. 153–5 (9 February 1884).

16 Al-Gaddal, *Lawha*, p. 123.

17 Kramer, 'Holy City', pp. 269–70; Fawzi, *Al-Sudán*, vol. 1, pp. 234–6, alleges that Aisha's father had tried to persuade the Mahdi to marry her two sisters as well, demanding a bride price for each; he was sternly rebuked by Muhammad Ahmad.

18 Abú-Salím, *Al-athár al-kámila*, vol. 1, pp. 397–8, dated 19 October 1883 (17 Dhú al-Hijja 1300).

19 Ahmad wad Sa'ad, '*Al-Mahdi abqúla yasr*' ('Al-Mahdi, the One with Pleasing Speech'), in Qurashi Muhammad Hassan, *Qasá'id min shu'rá' al-Mahdía* (Khartoum Ministry of Culture, 1974), p. 48;

Heather Sharkey, 'Popular Historiography and the Mahdiya' (lecture delivered at the 3rd international meeting of Sudanese Studies Associations, Boston, 22 April 1994).

20  The Qorán, Súrat al-Ahzáb (33/36).

21  Abú-Salím, *Al-athár al-kámila*, vol. 1, pp. 237–41; dated 27 January 1883 (17 Rábí' I 1300).

22  Ahmad 'Ali had served under Rudolf Slatin at Shakka; he served the Mahdi until Muhammad Ahmad's death, then his successor the Khalífa for another seven years until an unrecorded dispute caused him to fall out of favour; Hill, *Biographical Dictionary*, p. 29; SOAS, Holt Paper PP MS 07 Box 1 File 1/vi, MSS Qádi al-Islam's correspondence.

23  Layish, 'Legal Methodology', p. 39.

24  Abú-Salím, *Harakat*, pp. 44–5, citing Mahdi's letter to Faqí Balal Sabún; the Mahdi had hinted at this course of action as early as the summer of 1882, when he authorised Muhammad al-Amín al-Hindi 'not to adhere to the jurists'; Abú-Salím, *Al-athár al-kámila*, vol. 1, pp. 162–4, dated between 18 June and 16 July 1882 (Sha'bán 1301).

25  Ibid., pp. 45–8, quoting letter from Khalífa 'Abdulláhi, dated approximately to early 1884.

26  NRO, CAIRINT 11/1/8; undated proclamation.

27  Manshúr dated 11 Rabí' II 1300 (19 February 1883), though the 1299 seal is outdated; RLWC, RCIN 1005008, MS 'The Diary of 'Abbás Bey'; SAD, 178/2/48–51, MS translation (anon.).

28  Mahmúd 'Abbás Hammúda, *Ahmad Suleimán: amín beit al-mál al-Súdán* ('Commissioner of the Sudanese Treasury') (Cairo, Dár al-Thaqáfa, 1983).

29  NRO, CAIRINT 11/1/15, MS undated proclamation (tr. Na'úm Shuqair); SOAS, Holt Papers PP MS 07 Box 5 File 7/iv, p. 39; Holt, *Mahdist State*, pp. 125–6.

30  Kramer, 'Holy City', p. 271.

31  Nur, 'Yúsif Mikhail', p. 55; Holt translation, p. 136.

32  Holt, *Mahdist State*, pp. 125–7.

33  Abú-Salím, *Al-athár al-kámila*, vol. 1, p. 245; dated 10 February 1883 (2 Rabí' II 1300).

34  The Qorán, Súrat al-Záryát (51/10).

35  Abú-Salím, *Al-athár al-kámila*, vol. 1, pp. 359–60; dated 30 June 1883 (24 Sha'bán 1300).

36  Salmon, 'Vicar of Bray', p. 91.

37  The Qorán, Súrat al-Ahzáb (33/59).

38  Abú-Salím, *Al-athár al-kámila*, vol. 1, pp. 278–82; dated 4 April 1883 (25 Jumáda I 1300); the last phrases quote a saying ascribed to the Prophet Muhammad.

## 13. Hicks Pasha

1 Wood, *Field Marshal*, vol. 2, p. 155.

2 Lord Dufferin in *Egypt No. 6, 1883*, 6 February 1883, p. 70; in *Egypt No. 2, 1883*, he described Darfur as a 'profitless . . . incumbrance' [*sic*].

3 Omar, *Soudan Question*, pp. 5–6.

4 A 52-gate dam, built by Wáli Muhammad 'Ali, on the Nile at Qanater, after which the Nile divides to form the Delta.

5 Broadley, *Arabi and His Friends*, pp. 497–8.

6 Hill, *Biographical Dictionary*, pp. 164–5.

7 'Reminiscences of Egypt', unpublished memoirs of General Stuart-Wortley, cited in Henry Keown-Boyd, *A Good Dusting: A Centenary Review of Sudan Campaigns 1883–1899* (London, Leo Cooper, 1989), p. 10; Shepheard's Hotel burned down in 1952.

8 Thompson, *Imperial Vanities*, pp. 160–7; Queen Victoria was said to have 'intimated' that she would not permit Baker to command 'English full-pay officers'; Haggard, *Crescent and Star*, p. 25.

9 Morley, *Gladstone*, p. 146 fn, dated 2 November 1882.

10 Lord Dufferin to the Foreign Secretary, 14 December 1882, quoted in Omar, *Soudan Question*, p. 7.

11 Faríq; it was standard for foreign officers attached to the Egyptian army to be promoted two ranks.

12 *The Times*, 24 January 1883, p. 5.

13 Hicks, *Road to Shaykan*, p. 25.

14 Ibid., pp. 12–13.

15 Ibid., pp. 16–17.

16 News of the surrender of Bara (5 January) and Obeid (19 January) to the Ansár did not reach Khartoum until 11 February; SAD 867/7, pp. 26–7, MS Wingate, 'Chronological Events'.

17 Ibid., pp. 349–50.

18 Giegler, *Sudan Memoirs*, p. 213.

19 Hicks, *Road to Shaykan*, p. 40.

20 Evans was subsequently commissioned as an officer (Bimbashi or Major) by Hicks; as the Kordofan campaign approached he tried to resign but Hicks refused to accept the resignation; Evans was killed with the general at Sheikán.

21 Casati, *Ten Years*, vol. 2, p. 4.

22 Stewart, *Report on the Soudan*, p. 25.

23 Hicks, *Road to Shaykan*, p. 33.

24 Leverson, 'Insurrection', vol. 1, p. 10.

25 NRO, CAIRINT 1/3/14, MS outlining salaries; Hicks was paid

£1,200 per year. Colonel John Colborne, whom Hicks despised, contributed to the *Daily News* and Colonel Farquhar wrote campaign diaries for the *Egyptian Gazette*.

26  Giegler, *Sudan Memoirs*, pp. 216–17.

27  The European officers attached to the Hicks expedition were: Lt-Col The Hon John Colborne (11th foot), Lt-Col Arthur Farquhar (Grenadier Guards), Lt-Col H. de Coëtlogon (70th foot), Major A. Bentick Martin (Baker's Horse, South Africa), Captain Forestier-Walker (East Kent Regt), Captain N.W. Massey (Middlesex), Surgeon-General Giorgis Dimitrios Douloglu (known as 'Georges Bey'), Surgeon-Major Rosenberg, Major E.R. Warner, Major Evans, Major Artur Herlth (Austrian imperial army), Captain W. Page Phillips (who may not have reached Sudan), Major Baron Alfred Freiherr Götz von Seckendorf (Prussian army), Capt Alexander Matyuga (Austrian imperial army) and Lt Morris Brady (promoted from Sgt-Major). The *Illustrated London News*, 10 March 1883, p. 236, Colborne, Martin and Forestier-Walker were evacuated to Egypt on medical grounds before the Kordofan campaign; de Coëtlogon returned to Khartoum; the others were all killed.

28  Hicks, *Road to Shaykan*, pp. 21–2 and 30–1.

29  Donald Featherstone, *Khartoum 1885: General Gordon's Last Stand* (Oxford, Osprey, 1993), p. 24.

30  Hicks, *Road to Shaykan*, pp. 37–8.

31  The ninety-foot-long *El Fasher* had been used on the upper White Nile since 1870; it would be captured (along with the *Musselemieh*) by the Mahdists at Berber in 1884; Hill, 'River and Marine Harbour Craft', p. 132; Watson, 'Gordon's Steamers', pp. 121–3.

32  'Omar al-Makáshfi was among the leading Mahdists killed; Hicks, *Road to Shaykan*, pp. 52–3.

33  Colborne, *With Hicks*, pp. 160–2.

34  Hicks report to Cairo, dated 11 May 1883, quoted in Omar, *Soudan Question*, p. 9.


14. *'The Sunset of their Lives'*

1  *Abú durá‘ dagal*; Sheikh 'Ali Gulla (as told to L.F. Nalder), 'The Defeat of Hicks Pasha', *SNR*, 8 (1925): 120; SAD 643/4/29, MSS John Longe (Sudan government administrator, 1925–53); Nur, 'Yūsif Mikhail', p. 56; Holt translation, p. 139.

2  Hicks, *Road to Shaykan*, pp. 77–8.

3  Stewart, *Report on the Soudan*, p. 8.

4  Power, *Letters*, p. 23, dated 1 September 1883.

5  Ibid., pp. 23–4.

6  Known colloquially as a *fantass*.

7  Hill, *Biographical Dictionary*, p. 123.

8  Hicks, *Road to Shaykan*, pp. 65–6.

9  Letter from Saʿíd Pasha to Hicks, quoted in Colborne, *With Hicks*, pp. 222–3; Saʿíd Pasha subsequently disgraced himself during the siege of Khartoum and was shot for murder and treason.

10  O'Donovan had made his name as a correspondent in Central Asia; Hicks complained that he and Vizetelly would go on violent drinking sprees in Khartoum, giving the Europeans a bad name.

11  NRO, CAIRINT 1/3/14, p. 15, MS correspondence re. Chiene's personal effects.

12  Power, *Letters*, pp. 18–20, dated 2 August 1883.

13  Ibid., pp. 26–9, dated 9 October 1883.

14  His title was *Bash-Maawin*; RLWC, RCIN 1005008, MS 'Diary of ʿAbbás Bey'; Waley, 'Islamic Manuscripts', p. 9; 'The Diary of ʿAbbas Bey', *SNR* 33 (1952): 179–96. The journal is bound in simple marbled boards with a red morocco leather spine and written in densely scribbled pencil. It was discovered on the body of a dead Sudanese fighter after the battle of Karari in 1898 and, after scrutiny by Egyptian Army Intelligence, presented 'as a trophy of war' to Queen Victoria. Publication of the diary was ruled out by Wingate because, as he wrote to to Major G.L. Holford at Buckingham Palace on 28 October 1899, 'the obvious criticisms that there was huge mismanagement both in regard to the dispatch of the Hicks Expedition and in various other details connected with the operations would appear to be only too clearly justified'; NRO, INTEL 4/2/11, p. 105; in another letter (dated 27 April 1899), Wingate observed that there were many 'passages that might be used by anglophobes'; NRO, INTEL 5/2/11, pp. 98–9.

15  Peter Clark, 'The Hicks Pasha Expedition', in *Three Sudanese Battles*, Occasional Paper (No. 14), Institute of African and Asian Studies (University of Khartoum, Khartoum, 1972), p. 15.

16  Hicks, *Road to Shaykan*, p. 97.

17  Leverson, 'Insurrection', vol. 2 (27 February 1884), p. 4; *Egyptian Gazette*, 27 November 1883.

18  NRO, INTEL 1/1/10, MS khedivial firman (29 July 1883) appointing Hussein Mazhar as Deputy Governor-General to replace Giegler (while Hicks was away on the White Nile campaign).

19  Hicks, *Road to Shaykan*, p. 98.

20  Power, *Letters*, p. 46, dated 13 November 1883.

21  Account narrated to Lt-Col Colborne in Baron Samuel de Kusel, *An*

*Englishman's Recollections of Egypt 1863–1887* (London, John Lane, 1915); SAD 643/4, pp. 1–5, MS copy among John Longe papers.

22  Ramadan 1300; 'Defeat of Hicks Pasha', p. 119.

23  Ismail 'Abd-al-Gádir, *Sírát al-Imám al-Mahdi*, pp. 223–4; Shaked, *Life*, pp. 120–1.

24  Slatin, *Fire and Sword*, p. 230.

25  NRO, CAIRINT 3/9/197, pp. 1–2, MS account of Hassan Muhammad Habashi, scribe to the amír 'Abd-al-Halím Musá'id; Holt, *Mahdist State*, p. 72. Muhammad Abú-Girja would play an important role in the siege of Khartoum and in the east; he was one of the few senior umará' to survive into the post-Mahdist era; Hill, *Biographical Dictionary*, p. 279; Reid, 'The Mahdi's Emirs', p. 311.

26  Abú-Salím, *Al-athár al-kámila*, vol. 1, pp. 406–7, dated 21 October 1883 (19 Dhú al-Hijja 1300).

27  Ibid., vol. 1, pp. 404–5 (same date); SAD, 178/2, pp. 47–8, MS translation of 'Diary of 'Abbas Bey'.

28  NRO, CAIRINT 3/9/197, p. 3, MS account of Hassan Muhammad Habashi.

29  SAD 178/2, p. 6.

30  Ibid., pp. 8–9.

31  Hicks, *Road to Shaykan*, p. 99.

32  NRO, CAIRINT 3/9/197, pp. 4–9, MS account of Muhammad Núr Barúdi, Hicks Pasha's assistant cook.

33  SAD 178/2, pp. 22–3.

34  Muslim 'Festival of the Sacrifice', which marks the end of the month of pilgrimage to Mecca, falls on 9 Dhú al-Hijja; the 'Eid usually lasts for three days and commemorates Ibrahím's willingness to obey God by sacrificing his son; the *'Eid al-Fitr* (or 'Lesser Bairam') marks the end of the month of fasting in Ramadan.

35  'Diary of 'Abbas Bey', p. 190.

36  Sent out on 15 October 1883 (13 Dhú al-Hijja 1300); SAD, 178/2, pp. 30–1.

37  NRO, CAIRINT 1/3/14, p. 12, MS 'Contract: English Officers serving with Soudan Field Force': 'To the representatives of any English officer dying in the service of His Highness, a sum equal to six months' pay shall be given. If the officer be killed in action, a sum equal to two years' pay shall be allowed. These grants shall be in lieu of all pensions. . . . [For Egyptian officers, meanwhile,] pension to family equal to one quarter the officer's pay at time of death'.

38  Power, *Letters*, p. 50, dated 24 November 1883.

39  'Diary of 'Abbas Bey', p. 192.

40  SAD, 643/4, p. 3, MS Baron de Kusel.

41 Account in diary of Major Artur Herlth, seen and quoted (from memory) in Ohrwalder, *Ten Years*, p. 79.

42 Diary of Col Farquhar, seen and quoted (from memory) in Slatin, *Fire and Sword*, p. 242.

43 Slatin, *Fire and Sword*, p. 133, describes him as 'assistant' to Ilyás Um Bireir.

44 NRO, CAIRINT 3/9/197, p. 26, MS Muhammad Núr Barúdi account; SAD, 178/2, pp. 61–4; 'Abbás Bey's pencilled scribble breaks off in mid-sentence on 1 November at Alloba; Bannaga survived the battle at Sheikan with the loss of one eye; Ohrwalder, *Ten Years*, pp. 88–9.

45 Ohrwalder, *Ten Years*, pp. 80–4.

46 1 Muharram 1301. The various eye-witness accounts for the final days of the Hicks expedition provide often contradictory dates; the majority, however, agree that the final annihilation of the government army occurred on a Monday, which was 5 November. The Mahdi's own proclamation of 8 Muharram 1301, at Sudeley Castle in Gloucestershire, southern England, confirms the date of the battle as 4 Muharram; Ismail 'Abd-al-Gádir, *Sírát al-Imám al-Mahdi*, pp. 227–36; Shaked, *Life*, pp. 122–6; E.F. Aglen, 'Sheikan Battlefield', *SNR*, 20 (1937): 145, includes an account by Mek el-Tahir Toyan el-Dud.

47 'Abd-al-Gádir, *Sírát al-Imám al-Mahdi*, p. 230; Shaked, *Life*, pp. 123.

48 Account of Bela Ahmed Sirag el-Nur in E.F. Aglen, 'Sheikan Battlefield', p. 144.

49 SAD, 643/4, p. 3, MS Baron de Kusel.

50 Ohrwalder, *Ten Years*, p. 86.

51 Clark, 'Hicks Pasha Expedition', p. 18.

52 NRO, CAIRINT 3/11/197, MS account of Hassan Muhammad Habashi, includes detailed sketches of Hicks' formations on 3 and 4 November.

53 'God is great'.

54 Nur, 'Yūsif Mikhail', p. 57; Holt translation, p. 141.

55 NRO, CAIRINT 3/9/197, pp. 43–4, MS account of Muhammad Núr Barúdi.

56 SAD, 643/4, p. 4, MS Baron de Kusel.

57 NRO, CAIRINT 3/14/240, MS report of Bimbashi Mahmud Effendi 'Abdallah, a prisoner from the Mahdist capture of Bahr al-Ghazál province.

58 Power, *Letters*, pp. 79–80, dated 9 February 1884.

*15. 'In God's Fist'*

1   Darfur had only been formally annexed in October 1874.
2   Holt, *Mahdist State*, pp. 75–6.
3   Hill, *Biographical Dictionary*, pp. 339–40.
4   Leverson, 'Insurrection', vol. 2 (27 February 1884), p. 7, states that there were 4,863 troops remaining in Darfur.
5   Slatin, *Fire and Sword*, pp. 151–2.
6   Hill, *Biographical Dictionary*, pp. 261–2; 'Abd-al-Gádir, *Sírát al-Imám al-Mahdi*, p. 287 fn; Reid, 'Mahdi's Emirs', pp. 311–12.
7   This weapon was known colloquially as *Abú-Ruhein*, 'the one with [control over] two lives'.
8   Slatin, *Fire and Sword*, pp. 186–7.
9   Wilson and Felkin, *Egyptian Sudan*, vol. 1, p. 250.
10  Slatin, *Fire and Sword*, p. 215.
11  'Abd-al-Gádir, *Sírát al-Imám al-Mahdi*, pp. 290–1, calls Slatin a *dhimmi* (defined as 'a free non-Muslim under Muslim rule') with 'inclinations towards Islam' who had already converted before Muhammad Khálid's journey to Obeid. According to this account, news of the Hicks Pasha expedition 'deluded' Slatin 'and his adherence to the Mahdia lapsed'; Shaked, *Life*, pp. 152–3.
12  NRO, INTEL 1/43/357, MS 'The Family Tree of the Mahdi'.
13  'Abd-al-Gádir, *Sírát al-Imám al-Mahdi*, p. 287; Shaked, *Life*, p. 151.
14  The Qorán, *Súrat al-An'ám* (6/152–3); Abú-Salím, *Al-athár al-kámila*, vol. 2, pp. 21–2, dated 11 November 1883 (10 Muharram 1301); NRO, MAHDIA 1/1/8, original MS; Muhammad Khálid's title was amended the following May to '*Amil al-Mahdía* ('Governor of the Mahdía') in Darfur; NRO, MAHDIA 1/10/8.
15  A kavass was, variously, a manservant, an armed constable or a courier (from the Turkish *kavas* and Arabic *qawwás*, 'archer').
16  Slatin, *Fire and Sword*, pp. 261–2.
17  'Abd-al-Gádir, *Sírát al-Imám al-Mahdi*, pp. 294–5; Shaked, *Life*, pp. 154–5.
18  Date from Slatin, *Fire and Sword*, p. 270; Shuqair, *Taríkh*, vol. 3, pp. 185–91, gives 14 January (quoting Sa'íd Juma); 'Abd-al-Gádir, *Sírát al-Imám al-Mahdi*, p. 294, gives Rabí' II (30 January–27 February), which must be a typographical error for the previous month, Rabí' I; Hill, *Biographical Dictionary*, p. 325.
19  Hill, *Biographical Dictionary*, pp. 367–8; 'Osmán Digna was one of the very few umará' to survive into the Anglo-Egyptian Condominium period in the twentieth century.
20  H.C. Jackson, *Osman Digna* (London, 1926), pp. 22–3.

21  Abú-Salím, *Al-athár al-kámila*, vol. 1, pp. 71–2, 76–81 and 315–18.
22  Leverson, 'Insurrection', vol. 2 (27 February 1884), p. 7, states that there were 8,814 troops remaining in the Red Sea region (including 1,800 at Suakin and Sinkát, 2,442 at Massawa and 3,595 at Harrar) and another 4,304 on the Abyssinian frontier (including 1,259 at Kassala and 1,571 at Senheit).
23  The Qorán, Súrat al-Máʿida (5/56).
24  Ibid., Súrat al-Baqara (2/249).
25  Abú-Salím, *Al-athár al-kámila*, vol. 1, pp. 322–5, dated 1 Rajab 1300; Wingate, *Mahdiism*, pp. 92–3. This letter is addressed to *fulán* ('Mr So-and-so'), and was a generic template letter 'to whom it may concern', to be personalised as required. Because this letter sets out the Mahdi's claim so succinctly – and, to the 'ulamá' of Khartoum, heretically – they sent it as an attachment when they appealed to their masters at al-Azhar for a fatwa on that claim. An almost identical letter of the same date (addressed to the 'people of Suakin', *aháli Suakin*, as opposed to the 'people of the region of Suakin', *aháli burúr Suakin*) omits the plentiful Qoránic quotations.
26  Jackson, *Osman Digna*, p. 27.
27  Holt, *Mahdist State*, pp. 81–7.
28  Spring, *Arms and Armour*, p. 41; Featherstone, *Khartoum 1885*, p. 31.
29  Hicks, *Road to Shaykan*, p. 83; the same letter (dated 25 August 1883) states that 'Osmán Digna has been successful in that 'the road to Souakin is blocked'.
30  Hill, *Biographical Dictionary*, p. 276; appointment by firman of the Khedive on 14 February 1883; NRO, INTEL 1/1/10.
31  Hill, *Biographical Dictionary*, pp. 226–7.
32  Ibid., pp. 240–1; Moncrieff was supporting General Mahmúd Táhir, who was subsequently court-martialled for incompetence.
33  'Abd-al-Gádir, *Sírát al-Imám al-Mahdi*, p. 262; Shaked, *Life*, p. 136; Holt, *Mahdist State*, p. 84 fn, explains the misunderstanding of the Beja vernacular name, Andetteib ('The place where camels are hobbled'), by Arabic speakers as 'at al-Teb'.
34  Haggard, *Crescent and Star*, p. 24.
35  Brian Robson, *Fuzzy-Wuzzy: The Campaigns in the Eastern Sudan 1884–85* (Tunbridge Wells, Spellmount, 1993), pp. 32–4; Thompson, *Imperial Vanities*, pp. 222–4.
36  *The Evening Standard*, 6 February 1884, p. 8.
37  The Qorán, Súrat al-Baqara (2/255); this verse, the *áyat al-kursi*, is among the most important single verses of the Qorán, which defines the attributes of God as 'the living, the self-subsisting, the eternal'.

'Osmán Digna's banner is preserved in the Beit Khalífa museum in Omdurman.

38 1854–88; Hill, *Biographical Dictionary*, p. 218; E. Macro, 'Frank Miller Lupton', *SNR*, 28 (1947), 50–61.

39 Arabic for 'market settlement'; pl. *diyúm*.

40 Mashra' al-Req was the southernmost of nine sub-divisions of the navigable Nile, each of which had a landing-post; the others (from south to north) were (1) between Dueim and Fashoda on the White Nile; (2) between Omdurman and Dueim on the White Nile; (3) between Wad Medani and Fazogli on the Blue Nile; (4) between Tuti Island and Wad Medani on the Blue Nile; (5) the Khartoum area, centred on the Moghran; (6) the Berber region; (7) and Merowe region; and (8) the Dongola region; Musa, 'Judiciary', pp. 6–7.

41 Holt, *Mahdist State*, pp. 76–80.

42 Francis Mading Deng, *The Dinka and Their Songs* (Oxford, Clarendon Press, 1973), p. 2.

43 2 Shawwál 1299; NRO, CAIRINT 3/14/240, MS report of Bimbashi Mahmúd 'Abdallah, pp. 9–10; the author was the provincial Inspector for the prevention of the slave trade; this file has two translations of the report (the second by Na'úm Shuqair), which contain many contradictory dates.

44 Gessi, *Seven Years*, p. 292.

45 Wingate, *Mahdiism*, pp. 100–3.

46 NRO, Mahmud 'Abdallah, pp. 24–6.

47 Ibid., p. 30.

48 Sá'ti Abú-al-Qásim reached Khartoum on 24 January 1884 after a hazardous journey of more than three months but owing to the tightening siege was unable to return; he served Governor-General Gordon loyally during the siege of the capital until he was killed in a skirmish outside the city at Gateina; Macro, 'Lupton', p. 53, is wrong to say that he 'went over to the Mahdi'; Hill, *Biographical Dictionary*, pp. 332–3.

49 Hill, *Biographical Dictionary*, pp. 196–7.

50 NRO, Mahmud 'Abdallah, pp. 34–7.

51 Wilson and Felkin, *Egyptian Sudan*, vol. 1, pp. 193–4.

52 Administrator, doctor, natural historian and explorer whose real name was Eduard Schnitzer (1840–92); his nickname came from an informal title, *amín hakím* ('faithful doctor'); Hill, *Biographical Dictionary*, p. 333.

53 Stanley, *In Darkest Africa*, vol. 1, p. 418; Wingate, *Mahdiism*, p. 103.

54 Macro, 'Frank Miller Lupton', p. 54; Wingate, *Mahdiism*, p. 136.

55 Following imprisonment at Obeid, Lupton died in his chains at

Omdurman in May 1888, 'after four years of torturing captivity';
Macro, 'Lupton', p. 60.
56 Abú-Salím, *Al-athár al-kámila*, vol. 3, p. 128 (Karamallah's letter)
and p. 129 (the Mahdi's reply).
57 Stanley, *In Darkest Africa*, vol. 1, p. 25.

## 16. 'The Place of a Native'

1 Letter dated 9 November 1883 (8 Muharram 1301), in the Emma
Dent collection at Sudeley Castle, Gloucestershire.
2 Leverson, 'Insurrection', vol. 2, p. 12.
3 Hake, *Gordon at Kartoum*, p. 552.
4 *The Times*, 26 November 1883, p. 5.
5 Leverson, 'Insurrection', vol. 2, p. 21.
6 Letter dated 1 January 1884; Power, *Letters*, p. 67.
7 Dr Emin later recounted how his Egyptian officers in Equatoria
planned to march to Khartoum, assess the situation and, if necessary,
try to make their individual ways back to Egypt; Stanley, *In Darkest
Africa*, vol. 1, p. 423.
8 *The Morning Post*, 12 January 1884, p. 5.
9 *Egypt No. 1, 1884* (HMSO, London 1884), p. 93 (original italics);
Theobald, *Mahdīya*, pp. 69–70.
10 SLUK, 8CM/261139, MS advisory paper to government officials,
dated 11 February 1884; PRO, CAB 37/12.
11 Telegram from Sir Evelyn Baring, dated 24 November 1883, cited in
Leverson, 'Insurrection', vol. 2, p. 5.
12 Telegram from Lord Granville to Baring, dated 13 December 1883,
quoted in Omar, *Soudan Question*, pp. 19–20; this 'recommendation'
was tantamount to an order.
13 *The Times*, 21 February 1884, p. 5.
14 A poem by R.St.J. Corbet sent to *The Morning Post*, 8 January 1884,
p. 2, illustrates the anger of Gladstone's political opponents in Britain:

> So the wily Egyptian is urged to 'withdraw',
> And retire from the sandy Soudan –
> To stop ere bloodguiltiness desecrates war,
> And to scuttle as fast as he can!
> He's been beaten, and therefore to peace should aspire
> (True Liberal policy this!)
> So Downing Street hastens to Baring to wire –
> 'Bid Tewfik give Mahdi a kiss!'

15 Statement of 7 January 1884, cited in Leverson, 'Insurrection', vol. 2, p. 16.
16 Long, *Three Prophets*, p. 230 fn; a further firman, dated 1 August 1879, formally prohibited the abandonment of imperial territory by the Khedive.
17 *Pall Mall Gazette*, 9 January 1884, p. 11.
18 Ibid., p. 1.
19 Chenevix Trench, *Charley Gordon*, pp. 196–7.
20 Stanley, *In Darkest Africa*, vol. 1, pp. 19–20, gets the order of events wrong, saying that Gordon 'had no sooner . . . parted from His Majesty than he was besieged by applications from his countrymen to assist the Egyptian Government in extricating the beleaguered garrison of Khartoum'; Gordon was replaced by Lt-Col Sir F.W. de Winton, personally selected by Wolseley and recommended to the King as 'a really good man'; Hove Library (HL), W/PLB.1, pp. 12–15, MS letter to King Leopold; NRA.1047, p. 102, MS Leopold's reply.
21 Long, *Three Prophets*, p. 40.
22 SAD, 700/7, MSS Papers of G.W. Bell, p. 35.
23 Account of Lord Wolseley, *The Strand Magazine*, January to June, p. 460.
24 Chenevix Trench, *Charley Gordon*, pp. 207–18.
25 Morley, *Gladstone*, p. 154, dated 22 January 1884.
26 Chenevix Trench, *Charley Gordon*, p. 203.
27 Power, *Letters*, p. 79, dated 9 February 1884.
28 Wood, *Field Marshal*, vol. 2, p. 162.
29 SAD, 630/5, pp. 28–30, letter to Capt Brocklehurst, dated 26 January 1884, from Cairo; Keown-Boyd, *A Good Dusting*, p. 20.
30 Hake, *Gordon at Kartoum*, p. xxx; a verbatim translation of the firman's formal and ornate wording can be found in the Appendices, p. 551.
31 Nubar Pasha, a Christian and europhile, was appointed to lead a new cabinet on 8 January 1884; SAD, 867/7/49, MS 'Chronological Events'; Hill, *Bibliographical Dictionary*, p. 296.
32 Shannon, *Gladstone*, pp. 329–30.
33 SAD, 631/1/1–29, MSS notes of meeting by J. Martin; Wood, *Field Marshal*, vol. 2, p. 164.
34 PRO, FO 78/3683, memorandum dated 22 January 1884.
35 SAD, 630/5, pp. 37–8, MS letter to Captain John Brocklehurst, dated 3 March 1884, from Khartoum.
36 PRO FO 78/3680, MS letter from Baring to Lord Granville, citing statement of Haj Mahmúd Maligi; Wolseley (who described Zubeir as 'the ablest and consequently the most dangerous man to the Egyptian

rule in the Soudan') believed that he could do no harm in Cyprus: 'I would let the sleeping dog lie'; HL, W/MEM/1/14, pp. 1–4.

37 SAD, 630/5, p. 29, MS letter to Capt Brocklehurst, dated 26 January 1884, from Cairo.

38 Hill, *Biographical Dictionary*, pp. 172–3.

39 Chenevix Trench, *Charley Gordon*, pp. 217–21.

40 PRO, FO 78/3667, telegram dated 8 February 1884.

41 Abú-Salím, *Al-athár al-kámila*, vol. 2, pp. 244–5; the tarboush was adopted as part of Egyptian military uniform by Viceroy Muhammad 'Ali in the 1830s; each soldier was issued with two a year as part of his uniform.

42 *Pall Mall Gazette*, 9 January 1884, p. 12.

43 Hill, *Biographical Dictionary*, p. 169.

## 17. *The Siege of Khartoum*

1 The reference would have been familiar to Muhammad Ahmad from The Qorán, Súrat Yúsuf (12/21–35).

2 The Qorán, Súrat al-Má'ida (5/51 and 55); the same verses are quoted in the Suakin proclamation.

3 King Solomon and the Queen Bilqís of Sheba (Saba, in what is now north-eastern Yemen), who are believed to have met between 950 and 930 BC; see The Bible, 1 Kings 10: 1–13.

4 The Qorán, Súrat al-Naml (27/36–7).

5 Letter dated 9 March 1884 (11 Jumáda I 1301). Nine letters from the Mahdi to Charles Gordon, written between this date and 12 January 1885, are extant and contained in Professor Abú-Salím's anthology (three in vol. 2, one in vol. 3 and six in vol. 4); Holt, 'Sudanese Mahdia', p. 280 fn 1; BL, Add. Ms. 34478, p. 99, MS letter dated 21 October 1884 (2 Muharram 1302).

6 Abú-Salím, *Al-athár al-kámila*, vol. 2, p. 254, same date, sent as postscript; Ohrwalder, *Ten Years*, p. 98.

7 Kramer, 'Holy City', p. 46.

8 Slatin, *Fire and Sword*, p. 283.

9 'Abd-al-Gádir, *Sírát al-Imám al-Mahdi*, p. 238; Shaked, *Life*, p. 127.

10 Ohrwalder, *Ten Years*, p. 102.

11 The amír Mahmúd Khalíl 'Abd-al-Wáhid, an uncle of the Mahdi; Hill, *Biographical Dictionary*, p. 226.

12 Ohrwalder, *Ten Years*, p. 106.

13 'Abd-al-Gádir, *Sírát al-Imám al-Mahdi*, pp. 301–17; Shaked, *Life*, pp. 157–66.

14 Quoted (from memory) in NRO, INTEL 5/2/12–14, MS Muhammad

Nushi Pasha 'Report on the Siege and Fall of Khartoum' and tr. Na'úm Shuqair, dated 2 July 1891; corroborated almost verbatim in Long, *Three Prophets*, pp. 63–4.

15 *Egyptian Gazette*, 18 February 1884, p. 3.

16 Long, *Three Prophets*, pp. 64–5; *The Times*, 21 February 1884, p. 5.

17 A contemporary portrait shows the Sheikh as a stern but contemplative, white-bearded figure in an elaborate turban; *The Graphic*, 3 May 1884, p. 428.

18 Hill, *Biographical Dictionary*, p. 50; the Mudír shot his family and himself as the city was overrun.

19 Ibid., pp. 124–5; the Court Martial also included Muhammad Nushi and Ibrahím Bey Fawzi.

20 Hake, *Gordon at Kartoum*, p. 206, lists (on 19 October) 3,737 regular troops, 1,906 'Cairo Bashi Bazouks', 2,330 Shaigía militiamen and 692 'townspeople enrolled', totalling 8,665 men.

21 NRO, INTEL 5/2/14, pp. 3–4; Nushi's Pasha's meticulous list includes 23,500 ardabs of durra (1 ardab = 5 bushels or 40 gallons), 1,250,000 *oks* of biscuit (1 oke = 2.8 lb), 14 kontars of honey (1 kontar = 120 lb), 872 Remington rifles and 315,740 packets of a dozen Remington bullets.

22 Haggard, *Crescent and Star*, p. 123.

23 Power, *Letters*, pp. 69–70, dated 2 January 1884.

24 Abú-Salím, *Al-athár al-kámila*, vol. 2, p. 258; almost verbatim in NRO, INTEL 5/2/14, pp. 26–7, MS Nushi Pasha.

25 Hill, *Biographical Dictionary*, p. 253; Holt, *Mahdist State*, p. 96; Bedri, *Memoirs*, pp. 18–19; his sons, al-Táhir and Abbás, both became leading Mahdist figures.

26 Chenevix Trench, *Charley Gordon*, p. 224; Gordon subsequently tried to blame this misunderstanding on his superiors in London; Hake, *Gordon at Kartoum*, pp. 59–60.

27 Hill, *Biographical Dictionary*, pp. 155–6 and 325.

28 NRO, INTEL 5/2/14, pp. 15–17, MS Nushi Pasha.

29 Muhammad Osmán Abú-Girja's appointment as *amír jihat al-bahr*, 'Commander of the River District', is mentioned in the Mahdi's letter of appointment to Muhammad Khálid Zugal; Abú-Salím, *Al-athár al-kámila*, vol. 2, pp. 21–2, dated 11 November 1883 (10 Muharram 1301); NRO, MAHDIA 1/1/8; Holt, *Mahdist State*, p. 98.

30 'Abd-al-Gádir, *Sírát al-Imám al-Mahdi*, pp. 318–19; Shaked, *Life*, p. 167.

31 NRO, CAIRINT 1/10/52, MS report of Bimbashi 'Abdallah Agha Muhammad; SOAS, PP MS 7/1/xiii, p. 3, tr. P.M. Holt.

32 4 Shawwál 1301.

33 Liwa; Hill, *Biographical Dictionary*, p. 250; Muhammad 'Ali Hussein was killed near Ailafún during a subsequent sortie by steamer.

34 *Wakíl*, meaning 'deputy' or 'agent'.

35 Handwritten report (dated 31 July 1884, 'end of 5th month of siege'), sent to Moberly Bell, Cairo correspondent for *The Times*, online at http://www.timesonline.co.uk/article/0,,700-55385,00.html.

36 Abú-Salím, *Al-athár al-kámila*, vol. 4, p. 236 or 274; Bedri, *Memoirs*, p. 20.

37 During the month of Dhú al-Qaida (23 August to 21 September); 'Abd-al-Gádir, *Sírát al-Imám al-Mahdi*, pp. 321–3; Shaked, *Life*, p. 169.

38 Hill, *Biographical Dictionary*, p. 7.

39 Bedri, *Memoirs*, p. 21.

40 'Abd-al-Gádir, *Sírát al-Imám al-Mahdi*, pp. 323–4; Shaked, *Life*, p. 170.


## 18. 'The Torture of Defeat'

1 Chenevix Trench, *Charley Gordon*, pp. 241–89, is a comprehensive account of the siege.

2 D.V. stands for *deo volente* (Latin for 'God willing'), the educated British equivalent of *insha'allah*.

3 PRO, FO 78/3761, dated 18 April 1884.

4 NRO, INTEL 1/15/74, dated 22 June 1884 (28 Sha'bán 1301).

5 Hake, *Gordon at Kartoum*, pp. 236–7 (Gordon's emphasis).

6 3 Jumáda 2 1301; Muhammad al-Kheir's commission as amír is in NRO, MAHDIA 1/10/8; Holt, *Mahdist State*, p. 98 fn 3.

7 Appointed Governor of Northern Sudan, Dongola and Berber on 30 September 1871; the influential Khalífa clan traditionally controlled the desert crossing from Upper Egypt; Hill, *Biographical Dictionary*, p. 169; Hill, *Egypt in Sudan*, pp. 59–60.

8 22 Rajab 1301.

9 'Abd-al-Gádir, *Sírát al-Imám al-Mahdi*, pp. 295–300; Shaked, *Life*, pp. 155–7; NRO, CAIRINT 1/8/36, MS Hussein Khalífa's account of the fall of Berber; SOAS, PP MS 7/1/xvi, MS tr. P.M. Holt.

10 Ibrahím Bey al-Burdeini, commenting on Nushi Pasha's report, alleged that Nushi and Ibrahím Fawzi were imprisoned for a month for taking bribes from officers hoping to be awarded the siege medal.

11 All the banknotes were numbered and bore the date 25 April 1884; Khartoum merchants were initially suspicious of the new notes and reluctant to take them seriously.

12  NRO, INTEL 5/2/14, pp. 43–53, MS Nushi Pasha.

13  Abú-Salím, *Al-athár al-kámila*, vol. 2, pp. 256–7 (no date).

14  Hake, *Gordon at Kartoum*, pp. 405–6, dated 12 September 1884 (21 Dhú al-Qaida 1301); BL, Add. Ms. 34474, pp. 90 and 105.

15  Mohammed Omer Bashir, 'Nasihat Al Awam', *SNR* 41 (1960): 59–65; Hill, *Biographical Dictionary*, p. 30.

16  SAD, 98/5, pp. 37–50, MS 'Nasíhat Awwám li'l-kháss wa'l-'ámm min ikhwáni ahl al-ímán wa'l-Islam' ('Awwám's Advice to the Educated and Common People Among the Brethren of the Family of Islam'), a work of five chapters; SAD, 98/5, p. 1, MS translation. The treatise is dated 14 July 1884 (20 Ramadan 1301).

17  SAD, 98/5, pp. 12 and 33, the latter a reference to Sheikh Muhammad al-Amín Darír and his colleagues' earlier anti-Mahdist manifestos.

18  Ibid., p. 20.

19  SAD, 98/5, p. 20.

20  The official Mahdist court biographer, Ismail 'Abd-al-Gádir, agreed. 'How strange were the 'ulamá' of Egypt,' he wrote. 'They had given a fatwa to Ahmad 'Arábi to fight the Wali of Egypt and decreed that it was a duty to fight him – yet they disbelieved the rise of the Mahdi . . . That first fatwa was really a testimony in support of the Mahdi. As a poet once wrote: "There is a beautiful maid whose co-wives testified in her favour" – in other words, true virtue is that which is conceded by your enemies'; 'Abd-al-Gádir, *Sírát al-Imám al-Mahdi*, pp. 155–7; Shaked, *Life*, p. 93.

21  Bashir, 'Nasihat', pp. 59–61; Awwám had hoped to complete his 'Advice to the Educated and Common People' with a chapter on the Mahdi after meeting him in person, a wish that remained unfulfilled.

22  Hake, *Gordon at Kartoum*, pp. 556–7.

23  PRO, FO 78/3683, MS memorandum dated 5 January 1884.

24  H. Herbin (first name unknown) was, like Power, a journalist who contributed to *Le Bosphore Egyptien*; Hake, *Gordon at Kartoum*, p. 273, has the names of the Greek passengers.

25  Ibid., pp. 442–5.

26  BL, Add. Ms. 34474, p. 111, MS letter dated 15 September 1885.

27  Cypher O had been developed by the Foreign Office in 1878 'for the Queen and special Embassies'; it was superseded and replaced in 1886 by Cypher Z; PRO HD/3/26, MSS correspondence dated 25 March 1878 and 23 July 1886; also FO 78/3683.

28  NRO, CAIRINT 11/1/14, MS undated proclamation citing hadhra of 7 Sha'bán 1301.

29  Slatin, *Fire and Sword*, p. 305; on the way, this party paid their

respects at the tomb of the Khalífa 'Abdulláhi's father at Abú-Rukba in Jimi' country.

30 Nur, 'Yūsif Mikhail', pp. 61–3; Holt translation, pp. 149–53; corroborated in Hake, *Gordon at Kartoum*, p. 203.

31 30 September–2 October 1884 (9–11 Dhú al-Hijja); for information on the 'Eid, see chapter 14, note 34.

32 The *khutba* is an important sermon, delivered at Friday prayers, during the 'Eid al-Adha and the 'Eid al-Fitr, as well as an extra sermon in times of hardship.

33 Slatin, *Fire and Sword*, p. 317.

34 21 October 1884 (1 Muharram 1302); Hake, *Gordon at Kartoum*, p. 213.

35 Abú-Salím, *Al-athár al-kámila*, vol. 4, pp. 8–13, dated 22 October 1884 (2 Muharram 1302); Hake, *Gordon at Kartoum*, pp. 522–30.

36 Known to the Ansár as *nugtat Omdurman*, 'Omdurman Post'.

37 Hill, *Biographical Dictionary*, p. 124.

38 Abú-Salím, *Al-athár al-kámila*, vol. 4, pp. 46–7, dated 28 Muharram 1302; Shuqair, *Taríkh*, vol. 3, pp. 281–2.

39 Bedri, *Memoirs*, p. 24; after 'Abdulláhi wad al-Núr was killed in intense skirmishing around Burri, his body was personally placed in the grave by his friend 'Abd-al-Rahmán al-Nujúmi.

40 James Darmesteter, *The Mahdi Past and Present* (New York, 1885), p. 117.

41 Wood, *Field Marshal*, vol. 2, p. 165.

42 HL, SSL.9, p. lvii, MS Lord Wolseley's notes for the (unpublished) third volume of his autobiography, *The Story of a Soldier's Life*, Field-Marshal Viscount Wolseley (2 vols, London, Ernest Russell, 1903).

43 Letter dated 8 April 1884; Morley, *Gladstone*, p. 163; Robert Wilkinson-Latham, *Sudan Campaign 1881–98* (London, Osprey, 1976), p. 24.

44 *The Times*, 1 April 1884, p. 5.

45 Graham's force included the Black Watch, the Gordon Highlanders and the 60th Rifles; they were joined by contingents of the York and Lancaster Regiment, the Royal Marines, the Royal Engineers, the 10th and 19th Hussars, the Royal Irish Fusiliers and the Royal Artillery.

46 Edgar Sanderson, *The British Empire in the XIX Century* (2 vols, London, 1897), vol. 2, p. 256.

47 HL, SSL.9, p. xlii.

48 Sketch by Melton Prior; Thompson, *Imperial Vanities*, p. 228.

49 Known to the British as 'Tamai'.

50 'Abd-al-Gádir, *Sírát al-Imám al-Mahdi*, pp. 269–71, glosses over these heavy defeats; Shaked, *Life*, p. 141.

51 Wolseley denounced the plan for a Suakin–Berber railway (championed by the Inspector-General for Fortifications, Sir A. Clarke) as a 'most costly undertaking' and an 'absurdly ridiculous proposal'; HL, SSL.9, pp. xxv and cccix.

52 BM, Add. MS 44147, p. 91, quoted in Chenevix Trench, *Charley Gordon*, p. 256.

53 Roy MacLaren, *Canadians on the Nile, 1882–1898: Being the Adventures of the Voyageurs on the Khartoum Relief Expedition and Other Exploits* (Vancouver, University of British Columbia Press, 1978), p. 50.

54 SLUK 8CM/261139, MS Capt W.H. Hall's memorandum 'Sir Samuel Baker's Suggested Relief of Berber and Khartoum from Cairo by the Nile Route', dated 13 May 1884; CAB 37/12.

55 Much of this area today lies deep under Lake Nasser; today's Wadi Halfa is at a different location.

56 Wood, *Field Marshal*, vol. 2, p. 171.

57 MacLaren, *Canadians*, p. 43–71.

58 The prize was won by the Royal Irish; Wood, *Field Marshal*, vol. 2, pp. 173–4.

59 The Mudír of Dongola was a Circassian; other government-held towns included Sennar (which surrendered on 19 August 1885), Kassala (30 September 1885) and Khartoum itself.

60 NRO, CAIRINT 1/3/11, MS message from Mudír of Dongola to the 'President of the Council' in Khartoum, begging to have the text of Telegram No. 31 corrected so that it could be decoded.

61 Lieut-General Sir G.J. Wolseley, *The Soldier's Pocket-Book for Field Service* (Macmillan, London, 1882), pp. 427–9; copy in NAM, 355.3 (02) '1882'.

62 *Relief of Gordon*, ed. Preston, p. 67; HL, SSL.9/Part 1, MSS notes for unpublished third volume of *Story of a Soldier's Life*, Lord Wolseley's autobiography; the latter key is resolved thus: twenty-one guns on the hill named after Capt Alexander Gordon RA (no relation); Charles Gordon's date of birth was 28 January 1833; and eight letters in General Sir Charles Staveley's surname; hence $A^2 \times B^2 + C = 345, 752$.

63 Sir Evelyn Baring's deputy, later Sir Edwin; Cromer, *Modern Egypt*, p. 432.

64 Hake, *Gordon at Kartoum*, p. 74 fn.

65 Watson, 'Gordon's Steamers', pp. 129–41, is a dramatic account of Nushi Pasha's mission; BL, Add. Ms. 52403, pp. 130, MS copy of Nushi's letter to Wolseley, dated 18 October 1884.

66  Known to the British as Gakdul and Abu Klea.

67  SAD, 695/7/1, MS 'With the Camel Corps: To the Relief of Khartoum' by Arthur Robeson.

68  Featherstone, *Khartoum 1885*, p. 59; the largest contingents were from the Guards Camel Regiment, the Heavy Camel Regiment, the Mounted Infantry Camel Regiment and the Royal Sussex Regiment; other units came from the 19th Hussars, Royal Engineers, Royal Artillery and Naval Brigade; *Relief of Gordon*, ed. Adrian Preston, pp. xxxv–xxxvi; Lehmann, *All Sir Garnet*, pp. 339–78; Colonel Colvile, 'History of the Soudan Campaign', Pt 1, pp. 45–9.

69  The Mahdi wrote to Muhammad al-Kheir with last-minute instructions on 31 December 1884; Abú-Salím, *Al-athár al-kámila*, vol. 4, pp. 165–6 and 168.

70  Músa wad Helu was of the Digheim Baggára in the White Nile region; Hill, *Biographical Dictionary*, p. 284.

71  Lehmann, *All Sir Garnet*, p. 369.

72  'Abd-al-Gádir, *Sírát al-Imám al-Mahdi*, p. 353; Shaked, *Life*, p. 184; the rifle used by the British was the .45-calibre Martini-Henry, which replaced the .43-calibre Remington in 1871.

## 19. *Victory*

1  NRO, CAIRINT 1/10/52, MS report of Bimbashi 'Abdallah Agha Muhammad; SOAS, PP MS 7/1/xiii p. 4, tr. P.M. Holt.

2  The Qorán, Súrat al-Nisá' (4/29).

3  Correspondence from al-Sayyid 'Abd-al-Rahmán al-Mahdí, including Arabic text and translation, *SNR* 24 (1941): 229–32; Abú-Salím, *Al-athár al-kámila*, vol. 4, pp. 207–8, dated 12 January 1885 (25 Rabí' 1 1302); Shuqair, *Taríkh*, vol. 3, pp. 289–90.

4  8 Rabí' II 1302; 'Abd-al-Gádir, *Sírát al-Imám al-Mahdi*, pp. 346–51; Shaked, *Life*, pp. 180–2.

5  Nur, 'Yúsif Mikhail', p. 66; Holt translation, p. 161; NRO, INTEL 5/2/14, p. 165, MS Nushi Pasha.

6  Bedri, *Memoirs*, pp. 28–9.

7  Account of Muhammad Mustafa 'Abd-al-Gádir, in Bedri, *Memoirs*, pp. 30–1.

8  The battalion commander, al-Sayyid Bey Amín, had been wounded in an earlier skirmish; during the capture of Khartoum he was stabbed with a spear and shot twice more but survived to contribute to Nushi Pasha's report-writing panel.

9  NRO, INTEL 5/2/14, pp. 169–70, MS Nushi Pasha.

10  Nur, 'Yúsif Mikhail', p. 68; Holt translation, pp. 163–4.

11 Shuqair, *Taríkh*, vol. 3, p. 300.

12 'Abd-al-Gádir, *Sírát al-Imám al-Mahdi*, pp. 350–1; Shaked, *Life*, pp. 181–2.

13 NRO, INTEL 5/2/14, pp. 171–2, MS Nushi Pasha.

14 Most likely the uniform of the Royal Engineers, his regiment since June 1852.

15 J.A. Reid, 'The Death of Gordon: An Eye-witness Account', *SNR* 20 (1937), pp. 172–3.

16 Slatin, *Fire and Sword*, p. 340. An inscription in the (now deconsecrated) Anglican Church in Khartoum reads: 'Praise God for Charles George Gordon, Manservant of Jesus Christ, Whose Labour was not in vain In the Lord'.

17 Bedri, *Memoirs*, p. 31.

18 SAD, 113/3, p. 285, MS notes by Na'úm Shuqair on the Shaigía, 29 July 1896.

19 Bedri, *Memoirs*, pp. 31–2.

20 21 Rabí' II 1302.

21 Bedri, *Memoirs*, pp. 32–3; Imám Sharif al-Dín al-Budíri (1212–*c.* AD 1294) was a poet acclaimed across the Muslim world for his *Qasídat al-Burda* ('Poem of the Cloak'); the lines paraphrased by Babikr Bedri are 'High mountains of gold lured the Prophet to turn against himself/But, yea, what haughtiness he showed them'.

22 Bedri, *Memoirs*, p. 33.

23 Warburg, *Islam*, p. 53, gives examples of the scale of the pay-outs made in 1884–5 to the khulafá', for distribution to their fighters and camp-followers.

24 Kramer, 'Holy City', p. 270.

25 Abú-Salím, *Al-athár al-kámila*, vol. 4, pp. 342–4, dated 27 February 1885 (11 Jumáda I 1302).

26 *Strand Magazine*, January to June, p. 460.

27 HL, W/P.14/3i.

28 Kitchener's count of the days of siege evidently begins with the abortive attempt to retake Halfáya on 16 March 1884.

29 PRO, 30/57/6, MS Major H.H. Kitchener, 'Notes on the Fall of Khartoum', dated 18 August 1885.

30 *Punch*, 14 February 1885, p. 75, in *Punch*, vol. 88 (London, 1885).

31 NAM, 8008–70, MS A.W. Money, 'Cost of Principal British Wars, 1857–1899', dated 23 December 1902, puts the total cost to Britain at £7,263,410.

32 SAD, 250/1, p. 202, MS translation; MS original Arabic proclamation, p. 201.

## 20. 'The Last Grave of Mahdism' *

1 'Abd-al-Gádir, *Sírát al-Imám al-Mahdi*, pp. 361–71; Shaked, *Life*, pp. 188–92.

2 The surrender of Kassala was accepted by the Islamic scholar al-Hussein Ibrahím wad al-Zahrá on 29 July 1885 (16 Shawwál 1301).

3 Featherstone, *Khartoum 1885*, p. 83, has details of General Graham's force.

4 HL, SSL.9, p. xlvi.

5 Ohrwalder, *Ten Years*, p. 279.

6 He had, however, not hesitated to use the government telegraph system to make his first contact with Governor-General Muhammad 'Abd-al-Ra'úf.

7 Ohrwalder, *Ten Years*, pp. 154–5.

8 Abú-Salím, *Al-athár al-kámila*, vol. 3, pp. 181–2, dated 26 July 1884 (2 Shawwál 1301).

9 Ibid., vol. 4, pp. 403–5; Holt, *Mahdist State*, p. 124.

10 In Arabic: *Akán al-Mahdi dák waladan qaddal foq 'izza/Hat wad al-Basír yissína fí tíz wizza*; the last phrase literally means 'pushes us up a goose's backside'.

11 'Amr ibn al-'As was a personal envoy of the Prophet Muhammad; his mosque (much rebuilt since 641 AD) is the oldest in continental Africa; Seton-Williams and Stocks, *Egypt*, pp. 393–4.

12 Letter dated 10 May 1885 (25 Rajab 1302); Holt, *Mahdist State*, p. 115; Shuqair, *Taríkh*, vol. 3, pp. 351–2.

13 Abú-Salím, *Al-athár al-kámila*, vol. 4, pp. 481–8, dated 8 May 1885 (22 Rajab 1302); Shuqair, *Taríkh*, vol. 3, pp. 352–3.

14 Abú-Salím, *Al-athár al-kámila*, vol. 5, pp. 241–5 (addressed to *Wali Misr*, 'the Governor of Egypt'), 246–50 ('to the 'ulamá' of Egypt') and 251–3 ('to the residents of Egypt'), all dated 17 June 1885 (3 Ramadan 1302), five days before the death of the Mahdi.

15 Abú-Salím, *Al-athár al-kámila*, vol. 5, p. 245; also Holt, 'Sudanese Mahdia', p. 281.

16 'Abd-al-Gádir, *Sírát al-Imám al-Mahdi*, pp. 389–91; Shaked, *Life*, pp. 197–8; Shuqair, *Taríkh*, vol. 3, pp. 358–9.

17 Slatin, *Fire and Sword*, p. 368.

18 Shuqair, *Taríkh*, vol. 3, p. 358.

19 The Qorán, Súrat al-Ikhlás (112/1–4); Nur, 'Yúsif Mikhail', p. 68; Holt translation, p. 165.

20 This 'proclamation of rest' (*al-manshúr al-ráha*) has been interpreted to mean that the Mahdi was handing over authority to the Khalífa 'Abdulláhi before his death, a claim denied by the Ansár community; Abú-

Salím, *Al-athár al-kámila*, vol. 5, pp. 207–8; Shuqair, *Taríkh*, vol. 3, p. 934; al-Mahdi, *Yasʿalúnaka*, pp. 188–9; Warburg, *Islam*, p. 43.

21 Abú-Salím, *Al-athár al-kámila*, vol. 5, pp. 257–8 and 262–3.

22 Hill, *Biographical Dictionary*, p. 254; Muhammad Bushára was a Taʿíshi amír who had fought with distinction against Hicks at Sheikán.

23 Slatin, *Fire and Sword*, p. 369.

24 9 Ramadan 1302.

25 ʿAbd-al-Gádir, *Sírát al-Imám al-Mahdi*, p. 391; Shaked, *Life*, p. 198.

26 Nur, 'Yúsif Mikhail', pp. 68–9; Holt translation, pp. 166–7.

27 An analogy copied from the Mahdi (see chapter 12).

28 Slatin, *Fire and Sword*, pp. 370–1; Holt, *Mahdist State*, pp. 136–7.

29 Literally, 'the religion is supported'; Ohrwalder, *Ten Years*, p. 162.

30 Holt, *Mahdist State*, pp. 141–6.

31 SOAS, PP MS 07, Box 3, File 3g, MSS statements of Omar Ahmad Hadra and Sheikh Ahmad Muhammad al-Egeil in 'Staff Diary and Intelligence Report, Eastern Sudan, No. 21'; Holt, *Mahdist State*, pp. 197–201.

32 After this incident, the corps of mulazimín was expanded to become a 'new bodyguard army' (*jeish al-mulazamín al-jadíd*) of more than 9,000 personnel, under the Khalífa ʿAbdulláhi's son, ʿOsmán 'Sheikh al-Dín' ʿAbdulláhi; Nur, 'Yúsif Mikhail', p. 94; Holt translation, p. 225 fn; one of the gates in the wall surrounding the mulazimín compound has been preserved in Omdurman.

33 Ahmad Suleimán was replaced by Ibrahím Muhammad Adlan (a merchant from Obeid), then by al-Núr Ibrahím (from Jireif) and various other Ashráf; Warburg, *Islam*, p. 54.

34 Holt, *Mahdist State*, p. 104.

35 The Qorán, Súrat Ibrahím (14/45–6); Kramer, 'Holy City', pp. 46–7.

36 NRO, MAHDIA 3/2/42; ʿAbd-al-Halím Musáʿid was the soldier who had harried the Hicks force during its doomed advance into Kordofan.

37 The campaign was begun by Hamdán Abú-Anja and concluded, following his death from illness, by Zaki Tamal.

38 Hill, *Biographical Dictionary*, p. 385.

39 Ibid., pp. 496–7, dated 9 May 1885 (23 Rajab 1302); Bedri, *Memoirs*, p. 35.

40 The famine struck in the year AH 1306; Holt, *Mahdist State*, pp. 175–83; Slatin, *Fire and Sword*, pp. 452–7; Ohrwalder, *Ten Years*, pp. 284–92.

41 Bedri, *Memoirs*, p. 73.

42 Ibid., p. 78.

43 Nur, 'Yūsif Mikhail', p. 99; Holt translation, p. 238.

44 Letter to Colonel Sir Reginald Wingate under letterhead of the Department of Egyptian and Assyrian Antiquities at the British Museum, dated 28 October 1898, among Wingate Papers, SAD 267/1/418–19.

45 Holt, *Source-Materials*, pp. 109–13.

46 Money, 'Principal British Wars', citing report by Lord Cromer (dated 26 February 1899), puts the total cost at £2,415,000, of which the British exchequer paid just £798,802; NAM 8008–70.

47 J.A. Reid, 'Story of a Mahdist Amir', 30 August 1926, SOAS PP MS 07/3/3/'Personalia'/d.

48 Hill, *Biographical Dictionary*, p. 31.

49 Under the command of an Egyptian officer, Captain Mahmúd Hussein.

50 'Report on the Death of Khalifa', Colonel Sir Reginald Wingate, dated 25 November 1899; SAD 867/6/1–11.

51 Reid, 'Mahdist Amir'; a brief Reuters telegram dated 9 December 1899 run by the *Morning Post* described the battle; clipping among Wingate Papers, SAD 269/12/11.

52 Letter to T.J. Franks, dated 28 November 1899, among papers of George Franks, SAD 403/2, pp. 34–7.

53 'The Opening of the Soudan', *Tablet*, 16 December 1899; clipping among Wingate Papers, SAD 269/12/15.

# Bibliography

1.   *Published Sources*

'Abd-al-Gádir, I. *Kitáb sa'adat al-mustahdi bi-sírát al-Imám al-Mahdi*, ed. Muhammad Ibrahím Abú-Salím (Oxford, Oxford University Press, 1972).

Abú-Salím, M.I. *Al-athár al-kámila lil-Imám al-Mahdi* (7 vols, Khartoum, Khartoum University Press, 1990–4).

—— *Al-Harakat al-Fikría fí'l-Mahdía* (Khartoum, Khartoum University Press, 1970).

Abú-Salím, M.I. and Vikør, K. 'The Man Who Believed in the Mahdi', *Sudanic Africa*, 2 (1991), 29–52.

Adams, W. *Nubia: Corridor to Africa* (Princeton, Allen Lane, 1977).

Aglen, E.F. 'Sheikan Battlefield', *Sudan Notes and Records*, 20 (1937), 138–45.

Ali, A.Y. *The Holy Qurán* (Brentwood, Amana Corporation, 1983).

Ali, A.I.M. *The Slave Trade and Slavery in the Sudan 1820–1881* (Khartoum, Khartoum University Press, 1972).

*The Army List* (London, HMSO, 1882).

Barr, G. 'Slavery in Nineteenth Century Egypt', in R.A. Oliver and J.D. Fage (eds), *Journal of African History*, VIII, Nos 1, 2 and 3 (Cambridge, 1967).

Bawa Yamba, C. *Permanent Pilgrims: The Role of Pilgrimage in the Lives of West African Muslims in Sudan* (Washington, Smithsonian Institution Press, 1995).

Bedri, B. *The Memoirs of Babikr Bedri*, ed. and tr. Yusuf Bedri and Peter Hogg (2 vols, London, Ithaca Press, 1969, 1980).

Bermann, R. *The Mahdi of Allah: The Story of the Dervish Mohammed Ahmed* (New York, Macmillan, 1932).

Beshir, M.O. 'Abdel Rahman ibn Hussein el Jabri and his Book "History of the Mahdi"', *Sudan Notes and Records*, 44 (1963), 136–9.

—— 'Nasihat al-Awam', *Sudan Notes and Records*, 41 (1960), 59–65.

Broadley, A. *How We Defended Arabi and His Friends: A Story of Egypt and the Egyptians* (London, Chapman and Hall, 1884).

Brooke-Smith, R. *Documents and Debates: The Scramble for Africa* (Basingstoke, Macmillan Education, 1987).

Brook-Shepherd, G. *Between Two Flags: The Life of Baron Sir Rudolf von Slatin Pasha* (London, Weidenfeld & Nicolson, 1972).

Brown, L.C. 'The Sudanese Mahdiya', in R.L. Rotberg and A.A. Mazrui (eds), *Protest and Power in Black Africa* (New York, Oxford University Press, 1970).

Bugaje, U.M. 'Shaykh Uthman ibn Fodio and the Revival of Islam in Hausaland', in *Al-Mizan*, 2/1.

el-Bushra, S. 'Towns in the Sudan in the Eighteenth and Early Nineteenth Centuries', *Sudan Notes and Records*, 52 (1971), 63–70.

Cailliaud, F. *Voyage à Méroé, au Fleuve Blanc, au-delà de Fâzoql* (2 vols, Paris, 1826).

Casati, G. *Ten Years in Equatoria and the Return with Emin Pásha* (London, 1891).

Cave, S. 'The Financial Condition of Egypt', in *Parliamentary Papers LXXXIII* (London, HMSO, 1876).

Chaillé Long, Colonel C. *The Three Prophets: Chinese Gordon, Mohammed-Ahmed (El Maahdi), Arabi Pasha* (New York, D. Appleton & Co., 1884).

Chenevix Trench, C. *Charley Gordon: An Eminent Victorian Reassessed* (London, Allen Lane, 1978).

Churchill, R. *Winston S Churchill*, vol. 1: *Youth 1874–1900* (London, Heinemann, 1966).

Churchill, W. *The River War*, abridged edition (London, Prion Books, 2000).

Clark, P. 'The Hicks Pasha Expedition', in *Three Sudanese Battles*, Occasional Paper 14 (Khartoum, University of Khartoum Press, 1972).

Colborne, Col. the Hon. J. *With Hicks Pasha in the Soudan: Being an Account of the Sennar Campaign in 1883* (London, 1884).

Cole, J. *Colonialism and Revolution in the Middle East: Social and Cultural Origins of Egypt's 'Arábi Movement* (Princeton, Princeton University Press, 1993).

Cromer, Earl of (Sir Evelyn Baring). *Modern Egypt* (2 vols, London, Macmillan, 1908).

Daly, M.W. *Empire on the Nile: The Anglo-Egyptian Sudan, 1898–1934* (Cambridge, Cambridge University Press, 1986).

—— *Imperial Sudan: The Anglo-Egyptian Condominium, 1934–56* (Cambridge, Cambridge University Press, 1991).

Darmesteter, J. *The Mahdi Past and Present*, tr. Ahmad Suleimán Ballin (New York, 1885).

Dekmejian, R. and Wyszomirski, M. 'Charismatic Leadership in Islam: The Mahdi of the Sudan', *Comparative Studies in Sociology and History*, 4/2 (1972).

Deng, F.M. *The Dinka and their Songs* (Oxford, Clarendon Press, 1973).

'The Diary of 'Abbas Bey', *Sudan Notes and Records*, 32/2 (1951), 179–96.

Drage, G. *Cyril: A Romantic Novel* (London, W.H. Allen, 1892).

Edwards, F.A. 'The Foundation of Khartoum', *Sudan Notes and Records*, 5 (1922), 157–60.

*The Encyclopaedia of Islam (New Edition)*, various eds (8 vols, Leiden, 1985).

Ewald, J. *Soldiers, Traders, and Slaves: State Formation and Economic Transformation in the Greater Nile Valley, 1700–1885* (Wisconsin, Wisconsin University Press, 1990).

Fahmy, K. *All the Pásha's Men: Mehmed 'Ali, his Army and the Making of Modern Egypt* (Cairo, American University in Cairo Press, 2002).

Fawzi, I. *Al-Sudán bein yedí Gordon wa Kitchener* (Cairo, 1901).

Featherstone, D. *Khartoum 1885: General Gordon's Last Stand* (Oxford, Osprey, 1993).

—— *Omdurman 1898: Kitchener's Victory in the Sudan* (Oxford, Osprey, 1993).

al-Gaddal, M.S. *Lawha li-tha'ir Sudani: al-Imam al-Mahdi Muhammad Ahmad b. 'Abdallah (1844–1885)* (Khartoum, Khartoum University Press, 1985).

Ganem, H. 'Europe's Stake in the Sudan', *Fortnightly Review*, 209 (1884).

Gessi, R. *Seven Years in the Soudan: Being a Record of Explorations, Adventures, and Campaigns Against the Arab Slave Hunters*, tr. Lily Wolffsohn and Bettina Woodward (London, Sampson Low, Marston & Co., 1892).

Giegler, C.C. *The Sudan Memoirs of Carl Christian Giegler Pasha, 1873–83*, ed. Richard Hill (Oxford, Oxford University Press, 1984).

Greenlaw, J.-P. *The Coral Buildings of Suakin* (London, Oriel Press, 1976).

Gulla, Sheikh 'A. 'The Defeat of Hicks Pasha', *Sudan Notes and Records*, 8 (1925), 119–24.

Haggard, A. *Under Crescent and Star* (London, William Blackwood, 1896).

Hake, E. *The Journals of Major-Gen. C.G. Gordon at Kartoum* (London, Kegan Paul Trench & Co., 1885).

Hammúda, M.A. *Ahmad Suleimán: amín beit al-mál al-Súdán* (Cairo, Dár al-Thaqáfa, 1983).

Hassan, Q.M. *Qasá'id min shu'rá' al-Mahdía* (Khartoum, Ministry of Culture, 1974).

Henderson, K.D.D. *Sudan Republic* (London, E. Benn, 1965).

Hicks, W. *The Road to Shaykan: Letters of General William Hicks Pasha, Written during the Sennar and Kordofan Campaigns, 1883*, ed. M.W. Daly (Durham, University of Durham, 1983).

Hill, R. *Biographical Dictionary of the Sudan* (Oxford, Clarendon Press, 1967).

—— *Egypt in the Sudan* (Oxford, Clarendon Press, 1959).

—— *Gordon: Yet Another Assessment* (Durham, Sudan Studies Society of the United Kingdom, 1987).

—— *On the Frontiers of Islam* (Oxford, Clarendon Press, 1970).

—— 'The Period of Egyptian Occupation 1820–1881', *Sudan Notes and Records*, 40 (1959), 101–6.

—— 'A Register of Named Power-Driven River and Marine Harbour Craft Commissioned in the Sudan 1856–1964', *Sudan Notes and Records*, 51 (1970), 131–46, and 53 (1972), 204–14.

—— Review of *Slatin Pasha*, *Sudan Notes and Records*, 47 (1966), 167–8.

—— 'Rulers of the Sudan 1820–1885', *Sudan Notes and Records*, 32 (1951), 85–95.

Hillelson, S. *Sudan Arabic Texts*(Cambridge, Cambridge University Press, 1935).

—— 'Tabaqāt Wad Dayf Allah: Studies in the Lives of the Scholars and Saints', *Sudan Notes and Records*, 6 (1923), 191–230.

Hiskett, M. *The Sword of Truth: The Life and Times of the Shehu Usman Dan Fodio* (New York, Ocford University Press, 1973).

Holt P.M. 'Archives of the Mahdia', *Sudan Notes and Records*, 36 (1955), 71–80.

—— *The Mahdist State in the Sudan, 1881–1898*, 2nd edn (Oxford, Clarendon Press, 1970).

—— 'The Place in History of the Sudanese Mahdia', *Sudan Notes and Records*, 40 (1959), 107–12.

—— *The Source-Materials of Sudanese Mahdia*, St Antony's Papers (Oxford, Oxford University Press, 1958).

—— 'The Sudanese Mahdia and the Outside World: 1881–9', *Bulletin of the School of Oriental and African Studies*, 21/2 (1958).

—— *Sudan of the Three Niles: The Funj Chronicle 910–1288/1504–1871* (Leiden, Brill, 1992).

—— and Daly, M.W. *A History of the Sudan* (London, Longman, 2000).

Hope, A.C. 'The Adventurous Life of Faraj Sadik', *Sudan Notes and Records*, 32/1 (1951), 154–8.

Hornell, J. 'The Frameless Boats of the Middle Nile', *Sudan Notes and Records*, 25 (1942), 1–36.

Hourani, A. *A History of the Arab Peoples* (New York, Warner Books, 1991).

Ibn Khaldun, A.W.D. *The Muqaddimah: An Introduction to History*, tr. Franz Rosenthal, 3 vols (New York, Pantheon, 1958).

Ibrahim, A.U. 'Some Aspects of the Ideology of the Mahdiya', *Sudan Notes and Records*, 60 (1979), 28–37.

*In Relief of Gordon: Lord Wolseley's Campaign Journal of the Khartoum Relief Expedition, 1884–1885,* ed. Adrian Preston (London, Hutchinson, 1967).

Al-Jabarti, A. *Ajá'ib al-Athár fí'l-Tarájim wa'l-Akhbár* (4 vols, Cairo, 1880).

Jackson, H.C. *Osman Digna* (London, 1926).

—— 'Sudan Proverbs', *Sudan Notes and Records*, 2 (1919), 105–11.

Job, H.S. 'The Coinage of the Mahdi and the Khalífa', *Sudan Notes and Records*, 3 (1920), 165–78.

Johnson, D. 'The Egyptian Army 1880–1900', *Savage and Soldier*, 8/1.

Karrar, A.S. *The Sufi Brotherhoods in the Sudan* (London, Hurst, 1992).

Keneally, T. *Bettany's Book* (London, Sceptre, 2001).

Keown-Boyd, H. *A Good Dusting: A Centenary Review of the Sudan Campaigns 1883–1899* (London, Leo Cooper, 1986).

de Kusel, Baron S. *An Englishman's Recollections of Egypt 1863–1887* (London, John Lane, 1915).

Last, M. *The Sokoto Caliphate* (London, Longmans, 1967).

Layish, A. 'The Legal Methodology of the Mahdi in the Sudan, 1881–1885: Issues in Marriage and Divorce', *Sudanic Africa*, 8 (1997), 37–66.

Lehmann, J. *All Sir Garnet: A Life of Field Marshal Lord Wolseley* (London, Jonathan Cape, 1964).

Lepsius, K.R. *Denkmäler aus Ägypten und Äthiopien* (Berlin, 1849–59).

Leverson, Capt. J.J. 'Insurrection of the False Prophet 1881–83' (4 vols, Cairo, War Office, 1883–4).

Lewis, B. *Race and Slavery in the Middle East: An Historical Inquiry* (Oxford, Oxford University Press, 1990).

Linant de Bellefonds, A. *Journal d'un voyage à Méroé dans les années 1821 et 1822,* ed. M. Shinnie (Khartoum, Sudan Antiquities Service, 1958).

Lobban, R., Kramer, R. and Fluehr-Lobban, C. *Historical Dictionary of the Sudan*, 3rd edn (Maryland, Rowman & Littlefield, 2002).

Long: see Chaillé Long.

McHugh, N. *Holymen of the Blue Nile: The Making of an Arab–Islamic Community in the Nilotic Sudan, 1500–1850* (Evanston, Northwestern, 1994).

MacLaren, R. *Canadians on the Nile, 1882–1898: Being the Adventures of the Voyageurs on the Khartoum Relief Expedition and Other Exploits* (Vancouver, University of British Columbia Press, 1978).

MacMichael, H.A. 'Notes on Old Khartoum', *Sudan Notes and Records*, 6 (1923), 110–11.

Macro, E. 'Frank Miller Lupton', *Sudan Notes and Records*, 28 (1947), 50–61.

al-Mahdi, 'A. Correspondence (including Arabic text and translation) on the Mahdi's last letter to Gordon, *Sudan Notes and Records*, 24 (1941), 229–32.

al-Mahdi, M.A. *Rátib al-Imám al-Mahdi* (Khartoum, 1885).

al-Mahdi, S. *Al-Jazíra Aba wa-dawraha fí nahdat al-Sudán* (Khartoum, 1981).

—— *Yas'alúnaka 'an al-Mahdía* (Beirut, 1975).

Mahmoud, M. 'Sufism and Islamism in the Sudan', in D. Westerlund and E.E. Rosander (eds), *African Islam and Islam in Africa* (London, Hurst, 1997).

Malet, Sir E. *Egypt 1879–83* (London, John Murray, 1909).

Mason, A.E.W. *The Four Feathers* (London, John Murray, 1902).

Mikhail, Y. *Mazkarát Yúsuf Míkhail* (London, Dár al-Nusairi, 1998).

Moorehead, A. *The Blue Nile* (London, Reprint Society, 1962).

—— *The White Nile* (London, Hamish Hamilton, 1960).

Morley, J. *The Life of William Ewart Gladstone* (3 vols, London, Macmillan, 1903).

Mubárak, A. *Al-Khitat al-Tawfiqía al-Jadída* (Cairo, 1887–8).

Muqaybil al-Máliki, M.M. *Nasíhat al-umma fí shurút 'aqd al-dhimma* (Khartoum, 1882).

Mynors, T.H.B. 'The Adventures of a Darfur Slave', *Sudan Notes and Records*, 30/2 (1949), 273–5.

Nicholls, W. *The Shaiķíya: An Account of the Shaiķíya Tribes and of the History of Dongola Province from the XIVth to the XIXth Century* (Dublin, 1913).

Núr al-Dá'im, A. *Azáhír al-riyád fí manáqib al-árif billah al-Sheikh Ahmad al-Tayib* (Khartoum, 1954).

Ohrwalder, Fr J. *Ten Years' Captivity in the Mahdi's Camp, 1882–1892* (facsimile edn, London, Darf, 1986).

Omar, A.-M. *The Soudan Question Based on British Documents* (Cairo, Misr Press, 1952).

*Omdurman 1898: The Eye-Witnesses Speak*, ed. Peter Harrington and Frederic Sharf (London, Greenhill, 1998).

*Omdurman Diaries 1898: Eyewitness Accounts of the Legendary Campaign*, ed. John Meredith (London, Leo Cooper, 1998).

*The Oxford Encylopaedia of the Modern Islamic World*, ed. Professor John Esposito (4 vols, Oxford, Oxford University Press, 1995).

*The Oxford History of Islam*, ed. Professor John Esposito (Oxford, Oxford University Press, 1999).

Padwick, C. *Muslim Devotions: A Study of Prayer-Manuals in Common Use* (Oxford, Oneworld, 1961).

Page, C.H. 'Inland Water Navigation', *Sudan Notes and Records*, 2 (1919), 293–306.

Palmer, A. *The Decline and Fall of the Ottoman Empire* (London, John Murray, 1992).

Power, F. *Letters from Khartoum; Written During the Siege* (London, 1892).

de Pruyssenaere, E. *Reisen und Forshungen im Gebiete des Weissen und Blauen Nil* (Gotha, 1876).

Rehfisch, F. 'Omdurman During the Mahdiya: Extract from *I miei Dodici Anni di Prigionia in Mezzo ai Dervisci* by C. Rosignoli', *Sudan Notes and Records*, 48 (1967), 33–61.

—— 'A Sketch of the Early History of Omdurman', *Sudan Notes and Records*, 45 (1964), 35–47.

Reid, J.A. 'The Death of Gordon: An Eye-witness Account', *Sudan Notes and Records*, 20 (1937), 172–3.

—— 'The Mahdi's Emirs', *Sudan Notes and Records*, 20 (1937), 308–12.

—— 'Some Notes on the Khalifa Abdullahi from Contemporary Sudanese Sources', *Sudan Notes and Records*, 21 (1938), 207–12.

Robinson, A.E. 'The Mamelukes in the Sudan', *Sudan Notes and Records*, 5 (1922), 88–94.

—— 'The Rulers of the Sudan since the Turkish Occupation until the Evacuation by Order of the Khedive', *Journal of African Studies* (1924), 39–49.

Robson, B. *Fuzzy-Wuzzy: The Campaigns in the Eastern Sudan 1884–85* (Tunbridge Wells, Spellmount, 1993).

Rodinson, M. *Muhammad*, tr. Anne Carter (New York, New Press, 1980).

Rollet, B. *Le Nil Blanc et le Soudan* (Paris, 1855).

Salmon, R. 'The Story of Sheikh Abdullahi Ahmed Abu Galaha, A Sudanese Vicar of Bray', *Sudan Notes and Records*, 21 (1938), 84–90.

Sanderson, E. *The British Empire in the XIX Century* (2 vols, London, 1897).

Sanderson, G.N. 'Conflict and Co-operation between Ethiopia and the Mahdist State, 1884–1898', *Sudan Notes and Records*, 50 (1969), 15–40.

Seton-Williams, V. and Stocks, P. *Blue Guide: Egypt*, 2nd edn (London, A. & C. Black, 1988).

al-Shahi, A. 'The Distinctiveness of the Shaygiya', in H. Bleuchot, C. Delmet and D. Hopwood (eds), *Sudan: History, Identity, Ideology* (Reading, Ithaca, 1991).

Shaked, H. *The Life of the Sudanese Mahdi: A Historical Study of Kitáb sa'adat al-mustahdi bi-sírát al-Imám al-Mahdi by Ismá'íl bin 'Abd-al-Gádir* (New Jersey, Transaction Press, 1978).

Shannon, R. *Gladstone: Heroic Minister 1865–1898* (2 vols, London, Hamish Hamilton, 1999).

Sharkey, H. 'Ahmad Zayni Dahlán's al-Futuhát al-Islámía: A Contemporary View of the Sudanese Mahdi', *Sudanic Africa*, 5 (1994), 67–75.

—— Review of Neil MacHugh's *Holymen of the Blue Nile*, *Sudanic Africa*, 5 (1994), 266–9.

Shibeika, M. *British Policy in the Sudan, 1882–1902* (London, Geoffrey Cumberlege, 1952).

—— *The Independent Sudan* (New York, Oxford University Press, 1959).

Shuqair, N. *Taríkh al-Súdán al-qadím wa al-hadíth wa jughrafíyátuhu* (Cairo, 1903).

Sienkiewicz, H. *In Desert and Wilderness* (Edinburgh, Polish Book Depot, 1945).

Slatin, R.C. *Fire and Sword in the Sudan: A Personal Narrative of Fighting and Serving the Dervishes, 1879–1895* (London, Edward Arnold, 1892).

Speedy, C.M. *My Wanderings in the Sudan* (London, R. Bentley and Son, 1884).

Spring, C. *African Arms and Armour* (London, British Museum Press, 1993).

—— and Hudson, J. *North African Textiles* (London, British Museum Press, 1995).

Stanley, H.M. *In Darkest Africa: Or the Quest, Rescue and Retreat of Emin, Governor of Equatoria* (2 vols, London, Sampson Low, 1890).

Stevenson, R.C. 'Old Khartoum, 1821–1885', *Sudan Notes and Records*, 47 (1966), 1–38.

Strachey, L. *Eminent Victorians* (Oxford, Oxford University Press, 2003).

*The Strand Magazine: An Illustrated Monthly*, 3 (Jan.–June, 1892).

Taylor, B. *A Journey to Central Africa* (New York, Sampson Low, Son & Co., 1854).

Theobald, A.B. *The Mahdīya, A History of the Anglo-Egyptian Sudan, 1881–1899* (London, Longmans, Green & Co., 1951).

Thomas, G. *Sudan: Death of a Dream* (London, Darf, 1990).

—— *Sudan: Struggle for Survival* (London, Darf, 1993).

Thomas, G. and Thomas, I. *Sayed Abd El Rahman Al Mahdi, A Pictorial Biography, 1885–1959* (London, Sayed Abd el Rahman Centenary Fund, 1986).

Thompson, B. *Imperial Vanities* (London, Harper Collins, 2002).

*Travellers in Egypt*, ed. Paul and Janet Starkey (London, Tauris Parke, 2001).

Trimingham, J.S. *Islam in the Sudan* (London, Frank Cass, 1965).

Vikør, K. *Sufi and Scholar on the Desert Edge: Muhammad b. 'Ali al-Sanúsi, 1797–1859* (London, Hurst, 1995).

Waley, M.I. 'Islamic Manuscripts in the British Royal Collection: A Concise Catalogue', *Manuscripts of the Middle East* 6 (1992) (Leiden, 1994).

Walkley, C.E.J. 'The Story of Khartoum', *Sudan Notes and Records*, 18 (1935), 221–41, 19 (1936), 71–92.

Warburg, G. *Historical Discord in the Nile Valley* (London, Hurst, 1992).

—— *Islam, Sectarianism and Politics in Sudan* (London, Hurst, 2003).

Watson, Col. Sir C.M. 'The Campaign of Gordon's Steamers', *Sudan Notes and Records*, 12/2 (1929), 119–41.

Wilkinson-Latham, R. *The Sudan Campaigns 1881–98* (London, Osprey, 1976).

Willis, J.R. 'Jihād Fī Sabīl Allāh: Its Doctrinal Basis in Islam and Some Aspects of its Evolution in Nineteenth-Century West Africa', in *The Journal of African History*, vol. VIII (Cambridge, 1967).

Wilson, Revd C.T. and Felkin, R.W. *Uganda and the Egyptian Sudan* (2 vols, London, Sampson Low, 1882).

Wingate, F.R. *Mahdiism and the Egyptian Sudan* (London, Macmillan, 1891).

—— 'Note on the Dervish Wounded at Omdurman', in *Egypt No. 1* (1899) (London, HMSO, 1899).

—— 'The Siege and Fall of Khartoum', *Sudan Notes and Records*, 13 (1930), 1–82.

Wingate, R. *Wingate of the Sudan: The Life and Times of General Sir Reginald Wingate, Maker of the Anglo-Egyptian Sudan* (London, John Murray, 1955).

Wolseley, Field-Marshal Viscount G.J. *The Soldier's Pocket-Book for Field Service* (London, HMSO, 1882).

—— *The Story of a Soldier's Life* (2 vols, London, Ernest Russell, 1903).

Wood, E. *From Midshipman to Field Marshal* (London, Methuen, 1906).

Ziegler, P. *Omdurman* (London, Collins, 1973).

Zulfo, I.H. *Karari*, tr. Peter Clark (London, Frederick Warne, 1980).

2. *Unpublished Sources*

Bedri, G.A. 'A Critical Analysis of British Historical Writing on the Mahdiya of the Sudan', MA thesis, American University of Beirut, 1971.

Bugaje, U.M. 'The Jihad of Shaykh Usman Dan Fodio and its Impact Beyond the Sokoto Caliphate', paper read at a symposium in honour of Usman dan Fodio at the International University of Africa in Khartoum, 19–21 November 1995.

Kramer, R. 'Holy City on the Nile: Omdurman, 1885–1898', PhD thesis, Northwestern University, 1991.

Musa, F.M. 'Judiciary and the Nile Fleet in the Mahadya State in the Sudan', lecture given at 5th International Conference on Sudan Studies at Durham University, 1999.

Sharkey, H. 'A Jihad of the Pen: Mahdiya History and Historiography', draft article, 18 November 1993.

—— 'Popular Historiography and the Mahdiya', lecture given at the 3rd International Meeting of Sudanese Studies Associations, Boston, 22 April 1994.

Udal, J. 'Ja'afar Pasha Mazhar: A Worthy Governor-General, 1865–1871', paper presented to 5th International Conference on Sudan Studies at Durham University, 30 August–1 September 2000.

Yagi, V. 'Le Kalifa 'Abdullahi: Sa vie et sa politique', PhD thesis, Université Paul Valery, Montpellier, 1990.

## 3. *Manuscript sources*

### (A)  NATIONAL RECORDS OFFICE, KHARTOUM (NRO)

| | |
|---|---|
| CAIRINT 1/3/8 | Khedive Ismail's firman to Gordon (16 February 1874) |
| CAIRINT 1/3/14 | Officers of the Hicks expedition and their contract |
| CAIRINT 1/3/15 | 'Insurrection of the False Prophet 1881–83' (report by Captain J.J. Leverson, 1883–4) |
| CAIRINT 1/8/36 | Account of Hussein Pasha Khalífa on fall of Berber |
| CAIRINT 1/10/51 | Accounts of sieges and battles in Kordofan (1882–3) |
| CAIRINT 1/10/52 | Account of 'Abdallah Agha Muhammad (1881–5) |
| CAIRINT 1/10/53 | Account of fall of Sennar |
| CAIRINT 1/25/129 | Sa'ad Rifa'at report on Red Sea Province uprising |
| CAIRINT 3/9/189 | 'Mahdism in the Sudan' (report by Chermside, 1885) |
| CAIRINT 3/9/197 | Statements on destruction of Hicks expedition |
| CAIRINT 3/14/240 | Report of Bimbashi Mahmud Effendi 'Abdallah |
| CAIRINT 11/1/3 | Undated manshúr on banning use of 'dervish' |
| CAIRINT 11/1/13 | Letter from Mahdi to Gordon (12 Jumáda II 1304) |
| CAIRINT 11/1/15 | Mahdi's vision of people of Khartoum and fall of Sennar |
| CAIRINT 11/1/20 | Mahdi's proclamation in obedience and piety |
| INTEL 1/1/7 | 'List of Names of Hakimdars and Mudirs of the Sudan' and 'Names of Hakimdars, Mudirs and Governors of the Sudan from 1878 to 1882' |

| INTEL 1/1/10 | Appointment of Hussein Mazhar as Deputy Governor-General by Khedivial firman on 29 July 1883 |
| INTEL 1/15/74 | Gordon's pamphlet on activities of Zubeir Pasha (1879) and smuggled message to Dongola during siege |
| INTEL 2/43/357 | 'The Family Tree of the Mahdi' (1924) |
| INTEL 3/1/4–8 | Accounts of 'dervish' prisoners (1916–20) |
| INTEL 5/1/4 | Notes on Sheikh al-'Ubeid, Siraj al-Salikin (1881–1920) |
| INTEL 5/1/7 | Governors-General of Sudan |
| INTEL 5/1/8 | Tax information and various maps, including Khartoum |
| INTEL 5/1/10 | Khedivial decrees affecting Sudan (1883–7) |
| INTEL 5/2/11 | Copy of 'Abbás Bey's diary |
| INTEL 5/2/12–14 | Nushi Report on fall of Khartoum |
| INTEL 9/1/1 | 'History of the Mahdía' by 'Abd-al-Rahmán Hussain al-Jabri and related British commentary |
| INTEL 9/1/2 | Reading of the Rátib |
| INTEL 1/1/7 | Officialdom during the Turkía |
| INTEL 5/1/7 | Officialdom during the Turkía |
| INTEL 1/15/74 | 'Account of the Actions of Zubeir Pásha' |
| MAHDIA 1/1/8 | Appointment of Muhammad Khálid as amír of Darfur |
| MAHDIA 1/10/8 | Appointment of Muhammad al-Kheir as amír of Berber |
| MAHDIA 1/42/5 | Papers of the Qádi al-Islam, Ahmad 'Ali |
| MAHDIA 1/43/6 | Mail, etc., captured by Ansár |
| MAHDIA 2/51 | Egyptian official papers |

## (B)   SUDAN ARCHIVE, DURHAM UNIVERSITY LIBRARY (SAD)

| 98/5 | MS of 'Nasíhat al-Awám' and translation |
| 99/6 | MS of Kitáb sa'adat al-mustahdi bi-sírát al-Imám al-Mahdi (The Life of the Imam the Mahdi), Ismail bin 'Abd-al-Gádir |
| 100/6/1–3 | Mahdi's proclamation dated AH 1299; MS and translation |
| 100/10/1 | Mahdi's letter dated 10 August 1877 (3 Sha'bán 1294) |
| 106/2 | 'Dervish Who's Who' |
| 113/3/245–9 | 'Chronological Table of Recent Events in Egypt and the Sudan', British military intelligence, Cairo |
| 113/3/282–6 | Na'úm Shuqair memorandum on the Shaigía |
| 178/2/4 | 'Diary of 'Abbás Bey', translation (anon.) |

# BIBLIOGRAPHY

| | |
|---|---|
| 218/4 | Copy of *Report on the Soudan, Egypt No. 11* (1883), Lt-Col J. Donald H. Stewart |
| 228/15 | Translation of Fr Joseph Ohrwalder's preface to *Ten Years' Captivity*; other papers relating to the book |
| 230/1/10 | Fr Joseph Ohrwalder's hand-written German preface to English edition of *Ten Years' Captivity* |
| 230/17/69 | Wingate's correspondence with Fr Ohrwalder |
| 247/1 | Translation of Mahdi's *Rátib* |
| 247/4 | Translation of *Kitáb sa'adat al-mustahdi bi-sírát al-Imám al-Mahdi* |
| 260/2/1–6 | Na'úm Shuqair on Ismail 'Abd-al-Gádir's biography of the Mahdi |
| 267/1 | Wingate Papers, including details of Karari |
| 269/12 | Wingate Papers, including details of Um Dibeikarát |
| 403/2 | Papers of (later, Major-General Sir) George Franks |
| 404/10/8 | Papers of James Macphail |
| 430/6/4–6 | Letter to Kitchener from notables of Omdurman with translation |
| 605/6/4–12 | Papers of A.N. Gibson, including correspondence on slavery |
| 621/6/1–8 | Picture of Umm Dibeikarát (Papers of A. Cameron) |
| 630/5/28–30 | Copy of letter from Gordon in Cairo to J. Brocklehurst |
| 630/5/37–8 | Copy of letter from Gordon in Khartoum to J. Brocklehurst |
| 631/1/1–29 | Notes by J. Martin of meeting between Gordon and Zubeir in Cairo, 26 January 1884 |
| 643/4/29 | Papers of John Longe, Sudan government administrator, 1925–53 |
| 643/15/1 | Picture of Col. J.D.H. Stewart (Papers of J. Prendergast) |
| 646/7/21 | Map of Egyptian Sudan (Papers of J.F.E. Bloss) |
| 686/1/7 | Picture of Ansár in jibbas (Papers of E.G. Sarsfield-Hall) |
| 692/18/3 | Photograph of 'Osmán Digna (Papers of Col. Abu Qurun) |
| 695/7/1 | 'With the Camel Corps: To the Relief of Khartoum', among Papers of Arthur Robeson |
| 721/1/58 | Diary of Clarence Brownell |
| 777/14 | Papers of Peter Acland, Sudan government administrator, 1925–46 |
| 867/6/1–11 | 'Report on the Death of Khalifa' by Colonel Sir Reginald Wingate |
| 867/7 | 'Chronological Events in the Sudan for the Years 1881–1889 inclusive', F.R. Wingate |
| 878/3/1 | Destruction of the Mahdi's tomb (Papers of R.G. MacComas) |
| 97/1 | MS of Mahdi's *Rátib* (printed in Omdurman) |

(C)   SCHOOL OF ORIENTAL AND AFRICAN STUDIES, LONDON (SOAS)

| | |
|---|---|
| LP962.403/332255 | Salih Muhammad Nur, 'A Critical Edition of the Memoirs of Yūsif Mikhail', (unpublished) PhD thesis, School of Oriental and African Studies, University of London |
| LP962.403/332259 | Autobiography of Yúsuf Mikhail (translation by P.M. Holt, 1954) |
| PP MS 07 | Holt Papers (Boxes 1–12) |
| Box 1, File 1 | (i) Dreams and Visions (Ar.) |
| | (ii) Bahr al-Ghazál |
| | (iii) Darfur |
| | (iv) Abyssinia (Ar.) |
| | (v) Fadl al-Mawla (Ar.) |
| | (vi) Papers of Qádi al-Islam Ahmad ʿAli |
| | (vii) Log of SS *Safiya* (1313) |
| | (viii) Papers of the Mint (1310) |
| | (ix) Suleimán al-Hajjaz (1308–9) |
| | (x) ʿOsmán Digna (1306) |
| | (xi) Slavery (1306) |
| | (xii) Ibráhím Bordeini report on siege and fall of Khartoum |
| | (xiii) ʿAbdallah Agha Muhammad report (1887) |
| | (xiv) Saʿad Effendi Rifaʿat report on rising in the east (1889) |
| | (xv) Report on fall of Sennar |
| | (xvi) Hussein Pasha Khalífa's report on fall of Berber |
| | (xvii) Letters of the Mahdi and the Khalífa (1300–2) (Ar.) |
| | (xviii) Battles of Kordofan (various brief accounts) |
| Box 2, File 2, | 13 folders containing notes on 22 shorter documents |
| Box 3, File 3, | Misc. notes on a variety of topics including finance, commerce and the Mahdist legal system |
| File 4, | Letters of the Khalífa (1300–14) (Ar.) |
| File 5, | Misc. notes |
| Box 4, File 6, | Notes and correspondence of the Mahdi and the Khalífa (Ar.) |
| Box 5, File 7, | i. Photostats of manshúrát (Ar.) |
| | ii. Photostats of the Rátib (Ar.) |

|                    | iii. Photostats of Kitáb al-Indhirát (Ar.) |
|                    | iv. Letters, etc. (Ar.) |
| Box 6, File 8,     | Photostats of Funj Chronicle MSS (Ar.) |
| Box 7, File 9,     | i. Yúsuf Mikhail letter-book (Ar.) |
|                    | ii. Photostats of Yúsuf Mikhail's memoirs (Ar.) |
|                    | iii. Translucencies of Yúsuf Mikhail's memoirs (Ar.) |
| Box 8, File 10,    | i. 'Osmán Digna letter-book (Ar.) |
|                    | ii. Report to the Mahdi (Ar.) |
| Box 9, File 11,    | i. Photocopy of 'Abd-al-Rahmán al-Nujúmi letter-book (Ar.) |
| File 12,           | Fatwa against the Mahdi (Ar.) |
| File 13,           | Ibn Shaddad Tartch Baybars; MS of Edirne Selimiye |
| Box 10, File 14,   | Microfilm of Sírat al-Mustahdi (Ar.) |
| File 15,           | Microfilm of Yuhanna al-Hubush (Ar.) |
| File 16,           | Megillat Mitzrayim and MS belonging to amír Núr Angára (captured during Sudan Campaign) |
| File 17,           | Microfilm of Sudan Intelligence Reports (1889–92) |
| File 18,           | Microfilm of Sudan Intelligence Reports (1892–8) |
| Box 11,            | File 19, Maps of Nilotic Nubia |
| Box 12,            | File 20–4, P.M. Holt correspondence |

## (D)   NATIONAL ARMY MUSEUM (NAM)

| 6403–5 | Small Arabic prayer (1885) |
| 8008–70 | 'Cost of Principal British Wars, 1857–1899', A.W. Money |
| 6604–44 | Letter from Col. Sparkes on Battle of Omdurman and aftermath |
| 6012–119 | Sudanese documents seized after Battle of Omdurman |
| 6204/4 | Qorán taken from Khalífa's tent by Hugh Simpson-Baikie |
| 6012/406 (1884) | Panoramic map of Nile between Cairo and Khartoum |
| 6807/338 | Treatise on Mahdism by al-Hussein al-Zahrá |
| 6807–521–1 | Photo of Hicks Pasha and staff in Cairo (1883) |

## (E)   HOVE LIBRARY

| SSL.9 | (2 vols.) Lord Wolseley's notes for the (unpublished) third volume of his autobiography, The Story of a Soldier's Life |
| W/MEM/1 | Misc. Wolseley memoranda |
| W/P.14 | Letters from General Wolseley to his wife |
| W/PLB.1 | Misc. Wolseley correspondence |

## (F)   BRITISH LIBRARY, BRITISH MUSEUM

| | |
|---|---|
| Add. Ms. 34474/76 | Coded message from Egerton to Gordon |
| Add. MS 34474/85 | Letter from Qádi of Kalakla to Gordon (Ar.) |
| Add. MS 34474/90 | Letter from Nujúmi and al-Núr to Gordon (Ar.) |
| Add. MS 34474/98 | Letter from officer on Hicks expedition (Ar.) |
| Add. MS 34474/103 | Letter from Qádi of Kalakla to Gordon (Ar.) |
| Add. MS 34474/105 | Letter from Nujúmi and al-Núr to Gordon (Ar.) |
| Add. MS 34474/111 | Original of Herbin's last letter to Gordon |
| Add. MS 34478/110 | Mahdi's manifesto (Ar.) |
| Add. MS 34478/115 | Coded message from Wolseley to Gordon |
| Add. MS 34479/118–21 | Letters from Mahdi's lieutenants to Gordon (Ar.) |
| Add. MS 51299/56–59 | Wolseley letters to Lord Hartington |
| Add. MS 52388/133 | Wolseley letter to Gordon |
| Add. MS 52395B/45 | Gordon's 1880 medical examination |
| Add. MS 52395B/51–6 | French translation of anti-Mahdi proclamation |
| Add. MS 52403/130 | Nushi's letter to Wolseley from Metamma |
| Add. MS 52403/131 | Gordon's letters to Nushi at Metamma |

## (G)   SUDAN LIBRARY, UNIVERSITY OF KHARTOUM (SLUK)

'Al-nafahat al-wardía wal-shajarat al-Mahdía' ('The Odours of Roses and the Tree of the Mahdía'), 'Abd-al-Rahmán Hussein al-Jabri

## (H)   BRITISH LIBRARY NEWSPAPER LIBRARY, COLINDALE, LONDON

*The Graphic*, London
*The Times*, London
*The Egyptian Gazette*, Cairo
*The Illustrated London News*, London
*The Levant Herald*, Cairo

## (I)   WINDSOR CASTLE

| | |
|---|---|
| RCIN 1005006 | MS of Muhammad's al-Hasani's *Nasíhat al-umma fí shurút 'aqd al-dhimma* |
| RCIN 1005008 | MS of the 'Diary of 'Abbás Bey' |

# BIBLIOGRAPHY

## (J)  PUBLIC RECORD OFFICE, KEW (PRO)

FO 633/53–4     Correspondence relating to Egypt and Sudan
FO 78/3680–4     Correspondence relating to Egypt and Sudan (1884)
HD/3/26 and 80     Correspondence relating to codebooks
WO 32/6112     Wolseley correspondence
PRO 30/57     General Kitchener's papers on the Gordon Relief Expedition

# Index